THE CONDEMNATION OF BLACKNESS

THE CONDEMNATION OF BLACKNESS

RACE, CRIME, AND THE MAKING OF
MODERN URBAN AMERICA

WITH A NEW PREFACE

Khalil Gibran Muhammad

HARVARD UNIVERSITY PRESS

Cambridge, Massachusetts

London, England

First Harvard University Press paperback edition, 2011
Second printing

Library of Congress Cataloging-in-Publication Data

Muhammad, Khalil Gibran, 1972–
  The condemnation of blackness : race, crime, and the making of modern urban America /
Khalil Gibran Muhammad.
    p.   cm.
Includes bibliographical references and index.
  ISBN 978-0-674-03597-3 (cloth : alk. paper)
  ISBN 978-0-674-23814-5 (pbk.)
  1. Crime and race—United States.   2. African Americans—Social conditions.
3. Discrimination in criminal justice administration—United States.   4. United States—
Race relations.   I. Title.
  HV6197.U5M85 2010
  364.2'56—dc22   2009014930

For Stephanie, Gibran, Jordan, and Justice,
and for my parents, Ozier and Kimberly

CONTENTS

List of Illustrations   *ix*

Preface 2019   *xi*

Introduction: The Mismeasure of Crime   1

1 Saving the Nation: The Racial Data Revolution
and the Negro Problem   15

2 Writing Crime into Race: Racial Criminalization
and the Dawn of Jim Crow   35

3 Incriminating Culture: The Limits of Racial Liberalism
in the Progressive Era   88

4 Preventing Crime: White and Black Reformers
in Philadelphia   146

5 Fighting Crime: Politics and Prejudice in the
City of Brotherly Love   192

6 Policing Racism: Jim Crow Justice in the Urban North   226

Conclusion: The Conundrum of Criminality   269

Manuscript Sources   *279*

Notes   *281*

Acknowledgments   *369*

Index   *375*

"A Downtown 'Morgue,'" c. 1890   55

"How Criminals Are Made," c. 1907   102

"American Logic," c. 1913   142

Youth of the Friends Neighborhood Guild, c. 1901   156

"The Washington Party," c. 1901   159

Staged Charity Photo of Black Children as Pickaninnies, c. 1905   162

Handbill of the Joint Organization of the AEIO and LCPR,
   c. 1909   184

Pledge Card of the Association for Equalizing Industrial Opportunities,
   c. 1909   186

Adella Bond Defends Herself in Philadelphia Race Riot, c. 1918   212

Stoned to Death by a White Mob during the Chicago Race Riot,
   c. 1919   237

Police Search African Americans for Weapons during the Chicago Race
   Riot, c. 1919   239

"Puzzle: Find the 'Keepers of the Peace,'" c. 1928   250

"Be First to Let Him Out," c. 1929   264

In the late fall of 2007, around the same time I was putting the final touches on the first edition of this book, I was administering the final exam in my urban history course. One of my students handed in his blue book with an unusually cheerful smile. He was excited to share the news that he would soon be heading to campaign in Iowa for Senator Barack Obama. The moment has stayed with me because until then I had given little thought to Obama's candidacy. Voting in the Democratic primaries had yet to begin. And if I'm honest, at that point, I didn't think he had much of a chance against Hillary Clinton.

A couple of weeks later Obama won the 2008 Iowa Caucus, and in November he was elected the nation's first black president. This incredible historical moment found me both awestruck and, I have to admit, panicked. My book was headed to press with a "divisive" race title that I feared no one would pay any attention to. Yes, I could still count on other historians and some research librarians to notice the book. They would appreciate my findings that northern white liberals and progressives were a big part of the history of racism in America's criminal justice system, a major correction to most histories that focused exclusively on southern racists with their lynch mobs and chain gangs. I trusted that academic readers would see my novel claim that today's crisis of mass incarceration had its roots not only in the Jim Crow South but also in northern cities.

But I was convinced, like most authors, that everyone should read my book. Not just because I had poured nearly a decade into writing it, but because I thought it could genuinely transform how we thought about race, crime, and punishment. By population, by per capita incarceration rates, and by expenditures, the United States exceeds all other nations in how many of its citizens, asylum seekers, and undocumented immigrants are under some form of criminal justice supervision. The number of African American and Latinx people in American jails and prisons today exceeds the entire populations of some African, Eastern European, and Caribbean countries. The United States didn't get to mass incarceration without mass participation in the criminalization of black and brown people by liberals and conservatives, northerners and southerners, Republicans and Democrats, whites and blacks. By a long shot, the United States is the world's leading jailer. And no aspect of national life—from the economy to education to electoral politics—has been untouched by the scale and scope of racialized policing and punishment. With a more honest and complete record of the nation's punitive past, I hoped more people would learn from this history and choose to create a more compassionate, fairer, and racially just criminal legal system.

Yet in the hype of what many claimed was a new post-racial America, I fretted that my book would be drowned out by the euphoria of all that "hopey-changey stuff." So, I got the bright idea to change the title to *The Condemnation of Blackness: Before the Election of Barack Obama.* In addition to making my message less gloomy, I thought I might even be able to sell more copies by attaching my work to the wildly popular new president. Needless to say, I didn't change the title. The first black president has come and gone, but the history told here remains the same. If anything, the lessons are even more urgent.

When I first conceived this book, I wanted to answer a pretty straightforward question. I had learned about the slavery loophole in the Thirteenth Amendment, which abolished slavery "except as punishment for crime." I had read extensively about the use of the law after slavery and Reconstruction to criminalize black people, strip them of their newly earned civil and voting rights, and then force them back onto plantations as sharecroppers under the threat of punishment or death. Knowing all this, I was curious about what happened in Chicago for people like my great-grandparents, who left the South during the early decades of the Great Migration.

I was particularly keen to examine the criminal justice system outside of the South because I came of age when the first viral video of police brutality sparked protests. In 1991, nearly a dozen California highway patrolmen severely beat an intoxicated black motorist named Rodney King on the side of the road for speeding. King was the Emmett Till of my generation, just as the slain seventeen-year-old Trayvon Martin and twenty-two-year-old Rekia Boyd are to my children's generation. None of the history I had learned helped explain the antiblack violence, the miscarriages of justice, and the callous disregard and cheapness of black life in a supposedly post–civil rights America.

When the first edition of this book was published in 2010, I had no idea that a new racial justice movement to end racial profiling, police brutality, and mass incarceration was on the horizon. No one knew that social media would set off protests across the nation, or that smartphone video would capture scenes of police in riot gear confronting activists harkening back to the late 1960s. What I saw through the lens of my work was not tragedy in the killings of unarmed people but the long arc of history. These were predictable outcomes based on the logic of weaponized fear in a legal system designed to associate blackness with dangerousness.

We hear a lot about implicit bias research these days and how our brains—especially white people's brains—see young black people as older than they are, more threatening, and less human. This research has led to implicit bias training in some police departments and prosecutors' offices. But implicit bias is not the whole problem, nor does it alone change the rules governing use of force or prosecutorial discretion. For a century and a half, many of the best and brightest minds in America have produced volumes and volumes of research proving that, on average, white people should be suspicious (and downright fearful) of black people. Our brains did not end up with blind spots on their own. We have all been taught early in life with whom to play, where to go to school, what neighborhood to live in, where to work, even where to shop based on the risk of criminal victimization by a black person. Racial bias, like segregation, is not accidental; it is deliberate.

The Condemnation of Blackness is not an easy book. Nor should it be. It explores a past that like our present is complicated. Simple history lessons are often simple lies. I've noticed over the years that some readers like to describe the book in the narrowest of terms: that it exposes the "myth of black criminality." I've heard others define the book as yet another study of racism. And while both statements are true, the point is to know precisely how racist myths were built in the first place—as well as understanding why they endure. In this, we might choose to discard them and to dismantle the policies they uphold.

If the myth that black people belong to a criminal race had died a shameful death in the South during the civil rights movement, there might be no new edition, or even a first edition, of this book. It is precisely because the idea persists and has metastasized into other forms of racial criminalization that we must continue to pay scrupulous attention to this past. Obama's successor in the White House, Donald Trump, has claimed repeatedly that Mexican rapists and criminals are flooding the country's borders. Such myths have been extremely harmful to their intended victims. These myths are also pillars of the economic, political, and cultural infrastructure of America.

Ideas about black criminality are part of slavery's legacy of justifying why black bodies have been used for white wealth creation, electoral politics, and popular culture. The end of the Civil War did not bring an end to plunder, political race-baiting, and blackface. White supremacy did not die with slavery. It evolved during Reconstruction. And modern ideas emerged, at the time, to rationalize removing black bodies out of government offices and back into cotton fields.

This book shows how crime statistics became an innovative and scientific way of communicating the inferiority and pathologies of black people after slavery. These statistics became what anthropologist Michael Ralph calls a new "technology of social difference." Despite the oppression of those early years of freedom, arrest rates and prison data were considered objective, nonpartisan, race-neutral, and even post-racial. As new citizens in a society many whites claimed was now free of racism, African Americans had no excuse for their alleged crimes. It is hard to truly appreciate how soon after slavery many northern white elites, and some black ones, used crime statistics to emphasize that personal responsibility—bad behavior and broken homes—and not systemic discrimination in the age of "separate but equal" accounted for racial disparities. Crime statistics fueled gendered notions of black male pathology, and when linked to illegitimacy rates, doubly burdened black women by defining them as sexually deviant and undeserving of the protections of womanhood.

The turn to racial crime statistics was a cutting-edge idea. Made for modern times. Built to last, like the electrical circuitry invented in Thomas Edison's New Jersey lab in the 1880s. That old technology is still hardwired behind the walls of our homes and workplaces even as it powers our smartphones and latest digital devices. The old and the new often go hand in hand. If we refuse to see continuity and insist only on change, then we will miss what's behind the walls of our society. Miss how it all works. We will not understand how it is possible that America built the greatest punishment system the world has ever known.

The hunt for crime data to prove black inferiority started in the 1890s, when the New Jersey–based demographer Frederick L. Hoffman began looking. Black people had only recently become citizens and therefore subject to criminal prosecution in courts of law. Hoffman mined census reports and the local arrest statistics of a half dozen cities from Chicago to Charleston. He showed that "the criminality of the negro exceeds that of any other race of any numerical importance in this country," and insisted that the causes had nothing to do with structural inequality. The real problem was a lack of personal responsibility. Until "the negro learns to respect life, property, and chastity," he warned, "until he learns to believe in the value of a personal morality operating in his daily life," crime will increase.[1]

Over a century later, the Department of Justice investigated the Ferguson Police Department in the wake of the killing of eighteen-year-old Michael Brown. Federal agents found systemic racism among police officers and unconstitutional law enforcement practices. And yet, in their report, federal investigators wrote that Ferguson officials claimed that the "harsh and disparate results" were not "problems with police or court practices, but instead reflect a pervasive lack of 'personal responsibility' among 'certain segments' of the community."[2]

Three threads weave Hoffman and Ferguson officials' ideas together. First, racial disparities in crime rates are interpreted as black traits and reflect group behavior. Second, neither criminal justice bias nor structural racism explain high crime rates among individual black people. Third, the language of personal responsibility implies a justification for anti-black discrimination. Despite the separation of more than a century, both moments occurred in post-civil rights eras when police agencies were on the front lines of regulating black citizenship.

Indeed, there has never been a moment in history when law enforcement wasn't playing this role. "Too often the policeman's club is the only instrument of the law with which the Negro comes into contact," wrote Kelly Miller, a black sociologist at Howard University and antiracist reformer, in 1935. "This engenders in him a distrust and resentful attitude toward all public authorities and law officers. None can doubt that such a kindly attitude would go far to convince the Negro of the value to himself and advantage of law obedience and good citizenship."[3] Miller's observations were part of a broader effort of by black reformers to fix policing a century ago. National Urban League researchers Anna J. Thompson and Ira De A. Reid conducted several studies of policing in the 1920s and 1930s and found widespread evidence of discrimination and abuse.[4] More than thirty years later, after the 1960s uprisings, the Kerner Commission came to a similar conclusion and made several recommendations. The commissioners believed nothing would change without first acknowledging the structural racism built into policing. They called for the better treatment of black citizens, more effective police protection, the establishment of independent citizen review boards, and an end to "aggressive patrol."

When the esteemed social psychologist Kenneth Clark, whose research informed the *Brown v. Board of Education* decision, testified before the Kerner Commission, he saw history repeating itself. "I read the report of the 1919 riot in Chicago, and it is as if I were reading the report of the investigating committee of the Harlem riot of 1935, the report of the investigating committee of the Harlem riot of 1943, the report of the McCone Commission on the Watts riot [1965]," he wrote, doubting that yet another report would make any difference. "I must again in candor say to you members of the Commission—it is a kind of Alice in Wonderland with the same moving picture reshown over and over again, the same analysis, the same recommendations, and the same inaction."[5]

Neither Miller nor Clark lived long enough to read the New York Police Department's Mollen Commission report (1994) or the Los Angeles Police Department's Rampart Investigation (2000). Nor did they witness all the federal consent decrees and justice department reports, documenting in city after city a "pattern and practice" of unconstitutional policing: Pittsburgh (1997), Cincinnati (2001), Detroit (2003), New Orleans (2010), Seattle (2010), Cleveland (2012), East Haven, CT (2012), New York (2013), Albuquerque, NM (2014), Portland, OR (2014), Baltimore (2015), Los Angeles (2015), Newark, NJ (2015), and Chicago (2017). All except one are places outside of the South where law-abiding residents were systematically profiled, harassed, and abused. Countless men, women, and children—cis, trans, and queer folk—were harmed, with over four million stops in New York City alone. Their crimes: living while black.

A hundred years of police brutality reports reminds me of a lynching roll published in a 2014 report by the Equal Justice Initiative in Montgomery, Alabama. Four years later, Bryan Stevenson, the founding director of the initiative, opened the National Memorial for Peace and Justice to honor the lives of over four thousand victims of racial terror lynchings. The roll illustrates a state-by-state tally of every documented lynching from 1877 to 1950. The lynching roll and the memorial itself are devastating proof of systemic racism in America. No matter the guilt or innocence of the victims, the state was complicit in the killings, given that there are no known prosecutions for these murders.

There is an arc of history that connects lynching's past to policing's present. But some Americans reject this view. They exclaim Blue Lives Matter in utter defiance of Black Lives Matter activism. And they falsely equate doing a job, even if at times a dangerous one, with living in one's own skin. But there are no blue lives. Blue is not a shade of humanity. Blue is not protected by civil rights laws.

The year 2019 marks the hundredth anniversary of the Chicago Race Riot, which led to the first blue-ribbon commission on racialized policing in America. In the summer of 1919, white beachgoers stoned a black child swimming in Lake Michigan to death because he had crossed an aqueous color line. While blacks protested and pursued justice, white mobs attacked black pedestrians and homeowners. Blacks fought back. Thirty-eight people died. Hundreds more were injured. The Chicago Commission on Race Relations found evidence of systemic profiling, abuse, and corruption. Officials testified that officers routinely arrested blacks on suspicion and brought them "into court without a bit of evidence of any offense." A former chief of police admitted that black migrants "naturally" attracted "greater suspicion than would attach to the white man." Such startling testimony proved that police bias and discrimination were baked into the arrest statistics, leading the commissioners to abandon racial crime statistics altogether.

From the beginning, the collection and dissemination of racial crime data was a eugenics project, reflecting the supremacist beliefs of those who created them. It was an intentional way of sorting humanity not by an objective standard but by a convenient tool that simplified reality, justified racism, and redistributed political and economic power from black to white. The influential Harvard scientist Nathaniel Shaler wrote in the *Atlantic Monthly* in 1890 that statistics can lead the way to a new understanding of black people's "true racial capacity."[6]

The statistics Shaler called for were not facts. They were artifacts or traces of intense social conflict and ideology. They also underwrote discrimination in all areas of public life. With vicious circular reasoning, a new data revolution became the basis for labeling an entire group of people "criminal" and then stripping them of their human and civil rights. Felony disenfranchisement spread state by state and is still with us. Law enforcement's dogged faith in the numbers to this day is, as the late federal Judge A. Leon Higginbotham once wrote, "the same old poison of racial prejudices poured into new bottles."

Once we committed to measuring black lives and their worthiness as citizens and human beings by crime statistics, we never stopped. One of the most perverse uses of racial crime statistics by liberals and conservatives was to measure educational effectiveness by crime rates. Researchers published reports of how many black vocational schools and colleges had alumni with criminal records. Politicians pounced. Southern leaders claimed education actually turned blacks into criminals, citing census data that showed black people were better educated in northern states but still had disproportionately higher crime rates. President Theodore Roosevelt used crime data in a commencement address at Hampton Institute in 1906, where he told the graduates they should be proud that only two students out of six thousand had marred the reputation of their school. He then warned that no challenge in Jim Crow America was a "greater danger" to them than fighting the "criminality in your own race." Imagine the cognitive dissonance and psychological toll on those graduates that year when sixty-two black people were lynched, and no one punished.

We are still asking some of the same questions. "What have the thousands of [black] churches and schools and colleges, maintained at the cost of more than a hundred and fifty million dollars, produced?" inquired Thomas Nelson Page, a prominent white southern intellectual, in 1904. "We may inquire first: Has the percentage of crime decreased in the race generally?"[7] Since the end of slavery, access to public education for black people has been optional, or at least contingent, based on crime rates in ways that have not been true for the majority of white Americans. A Harvard economist published a study in 2012, "Does School Choice Reduce Crime?" He found that it did in fact "greatly reduce criminal activity." Should we be relieved?

I often say to my students that any serious analysis of Harvard alumni's criminal activity over the span of the school's 383-year history would likely register huge economic costs to millions of people with severe collateral consequences. No one is counting. I'm happy to be proven wrong, but whether I'm right or not misses a larger point. No one is asking the question because no matter how big the financial crimes are or how repugnant the corruption and illegal behavior of white elites is, there are no racial stakes.

Underlying every education and crime study rests a preposterous racial assumption from the past: are black people criminals and uneducable? Maybe schools don't matter? Maybe schools cost too much? Maybe schools are incapable of fixing these people? The early innovator Hoffman designed the education and crime blueprint: "In the statistics of crime and the data of illegitimacy the proof is furnished that neither religion nor education has influenced to an appreciable degree the moral progress of the race. Whatever benefit the individual colored man may have gained from the extension of religious worship and educational processes, the race as a whole has gone backwards rather than forwards."[8] One generation after slavery, Hoffman's use of crime and illegitimacy rates established the view that black education was a waste of time and money. To him and many others, the statistics proved resources were better spent educating whites. Even today's studies that pursue such research in the name of educational equity affirm the legitimacy of the enduring assumption.

We're still counting and correlating and making "tough on crime" or "smart on crime" decisions about what black people do or don't deserve in America. By always centering the conversation about how many black people are currently under some form of criminal justice supervision, the collective guilt of black people remains the core logic that continues to drive policy debates. In education, school effectiveness is not only judged on the basis of crime statistics. School itself, in too many instances, has become a correctional institution.

In his Pulitzer Prize–winning book *Locking Up Our Own*, James Forman describes a series of "terrifying and humiliating" police raids at the Maya Angelou Public Charter School in Washington, D.C., during the spring of 2000. School officials organized a town hall meeting with police officers. The students told the officers what it felt like to be treated like criminals. The black cops responded that the school was in a "high-crime neighborhood" and suggested that maybe they should "wear large student IDs." Many of the students had learned about the history of antebellum slave laws requiring manumission papers and South African apartheid-era passbooks. "Even those students who had studied none of this history could intuit the problem with IDs," Forman writes. "As free citizens, they deserved the presumption of innocence." This realization was a crushing blow to student morale. "We can be perfect, perfect, doing everything right, and they still treat us like dogs," said one student to Forman. This is what collective guilt looks like.

It does not have to be this way. One of the most rewarding aspects of sharing my work with others is making the case that although the past is still with us, it does not have to be the future. I've served on a New York City Council Anti-Gun Violence taskforce, contributed to a National Academy of Sciences report on the causes and consequences of mass incarceration, testified before congressional staffers for Senator Mike Lee and others on criminal justice reform, and participated in MacArthur Foundation–funded projects, such as a 2015 international trip to study German prisons. In the winter of 2018, I presented my research at a Vera Institute of Justice national convening of a dozen police chiefs, including retired chief Charles Ramsey, who cochaired President Obama's 21st Century Task Force on Policing. My presence at these tables, often alongside another historian, Heather Ann Thompson, the Pulitzer Prize–winning author of *Blood in the Water: The Attica Prison Rising and Its Legacy,* is a good sign.

Still, in conversations with empirical researchers, policymakers, and criminal justice practitioners over the years, I have seen up close how unevenly historical scholarship informs their work. They tend to prefer quantitative data and are often a little suspicious of academic history. One of my economist colleagues admitted to me that she didn't really understand history. Another colleague told a fellow historian at my university that she didn't get race. A senior criminal justice policy official in the Obama administration told me that he didn't have time to read much history. It is clear to me that they are influenced by history in the way James Baldwin described in a 1965 essay "The White Man's Guilt": "The great force of history comes from the fact that we carry it within us, are unconsciously controlled by it in many ways, and history is literally present in all that we do." Their own personal sense of the past most certainly shapes what they want to study, the theories they apply, how they design their research, what data they create or collect, and how they interpret their findings. And yet, some quantitative researchers are either oblivious or duplicitous about how race and racism shape their work.

When I asked the leading crime economist at the University of Chicago, who works closely with the Chicago Police Department on various gun violence research initiatives and policy interventions, how he accounted for the department's enduring problem of racism and police violence, he was speechless. He indicated that race was not central to his work. That surprised me. We spoke in late fall 2017, not long after revelations about the killing of seventeen-year-old Laquan McDonald, shot sixteen times by the recently convicted Chicago police officer Jason Van Dyke. When the cover-up of McDonald's murder was made public, protestors took to the streets. Black activists helped bring down police chief Gary McCarthy, Cook County state attorney Anita Alvarez, and some believe, Mayor Rahm Emanuel, who chose not to seek a third term in the 2019 election.

Moreover, our conversation happened just months after justice department officials released a damning report on "racially discriminatory conduct" among Chicago police, and after the first police brutality reparations payout in American history, $5.5 million to fifty-seven victims of police torture. Going back to the 1970s and lasting into the 1990s, Jon Burge, a Chicago police commander and a former military investigator in Vietnam, oversaw a "Midnight Crew" of officers who extracted false confessions from black citizens with cattle prods, plastic over their heads, and guns in their mouths. More than a hundred individuals were tortured, resulting in $83 million in abuse and wrongful conviction settlements.

I don't know exactly what to make of the disconnect with some social scientists, especially a prominent one in Chicago. The University of Chicago has a particularly well-documented history, as shown in this book, of pioneering studies on racial criminalization and discriminatory policing. One of its black sociologists, Charles S. Johnson, wrote the Chicago riot report (1922). Another graduate, E. Franklin Frazier, wrote the 1935 Harlem Riot investigation report, which was cited by Clark in his statement to the Kerner Commission. Frazier was the second most influential black sociologist of his generation after W. E. B. Du Bois. Other university researchers contributed to a 1929 Illinois Crime Survey. They found that African Americans made up 30 percent of the recorded police killings but only 5 percent of the population. In one case, a manhunt for a sixteen-year-old Chicago youth accused of breaking a restaurant window ended with police entering his home without a warrant, guns blazing; Alfred Lingle died in a hail of thirty-five bullets.

Despite resistance by some scholars, others are embracing history. Phillip Atiba Goff is a social psychologist and a leading expert on implicit bias in policing. He cofounded and directs the Center for Policing Equity. He told me that "the most important scholarship on race in policing to date is the work of historians who are able to shed light on how our traditions of discrimination live on." He cited a 2018 National Academies of Sciences, Engineering, and Medicine report, *Proactive Policing: Effects on Crime and Communities,* as evidence of how historical research led to the "most concrete conclusions" on which "a diverse group of quantitative scholars could agree" that discrimination mattered. "As with so many questions of race, the scientists lag distressingly behind the historians," Goff told me.

Goff's research examines how exposure to police contact itself may contribute to young people breaking the law, independent of other social influences. In other words, he asks: Is policing criminogenic? Back in the 1930s, remember, the sociologist Kelly Miller certainly thought so, linking the "kindly attitude" of police with "law obedience and good citizenship." Goff's work intrigues because it reflects similar questions raised not only by Miller, but also by white liberal researchers and reformers concerned about European immigrant criminality during the Progressive era.

For all that *The Condemnation of Blackness* has to say about the history of weaponized black crime statistics, racial profiling, and police brutality in northern cities, it also makes the case that crime did not (and does not) have to lead to more policing and more punishment. In showing how white liberals used high crime rates among whites in just the opposite way—to decriminalize the native poor and immigrant—it is possible to see what change looks like using the past. When I've engaged community members, social workers, congressional staffers, and even cops, this is the part of the story that really gets people's attention. It is the least well-known and most surprising.

Neither white crime nor violence justified harsh punishment and discrimination in the Progressive era. To the contrary, liberal researchers at the time called for less policing and more pro-social interventions. They avoided the language of personal responsibility. They rejected a focus on chastity and morality. They described struggling whites and immigrants as a "great army of unfortunates" driven "to madness, crime or suicide" by an unfair economic system. "It is the struggle of the masses and against the classes," Hoffman insisted, betraying his own racial double standards as the foremost proponent of using crime statistics to justify antiblack discrimination.[9] These compassionate white researchers and reformers redefined white crime and violence as symptoms of class oppression. And they built on-ramps to higher-paying jobs and exit ramps out of poverty. Like the brand-new interstate highways leading to the all-white suburbs of the 1950s, progressives paved the way for statistical white flight a generation before.

Gang-affiliated and criminally involved whites in America's fast-growing inner-city slums most certainly heightened public safety concerns. In 1903, a Boston researcher found that the Irish had the highest rates of petty crime and the Italians topped the list for major felonies. Chicago's Jane Addams, the most influential social worker and community activist of the early twentieth century, witnessed white-on-white violence daily for decades. After describing the grisly details of a gang-related shooting where a Polish youth shot the brains out of an Irish boy, Addams wrote, "this tale could be duplicated almost every morning; what might be merely a boyish scrap is turned into a tragedy because some boy has a revolver." Another white teenager from a "little farm in Ohio," she added, "had shot and killed a policeman while resisting arrest and was now awaiting the death penalty."[10]

A prisoner reentry organization in Chicago focused on the families of the incarcerated by calling attention to the struggles of white mothers who were left to rear their kids alone. In their 1907 annual report is an illustration of a single mother with five small children, standing on the porch of her dilapidated home. She holds an infant in her arms. One child stands behind her, another is at her side, and two are fighting in the street. She lives in a bad neighborhood with broken windows. There is a saloon behind her home and at the corner is a cop arresting a white male suspect. This is what urban disorder looked like before it was shaded black and brown.

Progressives did not fight crime with an early version of broken windows or stop and frisk policing. They focused on root causes. Below the illustration of the broken white family is a caption that speaks for itself: "HOW CRIMINALS ARE MADE: So long as there are bad tenements; sweat shops; brutal policemen; bad jails; child labor; dishonest and grinding employers; saloons and gambling dens; so long as boys are taught to fight and allowed to carry firearms; so long as fathers are indifferent deserters and mothers must maintain the family by the washboard—so long crime will continue. What will you do to help this Association to prevent it?"[11]

In the face of an epidemic of scenes like this one, liberals helped immigrants and poor whites by building a new and improved social and economic infrastructure to support them—new housing, new labor laws, new jobs, and new criminal justice policies. In 1904, fifteen thousand

youth, ninety percent white, came before Chicago's new juvenile court—
the first alternative to incarceration. According to Addams, none of the
young people or their parents were to blame for their crimes: "We certainly cannot expect the fathers and mothers who have come to the city
from farms or who have emigrated from other lands to appreciate or rectify these dangers."[12] Personal responsibility was off the table. And abusive police were part of the problem.

What happened, then, to the great-grandchildren of those troubled
white teens who had come "from other lands"? To judge by the standards
of how black descendants of the Great Migration are still assessed today,
we might ask: How many Italian Americans committed armed robbery
last quarter? How about Irish American burglars? Or Polish American
drug dealers?

The fact is no one knows. No such data exists any more. The numbers
stopped being relevant when immigrants became white. They still committed crimes, as individuals in all groups do. But when the leading criminologist Edwin Sutherland announced in 1934 that "the second generation appears to approach the native-born of native parentage in regard to
the kinds of crimes committed," he provided the scientific rationale for
statistical white flight.[13] From that moment until now, it was no longer
possible to use crime statistics to single out the Irish. They were decrimi-
nalized as a racial group. They became part of the statistical baseline of a
universal white norm. It is that baseline upon which black and brown
deviance is measured today.

By the late 1930s, local police agencies and the federal government
followed Sutherland's lead and stopped tracking arrest data by European
nationality. It was a remarkable achievement given the long, sordid history of antiwhite immigrant criminalization, xenophobic violence, and
eugenic sterilization campaigns. Liberal researchers had convinced progressive political allies that such data was not only racist but harmful to
America's future. By discarding European immigrant crime data altogether, researchers ceased dehumanizing immigrants and stopped promoting damage imagery. Instead, they and their political allies started
lifting them up. Progressive researchers and reformers extolled immigrants' virtues in spite of their vices because immigrants were, as Harvard economist William Ripley explained, "fellow passengers on our ship
of state."[14] They rejected the nativist politics that had already led to closing the borders to Asian immigrants in 1882, and would do the same to
additional waves of immigrants in 1924.

White liberals created a hierarchy that privileged white over black criminals. White people's crimes were a primary reason to help them. It was just the opposite for black people. Their crimes were used as evidence to contain and control them. Black people were redlined out of the decriminalizing, rehabilitative policies of the Progressive era, as well as the New Deal and the postwar suburbs. They were locked into a statistical ghetto that helped justify the physical one they would fight so hard to escape.

History shows that crime data was never objective in any meaningful political sense. Crime statistics have never been just about behavior no matter how obvious it may seem that numbers speak for themselves. They are proxies for beliefs, a way of defining reality and seeing things. Whatever truth they represent in counting actual arrests or real prisoners is itself a reflection of intense social and political struggles.

The choice to single out this group or that one in crime data has always been a reflection of ideological and political power, and still is. In the midst of the Trump administration's efforts to enact a Muslim travel ban, officials wanted to create new crime data. Section 10 of Executive Order 13769 called for enhanced statistical surveillance of the crimes of certain foreign nationals. No matter how many more white Americans commit acts of domestic terrorism than others, section 10 was aimed at stigmatizing and banning Muslim immigrants. The same held true in the administration's call for a national emergency at the border. No matter how law-abiding immigrants are compared to their native counterparts, Trump officials insisted—based on their own creative math—that Central Americans are a criminal menace.

Crime data never speaks for itself, nor does it lead inevitably to punishment. White House officials have labeled the opioid crisis of white drug addiction and premature death a "public health emergency"—echoing the call of Progressive era reformers to save the "great army of unfortunates" in white America. "For those already addicted, we are delivering lifesaving help" and spending $1 billion "to address prevention, treatment, and recovery," Trump announced in a White House speech in 2018. "Tremendous amounts of money and care have been given to specialty facilities" for heroin users. "People are hiring these inmates," Trump noted. "They're getting a second and sometimes a third chance."[15]

By contrast, candidate Trump evoked the language of the War on Drugs on the campaign trail in 2016. "We have to bring back law and order, in a place like Chicago," he said, citing crime rates as evidence of

African Americans and Hispanics "living in hell, because it's so dangerous." He frequently described urban violence as American "carnage." In his successful bid for the White House, he garnered universal support from police unions.

Nearly fifty years ago, at the dawn of the post–civil rights era, the black novelist and literary critic Albert Murray warned about the dangers and threats of social science data to underwrite "the contemporary folklore of racism in the United States" based on "white norms and black deviations." He cautioned black people to see the "social science statistical survey as the most elaborate fraud in modern times." African Americans "should never forget that the group in power is always likely to use every means at its disposal to create the impression that it deserves to be where it is," he insisted. "And it is not above suggesting that those who have been excluded have only themselves to blame."[16]

Looking back through the lens of *The Condemnation of Blackness,* it is hard to disagree with Murray. But many do. Law enforcement, especially, has doubled down on crime statistics in what is now the era of big data, artificial intelligence, and predictive analytics. Old ideas, yet again, have been programmed into the latest technology.

At the 2015 *New York Times* Cities for Tomorrow conference on the newest advances in technology and data analytics for everything from urban-based environmental sustainability to crime control, then Police Commissioner William J. Bratton spoke about the New York Police Department's latest crime-fighting tool. I sat in the audience anxious to hear him speak. With a broad smile and supreme confidence, he praised the newest release of the pioneering crime mapping software known as CompStat, which had been at the heart of stop and frisk policing when it began a generation ago. He likened the latest version to the 2002 film *Minority Report,* starring Tom Cruise as head of a special precrime unit. Set in Washington, D.C., in the year 2054, officers gathered intelligence from a trio of precogs, humanlike beings who can predict murders and identify killers before they act. Bratton was almost giddy about the comparison; the unintended pun on the film's title seemed to escape him.

Two years later at a 2017 Heritage Foundation summit on "Policing in America: Lessons from the Past, Opportunities for the Future," Bratton gave more details about the architecture of CompStat 2.0. The software is based on algorithms and "advanced data mining techniques, we call 'predictive policing,'" he said. "Effectively, it's the CompStat of the '90s

on steroids in the 21st century." And just like all new technology promises, it was guaranteed to be better than before. "It is discriminating, not
discriminatory," he bragged. "It is precise, not prejudiced."[17]

Until he retired, Bratton was known as America's Top Cop. Starting
his career as a military police officer in Vietnam and then onto Boston in
the 1970s, he spent the next five decades running the biggest and most
racially troubled police agencies in the country. Bratton served in six departments coast to coast, from New York to Los Angeles and back to the
Big Apple. Several of these departments were subject to federal investigations for police brutality either before or after he left. Over the years, he
developed a strong personal sense of history, covering the entire span of
the post–civil rights era in policing.

But unlike the many critics of aggressive policing tactics, Bratton has
rarely, if ever, publicly questioned the value of social science data, except
when the research critiqued police racism. In his Heritage speech, he celebrated the theoretical founders of broken windows policing, the criminologist George Kelling and the political scientist James Q. Wilson, "two
personal heroes of mine." He also repudiated the Kerner Commission
findings, which he said he had read in 1974 to pass the sergeant's exam
for the Boston Police Department: "They believed at the time that the
causes of crime were racism, were poverty, were police practices in many
instances, unemployment, demographics. They thought those were the
causes. They were not. They are not. And they never have been."[18] Bratton's emphatic dismissal of the Kerner report, and all the published evidence of police bias since, demonstrates just how enduring Hoffman's
original innovation with racial crime data has been.

At the summit, Bratton said that by the 1990s, the policing profession
had finally figured out how to get past the flawed Kerner legacy. Police
leaders started coming together at a series of executive sessions led by
faculty at the Harvard Kennedy School. There, "we began to get it right,"
he noted. "The cause of crime is people." Paraphrasing Al Gore, he said
"there is an inconvenient truth" that cops go where the criminals are.
"Data-driven or evidence-based policing is not bias policing." He continued: "The disparities are not a policing issue. It is about behavior. . . . You
have the crime numbers and they are self-evident."[19]

Future historians will have to place Bratton's legacy in its fullest context. For now, what's clear is that he has had an oversized influence on
how racial crime data continues to shape the lives of African Americans
and Latinx people in the post–civil rights era. But of course, he was not

alone. Near the end of New York City Mayor Michael Bloomberg's third term, when activists were demanding an end to stop and frisk and the New York Civil Liberties Union and Center for Constitutional Rights were suing the city, Bloomberg refused to change the policy. He consistently dug in, insisting that racial disparities in stops were not evidence of bias, but of criminality. And, at times, he ridiculed critics for not understanding how crime data works. "In that case, incidentally, I think, we disproportionately stop whites too much and minorities too little," he said in late June 2013 on his weekly radio show. "It's exactly the reverse of what they're saying. I don't know where they went to school, but they certainly didn't take a math course, or a logic course."

Less than two months later, the day after a federal judge ruled that stop and frisk was racially discriminatory and unconstitutional in the case of *Floyd, et al. v. New York,* Police Commissioner Ray Kelly went on national television to defend racial profiling. He suggested that black and brown people, subjected to stop and frisk policing, could not be innocent no matter that they had not broken the law. David Gregory, host of NBC's *Meet the Press,* asked him about the 4.4 million stops of New Yorkers, over 80 percent of whom were black or Latino, and 88 percent of whom were not even subject to a summons or arrest, between 2004 and 2012. Gregory said, let's start with the nearly nine out of ten people "not doing anything wrong." Kelly responded, "It doesn't mean that people are not doing anything wrong. If you look at the statute, it says reasonable suspicion that individuals may be about, are committing, or have committed a crime." Like precogs, the police were acting on data-driven predictions based on Compstat. "There's a preventive aspect to this. People say innocent," he said, stammering his way to an explanation. "That's not the appropriate word." Their crimes: living while black and brown. "This, by the way, is the standard law enforcement practice throughout America."[20]

Bratton, Bloomberg, Kelly, and so many other police and elected officials continue to defend their vision of policing today based on what they claim the data says and tells them to do. Former New York Mayor Rudolph Giuliani put it this way: "When I assigned police officers with Commissioner Bratton and Commissioner Safir, we did it based on statistics. We didn't do it based on race. If there were a lot of murders in a community, we put a lot of police officers there."[21] In the name of saving black people from themselves, they've turned policing into the most important legacy of the civil rights movement. "In our country, the first obligation of government is public safety," Bratton told the Heritage audience. But policing has always been at the heart of civil rights activism and the fight for equal citizenship. That is the civil rights movement's most enduring legacy and unfinished business. Even to take them at their word, by their own empirical standards, there is no research consensus on whether or how much violence dropped in cities due to policing.

The history in the following pages is as relevant now as ever and makes clear that racial crime statistics did not have to lead to racialized policing or lay the foundation for mass incarceration. When white communities, past and present, faced individual acts of crime and violence in a structurally unjust society, liberals chose to rebuild the economic and political infrastructure of white communities. They chose redistribution over retribution, and compassion over condemnation.

Notes

1. Frederick L. Hoffman, *Race Traits and Tendencies of the American Negro* (New York: American Economic Association, 1896), 228, 234.

2. United States Department of Justice, Civil Rights Division, "Investigation of the Ferguson Police Department," March 4, 2015, 5.

3. "Kelly Miller's Column: How To Restrain the Negro Criminal," February 9, 1935, Folder 80, Box 71–73, Kelly Miller Papers, Moorland-Spingarn Research Center, Howard University, Washington, D.C.

4. Anna J. Thompson, "A Survey of Crime among Negroes in Philadelphia," 1925, Box 8, Folder 131, Armstrong Association (Urban League affiliate of Philadelphia) Papers, Urban Archives, Temple University, Philadelphia, PA; Ira De A. Reid, "A Study of 200 Negro Prisoners in the Western Penitentiary of Pennsylvania," *Opportunity*, June 1925, 168–169; Reid, *The Negro Population of Denver, Colorado: A Survey of Its Economic and Social Status* (Denver Interracial Committee, National Urban League, 1929); Reid, *Social Conditions of the Negro in the Hill District of Pittsburgh* (Pittsburgh: General Committee on the Hill Survey, 1930); Reid, *Trojans of Color: A Social Survey of the Negro Population of Troy, New York* (New York: Department of Research, National Urban League, 1931); Reid, "Community Report No. VIII—Monmouth County," 26; "Community Report No. XV—New Brunswick and Perth Amboy," 37, Folder 10 and 11, Ira De Augustine Reid Papers, Schomburg Center for Research in Black Culture, The New York Public Library, New York, NY.

5. *Report of the National Advisory Commission on Civil Disorders* (New York: Bantam Books, 1968), 265.

6. Nathaniel S. Shaler, "Science and the African Problem," *Atlantic Monthly* 66 (July 1890).

7. Thomas Nelson Page, *The Negro: The Southerner's Problem* (New York: Charles Scribner's Sons, 1904), 74–75.

8. Hoffman, *Race Traits,* 236.

9. Frederick L. Hoffman, "Suicide and Modern Civilization," *The Arena* 7 (1893): 694.

10. Jane Addams, *The Spirit of Youth and the City Streets* (Urbana: University of Illinois, 1972; originally published 1909), 55–59, 61–62.

11. 1907 Annual Report of the Central Howard Association, Newberry Library, Chicago, IL.

12. Addams, *Spirit of Youth,* 15.

13. Edwin H. Sutherland, *Principles of Criminology* (Philadelphia: J. B. Lippincott Co., 1934), 115.

14. William Z. Ripley, "Race Progress and Immigration," Annals of the American Academy of Political and Social Science 34:1 (1909): 136.

15. "Remarks by President Trump on a Year of Historic Progress and Action to Combat the Opioid Crisis," accessed March 15, 2019, https://www.whitehouse.gov/briefings-statements/remarks-president-trump-year-historic-progress-action-combat-opioid-crisis/.

16. Albert J. Murray, *The Omni-Americans: New Perspectives on Black Experience and American Culture* (New York: Outerbridge & Dienstfrey, 1970), 31, 38.

17. William J. Bratton, "Cops Count, Police Matter: Preventing Crime and Disorder in the 21st Century," *Heritage Foundation Lecture* (Delivered September 21, 2017), March 27, 2018, 12.

18. Ibid., 5.

19. Ibid., 11.

20. "MTP Preview: Ray Kelly on Stop and Frisk," accessed March 15, 2019, http://www.nbcnews.com/video/meet-the-press/52776215.

21. Joanna Rothkopf, "Rudy Giuliani: Black people should be responsible for reducing police tensions," *Salon,* December 1, 2014, accessed March 15, 2019, https://www.salon.com/2014/12/01/rudy_giuliani_black_people_are_responsible_for_reducing_police_tensions/.

THE CONDEMNATION OF BLACKNESS

THE MISMEASURE OF CRIME

This book tells an unsettling coming-of-age story. It is a biography of the idea of black criminality in the making of modern urban America. The link between race and crime is as enduring and influential in the twenty-first century as it has been in the past. Violent crime rates in the nation's biggest cities are generally understood as a reflection of the presence and behavior of the black men, women, and children who live there. The U.S. prison population is larger than at any time in the history of the penitentiary anywhere in the world. Nearly half of the more than two million Americans behind bars are African Americans, and an unprecedented number of black men will likely go to prison during the course of their lives. These grim statistics are well known and frequently cited by white and black Americans; indeed for many they define black humanity.[1] In all manner of conversations about race—from debates about parenting to education to urban life—black crime statistics are ubiquitous.[2] By the same token, white crime statistics are virtually invisible, except when used to dramatize the excessive criminality of African Americans. Although the statistical language of black criminality often means different things to different people, it is the glue that binds race to crime today as in the past.[3]

How was the statistical link between blackness and criminality initially forged?[4] Who were the central actors?[5] By what means did black and white social scientists, social reformers, journalists, antiracist activists, law enforcement officials, and politicians construct, contest, and corroborate their claims regarding black criminality? How did they use crime among blacks to articulate their vision of race relations in modern urban America: what it was, what it is, and what it should be?[6] How did they incorporate others' ideas about race into their own suggestions about and solutions to the "Negro Problem"? How did they

1

produce, translate, and disseminate racial knowledge about crime to others? To put it another way, between 1890 and 1940, how and why did racial crime statistics become what Ted Porter calls a "strategy of communication"—a subject of dialogue and debate—about blacks' fitness for modern life?[7] Why did black criminality outpace, at times, many competitors—such as body odor, brain size, disease, and intelligence—in the national marketplace of ideas about, and "scientific" proofs of, black inferiority?[8]

In 1928 Thorsten Sellin, one of the nation's most respected white sociologists, argued that African Americans were unfairly stigmatized by their criminality. His article, "The Negro Criminal: A Statistical Note," captured the moment when nearly four decades of statistical research on black criminality began to be called into question.[9] In the aftermath of wide-scale racial violence during the Great Migration of black southerners to the urban North, African American researchers in the 1920s published a flurry of new statistical reports of racism among police officers, prosecutors, and court and prison officials. Convinced by the weight of evidence presented by these "New Negro" crime experts and crime fighters—the second generation of academically trained black sociologists and social workers—Sellin brought their work to the attention of his white academic peers.[10] Speaking as a representative of the white majority in a Jim Crow nation, he exposed the "unreliability" of racial crime statistics and the deeply troubling ways in which blackness and criminality shaped racial identity and racial oppression in modern America:

> We are prone to judge ourselves by our best traits and strangers by their worst. In the case of the Negro, stranger in our midst, all beliefs prejudicial to him aid in intensifying the feeling of racial antipathy engendered by his color and his social status. The colored criminal does not as a rule enjoy the racial anonymity which cloaks the offenses of individuals of the white race. The press is almost certain to brand him, and the more revolting his crime proves to be the more likely it is that his race will be advertised. In setting the hall-mark of his color upon him, his individuality is in a sense submerged, and instead of a mere thief, robber, or murderer, he becomes a representative of his race, which in its turn is made to suffer for his sins.[11]

Sellin's "we," linked to the notion of the Negro as a "stranger in our midst," marked not only his whiteness but also and more importantly, his position within a dominant racialized community with the power to define those outside it. That same power, Sellin implied, could be used to break with the past—to change the future of race relations—because crime itself was not the core issue. Rather, the problem was racial criminalization: the stigmatization of crime as "black" and the masking of crime among whites as individual failure. The practice of linking crime to blacks, as a racial group, but not whites, he concluded, reinforced and reproduced racial inequality.

The issue here was not whether crime was real. Instead, what struck Sellin as the key variable to expose and contextualize was the ideological currency of black criminality. Since the 1890s influential black crime experts such as W. E. B. Du Bois, a pioneering social scientist, and Ida B. Wells, an internationally-known antilynching activist, labored tirelessly to deracialize black criminality. Although their early efforts to convince white academic and activist peers failed repeatedly, Sellin owed a great debt to their struggle, and ultimately their vision of racial justice. Their vision of fairness and equality included a society in which innocent law-abiding blacks would not suffer the sins of individual black failures. They imagined African Americans within what sociologist Orlando Patterson calls the "broader moral community" of the United States.[12] Black scholars and activists pursued something akin to color-blind criminal justice by arguing that equal treatment, was the first step toward disentangling race and crime, destroying a pillar of racism, and creating a society in which blacks, like their white immigrant counterparts, were included within, as Du Bois wrote, the "pale of nineteenth-century Humanity."[13] They may not have set the terms of the initial discourse, but they most certainly altered it over time in unanticipated ways. Thus for Sellin and for the many black experts marginalized within the academy (but cited in his notes), black criminality had become the most significant and durable signifier of black inferiority in white people's minds since the dawn of Jim Crow. During the 1930s Sellin would leverage his influence alongside the persistent efforts of black scholars and activists to break the legacy of racial criminalization, to disentangle race from crime.[14]

The Condemnation of Blackness reconstructs the key moments, beginning one generation after slavery, when new sources of statistical data were joined to ongoing debates about the future place of African Americans in modern urban America. With the publication of the 1890 census, prison statistics for the first time became the basis of a national discussion about blacks as a distinct and dangerous criminal population. In the wake of the Civil War and Reconstruction, when the culture and politics of white supremacy in the South and across the nation were being reconstituted, African American freedom fueled far-reaching anxieties among many white Americans.[15] The census marked twenty-five years of freedom and was, consequently, a much-anticipated data source for assessing blacks' status in a post-slavery era.

New statistical and racial identities forged out of raw census data showed that African Americans, as 12 percent of the population, made up 30 percent of the nation's prison population. Although specially designed race-conscious laws, discriminatory punishments, and new forms of everyday racial surveillance had been institutionalized by the 1890s as a way to suppress black freedom, white social scientists presented the new crime data as objective, color-blind, and incontrovertible. Neither the dark color of southern chain gangs nor the pale hue of northern police mattered to the truth of black crime statistics.

From this moment forward, notions about blacks as criminals materialized in national debates about the fundamental racial and cultural differences between African Americans and native-born whites and European immigrants. These debates also informed questions about appropriate levels of African American access to the social and economic infrastructure of the nation. Calls for greater African American access to public education, for example, were challenged by statistical arguments that education turned black people into criminals.[16] Still, to friend and foe alike, black criminality offered both a discursive and a practical solution to healing the deep sectional divisions of a war-torn nation. For white Americans of every ideological stripe—from radical southern racists to northern progressives—African American criminality became one of the most widely accepted bases for justifying prejudicial thinking, discriminatory treatment, and/or acceptance of racial violence as an instrument of public safety.

Tracing the emergence and evolution of the statistical discourse on black criminality sheds new light on the urban North as a crucial site for the production of modern ideas about race, crime, and punishment. On the one hand, the dominant historical narratives about black criminality before the 1960s have been told through southern criminal justice practices and framed as premodern. Racist southern politicians, vigilante criminal justice officials, and body-parts-collecting lynch mobs during the long Jim Crow era have formed the core subject matter of these backward-looking studies.[17] On the other hand, the prevailing history of the northern criminal justice system, starting in the nineteenth century, has been a modernizing narrative, one in which the development of everything from prisons to policing to juvenile justice to probation and parole has turned almost exclusively on the experiences of native-born whites and European immigrants.[18] In this literature, it is as if black criminality had not been shaped by modern ideas or modern agencies, or that very little happening in the urban North pertained to black experiences until the post–World War II era.[19] Much historical and sociological scholarship proceeds from this vantage point, giving the impression that the history of racial criminalization began and ended in the Jim Crow South. Then in the late 1960s, according to most accounts, a latent subculture of violence erupted and spread across the nation's northern inner-cities.[20] But the statistical discourse on black criminality from the 1890s forward was a modern invention that encapsulated northern and southern ideas about race and crime. Many postbellum race-relations writers innovatively pointed out that the highest rates of black criminality could be found in the cosmopolitan, freedom-loving urban North. Since then, such "indisputable" statistical evidence from places like Chicago, New York, and Philadelphia has been at the heart of modern ideas about race and crime.[21]

At the dawn of the twentieth century, in a rapidly industrializing, urbanizing, and demographically shifting America, blackness was refashioned through crime statistics. It became a more stable racial category in opposition to whiteness through racial criminalization. Consequently, white criminality gradually lost its fearsomeness. This book asks, how did European immigrants—the Irish and the Italians and the Polish, for example—gradually shed their criminal identities while blacks did not? In other words, how did criminality go from plural to singular?

By examining both immigrant and black crime discourses in the urban North as they were mutually constituted by new statistical data and made meaningful to a Jim Crow nation, we can more easily discern distinct (and novel) patterns of talking about race and crime. Rather than following the lead of social historians of working-class immigrant and black communities who link ethnic culture to distinct patterns of criminal behavior, this book explores the genealogy of distinct patterns of racial crime discourses. In the period under investigation, crime, despite its variability in form and expression across groups, was a ubiquitous problem across the nation—so much a problem in the urban North that it was not clear that blackness would eventually become its sole signifier.

Even the wellsprings of violent crime, as historian and criminologist Jeffrey S. Adler found in his recent definitive study of homicide in Progressive era Chicago, flowed from the same broader cultural, social, economic, and demographic shifts and tensions affecting all non-elite urban people. "Contrary to the impressions of most observers," he writes, "African American violence was similar to white violence. It resembled white homicide in the form it took; and African-American violence paralleled white violence in how that form changed."[22] From the 1890s through the 1930s, from the Progressive era through Prohibition, African Americans had no monopoly on social banditry, crimes of resistance, or underground entrepreneurship; the "weapons of the weak" and "lower-class oppositional culture" extended far and wide and in many directions.[23] *The Condemnation of Blackness* demonstrates and explains how ideas of racial inferiority and crime became fastened to African Americans by contrast to ideas of class and crime that shaped views of European immigrants and working-class whites.[24]

Whiteness scholars have shown how crucial the attributes of skin color, European ancestry, and the gradual adoption of anti-black racism were to immigrant assimilation "into the singular 'white race.'"[25] Such benefits, Thomas Guglielmo found recently, even secured the whiteness of Chicago's "Sicilian Gunmen" because their criminality "never positioned them as non-white in any sustained or systematic way."[26] Building on whiteness and critical race scholarship, I explore how postbellum southern black out-migration to the urban North—to Philadelphia, Chicago, and New York in particular—fueled an invidious black migration narrative framed by crime statistics and reshaped broader racial discourses on immigration and urbanization during Progressive era. Evoking the specter of black rapists and murderers moving north one step ahead of lynch mobs, innovative racial demographers such as Frederick L. Hoffman explicitly sanitized and normalized the criminality of northern white working and immigrant classes. Consequently, the black southern migrant—the "Negro, stranger in our midst"—was marked as an exceptionally dangerous newcomer.

One of the strongest claims this book makes is that statistical comparisons between the *Foreign-born* and the *Negro* were foundational to the emergence of distinctive modern discourses on race and crime. For all the ways in which poor Irish immigrants of the mid-nineteenth century were labeled members of the dangerous classes, criminalized by Anglo-Saxon police, and over-incarcerated in the nation's failing prisons, Progressive era social scientists used statistics and sociology to create a pathway for their redemption and rehabilitation.[27] A generation before the Chicago School of Sociology systematically destroyed the immigrant house of pathology built by social Darwinists and eugenicists, Progressive era social scientists were innovating environmental theories of crime and delinquency while using crime statistics to demonstrate the assimilability of the Irish, the Italian, and the Jew by explicit contrast to the Negro.[28] White progressives often discounted crime statistics or disregarded them altogether in favor of humanizing European immigrants, as in much of Jane Addams's writings.[29] In one of the first academic textbooks on crime, Charles R. Henderson, a pioneering University of Chicago social scientist, declared that "the evil [of immigrant crime] is not so great as statistics carelessly interpreted might prove." He explained that age and sex ratios—too many young males—skewed the data. But where the "Negro factor" is concerned, Henderson continued, "racial inheritance, physical and mental inferiority, barbarian and slave ancestry and culture," were among the "most serious factors in crime statistics."[30]

Similar comparisons would echo for the rest of the twentieth century. The Progressive era was indeed the founding moment for the emergence of an enduring statistical discourse of black dysfunctionality rather than the 1960s, as is commonly believed. The post-Moynihan social-scientific and public policy view of black pathology that scholars such as Robin D. G. Kelley criticize as "ghetto ethnography" began, statistically speaking, in the 1890s. The racial project of making blacks the "thing against which normality, whiteness, and functionality have been defined," was foundational to the making of modern urban America.[31] Shaped by racial ideology and racism, the statistical ghetto emerged, study by study, in the Progressive era as the northern Black Belt formed block by block.[32] Inextricably linked at birth, they grew up together.

Northern black crime statistics and migration trends in the 1890s, 1900s, and 1910s were woven together into a cautionary tale about the exceptional threat black people posed to modern society. In the Windy City, in the City of Brotherly Love, and in the nation's Capital of Commerce this tale was told, infused with symbolic references to American civilization, to American modernity, and to the fictive promised land of unending opportunity for all who, regardless of race or class or nationality, sought their fortunes. In these imagined communities of a post-slavery, post-Reconstruction civil rights America, "color-blind universalism" added an additional thread of contempt to the narrative. In a moment when most white Americans believed in the declining significance of racism, statistical evidence of excessive rates of black arrests and the overrepresentation of black prisoners in the urban North was seen by many whites as indisputable proof of black inferiority.[33]

What else but black pathology could explain black failure in these modern meccas of opportunity? Unlike subsequent commentators in the 1920s and 1930s, Progressive era white race-relations writers frequently asserted that racism had nothing to do with black criminality. They self-consciously critiqued black criminality in what they perceived to be race-neutral language. The numbers "speak for themselves" was one frequent refrain, followed by "I am not a racist."[34] A variant attached to both rhetorical strategies accused black race-relations writers of being biased and sentimental toward their own. They were accused of "coddling" their own criminals and excusing their behavior. When black experts dug in, when they made forceful counterarguments of epidemic racism in the heyday of "separate but equal"—even in the North—they were often charged with playing the race card (a concept then still in its infancy). The familiar resonance of these statements and exchanges is a testament to their longevity in American culture and society.[35]

One explanation for the staying power of black crime rhetoric is that it had far more proponents than opponents compared to other racial concepts.[36] Beginning in the late nineteenth century, the statistical rhetoric of the "Negro criminal" became a proxy for a national discourse on black inferiority. As an "objective" measure, it also became a tool to shield white Americans from the charge of racism when they used black crime statistics to support discriminatory public policies and social welfare practices. Evidence throughout the first half of this book shows that the gap in the racial crime rhetoric between avowedly white supremacist writers and white progressives narrowed significantly when it came to discussing black crime, vice, and immorality. Progressive era white social scientists and reformers often reified the racial criminalization process by framing white criminals sympathetically as victims of industrialization. They described a "great army of unfortunates" juxtaposed against an army of self-destructive and pathological blacks who were their "own worst enem[ies]."[37] Race and crime linkages fueled an early antiliberal resentment that pushed African Americans to the margins of an expanding public and private collaboration of social, civic, and political reform.[38] Northern white settlement house workers, for example, drew on these ideas when they limited their crime prevention efforts "for whites only."[39] Local YMCA officials, playground managers, and recreation center supervisors drew on these ideas when they locked black youngsters out of constructive sites of leisure and supervised play. Trans-ethnic gangs of white men—backed by consenting police officers—drew on these ideas as they attacked black pedestrians and homeowners in an increasingly violent and enduring contest over racialized space in the urban North.

To be sure, racial liberals—a subset of white progressives—pushed back against the rising tide of northern segregation, discrimination, and violence during the Progressive era.[40] Such leaders as Jane Addams and Mary White Ovington distinguished themselves in their NAACP commitments to civil and political rights. Drawing on the pioneering work of cultural anthropologist Franz Boas, racial liberals also promoted new cultural explanations of black criminality and rejected the biological determinism of the racial Darwinists who had dominated scientific discourse on race since the mid-nineteenth century. But there were limits to Boas's culture concept.[41] The statistical evidence of black criminality remained rooted in the concept of black inferiority or black pathology despite a shift in the social scientific discourse on the origins of race and crime. The shift from a racial biological frame to a racial cultural frame kept *race* at the heart of the discourse. Although racist notions of (permanent) biological inferiority gave way to liberal notions of (temporary) cultural inferiority, racial liberals continued to distinguish black criminality from white and ethnic criminality. In effect, they incriminated black culture. Attempts to deemphasize blackness and provide social welfare for African Americans never matched the scale or intensity of the Americanization project among immigrants. The racial-cultural content of white ethnic criminality gradually began to lose its currency during the Progressive era, while black criminality became more visible (and more contested by blacks).[42]

Black crime researchers and reformers in fact contributed to and drew inspiration from the cultural discourse on crime. Many black elites had embraced Victorian ideals of morality and respectability in the late nineteenth and early twentieth centuries, often trumping their white elite counterparts in sophistication and refinement. Seeing themselves as walking billboards for the race's capacity for equal citizenship, and distinguishing themselves from "uncouth" and "criminally inclined" poor blacks, black elites often employed the language of racial uplift and the

9

"politics of respectability" to describe black criminality in terms of class and culture. Their race-relations writings and their social welfare efforts were often shot through with class bias and victim-blaming. At times, black northern elites were especially contemptuous of southern migrants. In rhetoric alone, when speaking to all-black audiences or when seeking credibility and financial support from white benefactors, their talk about black criminality seemed indistinguishable from that of their white counterparts. In the first post-civil rights era of the late nineteenth and early twentieth centuries—Jim Crow's early years—ideology often trumped race for African Americans vying for political, economic, and social resources among whites. Conservative black opinion makers and race reformers who dwelt on the self-destructive behavior of poor blacks were more likely than antiracist activists to be heralded as clear-eyed and unbiased by their influential white peers.[43]

For some African American writers and reformers, black criminality was a passport to relevancy in a wider white world in which black voices were actively suppressed.[44] Others, such as James Stemons, a Philadelphia race-relations reformer and local crime fighter, used black criminality to engage in a kind of double-speak: they used the rhetoric of black criminality to draw attention to themselves for the purposes of critiquing racism. Often out of genuine concern for public safety, Stemons, Du Bois, Wells, and many others did not ignore crime in their own communities. But neither did they ignore the racial double standards in the urban crime discourse, the mistreatment of black suspects and criminals, and the poor quality of police protection offered to black communities. Despite their elitism, many black reformers tended to offer "root-cause solutions" alongside their class-infused cultural critiques of black criminality.[45]

Progressive era black social scientists and reformers also exposed and challenged the limits of racial liberalism long before the post-World War II failures of residential and workplace integration in the urban North fueled a national civil rights movement and set the stage for a national political backlash against liberalism.[46] White social workers and white philanthropists failed to invest sufficient material resources into the uplift of African American urbanites, advising these communities to "work out their own salvation" before others could help them. But black progressives cried foul, and they pressed for the same responses to their needs that were being offered to white working-class and immigrant urbanites.

10

As much as they embraced the self-help ethos of the era, and as willing as they were to pull themselves up by their bootstraps and build churches, settlement houses, schools, businesses, labor organizations, and enter-tainment venues in their own communities, they recognized that, dollar for dollar, African Americans stood most in need of community invest-ment and economic resources but were least likely to be helped.[47] In the segregated black communities of the urban North, members of the work-ing class and the elite recognized that thoughtful, constructive crime prevention cost money, lots of it. White philanthropy was the dominant financial source for all crime-prevention efforts, but native-born poor whites and new immigrants received the lion's share of attention and aid. The hidden cost to black residents was not simply victimization by bad guys, but also brutality by bad police officers and the loss of faith in American society by the young and old, who saw the police as a repre-sentation of the government's malign neglect of black people in general.[48] As black sociologist Kelly Miller noted, thoughtful, caring policing was an important solution to inspiring blacks to invest in their own citizen-ship. Better policing would lead to better citizens in a feedback loop.[49] The empathy police officers brought to black communities would be one pathway, he argued, through which African Americans would come to know they were valued in modern urban America.[50]

Beyond their own need to distinguish themselves from social and cul-tural inferiors, black reformers noted time and time again that the stigma of criminality fell most heavily on the most disadvantaged, isolated, and neglected people of the urban North. As they saw it, the Progressive era discourse of black criminality was at its best a self-serving justification for segregation and black self-help even as its proponents—white elites—helped Europe's huddled masses by advocating for social welfare agen-cies, recreation facilities, better policing, economic fairness, and an end to political corruption. At its worst, the stigma of criminality was an in-tellectual defense of lynching, colonial-style criminal justice practices, and genocide.

The worst fears of black race-relations writers, crime experts, and social workers came true when widespread mob violence and race riots erupted across the urban North during the Great Migration years and beyond. Out of the bloodshed, black researchers and reformers rewrote black criminality in terms of racism in the criminal justice system. They tied testimonies of white police officers' complicity in anti-black violence

11

to evidence that Progressive era white vice had been deliberately relocated by police (and politicians) from immigrant communities into segregated black communities. Police misconduct, corruption, and brutality, they argued, helped to produce disproportionately high black arrest rates, the starting point for high juvenile delinquency commitments and adult prison rates. In this new formulation, New Negro researchers and civil rights activists such as Charles S. Johnson, Anna Thompson, and Walter White used statistical evidence of racial disparities in the northern criminal justice system as evidence that racial crime statistics were an unreliable index of black behavior. National Urban League and NAACP–affiliated black social scientists and reformers effectively appropriated the mainstream environmental discourse of white progressives and later Chicago School sociologists, breaking, for a time, the double standard that had long precluded such logic from working on behalf of African Americans. Sellin's 1928 article captured the ascendance of this formulation and its legitimacy among some of the most influential white sociologists and criminologists in the country.

Yet even as National Urban League reports and NAACP press releases brought unprecedented attention to new evidence of police brutality and called into question racial disparities in northern prisons in the 1920s and 1930s, black criminality remained a racial problem. Certainly, civil rights workers significantly transformed black criminality discourse among many white social scientists and white liberal social reformers. Their activism also contributed greatly to one of the most persistent themes within civil rights discourse—the fight for due process and equal protection within the criminal justice system. But an emergent civil rights critique of racial criminalization did not dissolve the link between race and crime.

By 1940, on the eve of the Second World War and a northward migration three times larger than the Progressive era migration, black criminality had not become a universal signifier of poverty and social marginalization; it had not become a universal social problem in the same way that Americanization helped to unbind nationality and criminality in the Progressive era. New knowledge of racial criminalization and a new awareness of the limits of black crime statistics had not guaranteed a New Deal for blacks or a fundamental shift in the scale or intensity of social, economic, or political reform directed toward black communities. New Negro antiracism and crime prevention gained a foothold in the broader ideological debate about the origins of black inequality just when America's inner-city landscapes were undergoing dramatic changes. The harvest of white ethnic succession—economic mobility, suburban home ownership, union membership, and whites-only schools, playgrounds, and recreation centers—sown in the seeds of Progressive era reforms and crime prevention fueled a growing antiliberal sentiment that northern blacks were still their own worst enemies because immigrants by dint of hard work escaped slums in spite of poverty, nativism, and police misconduct.[51]

But contrary to popular belief, the gradual quieting of the statistical discourse on white ethnic criminality was as much the consequence of racial ideology linking whiteness with class oppression as it was the result of new social and economic interventions at the state and federal levels.[52] Liberalism fueled immigrant success even as racial liberalism foundered on the shoals of black criminality. From the New Deal through the post-World War II period and for decades beyond, "the federal government, though seemingly race-neutral, functioned as a commanding instrument of white privilege." It was a period "when affirmative action was white," according to historian Ira Katznelson. "[A]t the very moment when a wide array of public polices was providing most white Americans with valuable tools to advance their social welfare—insure their old age, get good jobs, acquire economic security, build assets, and gain middle-class status—most black Americans were left behind or left out."[53]

African Americans were also left behind in the federal government's new *Uniform Crime Reports*, a breakthrough achievement in crime reporting developed in the 1930s. The new annual federal crime reports became the most authoritative statistical measure of race and crime in New Deal America, superseding decennial census data. Not only did these reports breathe new life into racial crime statistics, reversing gains made by black crime experts since the 1890s. The authors gradually removed the "Foreign Born" category from the crime tables, and by the early 1940s, "Black" stood as the unmitigated signifier of deviation (and deviance) from the normative category of "White."[54]

The preceding half-century of increasing statistical segregation and expanding residential segregation naturalized black inferiority, justified black inequality, and tended to mask black counter-discourses and resistance, shaping race relations into the second half of the twentieth

century. Although by the 1930s the statistical discourse on black criminality in the urban North was far more contested than it had been in
the 1890s, it remained largely rooted in segregationist thought and
practice and in competing visions of blacks' place in modern urban
America.[55]

1

THE RACIAL DATA REVOLUTION
AND THE NEGRO PROBLEM

In 1884 Nathaniel Southgate Shaler, a Harvard scientist and a prolific writer on late-nineteenth-century race relations, wrote his first article on what he and many others called the "Negro Problem." Like many contemporaries in the years following Reconstruction, Shaler believed that no other nation of the "civilized" world had a difficulty as great as America's Negro Problem. All evils old and new—militarism, monarchism, and the racial threat to Anglo-Saxon purity posed by the new global mobility of the Irish, Italians, and other so-called inferior races of Europe in the industrial age—paled in comparison, he warned, to the problem of the presence of black people in America. "There can be no sort of doubt that, judged by the light of all experience, these people are a danger to America greater and more insuperable than any of those that menace the other great civilized states of the world." Shaler believed that white men of the late nineteenth century—white men of science, white men of the industrial age, white men of the modern world—had inherited this predicament from their seventeenth- and eighteenth-century fathers, who had been "too stupid to see or too careless to consider anything but immediate gains" when they enslaved Africans in America. "It was their presence here that was the evil, and for this none of the men of our century are responsible," he wrote, assuaging the guilt of his *Atlantic Monthly* readers, who would now have to continue the heavy lifting of rebuilding and reconciling a war-torn nation racked by uncertainty and anxiety about its future.[1]

Shaler's articles emerged at a crucial moment in post Civil War debates about the future of black freedom in America. His studies and many others' illuminate regional instabilities—between the North and South—within scientific and popular discourses on the nature and meaning of blackness. Their ideas reveal the stakes for late nineteenth-century race-relations writers in search of an objective and unifying basis by which to measure and judge black fitness and behavior for survival, labor, and citizenship in a newly-modernizing nation. For these influential writers, postbellum census reports ushered in a racial data revolution that became the linchpin of an emerging white supremacist discourse on saving the nation through knowledge and acceptance of black death and self destruction.

This latest crisis had begun in the 1860s. In a moment equivalent to a historical blink of the eye, four million people were transformed from property to human beings to would-be citizens of the nation. Only a decade before, few white Americans other than abolitionists had anticipated that black people would become the legal equivalents of white people. In those outrageously heady days of the 1850s when slavery debates still raged, colonization schemes were still being hatched, and white optimism still percolated for black extinction if emancipation had to come, the possibility of living among and abiding black judges, politicians, and schoolteachers was, for many, unimaginable.[2]

By decade's end the unimaginable had become reality, and the prospect of settlement and incorporation of African Americans added urgency and confusion to what many whites already saw as a desperate situation. "Now, far more than at any time hitherto, the white people of the United States . . . seem to be particularly interested to know precisely what manner of man the negro [sic] is," proclaimed one writer in his 1868 introduction to *The Negroes in Negroland; The Negroes in America; and Negroes Generally,* a timely collection of previously published statements by some of the most respected European travelers to Africa and American men of renown. "Of these American writers, those from the North are here more particularly referred to; and it is trusted that the reader will ponder well the words of such truly able and representative men as John Adams, Daniel Webster, Horace Mann, Theodore Parker, Samuel George Morton, William Henry Seward, and others of scarcely less distinction." In a nutshell, "disinterested" and authoritative white men the world over, from European colonists and anthropologists to American presidents and statesmen, had the same warning to dispatch, according to Hinton Rowan Helper: "Negroes" with their "crime-stained blackness" could not rise to a plane any higher than that of "base and beastlike savagery." Helper presented his collection of expert opinions as an archaeologist uses fossils to reconstruct some prehistoric creature for the world to behold with gratitude that it no longer walks the earth. In

Helper's case, the caption for posterity read: terrible things await a nation bent on handing ballots to beasts. "Seeing, then, that the negro does,
indeed, belong to a lower and inferior order of beings, why in the name
of Heaven, why," he pleaded with his readers, "should we forever de-
grade and disgrace both ourselves and our posterity by entering, of our
own volition, into more intimate relations with him? May God, in his
restraining mercy, forbid that we should ever do this most foul and wicked
thing!"[3]

Helper's warning failed. Reconstruction proceeded, but not before
the seeds of dread, planted by Helper and many other post-emancipation
writers, spread across the nation like crabgrass in June. When Shaler began writing about the Negro Problem after federal troops had with-
drawn from the South, after ex-Confederates had returned to power, and
after the nation had set itself on a path of reconciliation, those seeds continued to produce apprehension about a future fraught with peril. "The
forecast of the unprejudiced observer was exceedingly unfavorable. Every
experiment of freeing blacks on this continent," Shaler wrote with seeming exasperation, "has in the end resulted in even worse conditions than
slavery brought to them." Haiti and Jamaica were perfect demonstrations of how blacks' "defects" could wreak havoc on civilization. Hai-
tians had once belonged to a colonial society of great "fertile lands"
and "great industries of sugar and coffee culture" built on "mild slavery."
But with a corrupt government and a failed economy, "the black race
[had] fallen through its freedom to a state that is but savagery with a little veneer of European customs." These were "a people without a single
trace of promise except that of extinction through the diseases of sloth
and vice." Jamaica was just as bad. It had once been a "garden land of
the tropics," the "British of the South," but had now become a land of
"barbarism."[4]

America must take heed, Shaler continued. Friends of the race who
had not simply fought for blacks' freedom but also demanded their
"complete enfranchisement as American citizens," who by blind faith and
by declaration tried to "fit them for a place in the structure of a self-
controlling society," did not realize that "resolutions cannot help this rooted
nature of man." "The real dangers that this African blood brings to our
state," Shaler cautioned, lay in "the peculiarities of nature which belong
to the negroes as a race." Unlike in "our own race inheritance," black brains
stopped developing sooner, leaving "the negroes" with an animal nature
unaltered by the "fruits of civilization." The results were devastating: blacks

were incapable of controlling their sexual impulses; they were unable to work together for a common purpose; and, most importantly, they had no power to delay gratification and plan for the future. Despite their "charming nature," their "quick sensibilities," and their "present Americanized shape," these "peculiarities" were easily overlooked by those who did not "know the negro by long and large experience," and who falsely believed that they were like them. With patience and "the opportunity to search closely into the nature of this race, they will perceive that the inner man is really as singular, as different in motives from themselves, as his outward appearance indicates." "There can be no doubt," Shaler proclaimed, "that for centuries to come the task of weaving these African threads of life into our society will be the greatest of all American problems."[5]

To some readers of Shaler's many race-relations articles, which spanned some twenty years beginning in the 1880s, Shaler might have been mistaken for a typical southern racist with a penchant for anti-black rhetoric and a fondness for scolding northerners for their radical excesses during Reconstruction caused by their belief that "the negro is only a black white man."[6] These readers would not have been totally wrong; he had much in common with writers like Helper. Shaler was a son of the South, born in 1841 in a slaveholding community in Kentucky, where his father practiced medicine. Reared in an environment of "southern racial paternalism," he certainly knew firsthand the customs and habits of the Old South.[7] Beyond that, however, Shaler saw himself as a "friend of the Negro." He supported emancipation. He was a vocal supporter of industrial education for freedmen, drawing extensively on the expertise and personal observations of General Samuel Chapman Armstrong, a white commander of a black regiment during the Civil War, founder of Hampton Agricultural and Industrial Institute in 1868, and Booker T. Washington's mentor. Although Shaler accepted legalized segregation as a short-term solution, he rejected it in the long run.[8] These positions marked him and many of his contemporaries, to varying degrees, as late-nineteenth-century racial liberals.[9]

Shaler also came to intellectual maturity in a far different milieu than the southern one in which he was reared. He attended Harvard for his undergraduate and graduate training, becoming a professor in paleontology at the university in 1870. As a young naturalist he was trained by or personally met some of the leading American and European race scientists of the day, including Louis Aggasiz, G. Stanley Hall, and Charles

Darwin. Through their influence and his own talents, Shaler built a career in the North that touched not only the lives of an estimated seven thousand Harvard graduates, but also the lives of countless others through his numerous articles in popular monthlies.[10] Historian John Haller notes that Shaler's "views about mankind, half scientific, half opinion and recollection, gave him a position of immense authority in the ripening of American attitudes on race."[11]

With one foot in the past and one foot in the future, Shaler was at the leading edge of post-emancipation racial science. He was one of the first naturalists and race-relations experts to call for the greater use of social scientific methods, particularly social statistics, to measure the behavioral characteristics of black people.[12] Key individuals, such as the pioneering racial demographer Frederick L. Hoffman, would make major contributions to the social scientific study of black people, answering Shaler's early call precisely because they made novel use of statistics, especially racial crime statistics. Equally important, Shaler was one of the first scientists of his stature and influence in the post-emancipation period to leverage his northern credentials against his homegrown southern sympathies in a call for national reconciliation—what he called "a union of endeavor on the part of those of North and South, of ex-slaveholder and ex-abolitionist alike"—in the scientific study of the Negro Problem. "In many ways Shaler's concern for the Negro typified the change taking place in the New England mind in the late nineteenth century," writes Haller. "Shaler accepted no justification for slavery, but he felt too much importance had been made of the southerner's sin and not enough of the Negro's place in nature."[13]

The post-emancipation period demanded a fresh and immediate inquiry into the new reality of black freedom in America. What grade of humankind were these Africans in America? What quality of citizenship did they truly deserve? What manner of coexistence should be tolerated? These were the burning questions that animated the minds of many white Americans, especially scientists, journalists, and reformers, a generation after the Civil War.[14] These pioneering post-emancipation writers set out to lead the way in analyzing this brand-new situation while producing new knowledge about the true nature of black people.

Since Thomas Jefferson had famously penned *Notes on the State of Virginia* in 1787, numerous American scientific and lay writers had speculated about the natural traits and tendencies of blacks and their fundamental differences from whites. Before emancipation, this had been a constantly evolving discourse tied to ideological perspectives on various aspects of black enslavement and resistance.[15] But never before had race experts faced an intellectual challenge of the scale of mass freedom that so clearly demanded fresh insight. Now in freedom, many of the experts reasoned, blacks would have to rise or fall on their own virtues or vices, no longer benefiting from American slavery, which many like Shaler praised as "the mildest and most decent system of slavery that ever existed." Since blacks' vices by far outweighed their virtues, the experts claimed, without the "strong control" of their masters the freedmen would "naturally" tend over the coming generations "to revert to their ancestral condition."[16]

On one level, such thinking demonstrates the urgency for Shaler's generation of race-relations writers to understand what, exactly, blacks' "ancestral condition" was. On another level, their a priori belief in black inferiority— that "the inherited qualities of the negroes to a great degree unfit them to carry the burden of our own civilization," as Shaler explained—meant that they really wanted to know the specific ways these inherited qualities made blacks harmful or helpful to America as citizens, not as slaves.[17] They set out to revisit and revise old race theories based on the new reality of freedom.

The monumental shift from slavery to freedom meant more than the transformation of slaves into freedmen—the realization of the hopes and prayers and resistance of four million people; it also meant a paradigm shift in the terms used to discuss, debate, and deal with them. The slavery problem became the Negro Problem. What began, in Shaler's words, as the historical problem of "African negro blood that an evil past" had "imposed" on the nation turned into a contemporary crisis centered on an array of social issues related to what places blacks would fill and at what pace they would enter the modern urban world as citizens.

Using new data from the 1870, 1880, and 1890 U.S. census reports, the earliest demographic studies to measure the full scale of black life in freedom, these post-emancipation writers helped to create the racial knowledge necessary to shape the future of race relations. Racial knowledge that had been dominated by anecdotal, hereditarian, and pseudo-biological theories of race would gradually be transformed by new social scientific theories of race and society and new tools of analysis, namely racial statistics and social surveys.[18] Out of the new methods and data sources, black criminality would emerge, alongside disease and intelligence, as a fundamental measure of black inferiority. From the 1890s through the first four decades of the twentieth century, black criminality would become one of the most commonly cited and longest-lasting justifications for black inequality and mortality in the modern urban world.

Throughout the first half of the nineteenth century, before freedom arrived, much of what passed as racial knowledge in the United States was rooted in the context of slavery and relied on personal observation as the basis for measuring the physical and social characteristics of black people. Beginning in the 1830s in response to the abolitionist movement, proslavery writers, many of them slaveholders, sought to justify chattel slavery as the natural state of existence for blacks.[19] In addition to what they claimed to see with their own eyes, they drew on the received wisdom of the day: a combination of Old World travel literature on African savagery; New World race-making through colonial and state slave laws; the pseudoscientific race ranking of Enlightenment naturalists, such as Carolus Linnaeus's *Systemae Naturae* and Johann Friedrich Blumenbach's *On the Natural Variety of Mankind*; and plain old common sense, given the daily reality of the master-slave relationship as a self-evident and God-sanctioned legitimation of white over black. It all seemed the natural order of things.[20] Southern lawyer William Drayton, for example, wrote in an anti-abolitionist pamphlet in 1836 that "personal observation must convince every candid man, that the negro is constitutionally indolent, voluptuous, and prone to vice, that his mind is heavy, dull, and unambitious; that the doom that has made the African in all ages and countries, a slave—is the natural consequence of the inferiority of his character."[21]

Proslavery writers' personal observations went far toward mobilizing the intellectual and political justification for perpetual slavery and eventual secession. Since so much hinged on their anecdotal claims in an ideologically charged and highly politicized context, their credibility and authority were constantly subject to challenge. Southerners generally assumed that northern writers—scholars trained in northern universities or journalists or reformers for northern publications such as the *Atlantic Monthly*—were sympathetic to blacks. Northerners assumed the opposite about southern writers. That is why Hinton Rowan Helper, heir to this problem, was so explicit about the credibility and objectivity of his sources, highlighting their spatial distance from slavery and their status as men of character and high principle who stood above the fray and whose opinions could be trusted. Even though the sectional differences

21

that had culminated in war never perfectly matched the ideological differences between northern and southern race-relations experts, writers tended to assume that they did. Although anecdotal evidence remained a key source of racial knowledge well into the twentieth century, it left writers vulnerable to regional suspicions and accusations of sectional bias, leading gradually to greater desire for and reliance on "scientific" evidence to overcome this credibility gap.[22]

The scientific effort to prove beyond doubt just how and why African Americans were inferior began in earnest among nineteenth-century scientists of the human body. Historians of scientific racism have variously called these men naturalists, physiognomists, anthropemetrists, physicians, and biologists because of their common efforts to measure every aspect of the human body in search of fundamental racial differences. Setting the gold standard for this research early on by linking cranial capacity to racial fitness, Samuel George Morton, a Philadelphia physician and naturalist and one of Helper's experts, began amassing eight hundred human skulls in 1820, the largest collection in the world. In 1849 he published findings that the English, the Germans, and the American whites were superior racial groups compared to American blacks, Chinese, and Indians. He based these findings on the volume of shot pellets or pepper seed it took to fill the skulls represented by each racial group. Although Morton himself later admitted that he had not accounted for the physical size and gender differences of those who had once been attached to the skulls—a serious lapse in his research methodology—his work was incredibly influential.

With the groundbreaking 1859 publication of Charles Darwin's *On the Origin of Species by Means of Natural Selection, or the Preservation of Favored Races in the Struggle for Life,* the pursuit of racial knowledge through the scientific study of the body reached unprecedented heights. Many scientists followed the path blazed by Morton and Darwin, searching for the holy grail of racial difference in brain size, gray matter, skin color, genitalia, body odor, hair texture, head shape, facial shape, and jaw angle, to name a few.[23]

Still others combined personal observation with the imprimatur of science, as did Josiah C. Nott, an Alabama physician, a student of Morton's, and the leading American ethnologist in the 1840s and 1850s. As a medical doctor, Nott was one of many clinical researchers at the cutting edge of racial research throughout the nineteenth century.[24] Much of his "expertise" came from observing patients in his medical practice, from which he "verified" polygenesis, the early-nineteenth-century religious theory that God had made blacks as a separate and distinct species of humans far beneath whites among His creations.[25] Nott believed that blacks were closer to primates than to whites. In correspondence with slaveholders and others interested in his work, the highly respected scientist liked to call his research the "nigger business" or "niggerology."[26]

As much a proslavery writer and racist propagandist as he was a scientist, Nott was not alone. "Many a racist awaited breathlessly some scheme of race classification which would withstand the testing methods of science and was prepared—once such a method was found—to pile mountains of ad hoc theory concerning the character and temperament of the races onto any discoveries concerning their measurable physical differences." Even when proof of such physical differences eluded them, writes Thomas Gossett, racist scientists assumed mental differences: "They did not really need proof for what they *knew* was there."[27] By the latter half of the nineteenth century, scientific research had become an irresistible temptation for opponents of black freedom.[28]

Despite this popularity, by the 1880s the best scientific efforts to prove the physical inferiority of African Americans had fallen short. Some leading scientists slowly recognized that variations within so-called races matched or exceeded those found between them.[29] This fact did not hinder the blind faith of most Americans, including a rapidly growing segment of northerners, that "negroes" were nearly subhuman.[30] But it did continue to undercut the many assertions of black inferiority by a growing cohort of white supremacists. White supremacist members of the Ku Klux Klan, the Knights of the White Camelia, and other terrorist groups in the South who shed the blood of black Republicans and enterprising black sharecroppers did not care about scientific corroboration.[31] Across the nation, however, white supremacist scholars of the new humanities and social science disciplines, who modeled themselves on the natural sciences, looked to societies, past and present, as the independent variable by which to measure the real fundamental differences between the races.[32] Just as Shaler had done with Haiti and Jamaica, most of these historians, economists, anthropologists, political scientists, and sociologists drew on and contributed to Anglo-Saxon civilizationist discourse, a global and Eurocentric spin on white supremacy. They extolled the Anglo-Saxon origins of democracy and modern political institutions, of which white Americans of English and German ancestry were the descendants and the natural-born leaders of the United States.[33] As Shaler put it,

"Every American, born to the manner of his kind, feels the world open to him" and "when called on [will] be ready for statecraft."[34]

These new scholars of race and society shifted the scientific study of race toward a behaviorist paradigm, measuring inferiority not just by physical differences but also by the historical and contemporary behavior of "primitive" races in civilized societies.[35] That is, they used evidence of political, economic, and social status found in society to shore up the physical evidence found in the body.

In nineteenth-century industrial America, the great scientific discoveries and technological innovations that unleashed the full potential of fossil fuels and set the United States on a course to be the world's leading manufacturer and first modern superpower also produced overwhelming economic misery, disease, and death among coal miners, canal diggers, railroad workers, and men, women, and children who populated factories across the country. Inequality in the shape of unprecedented wealth and epidemic poverty called into question the basic principle of a liberal society that all individuals possessed the sacred right to pursue their dreams based on their own abilities and ambitions. While "rapacity, conspicuous waste, and inequality were becoming as American as apple pie," in historian David Levering Lewis's words, captains of industry and their political allies considered themselves to be walking examples of modern industrial society at its best.[36] But the messy fact that millions demanded a fairer share of money and power created the need among elites to explain and justify their success. They could not sustain for long their plutocratic control in a democracy based on universal white male suffrage without ideological justification. Some decided that "a little socialism [was] now in order to avoid too much later."[37] Elites turned to universities and the new social sciences for a knowledge base for the defense of their ideological program.[38] As historian Dorothy Ross observes, they "believed the survival of the Republic virtually depended on their success."[39]

In this emerging social Darwinist context, all evidence of domination in society by one group over another—as explained by Herbert Spencer, the most influential founder of American sociology and creator of the term "survival of the fittest"—came to be seen as a natural consequence of that group's inherent superiority.[40] Inequality based on exploitation, coercion, duplicity, and genocide were subsumed within an understanding that the oppressed were dominated because of their own inherent weaknesses. Scientifically speaking, then, industrial elites naturally dominated the working poor, Anglo-Saxons naturally dominated the Celts and Mediterranean peoples of Europe, and whites naturally dominated blacks in America. "The superiority of a race cannot be preserved without *pride of blood* and an uncompromising attitude toward the lower races," proclaimed Edward A. Ross, an avowed Anglo-Saxonist and pioneering sociologist, at one of the earliest annual meetings of the American Academy of Political and Social Science.[41]

According to the dictates of Anglo-Saxonism, all lower races were not to be handled in exactly the same way. Although each race had its unique weaknesses, "colored" races in general were to be treated very differently from European races because the latter were within the pale of civilization.[42] "The problem of the proletariat, of the distribution of wealth and education, the dangers arising from the great social congestions in our cities, the difficulties of uniting one social order [out of] diverse branches of the Aryan peoples, are trials which we share with every important state in the civilized world," explained Shaler. European immigrants were indigenous whites; they were assimilable not just culturally and economically but biologically as well. "We can see how English, Irish, French, Germans, and Italians may, after a time of trouble, mingle their blood and their motives in a common race, which may be as strong or even stronger, for the blending these diversities."[43] In this formulation, as post-emancipation writers wrestled with the relative challenges of incorporating various Europeans "races" versus "Africans" into a rapidly growing U.S. economy, Anglo-Saxonism was indistinguishable from white supremacy. In the words of W. E. B. Du Bois, a student of Shaler's and the first black social scientist to attain national status as a race expert:

> [The] widening of the idea of common humanity is of slow growth and to-day but dimly realized. We grant full citizenship in the World Commonwealth to the "Anglo-Saxon" (whatever that may mean), the Teuton and the Latin; then with just a shade of reluctance we extend it to the Celt and Slav. We half deny it to the yellow races of Asia, admit the brown Indians to an ante-room only on the strength of an undeniable past; but with the Negroes of Africa we come to a full stop, and in its heart the civilized world with one accord denies that these come within the pale of nineteenth-century Humanity.[44]

Whatever geology Du Bois learned from Shaler at Harvard, he did not imbibe Shaler's view of the Negro Problem.[45] Numerous scholars have demonstrated that at the moment the Negro Problem was becoming a major subject of social thought and social scientific investigation, even as social Darwinists, Anglo-Saxonists, and later eugenicists produced volumes of literature on the inferiority of southern and eastern Europeans, late-nineteenth-century race-relations writers began to clearly articulate the modern foundations of white privilege.[46]

Being on the white side of the color line in the late nineteenth century was by no means adequate protection against oppression of all sorts, including racial violence. In the urban North, xenophobia and nativist violence were daily facts of life among, and against, various European immigrants competing economically, politically, and socially for a small share of the wealth accruing to mostly native-born whites.[47] Nevertheless, in a world where blackness presumptively defined savagery, whiteness had its privileges.[48] In Rayford Logan's classic study of the white racial attitudes portrayed in major newspapers and literary magazines of the North between the end of Reconstruction and the rise of Jim Crow, a period he called the "nadir," he wrote that "the 'belligerent' Irishman, the 'tight-fisted' Scotsman, the 'dumb' Swede were inherently less objectionable than the 'lazy, improvident, child-like, irresponsible, chicken-stealing, crap-shooting, policy-playing, razor-toting, immoral and criminal' Negro."[49] The anti-immigrant expressions of free blacks of the antebellum North also testified to the advantages of European newcomers; they observed firsthand the adoption of anti-black racism by new immigrants and the steady erosion of job opportunities for blacks. "Every hour," wrote Frederick Douglass, "sees us elbowed out of some employment to make room perhaps for some newly-arrived immigrants, whose hunger and color are thought to give them especial favor."[50] In his recent study of late-nineteenth- and early-twentieth-century Italian migration to Chicago, historian Thomas Guglielmo echoes the arguments and observations of Logan and Douglass:

> In the end, Italians' many perceived racial inadequacies aside, they were still largely accepted as white by the widest variety of people and institutions—naturalization laws and courts, the U.S. census, race science, anti-immigrant racialisms, newspapers, unions, employers, neighbors, realtors, settlement houses, politicians, and political parties.... For much of the turn-of-the century and interwar years, then, Italians were white on arrival not so much because of the way they viewed themselves, but because of the way others viewed and treated them.[51]

Although social Darwinism and nativism were defining ideological forces in the Gilded Age, they were not universally embraced by all social scientists. Many northern sociologists were "deeply committed to the study of social issues, and their basic stance was one of social reform."[52] In particular, they proactively sought to aid a new cohort of urban reformers called progressives who wanted to stem the violence, social disorder, and class conflict among native-born white Americans and new European immigrants. Together as scholars and activists, sometimes one and the same, they highlighted the need for reform of many social ills from sanitation to food regulation, from inadequate building codes to tenements, from monopoly power to political corruption, from alcoholism to prostitution. Like their reform counterparts, many northern sociologists believed that white immigrants possessed enough latent talent that, with outside help, they were capable of overcoming their shortcomings. Most believed that Europe's lower races, though uncouth, were still the beneficiaries of European civilization and were therefore much farther along on the evolutionary scale of progress than Africans who, as Georg Wilhelm Friedrich Hegel had argued earlier in the nineteenth century, were still in a state of nature.[53] On their way to a higher plane of civilization in the United States, new immigrants' advance in the "struggle for mastery" would take place in the northern inner city, as Anglo-Saxons' had triumphed in the Great Plains.[54] On the northern inner-city frontier, however, it would be urban progressives rather than the U.S. Army that would help to make their settlement possible through social reform. Yet in both places Native Americans and African Americans were either outside the boundaries of reform or stood in the way.

White progressives, it must be said, were unified only in their typically middle- to upper-class backgrounds, their high level of education, their belief in knowledge-based reform and advocacy, and their commitment to serving primarily the interests of white communities. Otherwise, they varied widely in temperament, in style, in the causes they pursued, in their belief systems, in their political affiliations, and in their views of black people.[55] By region, southern progressives tended to support industrial education for blacks. They often complained about the negative consequences of Jim Crow segregation, the isolation of blacks, and the loss of contact with white society; they tended to be among the few southerners who quietly criticized lynching as a "necessary evil."[56] Northern progressives were like their southern counterparts in their commitment to funding black education in the South, in their ambivalent acceptance of segregation, and in their intermittent expressions of disgust for lynch mobs.[57] Beyond that, however, they tended to have a limited view of the conditions facing black northerners and to varying degrees often practiced segregation and discrimination in the same communities in which they actively helped whites.[58]

Ray Stannard Baker, a northern journalist, observed the growing exclusion of blacks from northern reform efforts—what he called the extension of the color line from the South to the North. In his 1907 study, *Following the Color Line: American Negro Citizenship in the Progressive Era,* Baker reported on the racial attitudes of northerners in several cities, including Indianapolis, Cincinnati, Philadelphia, New York, Chicago, and Boston. "In Boston, of all places," he wrote:

> I expected to find much of the old [antislavery] sentiment. It does exist among some of the older men and women, but I was surprised at the general attitude which I encountered. It was one of hesitation and withdrawal. Summed up, I think the feeling of the better class of people in Boston (and elsewhere in Northern cities) must be stated: We have helped the Negro to liberty; we have helped to educate him; we have encouraged him to stand on his own feet. Now let's see what he can do for himself. After all, he must survive or perish by his own efforts. . . . Northern white people would seem to be more interested in the distant Southern Negro than in the Negro at their doors.[59]

Gone were the days of New England's firebrand antislavery activists and writers such as William Lloyd Garrison and radical Republicans such as Thaddeus Stevens and Charles Sumner. In reference to Garrison's diminishing influence as early as 1884, black journalist T. Thomas Fortune wrote, "There are no 'Liberators' today."[60]

Many northern white progressives rejected social Darwinism among whites while simultaneously espousing some variation of racial Darwinism among blacks, limiting their effectiveness as advocates of reform for blacks. According to Gossett, "It is an ironic fact that the men who challenged the conclusions of Social Darwinist individualism, who championed the cause of the lower classes and argued that their low state was not generally to be explained by their poor heredity, were, if anything, more given to racist theorizing than were their opponents . . . men whom we generally think of as liberals and who did the most to loosen the grip of the social and economic laws propounded by Spencer and [William

Graham] Sumner accomplished part of their task by appeals to race theory."[61] Even progressives, whose liberal credentials on racial matters were not in question, at times and especially in relation to black criminality disseminated anti-black ideas. Two years before Baker published his widely read book on the nationalization of the color line in the Progressive era, he condemned lynching because it degraded white men to the level of black men. "The man who joins a mob, by his very acts, puts himself on a level with the negro criminal: both have given way to brute passion. For if civilization means anything," he wrote, "it means self restraint," otherwise "the white man becomes as savage as the negro."[62]

In short, northern white progressives were often, or at various periods in their intellectual development and civic pursuits, liberals and racists.[63] In his critique of Richard Hofstadter's 1944 analysis of progressives, Lewis writes that Hofstadter was indifferent to the subtleties of "the left and right wings of Progressive reform."[64] The same can be said of much of the scholarship on progressives with regard to a recognition of two camps separated by how much they resisted the status quo on race relations. The smaller of the two camps, comprising the first generation of modern racial liberals, eventually helped to spearhead or lend their financial support to nascent civil rights organizations, such as the National Association for the Advancement of Colored People (NAACP), founded in 1910. NAACP founders were responding to increasing northern racial violence in the first decade of the twentieth century and to the outcries of local black activists.[65] But in many instances, northern white progressives neglected to think systematically about black people as one more struggling group like Italians, Russians, Jews, or poor native whites who needed their help. Consequently, whether by choice or unwittingly, many northern white progressives failed to act proactively on blacks' behalf. To be sure, there were courageous men and women who transcended the moment.

The Great Migration altered this general pattern of neglect, but the Progressive era was over by then. Reflecting the influence of post-emancipation writers like Shaler on their racial attitudes, many northern sociologists had pro-southern sympathies, according to historical sociologist John Stanfield, and "rarely inquired into black life mainly because they assumed that blacks were the South's problem." Many of them also believed that northern blacks were the primary source of their own problems.[66] As Frank Blackmar, a University of Kansas sociologist, put it, "Owing to his ignorance, superstition, indolence, childish nature, and racial characteristics, he is his own worst enemy."[67]

29

Shaler acknowledged the disinterest of his northern colleagues by calling for more of them to become involved, uniting "ex-abolitionist and ex-slaveholder alike." But until the Great Migration era, many of them followed the ideological temper of the times and left the bulk of the initial charting of the Negro Problem to southerners. Beginning in 1895, within the first fifteen volumes of the *American Journal of Sociology,* sociology's premier academic journal, the Negro Problem "was little discussed and not defined as reformable," according to historical sociologist James McKee. "From the 1890s on, the North was so focused on its own problems, particularly those of the new corporate economy and the new massive wave of immigrants from Europe, that it had little concern for the blacks in the South."[68] Lewis adds, "[T]he new northern wisdom in race relations counseled the sons and daughters of the abolitionists that it was unrealistic to expect African-Americans to measure up fully to obligations of citizenship, that it was both kinder and more expedient to entrust them to solutions devised by the white South."[69] This does not undercut the claims made above that a national discourse on the Negro Problem was ascendant at this time. It does, however, emphasize the sectional differences at play within the discourse as various reformers set out to save the nation by enacting Jim Crow in the South and Americanization in the North. Many northern sociologists pursued a proactive agenda on behalf of white immigrants and struggling native whites, just as southern sociologists pursued a proactive agenda on behalf of white supremacy.

The Negro Problem or Race Problem was, then, according to those who used these terms, partly an extension of the reconstitution of new economic roles for new groups in society, partly a product of a growing belief that black people could not and should not be assimilated as truly free members of a white society, and partly a new intellectual synthesis of the two. The vicious backlash against black southerners who were attempting to assert their freedom in every arena of life during and after Reconstruction gradually unfolded as a tale of national progress, of the triumph of a stronger race over a weaker race. Nearly every manner of anti-black terror, oppression, and exploitation, from lynching to convict leasing to political disenfranchisement, brought forth new intellectual efforts of racial justification.[70] The very health of the nation depended on legitimate and unprejudiced policies of subjugation when workable in light of African Americans' newly granted constitutional rights, and malign neglect otherwise. "I am far from blaming the Southern whites for their action in summarily excluding the enfranchised race from political advancement," Shaler wrote, as the long shadow of Jim Crow began to spread across the nation in the 1890s. "The ignorance of these Africans, their general lack of all the instincts of a freeman, have made this course, it seems to me, for the time at least, imperatively necessary."[71] The science of racial inferiority and the politics of racial subjugation converged in new ways in the 1890s.[72]

The new social scientific imperative of the late nineteenth and early twentieth centuries was to save the nation by measuring black inferiority through any sign of African Americans' failure to dominate or to lead or even to survive in modern society. These new scholars hoped that post-emancipation demographic reports, with their tallies of births, deaths, morbidity, and prisoners, would prove to be key indicators of black fitness or lack thereof. "Unhappily for our inquiry there is a lack of statistical data on which we can hope to base a definite conclusion as to the physical condition of the negroes of the southern States," Shaler wrote in 1890, just before the twelfth census was published.[73] Although the tenth census of 1870 provided the first large-scale data source on the general health and well-being of black people after slavery, it fell short for two reasons. First, given the challenges of counting the population of freedmen in the midst of the chaos and devastation after the Civil War, the sampling methods used were ultimately deemed too unreliable.[74] Second, like the 1870 data, the 1880 data were considered poor predictors of the future of the race, a future that would be shaped by children who were born outside of slavery, who had not been properly trained and cared for by beneficent masters, and who would be in their twenties by the time the 1890 census was published. The year 1890 was thus a crucial milestone, marking the twenty-fifth anniversary of the end of slavery, and initiating the first of many historical signposts social scientists used to evaluate the progress of black people.[75] Since most post-emancipation writers believed that slavery had sustained black people and protected them from their own defective biology and savage ways, this would be the first census to show how the race was truly faring on its own.[76]

The publication of the 1890 census was undoubtedly a highly anticipated event. Francis Amasa Walker, superintendent of the 1870 and 1880 censuses, wasted no time getting the word out in an 1891 article, "The Colored Race in the United States." Even before the population returns had all been counted, since only the "figures for all the late slave States" and Kansas were available, Walker used his Washington contacts to gain access to the data.[77] Table 1 presented the percentage of the "colored" population from 1790 to 1890. Though the "colored" population had grown ten times as large in absolute terms over this period, from 757,208 in 1790 to an estimated 7,500,000 in 1890, the figures, more importantly, showed blacks as a steadily declining population in relative terms: from the high-water mark of nearly 20 percent of the overall population in 1790, to roughly 14 percent on the eve of emancipation in 1860, to just under 12 percent in 1890.[78] From these figures Walker predicted continual declines in the future, leading "toward reducing the relative importance of this element in the population of the country." He claimed that the fear in the 1870s and 1880s of a possible "negro supremacy" because, according to some estimates, the black birthrate outpaced the white birthrate was unfounded. The "facts . . . show that the anticipations which so many Americans" have formed of the colored population increasing to a "very high point, have little foundation in recent experience."[79]

Walker's optimistic interpretation of the early data has been identified by several scholars of scientific racism as the "black disappearance hypothesis," and Walker is recognized as the first social scientist to interpret the 1890 census data as a ray of hope that blacks were steadily moving toward extinction in the United States.[80] In Walker's view of the relative decline in the population, the real sign of trouble for blacks was their high rate of mortality, especially in the urban North. Untrained and outmatched by white immigrants, Walker said, the race faced a virtual death sentence in the most advanced cities in America. "It will be seen from the foregoing data," he concluded, "that the colored population of the United States is at the present time maintaining" its slight absolute growth "only by means of a very high birth rate, just a little in excess of a very high death rate. . . . Indeed, in the case of an untrained and ill-developed race, any cause, whether diminution of marriages or persistence in the criminal practices, which diminishes the birth rate is more than likely to accelerate the death rate."[81]

Contemporaneous racial Darwinist and white supremacist scholars—some with liberal and northern credentials—explained this movement toward extinction as the natural fate of a primitive race, struggling to survive on its own in an advanced civilized society. They would also marshal and interpret statistical data to repudiate a new variation of the old abolitionist charge, soon to be reignited among the first generation of black scholars and their white liberal allies, that racism and racial inequality were important factors contributing to blacks' apparent inferiority.[82] Among race-relations experts, a new social scientific discourse on the Negro Problem had begun, set in motion by a racial data revolution.

In his 1890 *Atlantic Monthly* article "Science and the African Problem," Shaler perfectly articulated the imperative of this new moment. The need, he recognized, was for racial researchers to move beyond anthropometric and anecdotal evidence and to embrace the new racial demographic data. "By taking a broad statistical view of the field, it will be possible to found our conclusions on much surer ground," regarding African American potentiality. Statistics can lead the way to a new understanding of black people's "true racial capacity," he wrote, and he called for new research on morbidity and mortality.[83] Other scholars, especially American sociologists, were also on the cusp of promoting statistics as the key to "accuracy and precision" in unlocking the mysteries of various population changes in modern industrial society.[84] Richard Mayo-Smith, a Columbia University social scientist who was an avid promoter of statistics and trained some of the most successful economists of the period, wrote that "the sociologist must be acquainted with the technique of statistics, both the form of question and the methods of tabulation. He should seek to reduce his observations as far as possible to statistical form in order thereby to gain accuracy and precision."[85] Statistics, Mayo-Smith advised in a separate article, would put the "United States . . . in a position to analyze to better advantage than ever before the effect of race character upon institutions and of races upon each other."[86]

Sociologist Tukufu Zuberi notes that nationwide population statistics, which were "institutionalized by the mid-1800s," became a crucial source for social scientists in the late nineteenth century. "Especially important in this regard," he writes, "were their use of census data and the innovation of survey sample methods."[87] Since the search for certainty among racial scientists had been a continuous struggle throughout the nineteenth century, they embraced the new positivism in the social sciences as a way to close the credibility gap rooted in the sectionalism of the late war and its aftermath.[88]

With the ascendance of "statistical Anglo-Saxonism" at the "fore of the human sciences" and reform in the 1890s, abstract ideas of universal suffrage and abstract principles of equality, which had proven false and dangerous in the catastrophe that was Reconstruction, would no longer shape the future of race relations.[89] Statistical data on the absolute and relative growth of the black prison population in the 1890 census, for example, would now be analyzed and interpreted as definitive proof of blacks' true criminal nature. Such empirical evidence could then justify a range of discriminatory laws, first targeting blacks, then punishing them more harshly than whites.[90] It is important to note that Shaler did not at this point add criminality to his list of black facts to study, like disease and death, though within ten years he did, following a decade of the highest number of lynchings of black people in American history.[91]

As the twentieth century approached, it was left to others to justify this latest trend in racial terror, targeting black criminality for the newest statistical proof of black savagery and pouring racial crime statistics into the foundation of modern race-relations discourse. In the meantime, Shaler saw the handwriting on the wall even if he could not yet read it all. "It is clear that we are in the midst of a great darkness, which can be illuminated only by patient inquiry." Those who are best equipped to save the nation by helping to lead us in the "composition of our ideal society," Shaler concluded, are those who are interested in the Negro Problem and have data rather than just words to share with us.[92]

2

RACIAL CRIMINALIZATION AND
THE DAWN OF JIM CROW

With the 1896 publication of Frederick L. Hoffman's *Race Traits and Tendencies of the American Negro,* a tour de force in the annals of post-emancipation writing on the Negro Problem, statistical data on black criminality secured a permanent place in modern race-relations discourse in the United States for the first time. *Race Traits* was the first book-length study to include a nationwide analysis of black crime statistics, making it arguably the most influential race and crime study of the first half of the twentieth century. In his tone and in his findings, Hoffman, an actuary and statistician for Prudential, the insurance giant based in Newark, New Jersey, presented his work as innovative and essential. "Crime, pauperism, and sexual immorality are without question," he proclaimed, "the greatest hindrances to social and economic progress, and the tendencies of the colored race in respect to these phases of life will deserve a more careful investigation than has thus far been accorded to them."[1] Hoffman's rise to prominence, and the making of *Race Traits* and its intriguing aftermath reveals how racial criminalization linked to crime statistics helped usher in the age of Jim Crow.

Picking up where others had left off, Hoffman's pioneering statistical analysis of black criminality was embedded within a broader analysis and explanation of increasing black mortality rates as previously observed by former census superintendent Francis A. Walker.[2] In Hoffman's path-breaking formulation, crime was a major factor in the high mortality rate and was presented as a key finding in the black disappearance literature. Hoffman's emphasis on the innate self-destructive tendencies of black people, now a quarter-century removed from slavery, fueled his unequivocal argument that blacks' social and economic conditions, still largely attributed to white control, had absolutely nothing to do with black criminality. To drive this point home further, Hoffman touted his status as a northern-based race-relations expert. He highlighted data from the urban North, specifically Philadelphia and Chicago, to demonstrate that black criminality was as high in the racially liberal North as it was in the emerging Jim Crow South. The timing of the publication of *Race Traits*— the year the U.S. Supreme Court affirmed white superiority and signed off on segregation as the law of the land in *Plessy v. Ferguson*—coupled with the book's novel use of the statistical method and its cogent writing made the book the "most influential discussion on the race problem to appear in the late nineteenth century."[3] As it happened, Walker contributed to the immense success of Hoffman's study as an officer of the American Economic Association, the most prestigious social science organization in the nation, which published the book in its journal.[4]

The success of *Race Traits* also resulted from the way Hoffman marketed himself as a foreigner. His credibility was doubly secured by his unfamiliarity with American race relations and his reliance on data rather than words, as Harvard scientist Nathaniel S. Shaler had so presciently advised. "Being of foreign birth, a German, I was fortunately free from a personal bias which might have made an impartial treatment of the subject difficult," Hoffman wrote, emphasizing that he had limited his analysis to the "exclusive use of the statistical method" and had "in every instance" simply given the facts. "In the field of statistical research, sentiment, prejudice, or the influence of pre-conceived ideas have no place. The data which have been brought together in a convenient form speak for themselves. From the standpoint of the impartial investigator, no difference of interpretation of their meaning seems possible."[5] Given that nearly all race-relations writers of the late nineteenth century—self-identified experts on the Negro Problem—were tied to or associated with ideological positions rooted in the sectional conflicts of the Civil War and Reconstruction periods, Hoffman claimed that as a new arrival he had no blood on his hands.

Hoffman was indeed a German immigrant to the United States, landing at Castle Garden in New York City in 1884 as a jobless, penniless nineteen-year-old unable to speak English. Although he may have appeared to be one of Europe's huddled masses, he was in fact from an upper-middle-class family with Anglo-Saxon blood coursing through his veins. He would have received a university education in his homeland but for the untimely death of his father and his mother's insistence that he immediately begin working at the age of fifteen. Shortly thereafter, Hoffman made his way to the United States in hope of making a mark on the world. He arrived just as the *Atlantic Monthly* was publishing Shaler's first article on "The Negro Problem."[6] Although it would take roughly eight years for Hoffman to publish his own seminal article on the subject and another four to position himself as its foremost authority, by 1896 he was far from being the "impartial investigator . . . free from personal bias" he then claimed to be.

Hoffman traveled extensively throughout the United States during the first ten years after his arrival, trying to find his stride in the business world. Numerous dead-end and temporary jobs sent him to several cities and states in the Midwest, the Northeast, and the Deep South. As an avid reader of U.S. history and travel literature and a frequent visitor to museums, historical societies, and monuments, Hoffman became engrossed, biographer F. J. Sypher notes, in the "landscape, the people, and the culture around him." On his first trip south in 1887, traveling from St. Louis down the Mississippi River aboard the *City of New Orleans,* he was captivated by the Southland's beauty, noting in his diary that he had passed through a "veritable gateway to Paradise" upon reaching Natchez, Mississippi. He instantly fell in love with "the oleanders and magnolias, and especially the orange trees, which reminded him of holiday times in Germany, when his parents would receive oranges from southern Italy." But as any American well knew and Hoffman was quick to learn, when it came to race relations the postbellum South could be as brutal as it was beautiful. On the riverboat Hoffman witnessed, in his own words, the "truly horrible brutality practiced upon the negro deck hands."[7] Perhaps struck by the blatant contrast between his experience as a white immigrant who had never been the victim of racial violence while working in or freely traveling across the nation, he was no longer free of the taint of American racism. What was he to make of it?[8]

Hoffman would spend most of the next eight years, from 1887 through much of 1894, living in no fewer than six southern towns and cities in Georgia, Tennessee, and Virginia, experiencing southern culture, planting southern roots, and learning southern race relations. During a period of unemployment in 1888, he made a monthlong visit to the Georgia Historical Society in Savannah, where he was first introduced to black mortality research conducted by a local physician.[9] Eugene R. Corson's study, "The Future of the Colored Race in the United States from an Ethnic and Medical Standpoint," first given as a lecture at the society then revised and published in 1893, after the 1890 census data were published, noted higher rates of deaths from disease among southern blacks than among whites. This was a crucial finding, Corson maintained, given that the whites in his study lived under the same environmental conditions as the blacks. The difference, he argued, was the physical inferiority of blacks. Hoffman's reading of Corson's lecture was a life-altering experience. "This discussion laid the foundation of a lifelong interest in the mortality aspects of the so-called negro problem," he later recalled.[10]

More watershed moments in Hoffman's coming-of-age-in-the-South story soon followed. In the summer of 1891, in Atlanta, Georgia, Frederick Ludwig Hoffman married Ella George Hay. Reared in a "thoroughly Southern family," Ella was the daughter of a Confederate soldier and the granddaughter of a plantation slave owner.[11] The newlyweds quickly settled down in Hampton, Virginia, where Hoffman became familiar with Hampton Institute's program of black industrial education and racial accommodationism. By 1892 Hoffman had fully immersed himself in the "Negro question," expressing his private thoughts on the "worthlessness of certain negroes" and imbibing the racially conservative views of Frances Morgan Armstrong, a Hampton administrator and the daughter-in-law of Hampton's founder, General Samuel Chapman Armstrong.[12] Unlike her father-in-law and southern white progressives in general, Armstrong seriously questioned whether industrial education by itself was enough to correct blacks' racial defects. After the general died in 1893 she continued his work, "but without believing in its merits," according to Sypher.[13] Armstrong's private repudiation of industrial education for blacks, which she expressed to Hoffman, suggests that her beliefs were more in line with racial Darwinists. Hoffman, ever the quick student, learned much from Armstrong, who became his close adviser and confidant and a major influence on his writing of *Race Traits*.[14]

His residence in Hampton and his relationship with Armstrong marked the beginning of the end of Hoffman's neophyte years as a southerner and as a stranger to American race relations. A series of professional and intellectual developments during his last years in the South inspired Hoffman to combine his budding talent as a statistician in the insurance industry with his budding passion for shaping future race relations. In 1890 Hoffman wrote to Ella that he had come to realize his professional purpose in life. He saw in government statistics an effective means by which to expose problems in society and to help guide reform.[15] Although he was concerned at that time with industrial conditions among the white working class in northern mill towns, his interest shifted to the Negro Problem during his residence in Hampton. In 1892 he began corresponding with government officials, including Carroll D. Wright, a highly esteemed economist, census official, and commissioner of the U.S. Bureau of Labor, in order to collect statistical data on blacks' economic, social, and health conditions. His first published article, "Vital Statistics of the Negro," appeared in the April 1892 edition of *The Arena,* a Boston-based progressive journal. Hoffman's article was the fourth entry on the Negro Problem published by the journal subsequent to Shaler's three 1890 articles.[16]

In "Vital Statistics," Hoffman expanded on Walker's thesis that previous investigators had overestimated the "future colored population." Rather than analyze unreliable birthrate data as others had—the records were spotty and poorly kept—Hoffman turned to mortuary reports for eight southern cities.[17] He found that on average blacks died at nearly twice the rate as whites. Although environmental conditions were a factor for all groups living in poverty, the *"two main causes"* of high mortality among blacks were consumption and venereal diseases, which he linked to their "inferior constitution" and "gross immorality [Hoffman's italics]." The data, including statistics from the U.S. Army during the Civil War, clearly showed that more blacks than whites died of tuberculosis. In all these cases blacks and whites faced the same external conditions, according to the U.S. surgeon-general from whom Hoffman quoted directly in an 1889 report, demonstrating that the difference was the result of "a race proclivity to disease and death."[18]

In the expert opinion of the nation's foremost medical authority and Hoffman, health care discrimination plus the physical, emotional, and psychological toll of racial oppression apparently had nothing to do with black health and mortality disparities.[19] Although Hoffman liked to declare otherwise, it seems the data did not speak for themselves since there was more than one way to interpret them. As for venereal disease mortality, Hoffman had no actual data. Instead, he asserted that "any physician who practiced among the colored people" would attest that as many as 75 percent of them were "cursed" with a sexually transmitted disease. He followed up the anecdotal evidence with more death tables, showing that, across the board, black babies and black women died at higher rates than their white peers. From his perspective, every statistic or expert testimony was scientific proof of inferiority and degeneration. "Thus we reach the conclusion that the colored race is showing every sign of an undermined constitution, a diseased manhood and womanhood; in short, all the indications of a race on the road to extinction."[20] In his first article,

Hoffman was on his way to shaping racial statistics into a powerful, full-blown narrative of black self-destruction, racial decay, and the futility of reform. He asked rhetorically, why waste the nation's resources on a "vanishing race"?

With the forces of logic, reason, and statistics on his side, Hoffman appeared to foreclose the possibility of seeing blacks' situation any other way. Yet within the following year, in 1893, he presented a completely opposite interpretation of a high mortality problem among whites. In their case he blamed society and called for economic intervention. Suicide, the most literal act of self-destruction any individual can commit, was on the rise in the United States, and Hoffman collected mortality statistics to prove it. "Suicide and Modern Civilization," also published in *The Arena,* was, according to Hoffman, "the first time . . . the [suicide] statistics for American states and cities" had ever been presented.[21] Across the country, especially in the urban North where state and county agencies kept the best records, suicides had risen dramatically since the 1860s.[22] Massachusetts, the epitome of America's Puritan past and industrial future, recorded over 900 suicides in the last half of the 1880s, compared to 394 "self-killings" in the first half of the 1860s, a 130 percent increase. Connecticut's rising suicide rate, Hoffman found, was even more startling, growing 216 percent over a similar period. Always striking in its grandeur, New York City held the dubious honor of being the suicide capital of America in the late 1880s, recording 1,188 suicides that represented a 52 percent increase over the 1870s. Philadelphia and Baltimore had far fewer suicides but saw the rate of "voluntary destruction" increase by roughly 70 percent over the same period. If every suicide and attempted suicide were actually recorded, Hoffman wrote in a dire tone, "the army of those who seek in suicide a relief from earthly troubles would assume alarming proportions." The "plain but impressive language of statistics" had given "a picture of the darkest side of modern life." The stresses and strains of modern civilization were to blame, Hoffman wrote, and had contributed to increasing rates of insanity and brain diseases. According to an expert Hoffman cited, these individuals were victims not of "their own vices," but "of the state of society into which the individual is thrown." Hoffman agreed, insisting that the "total amount of misery and vice prevailing in a given community" was a manifestation of something fundamentally wrong in society. "The study of statistics of suicide, madness, and crime is one of the utmost importance to any society when such abnormal conditions are on the increase," he wrote in a plea for reform. "When such an increase has been proved to exist, it is the duty of society to leave nothing undone until the evil has been checked or been brought under control." The "*health* of the people" must come before the "wealth of the people." Hoffman concluded that "We must be far from truly civilized as long as we permit to exist, or accept as inevitable, conditions which year after year drive an increasing army of unfortunates to madness, crime, or suicide. . . . It is the diseased notion of modern life—almost equal to being a religious conviction—that material advancement and prosperity are the end, the aim, and general purpose of human life. . . . It is the struggle of the masses against the classes."[23]

Hoffman interpreted whites' self-destructive behavior as a consequence of a diseased society, not of a "diseased manhood and womanhood." White criminality was a response to economic inequality rather than a response to a "race proclivity." On the white side of the color line, it would take nothing short of "emergency measures" to save modern civilization from itself.[24]

Hoffman's emergent advocacy was bidirectional. On the one hand, he interpreted the data on black mortality as a race problem, a call to do nothing. On the other hand, he interpreted the data on white mortality as a social problem, a call to do everything possible—to "leave nothing undone." Taking one extreme position, then the other, Hoffman was becoming an outspoken partisan in debates about America's future well before he began writing *Race Traits*. Historian Lundy Braun writes that "he shared with other Progressive-era reformers . . . a faith in the expertise of middle-class professionals" to influence "the culture of knowledge production in the United States," and to "shape policies of the state and civil society in the late nineteenth and early twentieth centuries."[25] His tremendous influence in these areas was defined in part by his choice, and the decisions of many others, to see blacks' problems as uniquely their own, just as he chose to see whites' "struggle for mastery" as society's problem. In a society where the ideology of white supremacy was ascendant, Hoffman saw no inconsistency in his thinking. In his earliest writings he was not a social Darwinist in the sense that he thought helping the weak was antithetical to social progress and nature's plan; the problem was helping a race of people outside the pale of civilization who had, according to his interpretation of the latest data, proven themselves to be permanently inferior to all whites, including European immigrants like himself. "The city negro brought into direct competition with the white race has usually but one avenue out of his dilemma—the road to prison

41

or to an early grave," he wrote in an article following the suicide report.[26] In this racial Darwinist formulation, permanent racial inequality and premature death among blacks was a scientifically sound solution to the Negro Problem, and a progressive means to economic equality among whites through a more effective use of social resources.

In relation to the recurrent economic depressions of the late nineteenth century and related immigration and labor problems among whites, Hoffman's career was propelled by his attempt to outflank late-nineteenth-century racial liberals with novel racial statistics. Nondiscrimination laws in the 1880s forced insurance companies to offer blacks the same benefits for the same premiums that were guaranteed to whites. Prudential balked at the new laws and hired Hoffman in 1894 because of his expertise in the field of black mortality. The company wanted him to prove on actuarial grounds that discriminating against blacks was justifiable. "Prudential and Hoffman aimed to turn the racial fantasy of the extinction hypothesis into hard scientific numbers that could be deployed" for the purposes of profit and prejudice.[27] It was in this context that Hoffman made his most original contribution to the analysis of new racial demographic data by zeroing in on black criminality. Two years later he would elevate it to the national stage of race-relations discourse in an effort to silence northern racial liberals who had not yet been swayed into accepting black inferiority through biological evidence, such as small brains and diseased bodies.

Hoffman's decision to focus explicitly on black criminality was likely influenced by his encounter with a debate between two prison doctors on why black convicts died in prison at much higher rates than white convicts.[28] In the February 3, 1894, edition of *The Medical News,* R. M. Cunningham, a former Alabama prison physician, reported that "the negro mortality was three times greater than white," based on examination of "some 2,500 convicts" over several years ending in 1890.[29] Although, according to Cunningham, the site of investigation was a first, since no comparative racial study and explanation of mortality differences among prisoners had hitherto been attempted, the results confirmed previous research. The "well-known facts" of blacks' physical deficiency and asymmetrical development—their small thoracic regions versus their large stomachs and penises—predisposed them to diseases such as tuberculosis. "All one has to do is to see 300 or 400 negroes naked in a large bath-house, and then step through a door and see 75 or 100 white men in the same condition, to convince him of the correctness of this view." The statistical fact of black men dying in prison was written into the observed evidence of inferiority found in the body. Like life in the army, prison life was supposedly free of racism, eliminating it as a factor in the mortality differences. "This is certainly true at the place whence the foregoing statistics were obtained." That 85 percent of the prisoners were black, when before emancipation 99 percent of Alabama's prisoners were white, and that more than five times "as many negroes as whites [were] committed for crime" had nothing to do with discrimination. According to Cunningham, Alabama's laws were "impartially administered so far as race is concerned."[30] These disparities were also observable in northern prisons, where racial equality was a given, he explained as yet another proof that blacks were at the root of their own demise.

In rebuttal, M. V. Ball, a prison doctor at Eastern State Penitentiary, which housed Philadelphia's convicted felons, wrote that Cunningham's data were accurate but his interpretation was all wrong. Black prisoners were indeed far more likely than whites to die of tuberculosis in a Pennsylvania prison, as in other northern prisons, but the causes were related to childhood poverty, unsanitary living conditions, and poor hygiene. "In the early years are sown the seeds of tuberculosis," Ball wrote, "which require but the confinement of prison to mature and develop." He added that mortality statistics did not generally "take into account social distinctions," therefore masking the effects of poverty on populations that disproportionately suffered from it. Ball cited as an example data from the New York Board of Health "for various tenement districts" that revealed that childhood mortality rates among struggling Italian immigrants were similar to those of struggling blacks, and were much higher than for the city in general. "Make the conditions favorable for the negro from childhood up, and then first can we say that" blacks are more disease-prone. "The criminal nature of the negro must be viewed in the same light," Ball continued. Before ascribing the overrepresentation of blacks in Pennsylvania's prisons or in Georgia's or in Mississippi's to their inferiority, racial prejudice must be taken into account. "In the South, where lynch-law is most commonly dealt out to the negro, we might attempt to ascribe this greater criminality to lack of fair treatment, and prejudice on the part of the white man; but in the North we are supposed to be exempt from this accusation." Although Ball hesitated to say that northern racism was potentially as important to assessing black criminality as southern racism, he was certain that the current state of statistical analysis left much to be desired. "In criminal statistics, as in medical statistics, we do not compare classes." Until we do, he concluded, "I would refer the differences" to environmental conditions rather than to "physical distinctions." "Until the sociological factor is studied and taken into account, the so-called hereditary and racial characteristics as witnessed in the adult are liable to lead to wrong conclusions."[31]

If there was one moment when Hoffman, the young, ambitious, German-born statistical maven, had to step back and either reconsider his interpretation of racial statistics or charge ahead, fortifying his ideas with more forceful language and emphasis, this was the moment. This debate did not begin as his fight, but it most certainly ended that way when he published a rejoinder to Ball's article in the September 22, 1894, issue of *The Medical News*. Hoffman attacked Ball's every point with no fewer than twelve proofs of counter-data and counter-testimony. Most of the data and expert opinions he cited were recycled from his 1892 article, but this time his language was far more pointed and expressive, revealing a strong desire to eliminate any possible reason for interpreting the data in social terms or in a manner similar to his own position on white suicide and criminality. His strongest and most consistent argument against Ball was to unequivocally assert the total absence of racism and discrimination as determinative of the health and welfare of blacks in American society. Because "the negro is placed under exactly the same conditions, social and economic, as the white race," there was no way to explain the mortality and criminality differences other than their "race proclivity to disease and death." "Any city in the South will show that year after year, for the past twenty years," blacks died at rates 25 percent to 100 percent higher than whites. Records from the army presented similar data as "proof so convincing that it will be hardly necessary to add anything further in support of the theory of distinct race characteristics." Moreover, the surgeon-general, "a recognized authority," Hoffman continued, had come to the same conclusion "in such an emphatic manner."[32] Even the British troops in the West Indies outlived blacks in an environment where blacks had an advantage, "as life in the West Indian Islands is to the negro a paradise on earth, being an out-door rural life, with little manual labor," he wrote, echoing Shaler's words about Haiti and Jamaica.[33] Back in the United States, actuarial data "by all the life-insurance companies" confirmed that blacks on average died ten to twelve years younger (in their early twenties) than whites. With their economic incentive to seek healthy clients regardless of race and to perform routine "medical examination[s]," Prudential Insurance company's 50 percent higher payout to the beneficiaries of black policyholders was yet "another proof of the permanency" of racial difference. Hoffman continued, writing in an arrogant tone to show that Ball had missed or had refused to acknowledge what was plain for all to see: "Need more proof be brought forward to maintain the assertion that the negro and the white man differ fundamentally. . . . I could quote authority after authority to prove that such is really a fact."[34]

That Hoffman felt compelled to go to such lengths to refute Ball, given that it was not his research that had been directly challenged, demonstrates how passionately he believed that demographic evidence was the smoking gun for which so many racial scientists and race-relations writers, such as Shaler, had been looking.[35] But this was not just about one individual's pursuit of scientific certainty in solving the Negro Problem. Hoffman's was not the only voice of white absolution for the sins of America's founding fathers and mothers, nor was his the only voice speaking of black degeneracy, black savagery, and black extinction in the 1890s. He kept extremely good company in this regard, from scientists to academics to journalists to religious leaders to American statesmen.[36] Rather, this was about how one individual could make a difference in redefining a "scientific" problem and in pushing the boundaries of conventional knowledge and understanding into new research areas. At this time social scientists were attempting to raise their academic profile by becoming professionalized, by founding academic journals, and by adopting empirical methods to give their findings the veneer of scientific certainty like those of their senior colleagues in the natural sciences.[37] With a real knack for spotting emerging statistical trends in the United States and with a little help from his European counterparts, Hoffman identified key areas of demographic research, sometimes based on entirely new data that others had not yet noted or had only casually considered.

With black crime, like white suicide, Hoffman took Cunningham's and Ball's lead into the realm of black prison and arrest statistics and put himself on the cusp of yet another original contribution. Left with one final proof in order to dismiss all of Ball's interpretations, Hoffman cited a French physician's 1889 study that tied the physical differences between West Indians and "the white man" to "distinct social aptitudes," noting that "a similar study of the negro criminal in this country *would* lead to similar conclusions."[38] This was Hoffman's first published comment on "the negro criminal," demonstrating his dedication to searching for the data and to filling what was an obvious void in debates about the scientific origins of black disease, death, and self-destruction. A far more robust and pioneering crime analysis was to follow in the book. In the meantime, Hoffman haphazardly noted, without citing dates or using tables, wide racial disparities in Chicago arrest rates and Pennsylvania prison rates.[39] Unlike work on black mortality, the large-scale study of black criminality from the statistical standpoint was mostly uncharted territory.[40]

Anecdotal, anthropological, and journalistic assessments of black criminality had informed nineteenth-century popular opinion and social practices.[41] Colonial laws targeted unsupervised gatherings of enslaved men and women and conspiring free blacks to ensure against black uprisings. Antebellum blacks were often subject to discriminatory policing even as they suffered violence periodically at the hands of native-born white and immigrant mobs in northern cities.[42] Since nine out of ten blacks were enslaved until the late nineteenth century, the scientific measure of black criminality first awaited freedom, then reliable data. As late as 1893, as indicated by the absence of any mention of blacks in one of the first textbooks on what would later be considered American criminology, *An Introduction to the Study of the Dependent, Defective and Delinquent Classes* by University of Chicago social scientist Charles R. Henderson, quantitative research on black criminality had not yet begun.[43] Given how much Hoffman seemed to delight in pioneering the compilation and presentation of vital statistics on a national scale, he probably consulted Henderson's book before proceeding with his own study. The likelihood is further demonstrated by noting just how tightly drawn was the intellectual circle that encompassed Hoffman, Henderson, and others. In the second edition of *The Dependent, Defective and Delinquent Classes*, Henderson wrote on "the Negro factor" for the first time and cited Hoffman's *Race Traits,* which had been published in 1896, three years after the first edition.[44]

Another important report on the national crime situation that lacked statistical data on black criminality appeared the same year as Henderson's first edition, and Hoffman likely read it. The report was written by his colleague at the U.S. Bureau of Labor, Carroll D. Wright, from whom Hoffman had obtained data before writing his first race article.[45] Wright linked crime to unemployment and the exploitation of unskilled and uneducated workers. His only reference to African Americans was a slim mention in a discussion of general trends in industrial nations in the nineteenth century where, he argued, crime rose as a natural consequence of the transition from feudalism to wage labor and from slavery to freedom.[46] It seems likely that Hoffman noted the absence of vital statistics on black crime in Wright's article, then studied Wright's argument that preventing white crime required better protection of the white working-class against the ravages of economic depressions in the industrial marketplace. "The shutting down of the mines of Pennsylvania, or the reduction of work therein," Wright wrote, "throws large bodies of men out of employment. . . . Crime is the result, and the criminal statistics swell into columns that make us believe that our social fabric is on the verge of ruin." Wright's evocative language reflects the growing compassion of many American social scientists who, in the wake of a national recession in the 1890s, began to argue against social Darwinism. They were also arguing against the emerging biological determinism of European criminal anthropology, which was gaining popularity due to the efforts of its foremost promoter, Cesare Lombroso, an Italian prison inspector.[47] On the origins and solution to white criminality, Wright may have influenced Hoffman directly, given the tone and tenor of his suicide article.

Wright and Hoffman shared the same school of thought.[48] Society and the government had a responsibility, both argued, to protect the health and welfare of the white citizenry; otherwise crime, disease, and death were inevitable results. As Wright put it, "The health of the workers of a community is essential to their material prosperity, and the health of a community has much to do with the volume of crime." Within the general population, among Anglo-Americans and new European immigrants, the problems of disease, death, and self-destruction were rooted in industrialization and modern civilization. Harry Vrooman expressed similar views and was also a contributor to *The Arena*. A socialist writer and organizer of the Progressive Labor party, Vrooman argued that "the whole problem of crime, as to-day expressed in society, is summed up in the problem of poverty; we have churches enough, schools enough, moral sentiment enough, to regenerate the world in a decade, were it not for the awful pressure brought to bear on nine tenths of the human race, which all but forces them to be vicious." Moreover society owed the "the great army of unfortunates" not just economic security, but "goodwill" that encouraged "respect [for the ethical code]" and an obligation "to sustain . . . the social order." In other words, sympathy and compassion for working-class white Americans were as important as living wages and humane working conditions. Vrooman took his analysis one step further by attributing part of the blame for "Bowery crimes," a reference to a New York City immigrant slum, and "wage slave[ry]" to "Northern greed" during the Reconstruction period. Under "negro domination," he wrote, a "black horde of practical savages" controlled by "Yankee plutocrats" plundered the South.[49] Notwithstanding the challenge to universal white economic mobility posed by free black labor, Hoffman, Wright, and other progressives believed that at the nexus of crime and whiteness there was only a class problem. There was no race problem.

Ball agreed entirely with the conclusion that race was not the determinant factor in white mortality and white criminality, but he believed the same held true for blacks. In response to Hoffman's latest entry in what had turned into a nearly yearlong debate in the pages of *The Medical News,* Ball insisted for the second time, though much more forcefully, that mortality and crime statistics in and of themselves could not be trusted. "Figures in themselves mean nothing; they must be carefully analyzed and studied in connection with social conditions." Without taking into account a host of known "sociologic factors," statistics were an insufficient basis upon which to "draw conclusions" and could easily become misrepresentations of reality. Repeating a cliché, Ball wrote, "There are three kinds of lies, someone has said, 'white lies, black lies, and statistics.'"[50]

From Ball's perspective, the statistical lies told by Hoffman, Cunningham, and others had little to do with the actual mortality and prison data, which he admitted were not in "dispute." There was no doubt that more blacks than whites died of tuberculosis and went to prison, but explaining why was the essential problem. Ball rejected the racial meaning Hoffman obsessively gave to the statistics. He balked at Hoffman's omission of other kinds of demographic data that showed rates of mortality among the Irish and Italians living in impoverished neighborhoods of the urban North as similar to rates among blacks. According to Ball, even the 1890 census data, when read with a different interpretive lens, showed that "foreign-born whites and the children born of foreigners have the same death-rate as the colored, because they often dwell in the same surroundings and are under the same economic conditions."[51] Even when mortality differences seemed to point to racial differences, Ball found not biology, but more subtle environmental influences related to housing and hygiene. The extreme housing differences between whites of the "wealthy classes" and blacks "who live in the alleys back of their mansions" accounted for huge disparities in mortality.[52]

In regard to crime statistics, environmental factors, such as the misconduct and biases of criminal justice officials, were similarly as determinative, Ball continued. "All law-breakers are not sent to prison, and the more influential the criminal, the less likelihood of conviction. The police-court investigation in New York City shows us that morals cannot be determined by the number of arrests, and that the most disorderly element in New York City was most exempt from police interference."[53] Ball was citing the findings of the Lexow Commission of 1894, the first blue-ribbon investigation of police corruption and violence in American history, which made headlines at the same time his article appeared. According to historian Marilynn Johnson, the New York State Legislature launched an investigation of the New York Police Department after a series of high-profile corruption scandals. The investigation "produced more than ten thousand pages of testimony that detailed multiple cases of police graft, vice protection, racketeering, and election fraud." The investigation was nicknamed the "Clubbers Brigade" to highlight the connection between corruption and brutality by police officers, a hundred of whom appeared before the commission to explain their equal number of assault convictions. Like Ball, a lawyer for the commission noted the discriminatory effects of police misconduct. "Those in the humbler walks of life were subjected to appalling outrages. . . . They were abused, clubbed and imprisoned, and even convicted of crime on false testimony by police and their accomplices. . . . The poor, ignorant foreigner residing on the great East Side of the city has been especially subjected to a brutal and infamous rule by the police."[54] For Ball, then, the circumstances affecting disease and criminality among the "poor, ignorant foreigner" were likely to be as "active in the negro." Moreover, the tendency to compare blacks to the "whole white race with its four or five social divisions" exaggerated the racial distinctiveness of blacks, rendering invisible the commonality of "poverty and ignorance" among various subgroups. Such a method is "not scientific," he unequivocally asserted to Hoffman. "Thus, before we can call characteristics racial and dependent upon distinct organic differences, we must eliminate the sociologic factor."[55]

But Hoffman hardly looked back as he wrote *Race Traits and Tendencies of the American Negro*. In this full-length treatise on the racial deterioration of black people in America published two years later, he never explicitly acknowledged Ball's warnings. While he made a few veiled references to the environmental argument of "some authors," he insisted that the evidence of race deterioration was "indisputable" and that "no difference of interpretation . . . seems possible." With the notable addition of more mortality data, which he claimed had never been published or had "never been duly considered by those who believe so firmly in the all powerful effect of the 'milieux,'" much of the book was an expanded version of his previous articles.[56]

What was new in the book, however, was of no minor consequence. His major innovation was in presenting for the first time a statistical "study of the negro criminal." Whereas in slavery it was a "well-known fact that neither crime [nor] pauperism" existed, he began, in freedom the latest data positively proved otherwise. The 1890 census, according to Hoffman, showed 24,277 "negro criminals" out of the nation's 82,329 total prisoners, about 30 percent, and nearly three times the number of black men and women in the general population (12 percent). Although black men constituted more than 90 percent of all "colored prisoners" (just over 22,000), both sexes were most likely to be incarcerated for violence, "the most serious of all crimes." Out of nearly 7,000 men imprisoned for homicide, just over a third, 2,512, were black men. Black women made up nearly six in ten female prisoners convicted of murder, representing 227 women prisoners out of 393.[57] For rape, "the most atrocious of all crimes," black men composed 41 percent of convicts. For property offenses, arson ranked at the top among black men and women as a proportion of the total, at 46 percent and 61 percent respectively. Hoffman thus praised the "wisdom" of insurers in "restricting the amount of fire insurance obtainable by colored persons."[58] If the information in the book spoke for itself, as Hoffman frequently claimed, it seemed at times to have been too soft-spoken. The message apparently was worth repeating: black criminality justified black proscription.

Regarding lynching, for example, Hoffman interpreted press accounts of rape as justifying mob violence even as he admitted that there was no statistical evidence to link the two. "The evidence on this point is not such as would recommend itself to an investigation of this kind, in which official data are the main reliance," he wrote.[59] Instead he supplemented "newspaper evidence" with "the opinion of those most competent to judge," including the Virginian historian Philip Alexander Bruce, whose influential 1889 book *The Plantation Negro as a Freeman* was one of the most heavily cited postbellum race studies. Bruce, quoted by Hoffman, described the rape of white women by black men as "indescribably beastly and loathsome," without peer in the "whole extent of the natural history of the most beastial [sic] and ferocious animals."[60] Although

Bruce claimed to be impartial, dispassionate, and free of a personal connection to slavery, his book in general and his chapter on black criminality in particular represented the standard repackaging of proslavery beliefs for a postbellum audience.[61]

By relying on such experts, Hoffman combined crime statistics with a well-crafted white supremacist narrative to shape the reading of black criminality while trying to minimize the appearance of doing so. Thus the innovative and enduring significance of Hoffman's crime analysis was not only in presenting the data for the first time, but also in setting the terms and shaping the frame of analysis. Table after table of arrest and prison statistics from cities across the nation, such as Chicago, Philadelphia, Louisville, and Charleston (SC), and from states including New Jersey and Pennsylvania, Hoffman proclaimed, all "confirm the census data, and show without exception that the criminality of the negro exceeds that of any other race of any numerical importance in this country." When "the negro learns to respect life, property, and chastity, until he learns to believe in the value of a personal morality operating in his daily life, the criminal tendencies . . . will increase."[62]

Although anecdotally black criminality had already become a popular measure of black progress and potential among postbellum writers, in Hoffman's seminal statistical formulation it secured a more fundamental and permanent role in future race-relations discourse. It was now nearly impossible to read black crime statistics as symptomatic of the failed promises of racial equality in the wake of the Civil War and Reconstruction or, as Ball had suggested, to see crime beyond race as a sociological consequence of economic and social inequality in the industrial age. The construction of an avenue along which such thinking might have traveled was postponed indefinitely. Even suicide among blacks, according to Hoffman and in contrast to suicide among whites, was strictly viewed as pathological: "in most cases, to escape the consequences of his crimes."[63] Ultimately, by framing black criminality as a key measure of black inferiority in the same way that his peers and predecessors had done through anatomical measurements and mortality data, Hoffman wrote crime into race and centered it at the heart of the Negro Problem.

In *Race Traits* Hoffman brilliantly tied black criminality to a repudiation of abolitionists' and neo-abolitionists' claims that with freedom, education, and moral training blacks would gradually achieve equality with whites.[64] He framed black behavior as impervious to civilizing influences

51

by wedding increasing crime trends to the dramatic increase in black schools and churches over the three decades after slavery:

> I have given the statistics of the general progress of the race in religion and education for the country at large, and have shown that in church and school the number of attending members or pupils is constantly increasing; but in the statistics of crime and the data of illegitimacy the proof is furnished that neither religion nor education has influenced to an appreciable degree the moral progress of the race. Whatever benefit the individual colored man may have gained from the extension of religious worship and educational processes, the race as a whole has gone backwards rather than forwards.[65]

This was a powerful indictment of nascent liberal efforts for racial equality at the dawn of the Jim Crow era. Not only did Hoffman state that education and religion were a waste of time and money, but he also implied that they were harmful to the goals of racial uplift. The charge that black education by itself was a stimulus to crime would follow in the wake of *Race Traits*.[66]

It is entirely possible that, given the time Hoffman had spent at Hampton Institute, he owed some credit to Frances Morgan Armstrong for emphasizing the futility of black education.[67] "Unfortunately, for the negro," she stated, "the course of the race is influenced by those who have filled his mind with false ideals, who commencing with 'forty acres and a mule,' have ended with the prospect of an education in colleges or industrial schools." General Armstrong, with whom she disagreed, fit this description perfectly. The black crime problem, as diagnosed statistically by Hoffman and subsequent writers, undoubtedly struck a blow at the optimism of the liberal northerners who were major supporters of industrial education in the South and challenged their faith that education was the key to solving the Negro Problem.[68] From this point forward, white philanthropic and reform efforts on behalf of racial advancement would be evaluated to varying degrees by black crime statistics.

Hoffman's book was exceedingly influential across the nation, especially among leading students of American demography.[69] "The national white consensus emerging at the turn of the century," notes historian David Levering Lewis, "was that African Americans were inferior human beings whose predicament was three parts their own making and two parts the consequence of misguided philanthropy."[70] Hoffman played no minor part in building this consensus. Historian George Fredrickson writes that *Race Traits* "became a prized source of information and conclusions for anti-Negro writers for many years to come," in part because of its practical value.[71] Despite the few articles he had written as a newly minted southerner, Hoffman was a relative unknown to the vast world of race punditry prior to *Race Traits*. By 1896, however, he had remade himself in print as a foreign-born resident of New Jersey with no obvious past or association with the South. He worked as a statistician for one of the largest insurance companies in the country—an ostensibly polemics-free line of work. In the tradition of an Alexis de Tocqueville, he marketed himself as a clear-eyed, plainspoken, unbiased foreign observer of American race relations and demographic trends. Unlike Shaler, Hoffman had no obvious baggage to disclaim, but like him, Hoffman sought to transcend sectional strife by winning northerners to southerners' points of view. He reminded his readers that "racial inferiority was the keynote of the pro-slavery argument," which had been falsely "explained away" by the abolitionists.[72] With data and reason rather than passion and emotion, Hoffman tried to remove the stain of southern depictions of "black beasts," dressing up black criminality for the North. His citing of northern crime statistics and his use of *Chicago Tribune* lynching statistics were subtle ways of drawing northerners' attention to their own color-blind evidence that revealed the growing specter of black migrants "for whom," he wrote, "vice and crime are the rule and honesty the exception."[73]

In 1896 Hoffman sounded a national call to action. "Today, more than ever, the colored race of this country forms a distinct element and presents more than at any time in the past the most complicated and seemingly hopeless problem among those confronting the American people." The migration of blacks to "all sections of the country" was resulting in their increased population in "all the large cities," a fact heretofore unrecognized, Hoffman wrote, since "these tables, I believe, are the first to present with a considerable degree of accuracy the massing of the colored population of northern and western cities." The danger awaiting these cities due to this migration was cumulative. First, the rate of black population growth in large cities was faster than the rate for whites. Second, blacks "crowded into a very few wards," thereby creating segregated neighborhoods resulting in an "Africa" in the city. Finally, the black neighborhoods in northern cities were "as a rule . . . the most undesirable sections of the cities." In Philadelphia's "Africa" or Chicago's, New York's,

Boston's, or Cincinnati's, wrote Hoffman, "the colored population is found to be living in the worst section of the city" where "vice and crime are the only formative influences." The time was now for "individual states" and the "nation at large" to take heed of this "most serious aspect" of the Negro Problem—its northern population growth. This increasing presence of "undesirable characters" with their "evil effect" on northern cities was "a serious hindrance to the economic progress of the white race." "In the plain language of the facts brought together," Hoffman warned, "the colored race is shown to be on the downward grade, tending toward a condition in which matters will be worse than they are now."[74]

The fact that northern city leaders already blamed much of their crime on the slum communities of the foreign-born meant that warnings about the criminal tendencies of impoverished black migrants would have sounded more familiar than alarmist. Even the muckraking housing reformer Jacob Riis, author of an 1890 classic study of New York tenements and slum life, emphasized the common criminality of impoverished immigrants and blacks. According to Riis, "As the Chinaman hides his knife in his sleeve and the Italian his stiletto in the bosom, so the negro goes to the ball with a razor in his bootleg."[75] When Hoffman announced that Chicago's "Italians, Polanders and Russians" lived under conditions "without question more severe" than blacks, and blacks still showed the "most decided tendency towards crime in the large cities," he unequivocally marked the black urban migrant as a criminal of exceptional measure. On this one crucial point, Hoffman seemed to directly answer Ball's earlier criticism that poverty trumped race because the Irish and Italians showed similar death rates when compared to blacks in similar conditions. "Of the various nationalities enumerated," Hoffman wrote, "the Irish and Italians show a percentage of arrests decidedly above the average, yet small when compared with that of the colored element."[76]

In a milieu where environmental or sociological explanations of the criminality of native-born and foreign-born whites were ascending alongside the gradual segregation of northern blacks, Hoffman helped to legitimate the further isolation of blacks as a dangerous race with exceptional problems.[77] Historian and criminologist Jeffrey Adler observes that, as black migration to Chicago gradually increased in the next decade, "Chicagoans of European extraction, including both recent migrants and old-stock native-born Americans, often felt a powerful bond of racial solidarity," including a shared fear of blacks as criminals. Most "white city dwellers" in Chicago and "other northern cities," Adler

Figure 2-1   "A Downtown 'Morgue' " appeared in Jacob Riis's *How the Other Half Lives* to draw attention to the evil of New York's saloons that fueled crime and death rates. The large number of working-class white men of sordid appearance and likely immigrant origin pose a sharp contrast to Hoffman's marking of the black man as an exceptional threat. Photo by Richard Hoe Lawrence, c. 1890, Museum of the City of New York, The Jacob Riis Collection (Riis 162)

writes, "believed that African Americans were violent and deviant," and the whites sought various public policy measures to seal themselves off from them.[78] The first modern race-relations expert to evince the statistical connections between black migration to the North, urbanization, and criminality, Hoffman helped to certify the nationalization of the Negro Problem. He smartly anticipated that these three factors taken together would shape, to varying degrees, race-relations discourse into the next century and beyond.

The impact of Hoffman's ideas was detectable immediately following the book's publication. Among white reviewers, the reception ranged from adulation and critical acclaim to mixed praise.[79] All agreed on Hoffman's exceptional talents as a statistician, and all noted the significance of blacks moving to the urban North, spreading vice, crime, and disease in their wake.[80] In one of social science's premier northern journals, a white reviewer acclaimed that *Race Traits* was a pioneering achievement. It was a "most thorough and painstaking compilation" by a "competent" statistician to "deal with the vital and social statistics of the negro race in the United States," exclaimed Miles Menander Dawson, a New York actuary and a frequent reviewer of insurance-related publications. Thoroughly convinced by Hoffman's findings, Dawson summarized every section of the book without a single critical comment. No other race committed as much crime as blacks, wrote Dawson, despite the facts that about the same percentage of black children attended school as whites and almost the same percentage of blacks and whites were active Christians. "Even in northern cities, where abundant opportunities are given," Dawson noted, blacks are so inefficient that "comparatively few engage at skilled labor."[81] Hoffman's persistent efforts to render racism invisible were paying off.

Before launching into his own inspired denunciation of blacks, Frederick Starr, a white anthropologist at the University of Chicago and a proponent of Lombrosian criminology, praised Hoffman for being an "unbiased foreigner" instead of a "prejudiced observer"—a recognition of the stakes of post-racialism at the dawn of Jim Crow.[82] Starr's review, "The Degeneracy of the American Negro," was caustic, exhibiting the passion that Hoffman had perhaps intended to ignite. Starr's own summary of the "astonishing results" of "criminality in the two races" proved that Hoffman had unambiguously made his point to some of his white peers. "Conditions of life and bad social opportunities cannot be urged in excuse," Starr wrote, because immigrants' conditions "are fully as bad as for the blacks but their criminality is much less. *The difference is racial* [Starr's italics]." Starr reiterated Hoffman's conclusions in his own unequivocal terms: "What can be done? Not much. . . . Less petting and more disciplining is needed; fewer academies and more work-benches. Recognition of white men and black men is fundamental. The desire to turn bright black boys into inefficient white men should cease. It is imperative that we demand honesty toward the negro and decency from him. But we may expect the race here to die and disappear; the sooner perhaps the better."[83] Interestingly, the linking of crime to the folly of academic training reinforced an idea that Shaler had joked about in his 1884 article: A "little colored girl" had once said that "you can't get clean corners and algebra into the same nigger." She was right, Shaler added, noting that it was even "difficultly effected in our own blood. The world needs *clean corners,* it is not so particular about the *algebra* [Shaler's italics]."[84] In the near future, new evidence of black criminality would help to shape debates about the state of black education in America.

Not all white readers or critics of Hoffman's work, like Ball, unconditionally embraced his racialism even as they agreed that his data were sound. A notable exception was biologist Gary L. Calkins of Columbia University. This was somewhat ironic, given how much the first generation of American social scientists modeled natural scientists, and how much ideological support they drew from biologists in asserting the constitutional inferiority of African Americans.[85] Calkins described the book as an "admirable work," noting that Hoffman's logic was "convincing" and that his data clearly pointed to the "downward" trajectory of the race. But he was far from convinced by Hoffman's all-encompassing racial analysis, arguing that "racial difference" might account for some of the disparities between whites and blacks but "that it accounts for all . . . is hardly proved by the facts produced." The health-related disruptions of migration and urbanization make no racial distinctions, he argued. "Nor must it be forgotten that a race suddenly thrown upon their own resources under entirely new conditions, as were the negroes after their emancipation, must necessarily suffer change of circumstances, regardless of race tendencies." Likewise, their immorality, "which is constantly increasing," he added, "could" be viewed from the same perspective.[86]

Such initial cautions by white researchers such as Calkins and Ball gradually found greater currency among northern progressives when they began, somewhat half-heartedly, to apply their immigrant environmentalism to African Americans as the Great Migration era approached. For the moment, however, dissent was small by comparison to the attitudes of many whites who were already animated by thoughts of southern "black beasts" and who fully embraced Hoffman's empirically based, race-neutral depiction of a nationwide black crime problem.[87] For the moment, the bulk of the questioning of the new crime data and its racial interpretations was left to a new cohort of black scholars, reformers, and journalists.

These middle-class and elite black women and men were young; many had never been enslaved, and some had received first-rate educations at the most elite institutions in the nation.[88] Ironically, they were members of the generation captured by the 1890 census, the census that many scientific racists had eagerly anticipated would prove the race's inferiority once and for all.[89] Historian Glenda Gilmore calls them the race's "best men" and "best women" because they used their pedigrees and talents as personal testimonies to the race's infinite capacity for citizenship and excellence.[90] They considered themselves "their own best argument," writes historian Deborah Gray White, against the charge of racial inferiority.[91] Not all of them actively desired to be antiracist leaders, but those who did included Mary Church Terrell and the women who founded the National Association of Colored Women in 1896, and W. E. B. Du Bois and the men who launched the American Negro Academy in 1897.[92] Although they were hardly of one perspective or position on the Negro Problem—1895, for example, marked the rise of Booker T. Washington, the white-appointed accommodationist leader of the race—they tended to explain their circumstances quite differently than whites did, if for no other reason than that they overwhelmingly asserted their hopefulness, their humanity, and their inalienable rights to freedom and fairness.[93] "The present seems dark to the negro and that there is an increasing discontent, is perfectly evident, still I am far from despairing of his success in the future," wrote William Saunders Scarborough, a professor of classical languages at Wilberforce University, the first black author of a Greek college textbook, the first black member of the Modern Language Association, and a founder of the American Negro Academy. "If the South and North, white and black, will unite on lines of justice and humanity to man, the race question will work out its own solution with the least friction and best results."[94] Notwithstanding much intra-racial class and gender friction, many elite black men and women, in the words of historian Kevin Gaines, "sought to refute the view that African Americans were biologically inferior and unassimilable by incorporating 'the race' into ostensibly universal but deeply racialized ideological categories of Western progress and civilization."[95]

Ida B. Wells was the first of this generation of black scholars and reformers to link the language of civilization with statistics to defend the race against charges of criminality. She published her first two pamphlets, *Southern Horrors: Lynch Law in All Its Phases* (1892) and *A Red Record: Tabulated Statistics and Alleged Causes of Lynchings in the United States, 1892–1893–1894* (1894), at the same time that Hoffman authored his first articles. Although neither cited the other's work, Hoffman must have been aware of Wells's work and her British antilynching campaigns of 1893 and 1894 by the time he published *Race Traits* in 1896.[96] In 1892 Wells was a primary school teacher, a journalist, and an antiracist activist in Memphis who lost three close friends in a triple lynching after they defended their grocery store against a mob of white men intent on burning it to the ground.[97] This was not an uncommon occurrence. Professional and entrepreneurial blacks were frequent targets of mob violence in the South, especially when their commercial activities weakened the grip of white business owners who systematically exploited blacks. For Wells, the tragedy and personal loss were extremely difficult to accept, especially when the local white press applauded the violence. That she had long borne witness to white journalists' usual justifications for lynching as the only way to handle black criminals and "Negro rapists" left her no option but to speak truth to power. In the preface to *Southern Horrors,* she wrote, "Somebody must show that the Afro-American race is more sinned against than sinning, and it seems to have fallen upon me to do so. The Afro-American is not a bestial race. If this work can contribute in any way toward proving this, and at the same time arouse the conscience of the American people to a demand for justice to every citizen, and punishment by law for the lawless, I shall feel I have done my race a service."[98]

Historians of Wells's life and times credit her for inventing "forceful new arguments" and for being a "point of origin" in "American critical thought on lynching and racism."[99] Gail Bederman writes that Wells turned the Anglo-Saxon "discourse on whiteness, civilization, and manliness" on its head by redefining lynching as an act of barbarity by white men who "burned innocent black men alive for the 'crime' of sleeping with willing white women, while they themselves brutally and boldly raped black women."[100] In 1892 Wells's printing press was destroyed by arsonists; threatened with mortal harm, she left the South forever. She became a statistic, one of the soon-to-be-counted and much-discussed black migrants, first landing in New York, frequently visiting Philadelphia to draw support from the city's resourceful black religious and education leaders, and eventually settling in Chicago for the remainder of her life. There, after the turn of the century, she led a call for progressive-style crime prevention and outreach among young black men who suffered the triple burdens of labor-market discrimination, the stigma of criminality, and segregation from white- and immigrant-only social welfare agencies.[101]

Like almost everyone else in the twentieth century, Wells later witnessed and responded to the ubiquitous referencing of black crime statistics in all manner of race talk, which she had less to do with in the 1890s than did later black social scientists such as W. E. B. Du Bois, Kelly Miller, Monroe N. Work, Richard R. Wright, Jr., Sadie T. Mossell, and Anna Thompson.[102] In comparison to Hoffman, Wells neither identified herself as a statistician nor focused on the 1890 census. Still, her method for compiling lynching statistics was the same as Hoffman's. In preceding him by two years, she was doubtless one of the first race-relations writers, black or white, to analyze the *Tribune*'s lynching data. Though an overwhelmingly white-on-white American tradition of vigilante "justice" from the colonial period to the nineteenth-century Old West, lynching had only become a racist blood sport in the 1880s and 1890s.[103] On average in these two decades, "one person was lynched every other day, and two out of three were black." At the start of the twentieth century, lynchings fell to one every four days, but 90 percent of the victims were African Americans.[104] Like Hoffman, Wells was keenly aware of how her personal identity mattered to the reception of her study, proclaiming that her research had come strictly from white newspaper sources. "Out of their mouths," she boasted defiantly in the opening pages of *A Red Record*, "shall murderers be condemned." The heart of her condemnation was her meticulous reading, one by one, of press accounts of just over eleven hundred black men, women, and children who were "hanged, shot and roasted alive from January 1st, 1882 to January 1st, 1894," of whom 31 percent were actually "charged with rape."[105]

Her research findings defied most whites' understanding of lynching (and even, to a lesser extent, the way some elite blacks viewed the matter). Before Wells, few white people questioned the claim that the "majority" of lynchings in the country were, as Hoffman put it, "undoubtedly" the results of rape committed by black men.[106] Wells's aim was to debunk the myth that nearly every lynching of a black man represented a statistic of a ravaged white woman. She also wanted to challenge the emerging idea that any evidence of black criminality in the North was obvious proof of black inferiority, since many whites claimed that northern racism did not exist. In her retelling of northern press accounts, she highlighted how northerners contributed to the lynching craze and the scapegoating of black suspects by fabricating their own stories of black predators in their midst. In Philadelphia, for example, she told of an attractive and "well educated" white girl from a "good family" who had been stealing from her parents for some time. When a shadow of suspicion fell on the girl, she lied to the "daily papers" that a "colored man" had "gagged" and "bound" her and had stolen the money. In Cleveland, a mother and grand-mother conspired to have a black handyman disposed of by accusing him of "outrag[ing]" their four-year-old child. A preliminary hearing produced no evidence, but revealed that the women had concocted the scheme to avoid paying him a season's worth of wages.[107]

Wells's most provocative findings involved the rape or attempted rape of black women by white men. Of the dozen or so cases she cited, most took place in the South, but a few were from the Midwest and the North-east. Typically a white man or a "gang" of whites sexually attacked a young black woman. If the men were arrested, they were either acquitted or served minor sentences (far less than the many years similarly convicted black men received if they were lucky enough to make it to prison). None of them fell prey to a lynch mob. In Nashville, for example, Pat Hanifan "outraged a little colored girl," received a six-month jail sentence, and then became a city detective. In Baltimore "a gang of white ruffians as-saulted a respectable colored girl" who was out with her escort. Her date was held down while she was raped. All were acquitted. "Colored women," Wells wrote bitterly, "have always had far more reason to complain of white men in this respect than ever white women have had of Negroes."[108] In *A Red Record,* Wells exposed the enduring sexual violence perpetrated against black women, begun in slavery, and the unacknowledged hypoc-risy of the lynching hysteria.[109] She exposed the double bind of racial and sexual exploitation manifested in the figurative and literal dehumaniza-tion and destruction of black bodies.[110]

Given Wells's total repudiation of white supremacists' explanations for lynching and black criminality, it is easy to imagine Hoffman's incre-dulity when he came upon her work. It is not easy to imagine that he never knew of her work. He was extremely well read, curious, and thor-ough in his attempts to draw upon experts on topics of interest to him. That Hoffman probably ignored Wells's work is suggested by the fact that Robert Porter, one of his peers and the superintendent of the 1890 census whose signature appeared on the title page of the report on crime in the nation, publicly commented on the success of Wells's British cam-paign.[111] Although Wells's efforts created a storm of national controversy and an international scandal, for the most part she was not taken seri-ously by mainstream white race-relations writers like Hoffman, who from the beginning dominated the social scientific discourse on black criminality. Race and gender explain much of the "deafening silence," according to her biographer. Wells fit into no neat categories. She was a "kind of political exile." She was too bold as a female public figure, too outspoken in criticizing white women reformers for accepting lynching as a "necessary evil," too proud of her race to condone the conservative accommodationism of Washington-type black male leaders, and ultimately too unladylike and provocative in her sex talk for black club women. Her unequivocal antiracism may have marginalized her the most.[112]

Other black men and women of Wells's intellectual acumen and personal commitment to race work were slightly less marginal by comparison to Wells because they either believed that some blacks had racial tendencies toward criminal acts or because some, as racial uplifters, were more willing to traffic rhetorically in the high-value currency of black criminality so as to be taken seriously by whites.[113] But regardless of their gender or their class elitism or their rhetorical strategies, the first generation of professionally trained black social scientists, the vast majority of them men, were generally ignored by their white counterparts.[114] They were also few in number.[115] As one historian notes, in the early years of mass freedom "scholarly speculation among African-Americans was a luxury as rare as Mississippi snow."[116] From the 1890s until the 1920s, except when their words conceded, corroborated, or confirmed that blacks committed too many crimes—no matter their typically nuanced framing of the problem as primarily a symptom of industrial capitalism plus racism—"most white practitioners of racial science were able to silence the opposition of black thinkers."[117] Historian Davarian Baldwin explains that "the innovative Black scholarship on race relations was different enough from most ideas within the traditional organizational structure of" the field of sociology "that the work was systematically illegible, illogical and hence invisible."[118]

Nevertheless, black scholars responded to Hoffman's book with a mixture of ambivalence, sharp criticism, and restrained outrage. Neither W. E. B. Du Bois, the first black Harvard-trained social scientist and the first black academic to gain national attention as a race-relations expert, nor Kelly Miller, a pioneering black mathematician whose quantitative training and interest in the Negro Problem led him to launch a sociology department at Howard University, accepted Hoffman's prediction or Starr's endorsement of their race's impending disappearance.[119] In his review, Du Bois called it an "absurd conclusion" based on the "unscientific use of the statistical method."[120] Although Miller first conceded that the book was the "most thorough and comprehensive treatment of the Negro Problem, from a statistical standpoint," rivaling in its ability to "awaken" scientific interest in blacks what Harriet Beecher Stowe's *Uncle Tom's Cabin* had done to arouse "sentiment and generous feelings" for the race, he then agreed with Du Bois that Hoffman's conclusion was really a smokescreen for "*a priori* considerations."[121]

Miller's 1897 review, the first published paper of the American Negro Academy and itself a bestseller among African Americans, dissected the book chapter by chapter, allowing none of Hoffman's arguments to escape scrutiny. For example, he discounted Hoffman's entire treatment of the North as proof positive of blacks' hereditary shortcomings, arguing that social "captivity" and "isolation" were far more characteristic of the conditions facing the "Northern Negro." Blacks in the North were "completely submerged," he wrote. Their crime was primarily determined by their "social degradation." Not questioning the data but reversing Hoffman's statistical logic, Miller said that the census "nowhere" proved "any connection between crime and race but between crime and condition."[122] Northern black crime rates, from Pennsylvania's prisoners to Chicago's arrestees, were "six to eight times greater" per capita than whites because of racial discrimination.[123] "The criminal outbreak under the circumstances is only natural." If whites were to "exchange places" with blacks, then "the same story would be narrated of" them.

To be sure, Miller did not discount "this high criminal record" as simply a myth or a product of statistical sophistry. On a very basic level, he accepted Hoffman's charge of excessive criminality as partly the responsibility of blacks to fix. This was one of the earliest indications of the powerful rhetorical and ideological currency of black crime statistics even among African Americans. It is important, however, to note—for this was a point frequently ignored by Miller's white peers—that to admit that blacks played a role in the crime problem was not to concede racial inferiority but to insist that everyone had a part to play in the solution. Ultimately, Miller saw the problem in universal terms, both historical and sociological, that he believed held true for all groups: "The Jews in Egypt labored under circumstances remarkably similar to those of the American Negro" as they struggled to survive amid their own moral and physical "degeneracy" in the wilderness of freedom for forty years after emancipation. "Luckily for the Hebrews, there were no statisticians in those days. Think of the future which an Egyptian philosopher would have predicted for this people! And yet out of the loins of this race have sprung the moral and spiritual law-givers of mankind. We should not be discouraged because the Negro does not make a bee-line from Egyptian bondage to the Promised Land beyond Jordan. . . . If all the misdeeds of any people or individual were brought to light, the best of the race would be injured and the rest would be ruined."[124]

Along similar lines, Du Bois found much of Hoffman's data "interesting and valuable," but considered his interpretations highly suspect. There was no inherent reason why Hoffman had to emphasize "the bad as typifying the general tendency" of the race. Clearly the statistics showed mixed results: "increasing intelligence and increasing crime" as well as more wealth and more poverty. "Such contradictory facts are not facts pertaining to 'the race' but to its various classes, which development since emancipation has differentiated." Like Miller, Du Bois suggested an alternative reading of the data in both universal and antiracist terms. It was "natural" among "all races," he wrote, to experience in a "single generation" more material progress than moral progress. After all, the "dazed freedman" could comprehend the urgency of work "much easier" than how to rebuild the family life and moral foundation destroyed by slavery. The "younger generation" only turned to crime in the face of "dogged Anglo-Saxon prejudice" by which they were "subjected to different standards of justice" than "white malefactors." "To comprehend this peculiar and complicated evolution, and to pronounce final judgment upon it, will take far greater power of analysis, niceness of inquiry, and delicacy of measurement than Mr. Hoffman brings to his task."[125]

Du Bois's superior education, including a Harvard Ph.D. plus three semesters at the University of Berlin—the crème de la crème of academic training in the social sciences—prepared him to see the irony in Hoffman's German background and his "unscientific use of the statistical method." Turning the tables on Hoffman, the former student of Max Weber pointed out that in Hoffman's "own German fatherland" high death rates matched or exceeded those of blacks in the United States.[126] Were residents of Munich also headed for race extinction? What of Montreal, Naples, Belfast, Budapest, Breslau, and Madrid, which "all have shown within a few years, death rates equal" to or in excess of "American Negroes in cities"? Was illegitimacy among the inhabitants of Rome, Munich, Stockholm, Paris, and Brussels the beginning of the end of morality among Europe's elite races, given that their rates of out-of-wedlock childbirths were higher than the "Negroes of Washington [D.C.]"? The bottom line, argued Du Bois, was that the study of black life needed much more investigation at the local level and "from particular points of view."[127]

This was precisely Du Bois's point in "The Study of the Negro Problem," an address delivered at a meeting of the American Academy of Political and Social Science in the fall of 1897, several months after his review appeared.[128] By this time Du Bois was an assistant instructor at the University of Pennsylvania and was conducting the first-ever book-length sociological investigation of an American city. The study was "a breakthrough achievement," the seminal text on urban sociology, not soon to be matched by the research of the nation's inaugural sociology department at the University of Chicago, founded in 1892.[129] It seems an unlikely coincidence that his groundbreaking study, *The Philadelphia Negro*, was launched about the same time Hoffman's book was making headlines since, as Du Bois recalled many years later, he was brought to Philadelphia to conduct research to investigate the "theory" that the city "was going to the dogs because of the crime and venality of its Negro citizens."[130] Having already completed the fieldwork at the time of the annual meeting—835 hours of interviewing in 2,500 households, the life histories of 10,000 men, women, and children—Du Bois told his white peers that the "manifest and far-reaching bias" of race-relations writers should no longer substitute for the pursuit of a "reliable body of truth," that "deep, fierce convictions" must no longer guide the "uncritical study of the Negro." Systematic investigation of facts must supplant widely held opinions based on "faith [rather] than of knowledge."[131] "Intensive studies" should be conducted in "limited localities" by "competent and responsible agents." The use of "any general census," he warned finally, was likely to lead to "dangerously misleading" conclusions.[132]

Without naming names, Du Bois paused to highlight Hoffman's work as a case in point. The "foreigner's views, if he be not exceptionally astute, will depend largely on his letters of introduction"; like American pseudo-experts whose credibility is secured only by "birthplace and parentage," he will "fail" to capture the complexity of the Negro Problem and will "succumb to the vulgar temptation" to turn any "little contribution" into "general conclusions as to the origin and destiny of the Negro people in time and eternity . . . Thus we possess endless final judgments as to the American Negro emanating from men of influence and learning, in the very face of the fact known to every accurate student, that there exists to-day no sufficient material of proven reliability, upon which any scientist can base definite and final conclusions as to the present condition and tendencies of the eight million American Negroes; and that any person or publication purporting to give such conclusions simply makes statements which go beyond the reasonably proven evidence."[133] Unsurprisingly, given its dramatic rise as a national topic of discussion and debate, Du Bois singled out black criminality as a research area that was thoroughly awash in myth, stereotype, and ignorance. "It is extremely doubtful," he complained, "if any satisfactory study of Negro crime and lynching can be made for a generation or more, in the present condition of the public mind, which renders it almost impossible to get at the facts and real conditions."[134]

On that cool November day in Philadelphia, as Du Bois instructed a mostly white audience of social scientists and reformers on how to study the Negro, he may have found himself uncertain about how his own ongoing intensive study of Philadelphia's black criminals would be received by the public. By suggesting that no real knowledge could be ascertained for several years to come, he appeared to be hedging against his own contribution to reifying in white people's minds that too many blacks had "criminal tendencies." Even as he critiqued the "final judgments" of his white supremacist peers, he knew that eight months earlier he himself had verged perilously close to being guilty as charged.

Du Bois's March 5, 1897, speech "Conservation of the Races," delivered at the inaugural meeting of the American Negro Academy, put crime at the forefront of the Negro Problem.[135] Before the racial gifts of the American Negro—"our physical powers, our intellectual endowments, our spiritual ideals"—could be realized in that "broader humanity which freely recognizes differences in men" without inequality, we must seek unity and purification, Du Bois told an august gathering of Talented Tenthers, the upper crust of the educated black elite. "Weighted with a heritage of moral iniquity from our past history, hard pressed in the economic world by foreign immigrants and native prejudice, hated here, despised there and pitied everywhere; our one haven of refuge is ourselves." But eight million people can rise to greatness only by first being "honest, fearlessly criticizing their own faults, zealously correcting them." We must put an end, he continued, to political corruption, materialism, crime, and immorality. We must be "united to keep black boys from loafing, gambling and crime; united to guard the purity of black women and to reduce the vast army of black prostitutes that is today marching to hell." Members of the black vanguard must "bravely face the truth, not with apologies, but with solemn earnestness." Wagging a proverbial finger at poor southern blacks, his words nearing a crescendo, Du Bois stated that "a note of warning" should echo "in every black cabin in the land" that "unless we conquer our present vices they will conquer us; we are diseased, we are developing criminal tendencies, and an alarmingly large percentage of our men and women are sexually impure."[136]

Many historians see "Conservation" as a remarkable demonstration of Du Bois's youthful embrace of racial essentialism, a view that all blacks were endowed with the same special gifts only needing to be unlocked from the inside, part antidote to Hoffman's charge of self-destructive race traits. Lewis observes that Du Bois later looked back on this perspective as "something of an embarrassment."[137] What has not received the same attention in this speech, however, are Du Bois's earliest thoughts on black criminality. These profoundly significant ideas occupied a central place in his initial engagement with the race-relations discourse. The crime problem was so important to him at the outset of his scholarly and activist career that in his coming-out speech before his black mentors and esteemed peers, he recommended making crime fighting their top priority: "We believe that the first and greatest step toward the settlement of the present friction between the races—commonly called the Negro problem—lies in the correction of the immorality, crime and laziness among Negroes themselves, which still remains as a heritage from slavery. We believe that only earnest and long continued efforts on our own part can cure these social ills."[138]

The fact that Du Bois was still writing *The Philadelphia Negro* is crucial to capturing the complexity and tensions in his early crime analysis. This was an experimental period in Du Bois's intellectual development.[139] As a twenty-nine-year-old budding social scientist, he tried to approach the race problem by resisting preconceived conclusions. The "difficulties of studying so vast and varied a subject are so large that the first work to be done should be rather of an experimental or preliminary nature," he wrote two months after the "Conservation" speech in a letter to Carroll D. Wright, the census official who had worked with Hoffman years before and was now seeking Du Bois's expertise for an economic report on black southerners.[140] Du Bois was, after all, setting out to practice what he preached against in Hoffman's work.

But Du Bois could not entirely expunge his personal views from his own scholarship, a limit he recognized and fully admitted in the opening pages of *The Philadelphia Negro*.[141] From "Conservation" to the American Academy of Political and Social Science address to the final Philadelphia report, there is an unmistakable tension between his elitist sensibility and Victorian concern about individual moral accountability, and his professional view of crime as a "tangible phenomena of Negro Prejudice." In *The Philadelphia Negro,* Du Bois did not hesitate to moralize against the young black gamblers and prostitutes of Philadelphia's corrupt Seventh Ward, or to wage a full-scale rhetorical attack on the immorality of poor black southerners.[142] In Du Bois's early writings, in Hoffman's writings, and in the writings of many others who succeeded them, the data and discourse on black criminality at this founding moment masked the full range of ideological differences among many white and black race experts. When the statistical reality of black criminality was first making its way along the information railway of the industrial age, the critique of racism and the critique of racial inferiority were constantly overlapping. As numerous scholars have emphasized in their studies of racial uplift ideology, more often than not black elites' intraracial appeals for unity and progress in the Progressive era depended on one-sided jeremiads against poor and disreputable blacks.[143]

Contemporaries could hear or read in these statements the same condemnation of blackness, if that is what they chose to do. For example, among Hoffman's many proofs of crime and immorality as race traits, he wrote, "That an immense amount of concubinage and prostitution prevails among the colored women of the United States is a fact fully admitted by the negroes themselves."[144] He also cited evidence from the groundbreaking book *Hull House Maps and Papers.* The fact was "so forcibly brought out" by Jane Addams and Florence Kelley, Hoffman wrote, that wherever large numbers of blacks lived in the urban North, "houses of ill-fame and dives of the lowest order abound." Compiled by two white liberal pioneers of the settlement house movement, *Hull House Maps* was a proto-Compstat analysis, mapping vice and crime in Chicago's slum communities for the ultimate purpose of community-based crime prevention.[145] Context made all the difference in how both black and white experts expected their crime analyses to be interpreted and understood.

Du Bois claimed that *The Philadelphia Negro* was first and foremost a seminal study of the history and sociology of a black community in the urban North. It was the first of many local "intensive," systematic investigations of the facts and real conditions of black life in America. "The world was thinking wrong about race, because it did not know," Du Bois wrote years later, reflecting on his initial scholarly engagement with race-relations discourse. "The ultimate evil was stupidity."[146] *The Philadelphia Negro* was the first step in his multistep knowledge program to end the Negro Problem. With this purpose in mind, Du Bois produced an unprecedented in-depth analysis of the class structure of black Philadelphia. Considering the whole as greater than the sum of its parts, the four classes he identified—the "aristocracy of the race" (12 percent), the "hardworking, good-natured people" (52 percent), the "poor and unfortunate" (30 percent), and the "submerged Tenth (6 percent)"—amounted to a powerful rebuttal to the sweeping negative generalizations against all blacks, especially the charge of criminality. Du Bois saw the problem of black criminality much like the way Hoffman had characterized white criminality, as an "unfortunate" consequence of economic conditions. "We have here the [statistical] record of a low social class, and as the condition of a lower class is by its very definition worse than that of a higher, so the situation of the Negroes is worse as respects crime and poverty than that of the mass of whites." In the wake of a "period of financial stress and industrial depression," he continued, black and white crime both increased, but less so for whites "by reason of their richer and more fortunate upper classes."[147] Even his use of the term *submerged* shifted partial responsibility away from this "lowest class of slum elements" by implying that these individuals were oppressed by means other than just their own behavior.

Within this frame of analysis, Du Bois intended for crime to be seen as "a phenomenon that stands not alone, but rather as a symptom of countless wrong social conditions." In an unflinching chapter-long investigation of the serious crimes of the "submerged Tenth," Du Bois described mostly young black men who typically stole or assaulted others; who tended to be "ignorant," southern-born, repeat offenders; and who lived "in such [an] environment that they find it easier to be rogues than honest men." Yet all of the lawlessness did not alter his assessment that racism was the "vastest of the Negro problems." He reminded readers that since the colonial period these "perpetrators" had been subject to all the handicaps of being poor and black defendants in the criminal justice system. He redefined race traits as temporary deficiencies rooted in the moral debasement of slavery. He linked emancipation and northern migration to the universal experience of displacement and strain, like the wilderness period for the Hebrews of the Old Testament. He emphasized ongoing, not simply historical, acts of white discrimination in every sphere of black life. Beyond the "ordinary," all of these were aggravating causes of black criminality. According to Du Bois, they were the factors that made black people's crimes both excessive and peculiar. Otherwise, the heart of the Negro Problem was not crime but the exclusion of black

exclusion

people from within the "pale of nineteenth-century Humanity." In the work's final pages, he wrote:

> We have, to be sure, a threatening problem of ignorance but the ancestors of most Americans were far more ignorant than the freedmen's sons; these ex-slaves are poor but not as poor as the Irish peasants used to be; crime is rampant but not more so, if as much, as in Italy; but the difference is that the ancestors of the English and the Irish and the Italians were felt to be worth educating, help-ing and guiding because they were men and brothers, while in America a census which gives a slight indication of the utter disap-pearance of the American Negro from the earth is greeted with ill-concealed delight. . . . This is the spirit that enters in and compli-cates all Negro social problems and this is a problem which only civilization and humanity can successfully solve.

As was commonly expressed on the white side of the color line, Du Bois wanted Philadelphia's black crime problem to be greeted as a cause for concern and intervention rather than as a celebration of internecine genocide.[148]

Far less noted by historians was Du Bois's initial linking of crime fight-ing to racism.[149] Even in "Conservation," Du Bois did not simply wag a finger at black criminals and prostitutes, though the tone and tenor of his rhetoric suggested otherwise. He combined his primary call for an anti-crime self-help solution with a secondary call for whites to end racism. "We believe that the second great step toward a better adjustment of the relations between races," he stated, is the color-blind recognition and re-warding of talent in the "economic and intellectual world." In *The Phila-delphia Negro,* he tipped the balance toward equal responsibility, calling for a dual approach to the crime problem: "The Duty of the Negroes" was to first make every effort "toward a lessening of Negro crime" in spite of racial oppression; "[t]he Duty of the Whites" was to eliminate prejudice and discrimination in spite of "intermingling" with a "race so poor and ignorant and inefficient as the mass of the Negroes."

> That the Negro race has an appalling work of social reform before it need hardly be said. Simply because the ancestors of the present white inhabitants of America went out of their way barbarously to mistreat and enslave the ancestors of the present black inhabitants gives those blacks no right to ask that the civilization and morality

70

of the land be seriously menaced for their benefit. . . . But if their [whites'] policy in the past is parent of much of this condition, and if to-day by shutting black boys and girls out of most avenues of decent employment they are increasing pauperism and vice, then they must hold themselves largely responsible for the deplorable results.[150]

From "Conservation" to *The Philadelphia Negro,* even as he thought out loud and committed words to the page, the two sides of the problem were approaching inseparability in Du Bois's mind.[151] The complications in his own thoughts thus led him to doubt what the "public mind" was able or even willing to comprehend that November day before the American Academy of Political and Social Science.[152]

Du Bois's admonition against Hoffman's brand of racial analysis, two years before the final publication of *The Philadelphia Negro,* seems to have been his attempt at saying that it was possible to criticize bad behavior among blacks without eliminating racism as a major factor and passing final judgment on the inferiority of the entire race. Elsewhere during this period he would begin to express his personal despair over the tendency of whites to simplify the race problem and to see in the struggle and "strivings of the Negro People" justification for prejudice. In one of his most famous essays, first published in the August 1897 issue of *Atlantic Monthly,* midway between his "Conservation" speech and his American Academy of Political and Social Science address, Du Bois first described his own sense of living behind the veil, of being defined by others as a "problem."[153] "It is a peculiar sensation, this double-consciousness, this sense of always looking at one's self through the eyes of others, of measuring one's soul by the tape of a world that looks on in amused contempt and pity." He then linked the racialized oppression of black people in America to an enduring conundrum:

A people thus handicapped [by centuries of enslavement and degradation] ought not to be asked to race with the world, but rather allowed to give all its time and thought to its own social problems. But alas! While sociologists gleefully count his bastards and his prostitutes, the very soul of the toiling, sweating black man is darkened by the shadow of a vast despair. Men call the shadow prejudice, and learnedly explain it as the natural defense of culture against barbarism, learning against ignorance, purity against crime, the "higher" against the "lower" races. . . . But the facing of so vast

71

a prejudice could not but bring the inevitable self-questioning, self-disparagement, and lowering of ideals which ever accompany repression and breed in an atmosphere of contempt and hate.[154]

Here, before *The Philadelphia Negro* was finished, was the first articulation of the self-fulfilling prophesy of racism, poverty, crime, and inequality in modern America. Still, the Philadelphia study was Du Bois's most important scholarly contribution, an exegesis of this most complicated phenomenon. He opened the *Souls of Black Folk,* his most widely read publication—in which he intoned that "the problem of the twentieth-century is the problem of the color-line"—with a reprint (and slight revision) of the 1897 *Atlantic Monthly* essay. For many years to come, in numerous reports, essays, speeches, and editorials, he would press his two-pronged solution to the crime problem, shifting emphasis and blame ever so slightly to suit the biases and "stupidity" of his audiences.

Immediately following the completion of *The Philadelphia Negro,* Du Bois's tendency to move back and forth between emphasizing the need for self-improvement and emphasizing an end to racism, depending on the complexion of the audience, is perfectly illustrated by an article and a speech he gave in the same year. The article, "The Negro and Crime," appeared in the May 18, 1899, issue of the *Independent,* a northern liberal magazine. In responding to an earlier article in the publication that had blasted blacks for their vices ("the negro is the mongrel of civilization"), Du Bois firmly insisted that the history of slavery and the emancipation experience went a long way toward explaining the "Negro criminal class"—"it is astounding that a body of people whose family life had been so nearly destroyed . . . should in a single generation be able to point to so many pure homes." He then listed and explained four additional causes in the order of their significance: convict leasing, discrimination in southern courts, mob violence, and "the drawing of the color-line."[155]

By contrast, a few months later he delivered a speech, "The Problem of Negro Crime," at the Atlanta Negro Historical Society. According to a caption accompanying the January 1900 reprint in the *Bulletin of Atlanta University,* the address was "handled in such a way to make a deep impression upon those who heard." Du Bois began by asserting that the strictest test of the "Negro's progress is that of his criminal record." Citing the 1890 census, he said, "despite, then, all the discrimination and all other excuses that might be brought there can be no reasonable doubt but that the Negroes of this land furnish two or three times as many

72

criminals proportionately as the whites." In his usual way, he linked crime to the natural disruption of the emancipation period and concluded with five self-help recommendations: "establish better homes"; "educate our children"; inculcate a faithful and honest work ethic regardless of how menial the job; associate with "decent people" only; and unite with white Georgians to open a juvenile reformatory to keep young people from the "prison and chain gang." Herbert Aptheker, who first collected and assembled Du Bois's voluminous body of work, observes that around 1904 Du Bois "rejected" the views he expressed that day. In an October 1940 address, Du Bois publicly reflected on his change of perspective at that time.[156]

Still, despite all the moralizing and data crunching about black criminals, Du Bois's *The Philadelphia Negro* was "shamefully neglected."[157] The book never came close to attracting as large an audience as Hoffman's *Race Traits*. It did not become a nonfiction bestseller. It did not turn race-relations discourse on its head. Although it was reviewed in a few academic periodicals, it was ignored by the *American Journal of Sociology (AJS)*.[158] No mention of the book appears in that journal until 1903, when it was listed among texts used at Hampton Institute as part of a survey of sociology curriculums around the country.[159] Nearly a decade passed before it was first cited in the footnotes of an *AJS* article.[160] As late as the 1930s, not even the University of Pennsylvania's sociology department officially acknowledged, as historians Thomas Sugrue and Michael Katz write, "the most significant research in the history of the department."[161] It neither influenced a generation of sociology students nor garnered Du Bois critical praise and scholarly adulation befitting his accomplishment. It was an ominous sign, no less clear than in Ida B. Wells's case, of the outcome for a black race-relations expert or reformer who refused to let racism off the hook.

To be sure, Du Bois's Philadelphia research helped secure his next position at the historically black campus of Atlanta University. But in Lewis's assessment, he became a "scholar behind the veil." He wrote and supervised thirteen major research studies between 1898 and 1910, unmatched by most peers in quantity and quality, most of them cutting-edge reports that dissected all aspects of black life in the South. Du Bois nevertheless became an increasingly marginal figure to northern research foundations that repeatedly passed him over to fund white race experts who did not have a tenth of his training or experience.[162] Only with historical hindsight culminating around the centennial anniversary of *The Philadelphia*

Negro's publication have Du Bois's scholarly contributions been posthumously recognized within the academy. A 1991 appraisal of his work in the *American Economic Review* notes that "the extent of descriptive and statistical detail in Du Bois's studies is rarely matched even today."[163] Reflecting on the legacy of his exclusion from the "white car of scholarship," historian Ira Katznelson writes that American social science and history have suffered "intellectual conformity and normative bankruptcy" by failing to include the "first rate work" of Du Bois and other black scholars "relegated to the outer limit or edge of social standing."[164]

Du Bois's work was not totally unappreciated by white race-relations writers of his day. A review in the *American Historical Review,* the leading journal of historians, praised Du Bois for his candor. "He is perfectly frank, laying all necessary stress on the weaknesses of his people, such as their looseness of living, their lack of thrift, their ignorance of the laws of health, the disproportionate number of paupers and criminals among them as compared with the whites." The anonymous reviewer's only criticism was that some of his conclusions were overly optimistic that the Negro Problem could be solved in social terms. Du Bois had not sufficiently considered the saliency of racial inferiority. Speaking for the profession, the reviewer concluded, "We believe that separation is due to differences of race more than of status."[165] Du Bois's crime rhetoric did draw attention, but not exactly in the ways he had intended.

In September 1899 Walter Willcox, one of the most influential economists of his generation and the chief statistician of the United States Census Bureau, delivered one of his most widely quoted papers, "Negro Criminality," before the American Social Science Association meeting in Saratoga, New York.[166] The New England-born professor from Cornell University, promising a "fair-minded, clear-sighted and outspoken position," asked his audience to reconsider their ideas about racial bias in the nation's criminal justice system. Reminding them of familiar southern examples of racism, such as juror discrimination and sentencing bias, he asked whether the same arguments could hold true in the North. "Does it take less evidence to convict a Negro here, or is a Negro's sentence for the same offense likely to be longer? Such claims have never to my knowledge been raised." He then cited the latest prison data that showed that black prisoners in the North had higher per capita rates of incarceration than in the South (69 versus 29 of every 10,000 residents). In light of the numbers, there was not an obvious answer to his question other than the presumption among these good-hearted northern academics that northern racism could not explain the difference. So as to be clear, he stated: "These facts furnish some statistical basis and warrant for the popular opinion, never seriously contested, that under present conditions in this country a member of the African race, other things equal, is much more likely to fall in to crime than a member of the white race."[167] In other words, what many already believed to be true was now proven.

Willcox then cited the opinions of "representative Negroes" from the July 1898 annual Negro Conference at Hampton Institute. "The criminal record of the colored race in all parts of the country," Willcox quoted, "is alarming in its proportion." Like Booker T. Washington's annual Tuskegee conferences, Hampton's annual gatherings were intended to show southern moderates and northern philanthropists the benefits of industrial education as a worthy movement for black self-help or, as the *New York Times* noted in its coverage, "the aim in regard to each [topic discussed] was to find the faults for which the negro was responsible and to see how to supply the lack or find the remedy."[168] Given African Americans' own testimonies, then, racism was less the problem than racial inferiority. Considering that slavery "was never established" in the North, and that across the region the percentage increase of blacks going to prison was even greater than in the South, Willcox argued that the national black crime problem could no longer be ignored. "In these figures, one finds again some statistical basis for the well-nigh universal opinion that crime among the American Negroes is increasing with alarming rapidity." In a final attempt to dispel any remaining doubt about his conclusions, he read Du Bois's note of warning in "Conservation" and said, "I may quote the concession of the Negro who is perhaps doing as much as any member of his race to throw light upon its present condition."[169]

At the dawn of the Jim Crow era, writing crime into race became the latest trend among race-relations writers across the country. Hoffman's innovation of using crime statistics had helped to overcome the long-sought-after scientific goal of credibility within racial scientific discourse. Many of Hoffman's predecessors, who had once struggled to distance themselves from the charge of proslavery bias while objectively acknowledging the "feral state" to which blacks had returned since freedom, welcomed the "new scientific study of the negro." G. Stanley Hall, for example, a pioneering Harvard psychologist, founder of the *American Journal of Psychology* in 1887, and one of Shaler's mentors, described this period as a terrific opportunity to embrace the new social science research because it was a "more solid and intelligent basis" on which to end the sentimental notion of racial equality. Racial "differences are coming to be better understood," he wrote, "so that what is true and good for one is often false and bad for the other." As "an abolitionist both by conviction and descent," Hall instructed black people to stop "sympathiz[ing] with their own criminals" and to "accept without whining patheticism and corroding self-pity [their] present situation, prejudice and all."[170] With a growing body of evidence of the excessive crime rates of black people everywhere they could be counted—despite, or because of, the underlying social, political, economic, and racist realities underlying those statistics—the idea of black criminality quickly became a fundamental measure of black progress and potential in modern America.

Hall's racialized vision of crime prevention—a call for a separate solution to crime among blacks—was emblematic of how the idea of black criminality shaped the thinking of many white reformers, including neo-abolitionists and progressives, in this era. White criminality was society's problem, but black criminality was black people's problem. Such thinking contributed to discriminatory social work approaches and crime-fighting policies in black communities, with devastating consequences, including the worsening of social conditions. Among whites, struggling neighborhoods were considered a cause of crime and a reason to intervene. Among blacks, they were considered a sign of pathology and a reason for neglect. Against the grain, Du Bois called crime "a sinister index of social degradation and struggle."[171] Black criminality, he insisted, should be solved using "the very remedies which the world is using on all submerged classes" with "goodness," "beauty," "truth," and "faith in humanity." Such differences between Du Bois's vision and Hall's reflected the malleability of the concept depending on one's racial ideology.[172]

Still, the idea flourished even as some raised doubts about the accuracy of the census crime data as a source for comparing the criminal tendencies of different groups. One of the first academics in the United States to have "statistics" attached to his title, the pioneering University of Pennsylvania professor Roland P. Falkner, believed that comparative analysis "should be thorough, systematic and reasonable." More than a scientific issue, he wrote, "it is a matter of the gravest practical importance" since "popular interest" in crime is chiefly concerned with "the greater criminality of the foreign-born and colored elements as compared with the native and white." He argued that the census would have been more accurate if it had reported the total number of prisoners received during the year versus the population on a single day. The new method, he proposed, was able to account for new offenders who had served a short sentence but had been released before the census enumeration. It also avoided double-counting prisoners with sentences of one year or more. Falkner pointed out that by measuring new commitments instead of population, sentencing bias would have been eliminated. "If one class receives longer sentences than another, or commit classes of crimes for which longer sentences are given it will appear unduly magnified in the census report." Falkner concluded that the 1890 census had distorted the criminal tendencies of different groups. Blacks were shown to have committed more crimes than their total share and immigrants fewer.[173]

Falkner anticipated many of the criticisms of early prison and police data made by late-twentieth-century scholars. But, as social science historian Lawrence Rosen has pointed out, these limits were not generally "obvious to the criminologists and criminal statisticians of the nineteenth and the early years of the twentieth century." Their "uncritical generalizations," therefore, have to be understood in the historical context in which they informed early-twentieth-century popular and public policy understandings of criminality.[174] Similarly, historian Daryl Michael Scott warns contemporary scholars that too frequently social science "studies written prior to World War II have been interpreted not in light of the intellectual and political debates that prompted those research projects, but in connection with proposals and policies that originated during Lyndon Johnson's Great Society."[175] Significant doubts about the accuracy, reliability, and interpretive use of crime statistics for comparisons of racial groups did not emerge among white social scientists until the 1920s and 1930s in the midst of a nationwide campaign to standardize arrest statistics, culminating in the *Uniform Crime Reports*.[176]

In the meantime, Willcox acknowledged Falkner's doubts about the census data in a footnote. He agreed that prison statistics "exaggerated the criminal tendencies of Negroes" but felt that this distortion was offset by the fact that comparing prisoners to "persons of all ages" tended to "understate the true criminality of a race." This was a weak defense since age distortion—population inflation due to the inclusion of children and the elderly—impacted all races, which he also admitted. The sentencing distortion still adversely singled out blacks. Willcox nevertheless "[brought] the facts home" by ending his statistical proof of black criminality with a quotation from Du Bois.[177]

Black race-relations writers often contributed to the crime discourse with the intent of challenging white supremacists' interpretations.[178] As

Du Bois's and Wells's works demonstrate, black crime experts often used crime data and racial violence as symptoms of oppression to focus precisely on the "conditions of life" in the North and South that many white race-relations writers often dismissed. At times, however, they also unwittingly contributed to the writing of crime into race.

Monroe N. Work, for example, a graduate student at the University of Chicago and soon to be its first black sociologist, answered the challenge to the race posed by Hoffman's research.[179] Complementing Du Bois's Philadelphia findings, Work launched his own intensive five-month study of black criminality in Chicago from November 1897 to May 1898, which was published in late 1900. Focusing primarily on arrest statistics since 1872, he confirmed the then well-known trend that black criminality was proportionately highest in the North and was increasing.[180] He also found that black Chicagoans were arrested on average six times more frequently than immigrants. Written in a dry, clinical voice more characteristic of empirical reports today, "Crime among the Negroes of Chicago: A Social Study" was nearly devoid of antiracist tones and must have confirmed what many readers of the *American Journal of Sociology* believed to be true. In a somewhat incoherent final section, however, Work disagreed with Hoffman's "position that the negro is retrograding" by countering that blacks were "making progress in civilization." If the "hypothesis of his social advancement" was true, the graduate student tentatively suggested, the black man's crime is due to his "transitional state from a lower to a higher plane" and the "economic stress" accompanying it. Work observed that 75 percent of Chicago blacks "had, or gave, no occupation" at the time of their arrests compared to 38 percent of whites. In addition to economic factors that increased black criminality, Work added the causes of crime "common to all races" and "the race characteristics peculiar" to blacks.[181]

In comparison to Du Bois, Wells, Kelly Miller, and the future work of Richard R. Wright, Jr., whatever nod to racism Work intended by his final comments could not have been very convincing. Like other black writers, he mistook white social scientists' ability to cite white criminality as a symptom of the ravages of the industrial economy and modern civilization—"common" causes—as an invitation to apply the same logic on their side of the color line. Ultimately, the crime research and especially the intra-racial appeals for moral betterment by many black writers and reformers often achieved the opposite effect, reifying the tendency among most whites "to believe the worst about Negro character and prospects."[182]

The premium placed on the work of black writers whose crime discourse explicitly confirmed white supremacists' beliefs and practices was on full display in the reception of William Hannibal Thomas's 1901 book, *The American Negro: What He Was, What He Is, and What He May Become*. The Ohio-born black missionary, educator, and journalist in the postbellum South based his study on twenty-five years of personal observations. His methodology alone should have made his work marginal by the standards of the audience for whom he claimed to be writing, especially since he dismissed the reliability of existing data to measure the "actual crime instinct in the negro."[183] Nevertheless, the book was, according to the author, an indispensable "contribution to American sociology." Speaking directly to "American white people," Thomas gave his readers more justification for depicting the race as criminal than any "accurate" statistic could ever have accomplished by itself. His most recent biographer writes that Thomas's "list of negative qualities of Negroes seemed limitless."[184] Unmatched in his racist rhetoric by any other black writer of his day, Thomas insisted that the majority of blacks were mentally retarded, "savage[s] at heart," and amoral—"unable practically to discern between right and wrong." Most "negroes" were an "intrinsically inferior type of humanity" who preferred a "low order of living" and whose history was a "record of lawless existence, led by every impulse and passion." Equating the sum of black humanity to apes, Thomas wrote: "Really, the inferiority of the negro in mind, morals, judgement [sic], and character is such that there is no doubt that some very plausible confirmatory evidence of the justness of the simian theory of human origin might be derived from a close inspection of his demeanor."[185]

Controversial and attacked by the vast majority of African Americans of every ideological perspective, *The American Negro* was hailed by many whites as the most authoritative treatise to date on African American inferiority.[186] Even before the manuscript had been accepted for publication by the Macmillan Company, Franklin H. Giddings, one of the founding fathers of American sociology, the founder of Columbia University's sociology department, and the third president of the American Sociological Association, wrote in his reader's report that the book was the most complete, detailed account of the American Negro ever published: "As a sociological study it is one of the most valuable things to [be] put in the hands of genuine students of american [sic] conditions that I know of."[187] As news of its forthcoming release hit the market, the book was hailed not only for its thorough treatment, but for its objectivity as well. The writer "presents his subject without an atom of the sentimentality which has so often proved a blemish in many books otherwise most excellent," announced the *New York Times* book review section a month before the book's release.[188]

More impressive still was the fact that the author was a black man. After the book appeared in print, the *New York Times* gave it another rave review: "Mr. Thomas is probably, next to Mr. Booker T. Washington, the best American authority on the negro question" because of his race and his enlightened perspective on his own people. "No white man has ever so far as we can remember, arraigned the freedman with such scathing denunciation of his faults and vices" as Thomas. "Such a jeremiad, delivered by one belonging to the very race against which it is hurled, carries unmistakable conviction of the writer's sincerity and knowledge whereof he speaks." Thomas's observations lead to a "mental vision" of a "sinister and terrible figure still to be dealt with in our social economy." Finally cutting to the book's most damning observation, the unsigned review noted that there was nothing whites could do to help, "since the most ignorant and degraded examples of freedmen are to be found in the North, where they have enjoyed every advantage around them unrestricted. What better proof of racial incapacity is needed?" Without a fundamental change in the "negro's" nature, the situation was nearly hopeless.[189]

Thomas's observations, like Hoffman's data, revealed as much about the hardening of racial categories in the new century as they attempted to explain why crime was a growing problem in black communities.[190] The inseparable linking of the two social categories of race and crime was not inevitable; it was the conscious result of several writers' attempts to expand definitions of blackness beyond physical traits, historical association with slavery, and nineteenth-century romanticization of blacks as a child race. White or black writers who could marshal crime statistics from government data with alarmist predictions about the future of the race in urban places, especially northern cities, plus tie in a compelling narrative of the historical and biological factors that made American Negroes fundamentally different from American whites, and finally repudiate charges of racism, were sure to be noticed by many.[191]

In the same vein as the *New York Times*, C. C. Closson, a white reviewer for the *Journal of Political Economy*, praised Thomas as a candid and courageous black writer. Recommending the book, Closson wrote that despite some of Thomas's tendencies to exaggerate, "unfortunately, there is probably too much of truth in the picture."[192] Although the *American Journal of Sociology* never reviewed Du Bois's sociological treatise, it did review Thomas's. Ironically, the reviewer, Richard R. Wright, Jr., a theology student at the University of Chicago and a pioneer black Social Gospeler on the city's South Side, panned the book for highlighting only the worst elements of the race. "His book is as fair a characterization of the race as a detailed description of the slums and dens of vice of Chicago would be of the whole city," he wrote.[193] It may or may not have been considered a mistake by the journal to give Wright the opportunity to denounce the book. But in light of the high praise it received among whites Wright's review likely corroborated, for some at least, a sense that Thomas's study stood alone against a rising tide of black "sentimentality." Putting Du Bois in the ranks of those with a "rosy faith in the negro's prospects," one critic jointly reviewed *The Philadelphia Negro* and *The American Negro*, giving the edge to Thomas. "Professor Du Bois's statistics are worthy of careful study," but "they are a little weak in the pages devoted to showing that the negro is not so criminal as he is popularly represented to be."[194] That Du Bois was even compared to Thomas—two "negroes" of equal talent—was a sign that his credibility among white social scientists was in free fall. Du Bois nonetheless pointed out that the enthusiastic reception of Thomas's "virulent criticisms" was not at all surprising. "Mr. Thomas's book is a sinister symptom" of the times, witnessed in "the exigencies of the book market" and the "more or less unconscious Wish for the Worst in regard to the Negro," he explained. "If the Negro will kindly go to the devil and make haste about it, then the American conscience can justify three centuries of shameful history; and hence the subdued enthusiasm which greets a sensational article or book."[195]

The excitement surrounding *The American Negro* revealed just how quickly black criminality had captured the nation's imagination after 1896. To be sure, southern rhetoric about black criminals—racist justifications for lynching, convict leasing, prison farms, and chain gangs—preceded Hoffman's book. But in the wake of new national crime statistics, especially northern prison and arrest data from Philadelphia, Chicago, and New York, southern claims of blacks' criminal nature were finally exorcized of the ghost of their Confederate past. In the wake of the new crime discourse, Shaler's call for the scientific "union of endeavor on the part of those of North and South, of ex-slaveholder and ex-abolitionist alike" was finally being answered, even from the pen of a black man.[196]

Southern white writers wholeheartedly welcomed the new lines of communication as an important step toward national reconciliation. Thomas Nelson Page's 1904 book, *The Negro: The Southerner's Problem*, was one of the earliest and most explicit attempts in the new century to convince northern readers that white southerners were not inherently any more racist or violent toward blacks than northerners were. Page was a descendant of the Virginia planter class and a popular fiction writer of the Old South. He explained that "deep racial instincts are not limited by geographical bounds"; the increasing numbers of northern lynchings and mob attacks on "wholly innocent" and "unoffending Negroes" were proof of that. Southerners only appeared more brutal, reasoned Page, because of the "greater number of Negroes in that section."[197]

Page effectively used population and crime statistics the same way a Prudential Insurance statistician had in 1896: where blacks are, crime will follow. The ex-chief of the Census Bureau, Willcox, had helped clear the way for Page's argument by showing that black criminality in the North was increasing at a higher rate than in the South. Clearly, Willcox argued, a racially biased southern criminal justice system could not explain higher black criminality in the racially liberal North.[198] Either the North was not as tolerant of blacks as federal policy and some northern writers had made it appear, Page added, or black criminality brought out the worst in everyone. To argue the latter, Page relied on "the most remarkable study of the Negro which ha[d] appeared." Referring to Thomas's book, he ominously boasted:

> His chapter on this subject will be, to those unfamiliar with it, a terrible exposure of the depravity of the Negroes in their social life. . . . Unfortunately for the race, this depressing view is borne out by the increase of crime among them; by the increase of superstition, with its black trail of unnamable immorality and vice; by the homicides and murders, and by the outbreak and growth of the brutal crime which has chiefly brought about the frightful crime of lynching which stains the good name of the South and has spread northward with the spread of the Negro ravisher.[199]

With his northern readers at full attention at the "frightful" thought of more "Negro ravishers" and more northern lynchings—based convincingly on the "depressing view" of an "open-minded" black expert and increasing crime rates—Page made black criminality a rallying cry for national reconciliation. In his view, the fact that both sections of the country were vulnerable to being "drag[ged] down" by the "debased" Negro threatened the nation's future and whites' racial supremacy. "No country in the present state of the world's progress can long maintain itself in the front rank," he wrote, "and no people can long maintain themselves at the top of the list of peoples if they have to carry perpetually the burden of a vast and densely ignorant population." With ten million Negroes within its borders, the South needed understanding, not repudiation, from the North.[200]

Two years earlier, in 1902, Thomas Dixon, Jr., a southern lawyer, minister, and playwright, wrote a best-selling novel similarly focused on nationalizing white southerners' views on black criminality.[201] According to a reviewer, *The Leopard's Spots: A Romance of the White Man's Burden* was meant to justify white supremacy to northern readers by presenting as "vividly as possible the faults and crimes current among the Negroes of the South."[202] At the book's climax, a black man was burned at a stake for having raped and murdered a white woman. "Plainly the design is that the reader," a reviewer wrote, "shall exclaim in his indignation, 'I too would have helped to do the same, under the same circumstances!' "[203] The "circumstances" portrayed by Dixon gave the book's eye-catching title its significance, implying that there was no possibility of changing black people's brutal nature through philanthropy and education. By Dixon's rendering, then, the outlook was grim if northerners continued to try to elevate Negroes to the same level as whites. The two grand themes found in *The Leopard's Spots*—national unity and black retrogression—reached hundreds of thousands of Americans through its print run of nearly one million books.[204]

Dixon's work, with its commercial success, and Page's book, which followed shortly, demonstrated the increasingly popular appeal of thinking about black criminality and white responses on a national scale. Dixon's other bestseller, *The Clansman*, which was adapted for the big screen and became one of the first motion picture blockbusters as *The Birth of a Nation,* put the lynching of a black rapist at the heart of a national narrative about exterminating the danger within.[205] The general recognition of this trend in popular culture and social scientific thought inspired a major roundtable at the 1907 annual meeting of the American Sociological Association in Madison, Wisconsin. Some of the most prominent sociologists in the country gathered to hear and discuss Alfred Stone's paper, "Is Race Friction between Blacks and Whites in the United States Growing and Inevitable?" Stone, a southern sociologist and a Mississippi plantation owner "who controlled the lives of hundreds of black tenants," wanted his northern colleagues to be very clear about one thing.[206] Race prejudice was inevitable, but it was not a southern white phenomenon or a northern white aberration, he stated. It was the natural "antipathy" of whites, "an inherited part of his instinctive mental equipment," to the presence of a fundamentally different and inferior race. "The proposition is," Stone continued "too elementary for discussion, that the white man when confronted with a sufficient number of negroes to create in his mind a sense of political unrest or danger, either alters his form of government in order to be rid of the incubus, or destroys the political strength of the negro by force, by evasion, or by direct action."[207]

Stone's paper only implied a connection between black criminality and black inferiority as a source of race friction. Apparently stating that explicitly might have been too elementary, since four of the eight sociologists who published responses to Stone's paper—Walter Willcox of Cornell University, U. G. Weatherly of Indiana University, J. W. Garner of the University of Illinois, and Edwin L. Earp of Syracuse University—interpreted black criminality as the center of the problem. Willcox referred to it as a "rough index of race friction." Weatherly spoke of it as one of the most obvious indications of black inferiority: "Patience and toleration toward [the black man] are difficult when the facts that come most to the attention of the average white are those of crime, unthrift, and political corruption." Garner tied black criminality to migration and urbanization, while Earp, expressing the most liberal interpretation, saw it in relation to a lack of economic opportunities.[208] In a subsequent review of Stone's conference paper after it had been repackaged in *Studies in the American Race Problem* along with others of his essays (and Willcox's "Negro Criminality"), Frank Blackmar, a University of Kansas sociologist, praised the book for "being the most valuable contribution yet appearing on the race problem in the United States." Impressed by the race-relations interpretations of his esteemed northern colleagues, Blackmar added, "Owing to his ignorance, superstition, indolence, childish nature, and racial characteristics," the black man "is his own worst enemy."[209]

This roundtable discussion, published in the May 1908 issue of the *American Journal of Sociology,* crystallized the way in which African American criminality had gradually helped to bridge deep divisions over the meaning of black freedom since the end of slavery and Reconstruction, opening new lines of communication between the North and the South in search of a national solution to the race problem. In light of the conclusions reached at the Wisconsin meeting, Lewis writes, a "grim truth" emerged that "the march of science and industry tended to exacerbate race relations in the North as well as the South."[210] Two months later, in this "climate of national victimizing," New York feminist writer and evolutionary theorist Charlotte Perkins Gilman offered her own "suggestion on the Negro Problem." Since the problem was "the question of conduct" or preventing those "who are degenerating into an increasing percentage of social burdens or actual criminals," she recommended state-run forced labor camps.[211]

The race writers who conducted major studies or seminal works with a new emphasis on crime as *the* Negro Problem at the dawn of the Jim Crow era identified the transition from slavery to freedom as the origin of the problem. Frederick Hoffman argued that it was a "well-known fact" that crime did not exist during slavery, but in freedom, and especially in large cities, blacks were being reduced by their inferiority and immorality to "the anti-social condition" that "before many years will be worse than slavery." Walter Willcox insisted that slavery had not built up moral capital in black people; therefore they were unprepared and irresponsible in freedom. W. E. B. Du Bois believed that crime was a normal result of a "vast and sudden change like that of emancipation," especially for those "unable to adjust themselves to the new circumstances." William Hannibal Thomas noted that slavery had effectively restrained the "abeyant passions of [negroes'] undisciplined nature." Thomas Nelson Page observed that slavery had civilized the "savage from the wilds of Africa." It was precisely the blacks who had not grown up in slavery, whom he called the "new issue," who were fueling black crime rates. Thomas Dixon, Jr., like Page, pointed out that crime was an immediate consequence of the loss of southern whites' control during Reconstruction.[212] While it is obvious that these writers did not all agree about whether slavery had bred crime—Du Bois called crime a "heritage of slavery"—or had restrained it, they did agree that the present situation represented a sharp break from the past.

Many white race-relations writers hoped to blaze a research trail to solve the Negro Problem by writing crime into race. In the process, they also hoped to save the nation by using black criminality as a rhetorical bridge to heal deep sectional divisions and distrust rooted in the postbellum era. These writers saw vital racial statistics as a pathway to certainty and serenity. Beginning with Hoffman, they wanted their fellow Americans to see the indisputable evidence of black criminality as the key to binding the nation together in a campaign to keep the "negro" in his place.

Although the notion of black people as a race of criminals was pervasive and ubiquitous, the future was not all bleak. Some white race experts were not entirely convinced despite the new crime statistics. Like most black scholars and reformers, they resisted the temptation to completely dismiss "conditions of life" and racism as factors in the crime problem. M. V. Ball had been among the first northern whites to call the racialization of crime statistics into question, just as Ida B. Wells had been among the first southern black women to do the same. Even the popular science writer and Harvard scholar Nathaniel Southgate Shaler, who had done as much as any northern race-relations expert in the postbellum period to call for statistical investigations of black inferiority, balked at the new crime data. "The statistics of crime are not in such form as to make it clear in what regards they depart from the averages of the white population," he wrote in a 1900 *Popular Science Monthly* article. Even the most horrifying crimes, Shaler believed, were not "peculiarly common among the blacks." Given that of five million black men "probably not one in ten thousand" was guilty of rape, and given that rapes by white men tended to be underreported, Shaler was "inclined to believe that, on the whole, there is less danger to be apprehended from them in this regard than from an equal body of whites of the like social grade."[213] Shaler's speculation that white men were as guilty (if not more so) of rape as black men was surely perceived by some whites as an act of racial treason. Wells's work might have influenced him.

Seeing the arc of the discourse after nearly twenty years had passed from Shaler's first article on "The Negro Problem," the self-described racial liberal took an optimistic view of "the future of our American negroes." Though still a "half-savage people" and an "unexplored race," Shaler remained hopeful that over time, through industrial training and with the "masterful race's" help, blacks could become "valuable citizen[s]." That black people actually had the inherent capacity for citizenship, in Shaler's assessment, was a repudiation of the racial Darwinism of Hoffman and many others, and spoke to the shifting winds of the discourse among northern liberals. Du Bois's efforts, like Wells's, it seems, were not totally in vain. A dim light was beginning to shine on northern racism. "Sambo," Shaler wrote, was deprived "of opportunities in all the higher walks of life" in the North *and* the South. "In this matter there are but two courses open to us—one of folly, the other of wisdom. We may leave the black people to work out their own salvation as best they may, to lie as a mass at the bottom of our society. . . . Or we may set to work" with knowledge and strength to meet the great challenge ahead.[214]

Although Shaler passed from the world a few years later, in one of his last articles he renewed his call to solve the Negro Problem and to save the nation. But this time, well into the Progressive era, he was insisting that a rising cohort of racial liberals pursue a middle ground between racial research and racial reform:

> A necessary part of the work of true emancipation of the negro is a careful inquiry into the history and former status of the people. Such an inquiry, placed and kept in good hands, is a necessary preliminary to sagacious action. It may serve to unite the men of all parts of the country in a work that so nearly concerns us all. There is not, nor is there likely to arise, a situation that so calls for intelligent patriotism as this we are sorely neglecting. We may go far away and rear an empire with our armies; but if we leave these, our neighbors, without a fair chance to develop the good that is in them, we shall have lost our real opportunity for great deeds—mayhap we shall fix among us evils that in the end will drag us down.[215]

3

INCRIMINATING CULTURE:

THE LIMITS OF RACIAL LIBERALISM
IN THE PROGRESSIVE ERA

As if inspired by Nathaniel S. Shaler's parting words, one year after his call for a change in direction, a University of Chicago sociology graduate student joined the black crime debate, publishing a series of articles titled "The Criminal Negro" in *The Arena,* the favorite progressive journal of Shaler, Frederick L. Hoffman, and many others. Frances Kellor was the first white female social scientist to publish a major study of black criminality, and more importantly the first bona fide racial liberal to seriously investigate the subject following W. E. B. Du Bois.[1] In her 1901 publications she used more ink writing specifically on black criminality than any other white racial liberal to that point.[2] Whereas Hoffman had come to the fore as an innovative racial Darwinist and Shaler as a nationally renowned natural scientist whose homegrown southern sympathies and rosy views of slavery trumped his abolitionist credentials, Kellor made her debut as a northern-born-and-bred liberal scholar with working-class roots, a deep commitment to real-world reform, and an optimistic view that the black crime problem was not insurmountable.[3]

Kellor was at the leading edge of a new direction in the national black crime discourse. Directly responding to the groundbreaking and influential work of Hoffman, Du Bois, Walter Willcox, and Jane Addams,[4] she reframed the debate over heredity and environment as an open research question, staking an a priori claim to a middle ground between the two: "The problem of the causes of crime resolves itself into one of heredity and environment" that "racial tendencies alone cannot explain."[5] Kellor conducted a battery of anthropometric and psychological tests on ninety black female prisoners in eight southern states, comparing their body sizes and shapes, their sensory sensitivity, and their memory capability against her findings on sixty-one white female prisoners in "northern institutions." At the time of publication, she was also beginning to conduct some of the first race experiments at Tuskegee by measuring black female college students in order to compare them to the prisoners.[6] Until Kellor, no one had attempted to identify a black criminal type in the United States. Following Cesare Lombroso's criminal anthropological methods on Italian prisoners, she found no biological evidence that such a type existed.

Kellor's methods were unusual among mainstream white American sociologists, who leaned heavily toward an environmentalist view of white criminality, as was true of her mentor, Charles R. Henderson, author of a pioneering textbook in American criminology.[7] Within the still relatively new black crime discourse, by reproducing Lombroso's methods she attacked head-on the presumption that the black masses showed physical or mental traits that revealed criminal natures. By actually testing the theory, she was able to disprove it.[8] She was then able to move toward an environmental critique of the causes of black criminality, the true focus of her research.

"The Criminal Negro" was the first scholarly attempt by a white northern liberal to highlight southern conditions in relation to the national discourse on black criminality.[9] It revealed two systems in the United States: one northern, one southern; one reformatory, one punitive; one white, one black. "Only the North sustains theories worthy of the name *criminal sociology*, and only the North has adopted the reformatory idea," Kellor wrote. "The South is still in the age of revenge and punishment. Its system is neither systematic nor scientific. This is true" because "its criminal class is largely negro." With 90 percent of all African Americans residing in the South, Kellor painted a striking picture of a corrupt, vindictive, and racist criminal justice system that tailored its discriminatory laws through the county fee system, the all-white jury, felony enhancements targeting black agricultural workers, the chain gang, convict leasing, and the prison farm for the purposes of extracting financial profits from the bodies of black men, women, and children.[10] There were fewer than a handful of reformatories, she added. No kindergartens, no crime preventive agencies, nor any of the many progressive and constructive influences taking root among white northerners were available to black southerners. Tragically, in such circumstances and amid the poverty of large black families, even in the North, she revealed, the black man "has been left to look out for himself" while "we deplore and comment upon the morality of the negro." Yet "think of the cost and attention often required to save one [white] child in the North!" These were the circumstances, she emphasized like Hoffman's nemesis of old, M. V. Ball, that the census with its "bare statistics" could not explain. Implicitly repudiating Hoffman's work and explicitly questioning Willcox's denial of northern racism, Kellor argued that crime statistics had not proven that blacks were "incapable of advance." "The negro is more disadvantageously placed than is any other class in America," she concluded. "It is impossible to estimate the persistency of racial traits or of the limitations, mental or physical, imposed by racial development, until a parallel environment is removed; that is, the environment must be shown to be of such a nature that it offers every opportunity for development and improvement. In no phase of the negroes' life—domestic, social, industrial, political, or religious—does this appear to be the case."[11]

Kellor's analysis anticipated a new line of inquiry among northern progressives that linked black criminality not to hereditarian theories of race but to the absence of environmental interventions like those proliferating among whites in the urban North. By calling attention to the failure of whites to help black families overcome the "deteriorating influences" of city life, and by demonstrating through her anthropometric analysis that blacks had no biological defects that prevented their rising to meet the demands of an "advanced civilization," Kellor, like Du Bois, refocused the debate back to the old abolitionist question of what responsibility whites had in solving the Negro Problem.[12] Her work presaged two important changes in the black crime discourse that would gradually emerge among northern white racial liberals during the first two decades of the twentieth century. The first was the appeal for "remedial measures" in solving the Negro Problem, including expanded economic opportunities, education, social work, and crime prevention.[13] The second was the rejection of biological determinism, including redefining racial traits as cultural traits, a paradigmatic shift in the science of race that placed African Americans once and for all within the pale of civilization, at least in the minds of most liberal social scientists. The German-born anthropologist Franz Boas, the founder of cultural pluralism over these years, deservedly received much of the credit for this transformative moment.[14]

The intellectual landscape did not change overnight. William Hannibal Thomas's acclaimed *The American Negro* was published the same year as Kellor's articles, and *The Leopard's Spots* by Thomas Dixon, Jr., and *The Negro: The Southerner's Problem* by Thomas Nelson Page soon followed. Hoffman's 1896 predictions of blacks' eventual extinction due to inferior biology and self-destructive behavior were still very much in keeping with the dominant racial scientific discourse. Consequently, his ideological response to black migration and crime when it was but a trickle near the turn of the century remained a source of comfort to many northern and southern race experts seeking common ground in the spirit of white supremacy and national reconciliation. Even when that trickle turned to a flood at the onset of World War I, launching the Great Migration—the largest relocation of African Americans (a half million) prior to the World War II period—Hoffman's initial linking of migration, urbanization, and criminality remained a salient framework within which numerous experts continued to debate and discuss race relations. Moreover, as a national crime expert Hoffman remained extremely influential for many years to come, continuing to be the nation's premier source for the statistical reproduction of black criminality figures outside of census reports until the creation of the FBI's *Uniform Crime Reports* in the 1930s.[15] Praising his 1915 annual reports on homicide statistics, a reviewer for the *American Statistical Association* wrote, "That the only effort to present this branch of criminal statistics for the country as a whole is left to be undertaken year after year by a single individual in unofficial life is no less a tribute to Mr. Hoffman than it is a condemnation of the various agencies of government which should be concerned with accumulating and interpreting this information."[16] Part of his longevity was explained by the continued marginalization of black race-relations experts within the social sciences.

When Du Bois debated Hoffman's ideas around the turn of the century, he rejected the notion that blacks were racially inferior. Du Bois admitted that their criminality was high, their morals lacking, and their letters wanting, but these were not irrefutably racial traits. Du Bois and most other black race-relations writers countered the issue of the Negro Problem with evidence of racism and inequality, or instances of race progress, or themselves as their own best examples.[17] Equally important, black race-relations writers expressed their moral outrage about the failings and misdeeds of their social inferiors, emphasizing intra-racial class and culture distinctions as evidence that biology was not the problem. They described black women's high employment rate as an invitation to moral decay in the domestic life of black families. A working mother could neither nurture her children nor prevent them from falling into "evil ways." Underpaid black women domestics were constantly at risk for sexual immorality through the advances of white male employers who offered extra pay for sexual favors or a better paying job in prostitution. Black men's high unemployment rate and reputation for low efficiency led, black writers claimed, to idleness, drunkenness, and gambling. Assault or homicide were the by-products of bad friends, bad wine, bad bets, or a nasty brew of all three. Black men with decent jobs as service workers in hotels or restaurants picked up the vile habits of white men who vacationed in vice but did not live there. These otherwise hardworking black men imitated the worst habits of those they served without knowing how to break the cycle. The black household too often needed lodgers to pay the rent, an unfortunate breach of the sanctity of home, marriage, and family; too often the moral structure collapsed under the weight of too many people living too freely in too little space. The unsuspecting children, especially girls, would eventually be victimized by male boarders and thus start down the road to lives of sexual depravity. Children who were fortunate enough to keep their privates hidden from the stares and groping of strangers were still invaded by the "vicious elements" and "immoral characters" they passed daily on their neighborhood streets.[18]

Nevertheless, any evidence of northern black criminality or immorality presented by African Americans was filtered into the mainstream social scientific discourse as definitive "proof" of black inferiority. It did not matter to many of their most influential white peers that the black race-relations experts had intended their discourse and data to be interpreted within a broader critique of racial inequality and industrialization. The black writers had taken their cue partly from white writers, who located the source of white pathology in the economy. Even when white experts understood their intentions, their ideas were often dismissed as sentimental bluster. Upon reviewing Du Bois's most widely read collection of essays, *The Souls of Black Folk,* a classic of modern American literary realism and a canonical text of African American existentialism, Carl Kelsey wrote, "Not until he ceases to go about with 'chips on his shoulders' as it were, will he gain the influence to which his mental attainments entitle him." Kelsey, a prominent University of Pennsylvania sociologist and a visible player among Philadelphia's white racial liberals, sometimes collaborated with local black reformers such as James Stemons, a journalist, antiracist activist, and pioneering crime fighter.[19] Yet Kelsey dismissed Du Bois's personal expressions of racial victimization. "No doubt it is strange to 'be a problem,' he wrote, "yet one who knows the educational opportunities afforded Professor Du Bois, finds it hard to appreciate" his claims that prejudice is so widespread and debilitating. For black elites, promoting themselves like walking billboards for the race's mettle sometimes backfired, as evidenced by the thoughts of even some sympathetic whites who conflated the exceptional opportunities of a tiny minority with the circumscribed options of the masses. "The author is too much inclined to emphasize the bad," Kelsey concluded as he dismissed Du Bois's prediction that the twentieth century would be defined by the color line.[20] Not until the 1920s, in the wake of widespread racial violence across the urban North and mounting evidence of racist police violence and corruption, were national black crime experts able to construct a lasting alternative antiracist discourse.

For the moment, the trappings of the dominant racialist crime discourse limited the effectiveness of African Americans' rhetorical strategies. At the national level, race continued to trump class as the language of black inferiority until the culture concept was born. Between 1896 and the beginning of the Great Migration, writing crime into race had become more than the sum of white and black writers' data, discussion, and debate. Race-relations writers had inscribed criminality onto nearly every aspect of black people's existence. That crime became linked to migration, to education, to politics, to housing, and to philanthropy reveals the pervasive influence of those who had forced the question to the nation of whether African Americans should continue to have access to social resources at all. "What have the thousands of churches and schools and colleges, maintained at the cost of more than a hundred and fifty million dollars, produced?" asked Thomas Nelson Page. "We may inquire first: Has the percentage of crime decreased in the race generally?"[21] Until the Great Migration period ended, the underlying premise of criminality as the sine qua non of racial inferiority was extremely difficult to surmount. By debating the meaning of high versus low criminality or increasing versus decreasing crime rates, black writers unwittingly reinforced the importance of crime in defining black life.

Still, they had few options, given that the crime discourse framed serious policy proposals about the future of black life in America. Hoffman's and Page's linking of crime to education, for example, became part of a national debate about literacy as a stimulus to crime among blacks.[22] In the spring of 1904, Atlanta University held the Ninth Atlanta Conference on crime among Negroes in Georgia. Its published proceedings, *Some Notes on Negro Crime*, edited by Du Bois, was one of the first major studies to feature the opinions of southern black educators and reformers and a few southern white allies who examined the subject of crime in the South in relation to a broad range of social issues. According to Du Bois and the conference experts, "illiterate Negroes ... furnish more of the criminals than those who read and write." More importantly, because there was such little difference between the "wholly illiterate" and those "who [could] just barely read and write," Du Bois added, the "full degree in which ignorance causes Negro crime" was not clearly shown by the statistics.[23] He was subtly arguing that the poor quality of education for blacks rendered the classification "literate" too imprecise to be a reliable measure of the education levels of Negro criminals. In a letter Du Bois wrote to the editor of the *Nation* two winters before the Atlanta conference, he was more insistent that even the so-called literate Negro prisoners were barely educated. He revealed that of 24,277 black prisoners, fewer than 40 percent were considered literate, and only 321 of those "had any education above that of the common schools."[24] Kellor's mental tests of black women prisoners corroborated Du Bois's findings. Those "classed as literate on the prison records," she wrote, "in no exact sense could be regarded as able to read and write."[25]

After Du Bois failed to end the literacy-as-crime debate in 1902— when he cited the specific section and page number of the 1890 census where it was shown that the literate black population (42.9 percent) was underrepresented in the black prison population (38.8 percent)—he tried again in the 1904 conference proceedings. This time he relied on the opinion of a southern white man. Perhaps he was modeling white writers' co-optive strategies, just as Ida B. Wells had cited white press accounts of white rapists.[26] Du Bois quoted Clarence H. Poe, a white southern editor of the Raleigh *Progressive Farmer*, whose article had first appeared in the February *Atlantic Monthly*. Poe began by acknowledging the "oft repeated charge" that literate Negroes were more criminal than illiterate ones. He traced its origin to a speech given at a meeting of the National Prison Association in 1897; from there, Poe wrote, "it was printed in one of our foremost magazines, the *North American Review* (Philadelphia), in June 1900." Fiction substituted as fact, according to Poe, the "charge" toured the South from a Georgia governor's public address, to a Mississippi preacher's "broadcast over the South," and through the pages of "scores of [news]papers." Poe quoted the following rant against Negro education from a southern editorial: "To school the Negro is to increase his criminality. Official statistics do not lie, and they tell us that the Negroes who can read and write are more criminal than the illiterate. In New

England, where they are best educated, they are four and a half times as criminal as in the Black Belt, where they are most ignorant. The more money for Negro education, the more Negro crime. This is the unmistakable showing of the United States Census."[27]

Nearly a decade before the North Carolinian bristled at his fellow southerner's distortion, the New Jersey-based Hoffman had used the same statistics to argue similarly that "education ha[d] utterly failed to raise the negro to a higher level of citizenship, the first duty of which [was] to obey the laws and respect the lives and property of others."[28] But Hoffman and the southern editorialist were both mistaken. "To make the matter plain," Poe cited the same numbers Du Bois had used in the *Nation*. He also admitted, like Du Bois, that only in western states was there a slightly larger proportion of literate prisoners to the illiterate, but since the West had only 1 percent of the nation's black prisoners, no general conclusions could be drawn.[29]

The argument that Du Bois was refuting for the second time, albeit using Poe's testimony, had significant staying power because no one could deny that black crime rates were higher in the North or that the North had better schools for blacks. The presumption that white supremacy did not rule in the North—that blacks in the Land of Lincoln had as much freedom as their able minds and bodies entitled them to—weighed heavily among writers and readers who had been seduced by racial Darwinist thinking. The way this mind-set works, explained Howard University professor Kelly Miller, is that where "legal processes are acknowledged to be fair, and where the Negro has the fullest educational opportunity, he shows a criminal rate three to four times as great as his ignorant and oppressed brother in the South. And the conclusion is hastily reached that education makes the Negro a criminal." Miller refuted the reasoning behind the conclusion not just because it was a flawed deduction based on statistics, but because it was a prejudiced opinion against blacks. He argued that although blacks in Massachusetts had been five times more likely in 1890 to serve time than their Mississippi counterparts, the "white man in Massachusetts [had been] ten times as criminal as the white man in Mississippi." Miller wrote indignantly, "Shall we discount the superior education of the white man in the Bay State because he seems to be only one-tenth as saintly as his less enlightened white brother on the banks of the Mississippi? Or shall we foster the bliss of ignorance only when it is found under a black skin? Ordinarily one would explain the high criminal rate of the Northern States on the ground of congested population and more stringent enforcement of law; but logical processes seem to be of no avail against sweeping assertions to the detriment of the discredited Negro."[30]

Clearly, Miller believed that the dehumanization of black people was a prerequisite for the "bliss of ignorance" that substituted for nonracialist, environmentally focused statements that explained high crime and good schooling. Did not population density and better policing in the North affect blacks as it did whites, Miller asked, but for strictly viewing all blacks' behavior through the lens of racial inferiority? So much racist reasoning depended on perspective. Race seemed the least significant explanation for criminality and education when, from a national perspective, Miller compared per capita education costs. In Massachusetts twenty-five dollars was spent on education per white person; in South Carolina just under four dollars per capita was spent on whites and about seventy-five cents per capita on blacks. Miller had effectively exposed the underlying manipulation of statistics to bolster racist interpretations, specifically those that relied on the North as a sort of proving ground, ostensibly free of slavery's past and white supremacy's present, to illustrate just how futile it was to try to change "the leopard's spots" or black people's inferior nature.[31]

For years to come, counterevidence continued to be collected to show that educated African Americans were in fact law-abiding citizens. To use Kelly Miller's words, graduates of black colleges were no more likely to be criminals than "the alumni of institutions for the white race."[32] Gilbert Stephenson, a southern white municipal judge, polled officials at common schools, high schools, industrial schools, and colleges about the number of black graduates known to have committed crimes. He also asked prison wardens how many black inmates were skilled mechanics. "The records of the South, as a whole, show that ninety percent of the colored people in prisons are without knowledge of trades," wrote Stephenson. Based on Stephenson's study, educated blacks were far from overrepresented in the South's prisons.

In a separate study, Booker T. Washington conducted a similar investigation of black skilled workers in prison. One Alabama warden told him, "There is not a man in this prison that could draw a straight line."[33] As for the typical primary, secondary, or college graduate, school officials knew of very few who had turned to crime. In its first thirty-five years, Tuskegee had fewer than a half dozen graduates out of over two thousand who had "been arrested, convicted, or in any way charged with a crime." Hampton claimed four prisoners who had actually graduated and five who were dropouts; Fisk recorded only one.[34] At the pinnacle of higher education, Ray Stannard Baker wrote in 1907 that "no Negro student has ever disgraced Harvard and that no students are more orderly and law-abiding than the Negroes."[35] Despite increasing rates of literacy and ever-growing numbers of blacks attending school, tracking the criminal careers of black students kept black writers on the defensive and reinforced the appropriateness of using crime to measure black progress. James K. Vardaman, Mississippi's proudly racist governor, made the stakes painfully clear with his advice that "on the strength of [crime] statistics" southern states were "perfectly justified . . . in refusing to educate [blacks] at all."[36]

Even as the crime discourse continued to fuel the spirit of white supremacists determined to spread Jim Crow across every sphere of American society, it also pricked the conscience of a small number of northern progressives. "There must be a world of irony in the heart of the seeing Negro who reads in the papers the lurid descriptions of his own crime, while he lives in [New York's] Tenderloin district and looks out upon its . . . daily dangers" and "temptations" presented by "other races," wrote Mary White Ovington, a leading white settlement house advocate and a social survey researcher who specialized in documenting the struggles of northern African American families.[37] Although Ovington had begun her career as a social reformer after visiting London's East End slums, then plunging herself into the work of the Greenwich House, New York's first settlement for the struggling white and immigrant poor, shortly thereafter she became an influential researcher and advocate for the northern black urban poor. "She knows more about it than anyone I know," wrote an admiring Du Bois, who, according to his biographer deserved much of the credit for Ovington's background knowledge and inspiration. Over many decades she was Du Bois's closest white "confidante and advisor," beginning with her moral and financial support for his research program at Atlanta University not long after *Souls* had appeared. Ovington felt "it was impossible to read him and not be moved." She also became a founding member of the National Association for the Advancement of Colored People (NAACP).[38]

With some nudging from their black peers, a small number of white liberals like Kellor and Ovington increasingly recognized the lopsided nature of urban progressivism. They began to see their own desire to help struggling and self-destructive whites—the "great army of unfortunates"—as an incongruity worthy of further investigation, if not more. "The one class in the North with which the negro child is comparable," observed Kellor, "is the laboring class crowded in tenement districts. The habits, training, and opportunities are somewhat alike." Of those among both groups who ended up in reformatories, many are "largely [trained] in the street or in depraved homes." But "the agencies in the north reach whites far more effectively than they do negroes."[39] Reformers such as Kellor and Ovington began to see the inconsistency between a hopeful vision of white criminality as largely a symptom of industrial capitalism and a reason to intervene, and a pessimistic view of black criminality and the futility of reform.

From this consciousness-raising among northern white racial liberals came the seeds of a counter black crime discourse sown in the years leading to the Great Migration. In the midst of expanding black communities within or on the borders of much larger immigrant communities in the urban North, new cultural explanations emerged among an influential core of white liberal writers and reformers to reinterpret the places blacks would fill and at what pace they would enter the modern urban world as citizens. In this changing context, Franz Boas's new cultural anthropology laid the groundwork as the most influential social scientific source for rethinking blacks' potential to become full participants in American society.

Although Boas's cultural anthropology would not become widely known until the 1911 publication of *The Mind of Primitive Man,* his scientific ideas began to raise new questions and new doubts about heredity and environment as early as 1905. Based on his interpretations of anthropological accounts of the great cultural achievements of past African civilizations, Boas argued that there was no evidence to "countenance the belief in racial inferiority which would unfit an individual of the Negro race to take his part in modern civilization." Boas presented his early ideas in a special issue of *Charities* magazine, the premiere journal of northern charity workers and philanthropists. He was one of twenty-two contributors to a remarkable collaboration of nationally recognized white and black social reformers and a few leading race-relations experts sharing, for the first time since the abolitionist era, their own perspectives on the crisis of "the Negro in cities of the North."[40] "We do not know," Boas explained to his liberal peers, "of any demand made of the human body or mind in modern life that anatomical or ethnological evidence would prove to be beyond the powers of the Negro."[41] Like Kellor's publications, Boas's 1905 article would signal a new "scientific presumption" that "the Negro has the inherent capacity for progress, for civilization."[42]

With Boas's rejection of biological determinism, a fresh set of perspectives on black criminality and new arguments for racial advancement entered the race-relations discourse. Boas's interest in attacking biological racism was motivated in part by his primary concern with nativism in the urban North and related policy debates on restricting immigration. The assimilation of southern and eastern European immigrants was ultimately his central focus, as it was for the vast majority of Progressive era reformers.[43] Yet his 1911 treatise, *The Mind of Primitive Man*, undoubtedly opened the door for blacks to be accepted as full participants in America. Along with some of the most influential and outspoken northern progressives, Boas argued that black inferiority was not innate but was a temporary state perpetuated by whites' "social neglect." *The Mind of Primitive Man* thus marked a crucial transition moment for new cultural explanations of black criminality.[44]

As white racial liberals, Boas and those he influenced made great strides toward justifying racial equality in the urban North. In contrast to white racial Darwinists, including southern sociologists (or apologists), they constructed an alternative stage on which crime among blacks could be seen as a social problem rather than a biological one, as something temporary and reformable rather than innate and fixed. In light of modern capitalism's contradictory forces of expanded economic opportunities and social freedoms as well as new forms of misery and blight, these northern liberals brought blacks closer to their pro-immigrant structural critiques. For example, they recast black juvenile delinquency and prostitution partly as social dramas shaped by white racism and white privilege.

Still, they stopped short of where they went for white immigrants. They used culture as both a salve and a sieve, to mediate the line between racial oppression based on hereditarian theories of black inferiority and unambiguous color-blind appeals for social, economic, and political reform. Facing institutional racism and intensifying segregation and discrimination by the public at large, many racial liberals ultimately capitulated. By replacing biology with culture, sociologist Tukufu Zuberi argues, they did not overcome the problem of essentializing differences among groups. It "was a move from one type of essentialist perspective, the biological evolu-tionary, to another type of essentialist perspective, the cultural. This shift witnessed the birth of assimilation and a focus on unproductive behavior of the unassimilated as a dominant perspective—in a word, a return to view-ing the 'Negro as a [peculiar] problem.' "[45]

The limits of their cultural perspective were most clearly visible in discussions of black criminality and immorality. For all the new possi-bilities suggested by Kellor's crime analysis, there remained a dark side: "The negroes' criminality is that of an undeveloped race. That of the whites is more characterized by a capacity born of development. There are few professionals among the negroes, and there are no truly 'great criminals.' They may be 'prominent,' but the two are not identical. The negroes' crimes show an absence of social and personal responsibility, and are the outgrowth of impulse rather than of well-laid plans and com-plicated schemings." As Kellor discounted race traits and made signifi-cant strides toward an environmental or sociological perspective on black criminality, part of her analysis reified the inferiority of blacks even as criminals. "Negroes are notorious thieves, but they remain months and years in stockades that would not hold ordinary northern safe blow-ers twenty-four hours."[46] In this transitional formulation, not only were African Americans second-rate criminals but the sources of their criminal-ity were peculiar by comparison to whites. Black prostitutes, for example, were viewed differently from native whites and immigrants. They were not yet seen as victims of industrialization and its attendant dangers as were the young white factory girls and domestic servants no longer under the protective gaze of their mothers.[47] Black women's problem, Kellor wrote, was that they yielded "to white men quite as readily as in slavery." Even the constructive agents in the black community were not like their white counterparts, shining the light of salvation and education on the "wage slaves" of the urban North. Instead, "negro teachers and ministers are frequently the most immoral of their race," she explained.[48] Kellor's crime-as-culture proto-analysis foreshadowed the way the new discourse would continue to explain why black people's criminality was still funda-mentally different from that of whites and immigrants.[49] The new term *capacity* signaled a new language to measure historical and social differ-ences between blacks and whites. Terms that would come to be defined as cultural concepts attempted to place blacks on the same plane as whites, even if at the bottom.

The writing of crime into culture, then, became a counter-discourse that was deeply flawed not because it inherently examined the crimes and immorality of individual blacks but because it emphasized the cultural distinctiveness of black thieves, rapists, and murderers. Their ancestral victimization as the children and grandchildren of ex-slaves tied them to both an exceptional past and a peculiar present. Immigrants from dozens of European cities had their own distinctive histories of oppression and subjugation, but their trans-Atlantic voyage and landing at Ellis Island helped to wash away those distinctions. Relatively speaking, Progressive era social reformers were more willing to look beyond the "unproductive" behavior of the immigrant masses, excuse it, or do something about it than was generally the case with black migrants.[50]

These liberal social reformers did not ignore the illegal and immoral offenses of the transplanted either. Frederic Bushee, a leading Boston settlement worker and author of a pioneering 1903 study of immigrant life in the New England capital, described the Irish and Italians as the most criminal elements in the city, "excepting the Negroes." The Irish had the highest rates of petty crime, and the Italians topped the list for major felonies. "There is a moral degradation among Irish families as a result of drink which is not found among other nationalities," he wrote. "For quarrels which are serious affairs, for flashes of anger which mean a knife thrust, one must go to the Italian quarters."[51] Harvard economist William Ripley, who wrote the preface to Bushee's study, had his own nativist theories about the inferiority and criminality of the new immigrants: "The horde now descending upon our shores is densely ignorant, yet dull and superstitious withal; lawless, with a disposition to criminality; servile for generations, without conception of political rights."[52] Yet Bushee, Ripley, and many others insisted on seeing past the moral turpitude, violence, and "disposition to criminality" in all of its ethnic dimensions among the newcomers.

With a vision of European immigrants as "Americans in Process," many immigrant reform advocates insisted on focusing on the promises rather than the perils of assimilation. Bushee described the Irish and the Italians as extremely likable people despite their flaws. The Irish were especially well suited for contributing "many valuable traits to the American people." With their "happiness," "love of pleasure," and fondness for "games and sports," he wrote, "it is fortunate that they possess the char-

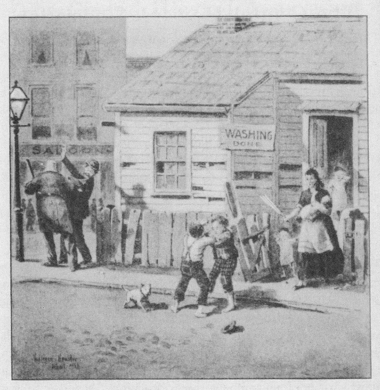

HOW CRIMINALS ARE MADE.

So long as there are bad tenements; sweatshops; brutal policemen; bad jails; child labor; dishonest and grinding employers; saloons and gambling dens; so long as boys are taught to fight and allowed to carry firearms; so long as fathers are indifferent deserters, and mothers must maintain the family by the washboard—so long crime will continue. What will you do to help this Association to prevent it?

Figure 3-1 "How Criminals Are Made" captures the environmental critique of crime made by Progressive era social reformers as they focused on helping struggling white and immigrant inner-city families. From the 1907 Annual Report of the Central Howard Association, courtesy of the Newberry Library.

acteristics which make them easily assimilable" in spite of their "weak personal characteristics." The Italians had good bones, he added, but needed a bit more direction and guidance. "They are a simple peasant class who respond readily to their environment." Yet they could not be "allowed to continue in unwholesome conditions," for "we may be sure the next generation will bring forth a crop of dependents, delinquents, and defectives to fill up our public institutions."[53] Put another way, "the great problem for us in dealing with these immigrants," Ripley stated, is not that of their nature but of their nurture. . . . They are fellow passengers on our ship of state; and the health of the nation depends upon the preservation of the vitality of the lower classes." Citing Chicago's Hull House and Boston's South End House as two of the nation's pioneering and premiere inner-city crime prevention agencies to be emulated, Ripley called for more playgrounds, schools, libraries, and all the "uplifting influences of these sorts to meet the needs of the women and children of the immigrant classes."[54] It was also in the nation's interest, added William S. Bennet, a plainspoken congressman from New York and a co-panelist at a 1909 immigration conference where Ripley made his remarks, to cease stigmatizing immigrants as a race of criminals. "Learn to treat the individual immigrant not as one of a nationality at all," he said, "and not allow the crime of one Italian, in a moment of passion to weigh for any more than the crime of an American."[55]

Like the legions of lesser-known settlement workers, most of whom were tireless college-educated white women who dedicated a tremendous amount of time and money to helping the less fortunate, many immigrant spokespersons were far less sanguine about the future of black people.[56] "The Negroes in general reveal the faults of an immature race," a consequence of the "evil effects" of slavery, which had saddled them with "peculiar forms of immorality." Their assimilation in the foreseeable future, Bushee advised, was not "desirable."[57] These urban reformers and immigrant advocates were not the exceptions, the historian Allen Davis noted in his classic study of social settlements, in an era when most "thought of the progressive movement as for whites only."[58] They were not the women and men who, at a minimum, investigated the conditions of African Americans in the midst of immigrant communities, recognizing that the fate of black people was in some way connected to the fate of poor white and immigrant urbanites. The racial liberals—Kellor, Boas, Ovington, Addams, and a handful of others—were exceptional in this way. In her recent study on "settlement folk," historian Mina Carson explains further: "The [typical] settlement leaders also showed what today we would see as 'blind spots' in their identification and condemnation of major social problems. In its first forty years the settlement movement did not ameliorate, or even directly address, white society's systematic discrimination against black Americans. Though several of the white founders of the NAACP had settlement connections, institutionally the settlements failed to make any significant contribution to white Americans' consciousness of racism or to furthering black peoples' rights and opportunities."[59] Among most liberal social reformers, among those deeply immersed in the on-the-ground work of establishing beachheads against the degradation of white youth and immigrant families, black criminality confounded the theory and the practice of racial equality.

Over time, white immigrants' escape from the slums by way of economic and social privilege—"becoming Caucasian"—and progressives' successful immigrant-focused legislative and social reforms raised and reinforced doubts about blacks' cultural readiness.[60] Most native whites and their newly minted cousins embraced these doubts because to them, perceptually, black life in urban ghettos was stagnant, if not dangerous. Even white racial liberals yielded to the contradiction that America guaranteed all of its citizens a fair shake when they knew, better than most, of "the world of irony" blacks faced daily on the tenement streets.[61] Like Ovington, they knew that whiteness was the precondition.[62] On the one hand, these exceptional race reformers—those who would gain their neo-abolitionist stripes as supporters of new civil rights organizations—helped to open a small number of settlements for black neighbors by 1910, while encouraging black reformers to open more of their own.[63] On the other hand, in an era when white supremacy was ascending, this was a surrender to segregation and a deeply flawed solution at best.[64] Black northern reformers had neither sufficient financial resources nor the sympathy of white philanthropists, who were interested mostly in industrial education for southern blacks, to fund the scale of work needing to be done.[65] "The settlements founded by the blacks themselves were the poorest equipped, the most severely underfinanced and understaffed, and the shortest-lived."[66] Besides, immigrants were not left to save themselves. Carl Kelsey's admonishing of Du Bois for his expressive antiracism in *Souls of Black Folk* was a telling sign of the liberal crime discourse to come. Prejudice, he wrote, "will cease when the blacks can command and compel the respect and sympathy of the whites."[67] For even the most sympathetic white social reformers, focusing on black criminality—even through the lens of Boas's new cultural pluralism— was a rhetorical and programmatic solution; it rationalized their gradu- alist approach to racial equality and limited black reform efforts.[68]

Kelsey was among the nearly two-dozen white and black liberal experts called on by *Charities* magazine in 1905 to provide a "suggestive survey" of the "typical facts" found among "Negroes in the northern cities."[69] This collaborative effort marked the moment when the North officially became the universally accepted proving ground of African American fitness for citizenship in modern America. For all the ways in which crime had in a decade become the linchpin of a national social scientific debate about black inferiority, with northern crime statistics commonly cited as defini- tive proof, northern liberal reformers were now ready to weigh in. "The Negro's worth as a citizen is to be tested in the great cities of the north as nowhere else in the world," wrote *Charities* contributor Fannie Barrier Williams, a black club woman and a vocal proponent for settlement work in black communities. The reformers "have begun to recognize that if the ever-increasing Negro population is treated and regarded as a reprobate race, the result will be an increase of crime and disorders of all kinds that will grow more and more difficult to handle and regulate."[70]

The editors of the special issue likewise expressed a sense of hopeful- ness and optimism and a desire to avoid emphasizing "statistical inquiry" and the perspectives of the "more bitter elements of the race conflict," citing "Mr. Page" as Exhibit A. Along with *Charities*' editor Edward T. Devine, secretary of New York's Charity Organization Society (COS), which sponsored the journal, and managing editor Paul Kellogg, many of the most influential progressive reformers in the nation edited the issue, including Hull House's Jane Addams, the housing muckraker Jacob Riis, and University of Pennsylvania political scientist Simon N. Patten, who was Devine's mentor and encouraged him to found Columbia Universi- ty's School of Social Work.[71] As leaders and innovators of urban reform movements, the editors privileged the value of local knowledge derived from clinicians, from people on the ground who could speak as social workers, probation officers, visiting nurses, ministers, and educators. Some of these men and women were already or soon to become national race-relations experts, such as Kellor, Du Bois, Ovington, Boas, Booker T. Washington, and John Daniels, a white Boston settlement worker who wrote *In Freedom's Birthplace: A Study of Boston Negroes*, a 1914 sequel to Bushee's immigrant study. Their contributions added to the credibility of the reports, but this was really about local knowledge in the service of shedding light on a regional controversy in the midst of a national debate.[72]

At the heart of the reports, according to the editors, was the problem of "deprivation." Whether in Philadelphia, New York, Chicago, or the border cities of Baltimore and Washington, D.C., the contributors had shown time and time again, black people lacked both opportunity and a sense of responsibility. For example, northern discrimination among industrial employers and unions kept black men on the economic margins of society in Boston, according to Daniels, and in Chicago, observed Richard R. Wright, Jr.. At the same time, too many recent southern migrants were deprived of the requisite fitness for industrial work. These "industrial scavengers" exhibited the "Negro traits of instability, and eat-drink-and-be-merriness," wrote Daniels, contributing to their limited job prospects. Lillian Brandt, an in-house white researcher for the New York COS, similarly observed that the single young black men and women arriving in the urban North were "seeking employment in conditions to which they are unaccustomed," which explained some of their "excessive criminality." Kelsey noted that some of the male migrants had no intention of working at all; instead, they had come in search of social intimacy with white women. "Possibly he hears the boast in the North [that] a Negro may enter a restaurant and be waited on by a white girl." Others, Kelsey continued, were "ex-convicts and otherwise undesirable individuals" on the lam from southern law enforcement.[73]

Whether black men arrived in trouble or ended up that way, Francis Kellor added that many black women migrants "left [their] happy-go-lucky, cheerful life in the South" only to end up "drift[ing] into immorality." They often had the best of intentions, but partly due to their "ignorance," their inflated ambitions, ("to them going to Philadelphia or New York seems like going to Heaven"), and the "sharks" posing as legitimate employment agents many became prostitutes.[74] To do something, Kellor gave up her scholarly career shortly after publishing "The Criminal Negro" to become a full-time reformer. She helped found the National League for the Protection of Colored Women, with branches in Philadelphia and New York. Kellor had always had one foot in the academy and the other in the reform community. Her research on southern prisons and Tuskegee had been funded by Celia Parker Woolley, a leader of the Chicago Women's Club and a local white settlement worker who, along with Ida B. Wells, opened the Frederick Douglass Center to promote interracial harmony through tea parties and parlor lectures.[75] Kellor's protective league aimed to "rescue" black female migrants at ports and train depots before they were lost to prostitution. The league was among the earliest of the small number of Progressive era agencies established to help black migrants. It was absorbed by the National Urban League (NUL) in 1910.[76] In the context of explaining why black people were falling short or, as the *Charities* editors wrote, "are not yet fitted to survive and prosper in the great northern cities to which so many of them are crowding," an Alabama black educator corroborated the connection between northern migration and criminality.[77] "It is the shiftless and unstable who make no effort to take advantage of the superior opportunities of the North, and whose only ostensible purpose is to seek social and moral degradation under the guise of domestic employment," wrote William E. Benson in a self-serving bid to promote his southern industrial school and Booker T. Washington's philosophy that blacks were best suited for the South and should cast down their buckets where they were.[78]

The most explicit linking of black criminality and the movement of blacks to northern cities in the special issue was made by another black educator, J. H. N. Waring, principal of Baltimore's High and Training School and also a physician. Using the language of an epidemiologist, Waring stated that crime among blacks was like a disease spreading at an alarming rate, no less direful than "the white plague of tuberculosis." With no desire to be a "prophet of evil," Waring nevertheless predicted "that some future day, unless conditions are definitely and radically changed, a Black Plague . . . will afflict us as one of the legitimate fruits of our present sowing of the seeds of indifference to the welfare of the millions of ignorant, half-taught, badly-housed, poorly-fed, and despised blacks in our population." Waring obviously expressed far less ambivalence about why blacks were not measuring up in the North, defining criminality much more clearly in relation to racism and neglect than to some underlying pathology migrants carried with them. He focused on racial disparities in education, housing, and law enforcement. "Schools for white children fulfill all the requirements of the ideal school and thousands of dollars are spent annually to make them architecturally beautiful, to adorn them with libraries and works of art, and to furnish instructors of the highest ability and skill." But black schools, he complained, were often "dilapidated buildings . . . abandoned by the whites as unfit for further use." Like the schools, black neighborhoods also suffered from a lack of "conscience of the American people." "City fathers" thought nothing of licensing liquor stores in "almost every colored neighborhood." The police frequently locked up "boys of tender age" with "hardened and depraved criminals, when a word of advice or reprimand would have served the purpose of the law." Instead, they have "done much to take away their sense of shame and self respect and really start them on criminal careers." With all of this, Waring surmised, "the wonder is not that there are so many criminals, but that there are any colored people who value honesty, honor, chastity and virtue!"[79] The racial disparities also troubled William L. Bulkley, a fellow contributor and a black principal of a Manhattan elementary school: "With the white child in America, everything industrial, civil, political, and social is possible. What of the black?"[80]

In the main, the *Charities* reports sent mixed signals about the conditions of life for African Americans in the urban North. Rooted in personal observation and survey research, the white and black liberal contributors shared a common recognition that life was hard for black newcomers to the urban North. In one of the earliest publications of its kind in the Progressive era, white liberal testimonies of racism above the Mason-Dixon line corroborated the claims of black writers who cried foul, but faced charges of sentimentality and bias by their racial Darwinist counterparts. Yet the editors' framing of the report suggested that white northerners were part of the problem but less the solution. With criminality and immorality as the fully accepted units of measurement, the editors billed the studies as a report card on how far black people had come in taking advantage of northern opportunities while "surmount[ing]" their own "difficulties." That many of these difficulties were self-inflicted (crime) and self-induced (inability to compete) raised serious doubts about the extent to which racism was the core problem. Some went so far as to argue that racism was justifiable.[81] Kelsey, for example, stopped just shy of defending economic discrimination when he wrote that white people across the nation were beginning "to demand efficiency, and the Negro is more and more left to himself to work out his salvation." To be sure, ambivalence and intimation characterized the editors' tone and Kelsey's, and were similarly notable in studies by Kellor and Daniels.

As an emerging counter-discourse to the likes of "Mr. Page," the white liberal vision was still not easily reconcilable with Waring's perspective or those of the other black contributors to the report, with the exception of Benson and Washington, who were pro-southern critics of northern migration. Fannie B. Williams, for example, was as optimistic a northern black reformer as any who contributed to the report, citing the opening of two new community agencies in Chicago—the Frederick Douglass Center and the Trinity Mission—as promising signs of change. But even she felt the need to remind her white liberal peers that black northerners could not do it alone. "It might be inferred that the colored people are quite capable of taking care of themselves and advancing their own condition in every direction. Let us not be undeceived [sic] in this," she wrote. "In every community the Negro is practically dependent, for nearly everything of importance, upon the dominant race." That black people are segregated in "the worst portions of the city," limited to the worst jobs despite "merit" and "education," and are even being replaced at the bottom of the job chain by new immigrants, she continued, were not conditions they alone could reverse. The Negro "is the victim of more injustice than is meted out to any other class of people." The real problem among blacks was their lack of "preparation" to deal with segregation and racism when those around them "among other nationalities" found "elevating and liberalizing influences." This was an entirely different kind of inefficiency or lack of training than what many white liberals had in mind.

For blacks overcoming their own difficulties or working out their own salvation was no simple matter of self-help and personal responsibility, according to Williams, when the spirit of the age was a "lowering of that public sentiment that formerly was liberal and more tolerant of the Negro's presence and efforts to rise." Moreover, the churches, the most dominant institutions of "moral uplift" in black communities, were in most cases, she wrote, saddled with "oppressive indebtedness."[82] "My friends," the bottom line is "that society . . . is doing everything that heart and brain can devise to save white young men and white young women, while practically nothing is being done for the colored young men and women, except to prosecute and punish them for crimes for which society itself is largely responsible."[83]

But if black inferiority was still viewed as a justification for racism even among northern white liberals such as the *Charities* editors and contributors, then according to Boas's new "scientific presumption," it was not to last forever. Most intellectual historians who have studied the construction of race within the social sciences have granted Boas the high honor of turning the direction of race writing on its head.[84] The German-born Jewish immigrant had experienced firsthand the consequences of racial ideology. In Germany of the late 1880s "antisemitism had become

re Bergson

an important political force," writes historian George Stocking, "and Boas had felt its impact personally—his face bore scars from several duels he had fought with fellow students who had made antisemitic remarks."[85] Based on studies and lectures he had begun in the early 1890s, Boas's first major book-length publication, *The Mind of Primitive Man,* helped lay the foundation for a generation of new thinking about the progress and poverty of blacks.[86]

The Mind of Primitive Man was a quasi-manifesto for social activism in the sense that it was organized as a chapter-by-chapter attack on the widespread scientific belief that heredity trumped environment in explaining the causes of social and economic inequality. As a leading proponent of the belief that European immigrants and African Americans were not racially inferior, Boas argued unequivocally that physical and mental traits could not be judged fairly by the racially imbued categories of "civilized" and "primitive" without properly accounting for differences in a people's history, social conditions, and habits of life that affected their bodies and minds. Moreover, he argued, physical and mental traits were not only alterable but were in fact not pure representations of the races. He made the point, which is now scientific orthodoxy, that there were more genetic variations among individual members of racial or national groups than there were between the groups. That is why, Boas explained, it was not hard "to find among members of the American race, for instance, lips and nose which approach in form those of the negro [sic]. The same may be said of [skin] color."[87]

That racial categories were hardening at this moment put Boas's statements directly at odds with an increasing public desire to believe in racial purity. White southerners were hysterical over the threat of "social equality" or what they took to mean the apocalyptic possibility of black men "ravishing" white women and passing on their "degenerate" traits to a "pure" white race.[88] A small but vocal group of white northerners leading the eugenics movement were equally apoplectic about "degenerate" new immigrant types mixing their inferior blood with old-stock Americans. In 1911 the eugenics movement had just begun to influence national public policy through its work with the Dillingham Commission on Immigration. In fact, the 1909 conference where Ripley, Bennet, and Kelsey expressed their pro-immigrant sentiments in rebuttal to the latest findings of leading American eugenicist Charles V. Davenport, whose Long Island laboratory attracted hundreds of thousands of dollars from wealthy philanthropists, was part of the national debate leading to the U.S. Senate investigation, which was named for its chairman.[89] In the commission's published reports, Boas wrote his dissenting opinion that no "biological chasm" separated old Americans from new immigrants.[90] Although, like most others in the mainstream social scientific and reform communities, Boas's work was intended primarily for the benefit of new immigrants, his rejection of racial determinism had an incremental and profound impact on the study of black life among liberal race-relations writers. This was due primarily to his ability to expose not only the fallacies of supremacist assumptions about race, but also about culture.

Boas argued that neither race nor culture was fixed by heredity. His definition of culture was rooted in civilizationist discourses that judged European or African societies by their historic achievements—their governments, technology, arts, and mastery over nature. Accordingly, cultural traits, like physical and mental traits, were shaped by environmental factors—climate, geography, natural disasters, war, and conquest. Boas's key intellectual move was to argue based on anthropological evidence, citing the historic achievements of African civilizations before European colonization, that there was no "close relation between race and culture." Instead, the future of the Negro would be determined not by a biological imperative but "on the basis of history and social status," a history, Boas insisted, that was civilized and prosperous before European contact. "In short," Boas concluded, "there is every reason to believe that the Negro when given facility and opportunity, will be perfectly able to fulfill the duties of citizenship as well as his white neighbor."[91] Racial Darwinists had already turned toward the use of vital statistics to prove that blacks' inferior social status was a reflection of their biological inferiority, but since many racial liberals were suspicious of their methods, Boas's research presented them with an alternative historical and scientific rationale for using social resources in the service of cultural rather than racial change. If Hoffman gave whites a reason for keeping a safe distance from blacks in the present, Boas gave them a reason for living next door in the future.

On another level, however, Boas erased the color line and replaced it with a culture line. Not in the sense that he supported another form of segregation—to the contrary, he had argued forcefully for the total inclusion of blacks into America's social fabric—but in the sense that he still linked inferior behavior with black people. He did not frame black pathology in universal terms like Ida B. Wells with her emphasis on white-on-black crime, or like Du Bois with his emphasis on high mortality and illegitimacy rates across European cities, or like Kelly Miller with his rhetoric of Hebrews struggling in the wilderness on their way to the promised land. Nor did he do what countless settlement workers and progressive reformers did to deemphasize pathology and nationality among various European immigrants by linking their fates to poor native-born white Americans struggling in the midst of massive demographic, economic, and social changes. As much as he had argued that in a global context American blacks were culturally more European than African, Boas also made it painfully clear that in a national context blacks were culturally inferior to all whites: "Undesirable traits . . . are at present undoubtedly found in our Negro population."[92]

Du Bois's large body of research on class differentiation among African Americans in the North and South and in urban and rural communities did not factor into Boas's blanket charge of cultural inferiority.[93] Boas, however, was not backpedaling on his debunking of racial determinism. To insist that black people's fates were not determined by their biology, that they had the inherent capacity for equality, and that they needed white people's support and greater opportunities to succeed were about as radical a set of precepts as any white scientist had uttered in the age of Jim Crow segregation. Nevertheless, he was stating to his readers what he considered the obvious in order to illustrate the consequences of their social neglect. "There is nothing to prove that licentiousness, shiftless laziness, [and] lack of initiative, are fundamental characteristics of the race," Boas wrote. "Everything points out that these qualities are the result of social conditions rather than of hereditary traits."[94]

Still, for many readers, culture was race even if the anthropological evidence showed otherwise.[95] By pointing out negative traits that had historically defined black people, Boas confirmed many white readers' a priori suspicions of blacks, with their "peculiar" or exceptional difficulties, even if they were now supposed to accept some of the blame. Failing to follow an important ingredient in the rhetorical assault on ideological racism, as demonstrated by the universal terms of his black counterparts and his white progressive peers, Boas undercut the value of his findings. Not until the 1920s would a new generation of scholars, with Melville Herskovits and Zora Neale Hurston in the forefront, begin to have a tremendous impact on dispelling many late-nineteenth- and early-twentieth-century racial myths about African and African American culture and history.[96]

Historians have noted that for all of Boas's pioneering racial egalitarianism, he was still very much a man of his times. Stocking argues that "given the atmospheric pervasiveness of the idea of European racial superiority," Boas's work amounted to an attack on orthodox racial beliefs rather than a "staunch" petition for racial equality. "Despite his basic liberal humanitarian outlook, he was a white-skinned European writing for other white-skinned Europeans at the turn of the century, and he was a physical anthropologist to boot," writes Stocking.[97] Historian Vernon Williams describes a "Boasian Paradox," identifying the contradiction between "his philosophical egalitarian sentiments" and his tentative acknowledgment that although most African Americans remained culturally inferior to whites, "in a just society" they would eventually approach equality. Given the repeated references beginning in 1894 to the culturally determined "undesirable" traits of African Americans in his speeches, personal correspondence, and minor publications, culminating in *The Mind of Primitive Man* in 1911, Boas's "racial vision [up to that point] had severe limitations." Most importantly, then, in the context of the history of ideas about African American criminality in modern America, the work of these scholars suggests that for Boas black immorality and cultural inferiority was a rhetorical bridge between a dominant racist discourse and an emerging racial liberal discourse. Williams consequently concludes that Boas "first adumbrated the position of modern-day liberals" that with cultural advancement and opportunity blacks could achieve equality.[98]

Writing crime into culture, therefore, represented a transition for social scientists and reformers who were beginning to explain black criminality in terms of environment rather than biology. In other words, it was the initial product of twentieth-century racial liberals' first successful attempts to defend the humanity of blacks and their right to fair play in American society, and at the same time to concede that blacks were still sufficiently inferior behaviorally or socially to warrant special attention, but not necessarily special help. This shift in argument articulated by Boas did not mark a clean break from writers who had failed to privilege the logic of an environmentalist view over their own racial prejudice. To the contrary, northern white progressives had placed structural problems at the forefront of their own reform activities. Yet at the turn of the century, they had shown relatively less interest or willingness to address urban problems complicated by segregation and discrimination that favored European immigrants over blacks. That began to change for a smaller

113

cohort after two hundred thousand southern blacks moved to the North and West between 1890 and 1910, nearly tripling the black population in New York State alone.[99] By the second decade of the twentieth century, some white racial liberals forged new interracial bonds and assumed greater commitments to the struggle for racial equality. Within a one-year period ending in 1910, for example, they helped to create the NAACP and the NUL—the two premier interracial civil rights organizations of the twentieth century.[100]

As a founding member of the NAACP, one of Du Bois's closest white allies, and a colleague of Boas, Mary White Ovington embodied the upper limit of racial liberalism in the Progressive era. Her study, *Half a Man: The Status of the Negro in New York* (1911), was the second major sociological study of black life in the urban North behind Du Bois's *The Philadelphia Negro,* published more than a decade before. Boas, who had worked with many settlement workers, including Ovington, on the Greenwich House Committee on Social Investigations that sponsored her study, wrote the foreword to *Half a Man.* He described her work as a "most painstaking inquiry" into blacks' "social and economic conditions, [that] brings out in the most forceful way the difficulties under which the race is laboring, even in the large cosmopolitan population of New York." He framed her study as an explicit rebuttal to "claims that the Negro has equal opportunity with the whites and that his failure to advance more rapidly is due to innate inability." Finally, Boas signaled that because anti-Negro ideology was so pervasive and segregation on the rise—as demonstrated by Ovington's book—African Americans would have to rise to a level "infinitely greater" than that "demanded from the white."[101]

Ovington's discussion of crime in *Half a Man* was similar to her *Charities* article. She began with her observations of the interaction between "colored children" and "their mischievous young white neighbors." Along the streets bordering tightly packed neighborhoods of a growing population of southern migrants and native black New Yorkers, some black children picked up the bad habits of their immigrant and white neighbors. Ovington wrote that of those who did, "many outdo the whites in depravity and lawlessness." Yet deeper within these neighborhoods, she suggested, the opposite was true: "The colored child, especially if he is in a segregated neighborhood is not greatly inclined to mischief." Contrary to her own integrationist interests and those of her fellow members of the NAACP, Ovington suggested that with respect to criminality blacks might be better off by themselves. "My own experience has shown me that life in a tenement on San Juan Hill is devoid of the ingenious, exasperating deviltry of an Irish or German-American neighborhood." While "there is plenty of crap shooting, rarely interfered with by the police," she conceded, "there is little impertinent annoyance or destructiveness."[102]

Ovington rejected the narrowly focused racial reasoning of many writers by identifying the development of some black children's aggressive behavior as a response to a racist social environment. These boys and girls learned how to be tough *because* of their interaction with white children, she explained. "To hold his own with his white companions on the street or in school, the Negro must become pugnacious, callous to insult, ready to hit back when affronted." Ovington also revealed a crucial aspect of black parents' responsibility to their children that did not register as family values capital among racial Darwinist and pro-immigrant writers: teaching black children to defend their self-pride and personal respect against racial insults from old and new Americans. She wrote of the lessons taught and learned by parent and child respectively: "Many are like the little girl who told me that she did not care to play with white children, 'because,' she explained, 'my mother tells me to smack any one who calls me a nigger, and I ain't looking for trouble.' The colored children aren't looking for trouble. . . . They believe if they had a fight, it wouldn't be a fair one, and that if the policeman came, he would arrest them and not their Irish enemies."[103]

Apparently black youth also learned well their lessons about how to respond to the police, according to Ovington. She regretted how "harshness, for no cause but his black face, has been too frequently bestowed upon the Negro by the police" and was "especially noticeable" in interracial conflicts when a "white officer, instead of dealing impartially with offenders, protected his own race."[104] In her *Charities* report, Helena Titus Emerson, a white New York kindergarten teacher, noted the same problem for black youth in a neighborhood dominated by Italians, Germans, and "the least desirable type of shiftless Irish." "The attitude of the [white] public school teachers is not always impartial," she wrote, "and police protection [of black children] is so often inadequate that, during the spring months, especially, there are such frequent clashes between the colored and white boys on the streets, that they sometimes assume the proportions of junior race riots. Even the little kindergarten children have been shamefully abused, and many an anxious parent has to accompany his boy on the street lest he be attacked by several white boys and be unable to reach school."[105] In the midst of New York City race riots in 1900 and 1905, Ovington described how policemen had abdicated their responsibility to dispense color-blind service and protection, resulting in an object lesson for youth: the indiscriminate mass arrests of blacks being attacked by white mobs.[106]

In November 1911 Du Bois, now research director for the NAACP and editor of its national *Crisis* magazine, listed in the monthly four un-related incidents of police officers' excessive use of deadly force against blacks. In states ranging from Pennsylvania to Florida, he wrote, "there are perhaps a half dozen other cases of this sort during the month." He also noted five cases in which blacks had committed the "slaying of of-ficers."[107] Self-defense may have been the cause in some of these in-stances. Based on dozens of letters written by black suspects and con-victs to the NAACP in the 1920s, self-defense was one of the most frequently cited causes of interracial homicide of white male citizens and police officers by black men.[108] In cities across the nation, such vio-lent confrontations with police officers would continue to show black children and adults alike that justice was, in Du Bois's words, "For White People Only."[109] On streets where black offenders and victims were perceived to be equally dangerous, clear limits were set on the actualization of blacks' rights to due process and equal protection un-der the law. "As it is," wrote Ovington, "there is no safety for any Ne-gro in this part of the city at any time."[110]

By highlighting the corrupting influences of "mischievous" immigrant neighbors, hostile youth armed with racial epithets, and racially abusive police officers, Ovington had broadened the social context in which black juvenile delinquency could be explained. Playing by the rules was clearly more than the product of black children's inherent capacity for self-control. To some extent their behavior, whether good or bad, was de-pendent on their interactions with whites of all ages. This was an atypical argument before a typically racist audience. "The average white resident in northern cities," migration historian Florette Henri writes, "was con-vinced that blacks had an innate proclivity toward crime." She explains that their certainty was derived from baseless talk, biased and inaccurate news reporting, and crime statistics with too much fine print. Such perva-sive thinking about blacks, Henri notes, even affected "some Negroes." For example, a black probation officer in Pittsburgh discovered her egre-gious error in concluding that the black juvenile delinquency rate had doubled in the previous year when she subsequently discovered that it had in fact "considerably decreased."[111] Nonetheless, Ovington knew from personal experience how many white New Yorkers believed that blacks, especially southern migrants, were preprogrammed to be inferior. According to this line of thinking, Ovington sardonically concluded, "there is nothing evil" that blacks are "not at the bottom of."[112]

Whereas Ovington had rightly targeted northerners' racialist views on black criminality, she was not immune from them. Seemingly puzzled by the "very large percentage of crime among colored women" and an "unduly large percentage of disorderly depraved colored" girls, Ovington was less certain about the current social origins of black female criminality than of male "colored prisoners." Given their low social status, she wrote, black men's criminality was "no higher" than could be expected. But her ambiguity about black women was unmistakable when she declared that "depravity among the girls and improper guardianship" were "the race's most serious defects." She meant that black girls had an exceptional record of being charged by the Children's Court for sexual improprieties, and their mothers were too often negligent about properly supervising them.[113] In her review of *Half a Man*, Sophonisba P. Breckinridge, a Chicago political scientist and settlement house reformer, observed that black women were "peculiarly subject to degrading temptation."[114]

These gendered charges were not unique to black females. Ovington knew that poor native-white and immigrant girls were subject to the same "degrading temptation." Northern progressives like Jane Addams, the patron saint of the settlement movement and a founding member of the NAACP; Louise De Koven Bowen, a Hull House donor and administrator and a leader in the child-saving movement; and Kellor saw these problems to varying degrees as a direct consequence of industrialization.[115]

Addams was particularly outspoken in her 1912 study of prostitution, *A New Conscience and an Ancient Evil*. She linked the rapid changes of a modern industrial economy, with its unprecedented need for mothers and their daughters to contribute cash wages to the household, to a rise in prostitution. From the reformers' perspective, working mothers left too many young children without adequate moral guidance. In other cases, mothers who managed to stay at home often could not avoid sending their daughters out to work, exposing them to the morally corrupting "cheap theaters and dance halls" or the evil designs of unscrupulous men. This was especially true for many immigrant girls, according to

Addams. Since factory work was undesirable due to its dangerous conditions, brutal hours, and low wages, and given the lures of the burgeoning mass consumer culture and its attendant pressure to look fashionably "American," prostitution, in a moment of "utter weariness and discouragement," was a ready alternative. By and large, Addams was unequivocal in her stance that the roots of prostitution were found in the broadest economic, social, and political context. She could not separate this "social evil" from the inadequacies of industrial legislation, trade unionism, police regulation, and political corruption. Ostensibly frustrated after pointing out that it was the state's responsibility to eradicate prostitution, Addams asked, "Is it because our modern industrialism is so new that we have been so slow to connect it with poverty and vice all about us?"[116]

Three years earlier Addams had examined the evils of modernization, urbanization, and industrialization among Chicago's white and immigrant youth, many of whom were clients of Hull House. In *The Spirit of Youth and City Streets,* she focused primarily on a startling rise in male juvenile delinquency and sharply criticized the ravages of modern city temptations such as dance halls, saloons, poolrooms, five-cent theaters, gangs, and drugs. Sorely lacking wholesome recreation, Addams observed, these children had few constructive outlets for their youthful energy and their "spirit of adventure."[117] In Chicago's hardscrabble neighborhoods, far from the Midwestern farms and Old World villages, their "sex susceptibility" was getting the better of them. "The newly awakened senses are appealed to by all that is gaudy and sensual, by the flippant street music, the highly colored theater posters, the trashy love stories, the feathered hats, the cheap heroics of the revolvers displayed in the pawn shop windows," she wrote. Recreation could win the war on vice, but the battle had to be led by city leaders.[118] "We certainly cannot expect the fathers and mothers who have come to the city from farms or who have emigrated from other lands to appreciate or rectify these dangers." Nor could "we . . . expect the young people themselves" to kill the "cancer" of "modern city conditions."[119]

Against tremendous odds, Addams and her Hull House staff worked with the new Juvenile Court of Chicago, founded in 1899 as the first modern alternative to youth incarceration. The goal was to save thousands of children from becoming hardened criminals.[120] *The Spirit of Youth* was originally to be titled "Juvenile Delinquency and Public Morality" or "Juvenile Crime and Public Morals," but Addams felt that these titles were "too sociological." They evoked statistics that missed the human element and the pathos of the growing white-youth-urban-crime problem.[121] In Addams's case and emblematic of how northern progressives generally wrote about white criminality and juvenile delinquency, sentimentality was a good thing.[122] "She has established a point of view at once sympathetic and optimistic which must characterize all efforts at improvement," wrote J. P. Lichtenberger, a University of Pennsylvania sociologist and a departmental colleague of Carl Kelsey. "The book will do much good." A review in the *American Journal of Sociology* concurred, adding that "sociology has published a classic. So exquisitely and poetically has Miss Addams revealed the precious stuff of which young hearts are made . . . that we gladly give her book a place besides Wordsworth's great Ode." Because of "her singularly comprehensive experience Miss Addams has rendered a notable service to society, which is just now coming into full consciousness of its long-neglected obligation to childhood."[123]

Citing dozens and dozens of cases, Addams knew firsthand that "many city boys" had been arrested and brought before the court for everything from playful vandalism to murder. She especially singled out a range of offenses along the city's railroad tracks—throwing rocks at trains, breaking signal lights, setting fires, stealing from freight cars, and committing armed robbery—as a way of "illustrating the spirit of [youthful] adventure" in relation to the locomotive, the ultimate symbol of modern industry. Many other instances turned tragically violent. A Polish youth shot and killed an Irish boy after a gang of Irish youths came to his house seeking retaliation for his "whipping" one of their own. "This tale could be duplicated almost every morning," Addams wrote. "What might be merely a boyish scrap is turned into a tragedy because some boy has a revolver." Chicagoans were growing "heartsick" over the mounting tragedies. Within the past month, another teenage boy, a transplant from a "little farm in Ohio . . . had shot and killed a policeman while resisting arrest and was now awaiting the death penalty." He was one of "the best type of Americans, whom we boast to be the backbone of our cities," Addams noted somberly, as she tried to reconcile white youth violence with the rhetoric of Anglo-Saxon superiority.[124]

Gang- and drug-related crimes, she continued, were also out of control. The "cocaine habit" had noticeably spread in recent years. A Hull House investigation in 1904 discovered a gang of truant and unemployed neighborhood boys addicted to the drug. "They stole from their parents, 'swiped junk,' pawned their clothes and shoes–did any desperate thing to 'get the dope,' as they called it."[125] Drugs were not the only means of satisfying their "desire to dream and to see visions" that had potentially deadly consequences. Inspired by a movie and taking "Dead Men Tell No Tales" as their mantra, three boys, "aged nine, eleven and thirteen" conspired to rob and murder the neighborhood milkman. Fortunately, the bullet missed him. Numerous youth robberies and burglaries had been a direct result of the five-cent theater or the "house of dreams," Addams explained. All told, fifteen thousand youths had been arrested and brought before the Juvenile Court in the past year. Most of them "had broken the law in their blundering effort to find adventure" and "self expression."[126]

Girls were counted in that number. Gangs of thieving young women were "discovered in Chicago last June" roaming the city streets, picking pockets, and shoplifting. Others were found on the precipice of prostitution after "revolt[ing] against the monotony of [factory] work." One young lady regularly sought refuge in dance halls. "I just had to go to dances sometimes after pushing down the lever of my machine with my right foot and using both my arms feeding it for ten hours a day—nobody knows how I feel some nights." The partying ended when a sympathetic man befriended her, only to try to steer her into prostitution. "Of course, I threatened to kill him," she told Addams; "any decent girl would."

For Addams, the situation born of the spirit of youths who were misdirected and unsupervised in the nation's cities called for a change in the nation's priorities. Is everyone "so caught in admiration of the astonishing achievements of modern industry that they forget the children themselves?"[127] Addams focused on the apathy, neglect, and exploitation facing white and immigrant youth in Chicago; the experiences of black boys and girls were nearly completely absent from her antimodernist critique.[128]

However, in her follow-up study, *A New Conscience and an Ancient Evil,* Addams, like Ovington, did not exclude black women, showing them as victims of the same "modern industrialism" affecting white women. To their credit, both recognized that racism made matters worse. As Ovington explained, "*She gets the job that the white girl does not want.* [Ovington's italics]"[129] Domestic work, the least attractive and lowest paid occupation for women, represented black women's subordinate position in the labor market.[130] In New York City, for example, 90 percent of black working women were domestics or personal servants, compared to 40 percent of the white women in the workforce.[131] Black women's employment options in Philadelphia, Chicago, and elsewhere were no better. Jobs in factories, workshops, department stores, and hotels open to black women were "extremely limited," according to Addams. "The majority of them," she wrote, "therefore are engaged in domestic service and often find the position of maid in a house of prostitution or of chambermaid in a disreputable hotel, the best-paying position open to them."[132]

Historian Elizabeth Clark-Lewis's study of African American domestics in Washington, D.C., offers a firsthand account of a black woman who recalled "making money all the time" in a "joint" that illegally sold liquor and "had gambling." So consistent was Beulah Nelson's income compared to that of her brother and his wife, with whom she lived, that she was able to use her earnings to prevent her family's eviction by paying the "back rent, rent due, and two months ahead."[133] Although Nelson had sought out her own "best-paying" job, many newly arrived southern migrants were sent unknowingly to such scandalous places by employment agencies, observed Louise De Koven Bowen, president of the Juvenile Protection Association of Chicago. In fact, Bowen wrote, the same agencies "would not take the risk of sending a white girl to a place where, if she was forced into a life of prostitution, the agency would be liable to a charge of pandering."[134] Based on its assessment of the situation, the Chicago Vice Commission of 1911 concluded that "The prejudice against colored girls who are ambitious to earn an honest living is unjust."[135]

By contrast, historian Roger Lane asserts that most black prostitutes, at least in Philadelphia, were not victims of broader social barriers. "Only a small fraction of them were physically forced into the life," he writes. Lane speculates that "the rest of them were there by choice" because black women preferred the additional freedom prostitution gave them over the "sexual harassment and the loss of dignity" endemic to domestic work.[136] Historian Kevin Mumford challenges Lane's portrayal of black women's autonomy in prostitution, suggesting that sexual racism prevailed even within prostitution. Black women were paid less overall and were more often limited to streetwalking, the most degrading sex work.[137] Nevertheless, compared to the wider "field of employment" for white women, black women's search for respectable and legitimate work was clearly circumscribed by racial discrimination, despite any individual preferences black women may have exercised when accepting domestic work in a "disreputable" place.[138]

Still, the association of black women with vice transcended the perils of limited economic opportunity for women and racial discrimination against blacks. Because the bugaboo of statistical disproportion now framed crime among blacks as excessive and unnatural, and most significantly as a reflection of the fundamental difference between blacks and whites, sympathetic writers like Boas, Kellor, Ovington, and Addams turned to culture rather than biology to account for this difference. Because these racial liberals truly believed that most blacks were indeed culturally inferior to most whites, they did not shrink from incriminating black culture, even as they passionately rejected the biological determinism of such conservative colleagues as Eleanor Tayleur, who in 1904 wrote in a progressive journal that a black woman had the "brain of a child and the passions of a woman steeped in centuries of ignorance and savagery, and wrapped about with immemorial vices."[139]

Beyond racial liberals' recognition of the limited employment options for black women, they emphasized culture to explain black women's disproportionate fall into prostitution. Ovington did this when she called sexual activity among black girls in New York city a racial defect. The historical reason for the defect, as expressed by "Negroes themselves," she wrote, was that slavery had fundamentally handicapped the black family to the point where "it is inevitable that numbers of their women should be slow to recognize the sanctity of home and the importance of feminine virtue."[140] Addams agreed entirely with this long-view explanation for present-day cultural inferiority. "Confessedly," she wrote, blacks have "the shortest history of social restraint." Coupling their "belated" moral development with current social conditions, Addams concluded that the results were not surprising: a "very large number of colored girls entering a disreputable life."[141]

In a February 1911 editorial for the first volume of *Crisis*, Addams's focus on the innate cultural weaknesses of black women compared to their white and immigrant counterparts is striking. The editorial was an early contribution to the NAACP in her role as a "spearhead" of the new interracial movement against racial violence and the further erosion of black political and civil rights. She began by acknowledging the growing problem of residential segregation in northern cities. It is clear, she wrote, "that not only in the South, but everywhere in America, a strong race antagonism is asserting itself, which has various modes of lawless and insolent expression." But the problem was not just racism, she continued;

it was that "in every large city we have a colony of colored people who have not been brought under social control":

> One could easily illustrate this lack of inherited control by comparing the experiences of a group of colored girls with those of a group representing the daughters of Italian immigrants, or of any other Southern European peoples. The Italian girls very much enjoy the novelty of factory work, the opportunity to earn money and to dress as Americans do, but this new freedom of theirs is carefully guarded. Their mothers seldom give them permission to go to a party in the evening and never without chaperonage. Their fathers consider it a point of honor that their daughters shall not be alone on the streets after dark. The daughter of the humblest Italian receives this care because her parents are but carrying out social traditions. A group of colored girls, on the other hand, are quite without this protection. If they yield more easily to the temptations of a city than any other girls, who shall say how far the lack of social restraint is responsible for their downfall? The Italian parents represent the social traditions which have been worked out during centuries of civilization. . . . it is largely through these customs and manners that new groups are assimilated into civilization.[142]

Within the progressive black crime discourse, Addams attacked racism but simultaneously excused it on the grounds that African Americans lacked sufficient "inherited" resources to deal with the challenges of modern city life. Within the progressive white crime discourse, Addams framed immigrant crime and immorality as social problems wholly divorced from any inherited defects of the Old World. Nationality as a factor explaining juvenile delinquency in Chicago hardly registered in *The Spirit of Youth* except when Addams described instances of interethnic violence. In this plea for public recreation, her silence on group deficiencies and ethnic patterns of criminality among immigrant newcomers was matched by her silence on the plight of inner-city black youth. Black youth victimization was rendered totally invisible, as were the added effects of racial violence directed at black youths by their white counterparts, as Ovington and Fannie B. Williams had observed. Indeed, Addams's only mention of a black person in relation to the dangerous temptations of city living was of a "colored man, an agent of a drug store," who had gotten several neighborhood kids hooked on cocaine.[143] Yet in "Social

Control" she clearly used Italian immigrants' whiteness (or Europeanness) as a measure of their superior fitness and assimilability—"worked out during centuries of civilization"—in a way that was meant to stress the temporal backwardness of "colored people." Moreover, the spirit of her comments to a mostly black readership gave a false impression that modernization and industrialization were not "wreaking [the] foundations of domesticity" among the nation's urban white and immigrant youth.[144] Were the happy, well-adjusted, and well-supervised "Italian daughters" of her NAACP editorial different from those in her other writings, one ten-hour shift away from prostitution? One can only speculate about whether Addams worried about fueling black sentimentality (or the excuse of racial victimization) and distorted the picture of young immigrant women so as not to excuse the immorality of young black women.

Without a doubt, Addams brought attention to black political and civil injustices, the horrors of lynching, and the evils of segregation and "race antagonism."[145] At times, she even gave direct assistance to antiracist campaigns to end de facto segregation in the urban North. In 1903, after Wells sought her assistance, for example, Addams successfully called upon influential white Chicago elites to put an end to a movement for segregating Chicago's public schools.[146] But in regard to delinquency and crime, Addams did not write about black youth the same way she wrote about white and immigrant youth. At the moment when black migration to the North was the subject of intense debate linked to what many believed was an impending crisis of black criminality nationwide, she did not include blacks in her repeated calls for public recreation, which she argued was a silver bullet against "the number of arrests among juvenile delinquents."[147] Addams's inconsistency may be partly explained by the fact that, according to Davis, she drew inspiration and guidance from the pioneering research on adolescence and juvenile delinquency of psychologist G. Stanley Hall.[148] Hall, a self-identified abolitionist and a proponent of scientific racism and segregated crime prevention, instructed black people in 1905 to stop "sympathiz[ing] with their own criminals" and to "accept without whining patheticism and corroding self-pity [their] present situation, prejudice and all."[149]

In most cases when the stark realities of antiblack violence were not foremost in the minds of white progressive race-relations writers, black criminality and immorality remained tangible signs of black pathology even among the most committed racial liberals. In the cases of Addams and Ovington, the implication of highlighting excessive immorality among black women was that social, economic, and political reform might not be enough to reverse blacks' cultural inferiority, especially since it was the duty of women to nurture the moral character of their families and therefore their race.[150] As necessary as structural reforms were overall in the context of black and immigrant communities in or on the borders of vice districts, liberal race-relations writers still suggested that black women needed an additional dose of moral tonic to help save their race. My argument that Boas had erased the color line only to unintentionally replace it with a culture line helps to explain the contradictory assumptions underlying progressives' limited on-the-ground reforms aimed at blacks on the eve of the Great Migration. When Kelsey wrote in 1909 that "much is now charged to the Negro, as a Negro, which should be charged to the Negro as an ignorant and untrained man," he was calling for a fundamental shift away from a biological determinism that he recognized as racist to a cultural determinism that he and other liberals recognized as race neutral or color blind.[151]

The problem, however, was that black male ignorance and inefficiency, like black female ignorance and immorality, were defined in relation to slavery and to white civilizationist discourses that already ranked all blacks at the bottom. Therefore black reform, by historical, sociological, and philosophical definition, ought to be separate and distinct since blacks, as the logic dictated, could rise to a higher plane only through their own struggle following emancipation. All whites of whatever nationality were, by definition (through centuries of struggle in the wilderness of Europe and colonial America), already on a higher plane capable of being saved by others.[152] When children are born to broken homes, when "the natural prop is gone, the normal limb removed," wrote Mabel Rhoades, a white University of Chicago graduate student in one of the first sociological investigations of the Chicago Juvenile Court, "we have always to make the best possible substitute," helping "the patient . . . get about to do his [or her] share of the great world's work."[153] Progressive era social reformers had come to intellectual maturity in a highly paternalistic and racialized milieu. That some of them as "friends of the Negro" represented a nascent neo-abolitionist movement in the urban North does not negate the fact that by incriminating black culture, they legitimized piecemeal urban reform efforts on behalf of blacks.

Too often white reformers settled for indexing racial injustice rather than fighting it. For example, Jane Addams could point out the perilous consequences of residential segregation for black families without ending the practice of segregated activities at her own Hull House. Historian Thomas Philpott argues in his study of Chicago's reformers that "in the main, settlement houses served blacks separately or did not serve them at all. Most settlement workers, like most reform-minded people and most Chicagoans, generally were racists, or, if not, they were conformists: They went along."[154] Even as late as the 1920s, when Chicago's black population had more than tripled to nearly 110,000 people and the flow of European immigration had been cut off by World War I and the National Origins Act of 1924, Hull House continued its policy of "exuding interracial good will but including almost no Negroes." By 1930 only about one-third of private welfare agencies in Chicago were willing to use 1 percent of their budgets to fund services for blacks.[155] In New York in 1929, the Children's Aid Society reported that Harlem had "only 15 percent of the recreation facilities it needs."[156] African American reformers continued to insist that blacks not only had very few places for constructive leisure activities but that they also could not improve conditions without help.[157] George Edmund Haynes, a Columbia University–trained black sociologist and the first research director of the NUL, insisted that the problems of black "maladjustment" must be fixed by "methods similar to those that help other elements of the population."[158] In a 1913 race-relations progress report commemorating the fiftieth anniversary of the Emancipation Proclamation, Haynes described the failure of liberal intervention as the "sequel of segregation":

> To make the view of the urban situation among Negroes full and clear, a number of conditions which exist in some cities but are absent in others should be included in the list. In many cities the sequel of segregation means less effective police patrol and inadequate fire protection, in others it means unpaved streets, the absence of proper sewerage and lack of other sanitary supervision and requirements. . . . Playgrounds in Negro neighborhoods are so rare as to excite curiosity, and organized play is just being heard of in the Negro world. . . . In these efforts for self-realization in the city the Negro needs the fair dealing, the sympathy and the cooperation of his white brother. For the problem of his adjustment is only a part of the great human problem of justice for the handicapped in democratic America.[159]

Yet almost no public facilities used by whites, like beaches and playgrounds, were open to blacks without serious risk of mortal harm. In the

Great Migration period and beyond, cities across the urban North experienced wholesale white-initiated attacks on their black residents. In the Red Summer of 1919, Chicago, one of more than twenty cities to see race riots, experienced unprecedented racial violence ignited by whites' stoning to death a black child who crossed an aqueous color line at a public beach on Lake Michigan.[160] Although racial violence was a constant reminder of the limits of racial reform among the white masses, ironically those limits were in part shaped by reformers' ambivalence about blacks' cultural—albeit moral—fitness. At the grassroots level of social work, white settlement workers largely failed to put their own ideals into action when it came to black neighbors. In the spirit of documenting racial disparities, Bowen revealed the paucity of crime prevention agencies open to African Americans. In a 1913 report for Chicago's Juvenile Protection Association, she observed that even when "colored people" did attempt various efforts to assist "dependent and semi-delinquent colored children," they did not have sufficient resources, all the more disturbing, she noted, since "all the public records give a high percentage of Negro criminals."[161]

Some observers came to see the ways in which racial violence substituted for social reform. Six years before Chicago's South Side beach became ground zero for the racial conflagration that enveloped the city, Bowen reported that a "little colored boy" had been "mobbed" the previous summer. She also noted in her 1913 investigation that blacks had begun a campaign to open a "model dance hall," but whites in the vicinity objected on the grounds that it would be a "public nuisance," and "[t]his effort toward better recreation facilities had to be abandoned."[162] At a 1920 meeting of the NUL, Bowen continued to emphasize the missed opportunities to include African Americans in all manner of inner-city social work. "We are not apt to think of the negro as an immigrant, but in reality he occupies the same position as does the foreigner who comes to us from other shores, except that the negro's position is more difficult, for he is subjected to racial discrimination, and while no limitations are imposed upon the children of the immigrant, this unfortunately, is not true of the negro."[163]

Even a white southern reformer stated in 1914 that it was just "good business economy to save . . . [Negro] children from vagrancy and crime" through public taxation, not to mention that in his opinion "playgrounds with directors [were] cheaper than penal institutions or probation officers." Thus it did not make sense to Charles H. McCord that during

1912 cash-strapped "Negroes" in Atlanta spent in excess of $100,000 in "fines and stockade sentences" related to crime. That money plus "lost time and lawyers' fees," he calculated, could have bought a "fifty-acre tract of land" to be developed into a "park for Negroes with greenhouses, wild animals, and a boating lake and swimming pool."[164] S. Waters McGill, a Nashville, Tennessee, YMCA official, captured the situation experienced by many blacks across the nation in verse:

> Plenty of room for dives and dens,
>   Glitter and glare and sin;
> Plenty of room for prison pens,
>   Gather the criminals in;
> Plenty of room for jails and courts—
>   Willing enough to pay;
> But never a place for lads to race,
>   No never a place to play.
> Plenty of room for shops and stores,
>   Mammon must have the best;
> Plenty of room for the running sores
>   That rot in the city's breast;
> Plenty of room for the lures that lead
>   The hearts of our youth astray;
> But never a cent on a playground spent,
>   No never a place to play.[165]

Whereas southern cities provided far fewer resources to combat juvenile delinquency for black or white youth, in northern cities white youth were still the overwhelming beneficiaries of public and private assistance.[166]

Following the poet's lead, historian Elisabeth Lasch-Quinn takes reformers to task for their "faulty interpretation of black culture" and "failure to address the problems of blacks." She argues that despite settlement workers' personal knowledge of poverty and discrimination, their "debilitating depiction of the black individual as lacking the most basic capacity for self-control buttressed the settlement movement's failure to redirect its efforts from white immigrants to black migrants." Historian Anne Meis Knupfer agrees, adding that "although Breckinridge, Addams, and Bowen had also expressed strong disapproval of such segregative practices, their actual involvement in establishing and sustaining the African American settlements, missions, girls' homes, and orphanages was minimal." As a result, Lasch-Quinn concludes that white settlement workers "largely ignored" black migrants, calling instead for "black self-improvement organizations, which they thought would begin the slow 'civilizing process.' " Meanwhile, for white immigrants they sought structural changes in the "local political economy and provision of social services."[167]

Additional studies by Dorothy Salem, Anne Firor Scott, and Judith Trolander that compare the involvement of white settlement workers with black neighbors with their involvement with whites and immigrants confirm the pattern.[168] "Huge private donors" were key to the efforts of settlement workers, but "fund-raising for agencies to serve blacks was difficult," writes Trolander. For whites, "it was the settlement workers' ability to move within the two worlds of the wealthy and the working class that gave them their unique identity." Bowen, for example, donated more buildings to Hull House out of her own pocket than there were black settlement houses opened in Chicago during the Progressive era.[169] Her contributions amounted to more than a million dollars, a sum equal to more than twenty-one million dollars in 2008 dollars.[170] From local, state, and national politicians to the wealthiest men and women of the industrial age, from beat cops to visiting nurses, from probation officers to real estate developers, white settlement workers had access to power, resources, and spheres of influence impossible for middle-class and elite black reformers to match.[171] By almost unanimous consent, dollar for dollar, black communities stood most in need.

Whether research dollars or seed money to cover the salaries and operating expenses of social welfare agencies were at stake, African American reformers were especially disadvantaged. Even Du Bois, the most prolific and accomplished black social scientist of the Progressive era, often complained about the difficulties of raising money to conduct the work he hoped to accomplish. It was a core struggle in his life as a scholar and activist, according to his biographer. "Without money, both scholarship and advocacy faltered." David Levering Lewis notes that not only did Du Bois frequently complain about losing research funds to white race-relations writers with far less experience and more sanguine views of racism, but his money worries also threatened to keep him from attending scholarly conferences because of the cost of travel.[172]

Similarly, Ida B. Wells described the financial challenges she faced in trying to open a crime prevention agency in the heart of a South Side Chicago vice district. The idea had come to her while conducting a men's Bible class at Grace Presbyterian Church. Among young men, "ranging from eighteen to thirty years of age," Wells facilitated topics relevant to their experiences, including the spread of racial violence in the North. In the summer of 1908, in Springfield, Illinois, about two hundred miles south of Chicago, a white woman accused a black man of assaulting her. In the manhunt for a suspect, three random black men were lynched and three others were shot. Although many African Americans defended themselves, many of their homes were burned to the ground, and as many as two thousand black residents were driven from town.[173] The Springfield riot led directly to the founding of the NAACP. The violence, Wells recalled discussing with her young male charges, "seemed to be becoming as bad in Illinois as it had hitherto been in Georgia." The following year, Will "Froggie" James was lynched by five hundred townspeople who fired bullets into his body as it hung from a downtown arch in Cairo, Illinois. His lifeless body was then decapitated (his head placed on a fence post) while his remains were burned to ashes. Horrified, Wells became determined to reach out to black men in trouble with the law and began visiting black male prisoners in Joliet Penitentiary.[174] Out of her conversations with the prisoners and the young men in church, Wells resolved to establish the Negro Fellowship League to extend a "helping hand" to new arrivals in the city's seedy settlement zone—because "with no friends, they were railroaded into penitentiary," she recalled saying to the Bible group. The league "would be on the lookout for these young people. . . . To this all were agreed, but as we had no money, they could not see how it could be brought together."[175]

Although Wells was a major figure in the black club woman's movement with many contacts among leading white club women, only luck allowed her to find a wealthy donor for the league. Shortly after the church meeting, she attended a five-hundred person banquet as an invited speaker of the Congressional Union Church at the luxurious Palmer House hotel in downtown Chicago. Another speaker was J. G. K. McClure, the head of the Chicago Theological Seminary, whose topic was "The White Man's Burden." According to Wells, in his statistically rich speech about black people as a national problem he said: "Even here in Chicago, which is the black man's heaven, although he is less than 3 percent of the population, last year he furnished 10 percent of the crime." Wells remembered that right then the presiding officer of the church whispered to her that he expected her to challenge McClure's statement. At first she demurred, since her subject was lynching and the need for fair trials and color-blind justice, plus she had not come to debate. But then she changed her mind, thinking that no wonder "race prejudice seemed to be growing in Chicago if that was the sort of addresses being given."[176] Wells told the audience that the statistics were misleading if they led people to assume that blacks were the "most criminal of the various race groups in Chicago. It does mean," she insisted, "that ours is the most neglected group. All other races in the city are welcomed into the settlements, YMCA's, YWCA's, gymnasiums and every other movement for uplift if only their skins are white. . . . Only one social center welcomes the Negro, and that is the saloon. Ought we to wonder at the harvest which we have heard enumerated tonight?" Among those listening was Mrs. Victor F. Lawson, the wife of the owner and publisher of the Chicago *Daily News,* who told Wells that she was "so surprised" to find out that her husband's "several thousand dollars" had been given to support segregation at the YMCA.[177] The Lawsons were outraged. After several months passed, Mrs. Lawson decided to bankroll the Negro Fellowship League for one year. She insisted, however, on being an anonymous benefactor because she told Wells she had given to a "colored church" in the past and as a result had been overwhelmed by "others soliciting aid." The league opened in May 1910, complete with a lodging facility, a reading and game room, and an employment bureau. Mrs. Lawson supported the league for three years until her death in 1912. With her passing, so too did the agency. Her husband withdrew funding, insisting that it should have been "self-supporting" by that time.[178]

For grassroots reformers and black social workers, acquiring the necessary funds to open, run, and sustain a settlement or community center was extremely difficult. "The settlements for 'colored people' never had the capacity to provide black Chicago with adequate, much less *equal* service. Several white settlements were in a position to relieve the strain on black centers by opening their own doors to blacks who lived nearby." Instead, they tended to "follow the color line."[179] Many scholars have observed that when black settlements and other social welfare agencies were opened with the financial assistance of white philanthropists, the racial vision of the white benefactors and board members often clashed with what black reformers had in mind.[180] Progressive era black social workers in Chicago, New York, Philadelphia, Cleveland, Boston, and across the South were frequently forced to choose between no funding or molding the programming of the institutions to accommodate the perspectives of their white sponsors. "Over and over again, the pattern repeated," writes historian Deborah Gray White.[181]

For example, when Wells worked with Celia Parker Woolley, the wealthy white leader of the Chicago Women's Club and sponsor of Frances Kellor's groundbreaking crime research, to open the Frederick Douglass Center in 1905, Wells assumed she would be tapped as the first director. To her surprise, Mary Plummer, a luminary among local representatives of the suffragist movement and the wife of George W. Plummer, one of Chicago's top corporate lawyers, was put in charge.[182] Wells went along, becoming vice president. As Woolley had planned, the Douglass Center was intended to focus mainly on promoting interracial dialogue.[183]

In the wake of the Atlanta race riot of 1906, the dialogue between Wells and Plummer imploded over a disagreement about the riot's causes. The violence had claimed the lives of twenty-five black people, with hundreds more injured, and not a single white person was arrested (out of thousands involved, including members of the police and the state militia).[184] Director Plummer, like white Atlantans, justified the racial violence because of the purported behavior of black criminals and rapists. After hearing J. Max Barber, an Atlanta-based black journalist, give firsthand testimony of the events, Plummer replied, "I do not know what we can say about this terrible affair, but there is one thing I can say and that is to urge all of you to drive the criminals out from among you." When Wells challenged her statement and reminded her of all she had told her about lynching over "these years," Plummer retorted, "Have you forgotten that 10 percent of all the crimes that were committed in Chicago last year were by colored men?" Besides, she added, "every white woman that I know in the South has told me that she is afraid to walk out after dark. I hope some day to find out for myself if it is true." With that, the interracial dialogue ended. "There was nothing more for me to say," Wells recorded in her autobiography.

Wells's memory may have distorted Plummer's actual words, but not the spirit of the exchange. Plummer left the Frederick Douglas Center due to resentment of Wells's challenging her authority, and Wells left because Woolley, the funder, still wanted a white woman in charge. In Wells's assessment, the center was never the same after she departed.[185] "A source of outrage and frustration," White observes, "the racism of some of the nation's most progressive white women reveal[s]" the limits black women reformers faced in doing the very thing they were encouraged to do. Saving their own in a context where all reformers, black and white, depended on the philanthropic and political support of white elites left African Americans at a distinct disadvantage.[186]

There were dire consequences for blacks given this disparity in the scale and nature of progressive reforms. For example, what began as a series of local attempts to save women from prostitution became a national movement and one of the twentieth century's "great crusades," culminating in the Mann Act of 1910.[187] Also known as the White Slave Traffic Act, its prosecutors targeted foreign-born whites and African American men for transporting white women across state lines "for the purposes of prostitution or debauchery, or for any other immoral purposes." Although the act itself was written in color-blind language, the racialized term *white slavery* culturally and politically prescribed victimization for whites only.[188]

The term *white slavery* had long been a trope of the nineteenth-century labor movement. To emphasize the industrial exploitation of the northern white working classes, labor leaders linked them rhetorically to a state of debasement associated only with black chattel slavery or the experiences of the racialized "Other."[189] The same idea worked in much of the writings of anti-vice crusaders.[190] Like Indian captivity narratives, white-slave narratives exploited white middle-class "anxieties" stimulated by the "migration of rural and small-town girls to the new urban wilderness."[191] According to historian Mark Connelly, at the heart of the tracts lies the sexual victimization of "beautiful native American country girls" by "dark" men or, as the author of *America's Black Traffic in White Girls* wrote, a "foaming pack of foreign hellhounds."[192] As in Addams's writings, "almost all of the white-slave tracts include discussion of the plight of immigrant white slaves, who are treated quite sympathetically."[193] "Alien women and girls" were the only group named in the legislation itself.[194] The popular success of the tracts helped to lead to a U.S. Senate investigation in 1909–1910, and the Mann Act passed soon after.

Black women's perceived moral shortcomings or racial "defects" disqualified them from the protective status of the law. As late as 1997, no historian had published evidence of a single Mann Act prosecution of a white man for "endangering the morals of a black woman," writes Mumford. "The racial basis of the movement—the exclusion of black women from the category of the deserving and redeemable—created a social policy that effectively relocated vice" in segregated black communities "and, ultimately, led to the abandonment of black prostitutes."[195] According to the findings of the Chicago Vice Commission in 1911, that also meant that white prostitutes were "invariably driven" into black neighborhoods by the police, adding to the "demoralizing example[s] and influence for the colored youth of both sexes."[196]

In contrast, Kellor's National League for the Protection of Colored Women, which based its work on the perception of southern black women's moral weakness and ignorance of northern city life, represented the height of white progressives' attempts to save black women from prostitution.[197] According to Hazel Carby, an interdisciplinary scholar of black female migration in the early twentieth century, Kellor's efforts appeared "on the surface" to be a defense of black women's "female virtue but it is quickly evident that she does not believe that women have any moral fiber or will of their own that can be mobilized in the defense of their own interests." The problem was "located in black women themselves."[198] Because of Kellor's views, Lasch-Quinn adds, she "helped further racist assumptions about the inferiority of blacks by blaming them for their situation."[199] Paradoxically, these two antiprostitution movements at the federal and the local levels represented two sides of the same coin, one that distinctly criminalized black women. In both cases the basis for black women's criminalization was their well-intentioned sponsors' belief in black cultural inferiority.

The confluence of victim blaming and expert knowledge of historical and structural inequalities by a reformer intimately connected with settlement houses reached its clearest expression on the eve of the Great Migration in John Daniels's *In Freedom's Birthplace: A Study of the Boston Negroes* (1914). After conducting six years of research (1908–1913) at the Robert Gould Shaw House in Boston, Daniels wrote with the utmost authority. The Shaw House was a segregated spin-off of the South End House, where Daniels had initially worked with Frederic Bushee beginning in 1904. Daniels's study picked up where Bushee's 1903 pro-immigrant study left off.[200] Like Du Bois's *The Philadelphia Negro* and Ovington's *Half a Man*, Daniels's *In Freedom's Birthplace* was a seminal investigation of the history and sociology of African Americans in a major northern city. In 1915, a year after the book came out, a reviewer called the books by Daniels and Ovington the "two most notable" monographs to appear in "the last few years" on "the Negro problem in various northern communities."[201]

Daniels began by tracing the earliest presence and achievements of black Bostonians from the colonial period, through the revolutionary era, to the moment when the great antislavery agitator David Walker rose to national prominence with his 1829 *Appeal*. Giving credit to

Walker, "a leader among his people," and Frederick Douglass, "the most remarkable of them all," for inspiring William Lloyd Garrison, Daniels narrated Boston's abolitionist movement as a triumphant era of blacks taking the lead in their own march toward freedom. "Thus, while by his part in the [American] Revolution," he wrote, "the Negro had contributed to his consequent emancipation throughout the North, by his part in the Civil War he himself proved the decisive factor in the establishment of his freedom throughout the nation." For all of this, by 1895, with the passage of the Massachusetts civil rights act that prohibited discrimination in all public arenas, blacks "had been made fully equal." White Bostonians were so pleased with race relations that, according to Daniels, "popular sentiment with reference to the emancipated people was generous to a degree of indulgence." Without a hint of sarcasm or insincerity, Daniels wrote, "the fact of being a Negro actually counted as an element of advantage," conferring "special sympathy and help."[202]

But in the wake of the "wretched exhibition" of black inferiority during the Reconstruction period and the passing away of the "Old Guard" in the North, the high tide of racial harmony in Boston was gradually heading back to sea. Like so many of his racially liberal peers, Daniels acknowledged that segregation and discrimination were on the rise in the North and that white northerners had begun to embrace the southern view. Like most of them, he also justified the change in "sentiment." At the sight of the "ignorant" and "uncouth," and "indeed brutish" new migrants from the South, white Bostonians could not help but recoil. "Never before had Boston experienced the Southern Negro en masse." Here Daniels paused for a bit of historical revision, noting that actually the "escaping slaves of Abolition days were sufficiently abject specimens," but most had been "kept out of sight" and had been over-shadowed by the "highly refined type" of Negro. But now, he explained, "in the face of the black horde" invading the North since the war the "present backward conditions" of the "race" were plain for all to see. The current problem was not the "possession of . . . rights and privileges" but "rather the underlying equipment for the proper exercise of such rights and privileges." "Nothing could be more unquestionable than the inherent weaknesses" of Negroes. So "morally backward" was the race that "to go into any extended citation of figures to prove that there is a more pronounced tendency to immorality and criminality among the Negroes than among the whites would be superfluous. That such is the case may be, indeed must be presumed."[203]

As was true in the assessments of so many of Daniels's peers, evidence of blacks' criminality and immorality fundamentally called into question how much whites could and should do to help them. Daniels insisted that the future would now depend not on "the bestowal of favor from without, but upon their own independent effort from within." Even white "settlements, clubs and classes of a social service nature" could not be blamed for the many agencies that "make it a hard-and-fast rule to have nothing to do with" Negroes. Among the majority, "it is more practicable" to adopt the "segregation plan" given the "general backwardness of Negroes, and the prevailing disinclination of the whites to be thrown into close association with them."[204] The real heavy lifting had to be done by blacks alone; doing it was the only effective path to "self-dependability," despite the fact that, as he noted, social work conducted by Boston's black club women was "of necessity of humble proportions." Struggling financially, they could count only on periodic fundraisers and dues not more than "twenty-five cents a month."[205]

Financial hardships aside, "the future of the Negro people," Daniels emphasized, called for fundamental improvement in "moral stamina."[206] In every way, organizationally, politically, industrially, and morally, Daniels stated plainly, blacks were the "most backward group in the community." All evidence of their base social status was a reflection of their "actual" inferiority, best measured by their pathology: "The Negro's disproportionate commission of crime and his flagrant sexual laxity are but two of the most obvious outcroppings of a generally discernible moral and ethical undevelopment, by which he is characterized." Moreover, Daniels, like Addams, suggested that blacks were "centuries of civilization" behind. He wanted his white readers to be clear that this pathology was not their fault and that his book was not yet another abolitionist attack on white racism as the cause. Citing Phillis Wheatley, Prince Hall, and David Walker, Daniels wrote that since "far back in the colonial days, the plaint that he was the object of contempt and ill-usage was raised by the Negro himself," and for too long was "fostered" and "indulged" by a "small minority of the white population." Given the "sorry spectacle" of Reconstruction and the "great numbers of raw and uncouth Negro immigrants" in Boston and across the nation, the sentimental cry of black victimization had to cease. Contrary to the "pathetic and monotonous refrain" of those who blamed their condition on prejudice, race hostility was, he argued, "roughly commensurate with extreme racial differences."[207]

So as not to be mistaken for a retrograde racial Darwinist or a liberal turned neoconservative, Daniels smartly turned to the most influential liberal social scientific research on race in the Progressive era. Incorporating Boas's groundbreaking research into his own, he insisted that "racial differences" were not biological, "nor can it be presumed that . . . this inferiority is necessarily permanent and insurmountable." After all, he noted, blacks and whites practically looked alike, spoke the same language, practiced the same religion, and were patriotic. "Except for color and certain other physical characteristics—the American Negro is very closely like the native white American." Even if one conceded that dark skin, "a strong natural odor, and kinky hair," were sufficiently offensive to warrant special attention, he added, it was "hardly probable" that prejudice would exist if blacks were, in fact, superior to whites in "knowledge and attainment."[208] The problem was not with the exceptional blacks whose "individual attainment really bears witness to," in Boasian terms, "the latent capacity of the Negro in general." It was "the past and . . . the present [of] the *average* Negro" who "has always been and still is inferior to the *average* white man" that proved the rule.[209] Boas had also used the fact of exceptional blacks who "outrun their [white] competitors" to discredit biological determinism, since variations within the race often exceeded those between races, while still insisting that blacks' "average achievement will not quite reach the level of the average achievement of the white race."[210]

In 1914, exactly a half century before the legislative victories of the modern civil rights movement would come to be known as the Second Reconstruction—a final act of national will to exorcize America of the ghost of her Jim Crow past—there was no irrational or unjustified racism, according to Daniels. Save for a few racist individuals, the free market dictated race relations in the Progressive era:

In Boston, as is the case in most American communities, affairs regulate themselves very largely on a simple business basis of sale and purchase, with material means, rather than race or color, as the determining element. The fact that the Negro is steadily becoming better able to pay for privileges is his best guarantee of possessing these privileges. Restaurants and theaters, for instance, find that a Negro's money goes as far as a white man's profits. A cab driver deems it wiser to pick up a fare from a Negro than to let his vehicle stand idle. Stores of all kinds, even the most select, see no good reason for declining to sell their wares to members of this race. Banks draw no color line in accepting deposits.

And for the right price, he added, the Negroes can live anywhere they choose, including "superior white neighborhoods." The bottom line, Daniels argued, is that for those without the means to "pay for privileges," those who are barred from the marketplace of American dreams, "the aversion in question is based upon recognition of the Negro's past and present inferiority." Unambiguously ascribing white prejudice and discrimination to black inferiority, Daniels concluded that "It is not race-feeling. It is not color-feeling. It is inferiority-feeling." White people "feel and act toward him accordingly." When "his present incapacities" disappear, so too will the "Negro problem."[211]

U. G. Weatherly, an Indiana University sociologist, positively reviewed *In Freedom's Birthplace* in the *American Journal of Sociology,* describing Daniels as a "clear, incisive critic, whose virile sympathy for the Negro is always held in check by his discriminating candor."[212] University of Pennsylvania sociologist J. P. Lichtenberger, who had praised Addams's *The Spirit of Youth,* likewise considered *In Freedom's Birthplace* among the best "local studies of the Negro Problem" ever written.[213] Although Addams's book was commended precisely for its sympathetic tone and for the "good" that it would do on behalf of white youth, Lichtenberger hailed Daniels's book for its frank honesty. It is "one of the most unbiased studies we have seen." Highlighting Daniels's finding that the "actual inferiority" was the root problem behind "the prevailing prejudice," he endorsed Daniels's conclusion that the most good would come when black people helped themselves.[214] Had Lichtenberger reviewed Frederic Bushee's study of Boston at the beginning of the Progressive era, he might have noted the striking similarity between Bushee's claim that black assimilation was undesirable and Daniels's recommendation a decade later.[215] Until African Americans embraced segregation and took the necessary time "to make a history for" themselves, Daniels argued, they were not "yet prepared to be received fully, or even in major degree, within the general fabric and organization of the white community."[216] A major litmus test for credibility among liberal experts on the Negro Problem was the degree to which one conceded blacks' shortcomings.

Such ideas were forged not only out of the groundbreaking research on race relations in the urban North of Frances Kellor, Frederic Bushee,

Carl Kelsey, Franz Boas, the many *Charities* contributors, and settlement workers such as Mary Ovington, Jane Addams, and John Daniels, but also out of the close professional relationships of these individuals. These northern white race-relations experts reviewed each other's work, vetted and corroborated each other's findings, collaborated on specific projects, worked in the same academic departments, and shared national leadership positions in social scientific and reform communities. J. P. Lichtenberger and U. G. Weatherly, for example, later served together as president and vice president of the American Sociological Association in 1921.[217] The intellectual and professional ties that bound these individuals together inspired mutual respect for each other's ideas. Their collaboration fueled their willingness to write crime into culture. They were responding to their black peers and critics, as was so clear in the special issue of *Charities* and in the work of Addams and Daniels. The perspectives of W. E. B. Du Bois and Fannie B. Williams and Ida B. Wells were subsumed by these writers even as they moved beyond, or devalued, antiracist critiques. From the opening of the Progressive era to its waning days on the eve of World War I and the Great Migration, black criminality had become not just a universal tool to measure black fitness for citizenship; it was also a tool to shield, to varying degrees, white Americans from the charge of racism, helping to determine the degree to which whites had any responsibility to help black people.

By the standards of liberal race-relations discourse in the wake of Boas's *The Mind of Primitive Man*, much of their work was recognized as, in Lichtenberger's reading of Daniels's study, "decidedly optimistic." Unlike Frederic L. Hoffman, they emphasized that neither black inferiority nor white racism were "irreducible nor necessarily permanent." Although the full impact of Boas's turn toward cultural determinism within the liberal race-relations discourse was still in the making at the time *In Freedom's Birthplace* was published in 1914, it was clear that liberal social scientists of the Progressive era were rejecting racial determinism in favor of a new language of racial inequality. Rather than "race traits and tendencies" to define the permanency of black pathology, the new term "inherent capacity" emerged among these writers to emphasize the remedial nature of black pathology.[218] In this counter-discourse there was a way out.

For the first time since the days of abolitionism, this small cohort of northern racial liberals of the Progressive era began to acknowledge northern white racism even as they remained deeply ambivalent about black immorality and criminality. Boas, for instance, reminded his readers that they could not fairly judge blacks' missteps without recognizing that society "does not give us [whites] a chance to step out of its limits."[219] Ovington scolded her audience for constantly making generalizations ("we classify and measure and pass judgement [sic]") about "colored Americans" when "we white Americans" do not do the same "concerning ourselves."[220] In brief moments, even their ambivalence receded before the double standards increasingly in vogue. Bowen, for example, told whites not to make the Negro "the universal scapegoat." "When a crime is committed," she explained, "the slightest pretext starts the rumor of a 'Negro suspect' and flaming headlines prejudice the public mind long after the white criminal is found."[221] An editor of a religious paper in Newark, New Jersey, confirmed Bowen's statements, noting that "the [daily] reader sees after the name of a lawbreaker the word 'Negro' or 'colored,' " but "never sees the word 'white' in this relation." To illustrate for whites the cumulative negative impact of linking race with crime, the editor added "white" to every headline in the morning paper for four consecutive days in 1911. Fifty headlines were revised; these five were some of the most interesting:

> SIX ON STOOP SHOT BY MAN (WHITE) ACROSS STREET; SHOOTS DETECTIVE FOUR TIMES AND IS SHOT TWICE HIMSELF (WHITE); BURGLAR (WHITE) SON OF BANKER ADMITS LOOTING EIGHTEEN HOMES; EX-POLICEMAN (WHITE) CAUGHT PASSING "PHONY" CHECK; and POLICEMAN (WHITE) ACCUSED OF EXTORTION.

Adding to the saliency of the editor's observations was the fact that no crimes committed by blacks had been reported in the four days of analysis. Sarcastically, the editor concluded, "If it were not for the whites, the papers would not be worth reading."[222]

Daniels was ideologically on the center-right of this emerging liberal discourse, which was still a counter-discourse rather than the prevailing one. Given the segregation and discrimination African Americans experienced in their own communities and not on some pages of liberal reform literature, Daniels's work veered close to the type of wholesale black denunciation made by racial Darwinists, in spite of his liberal credentials. For this reason, Lasch-Quinn calls his work "insidious."[223] Daniels wanted to incorporate and move beyond what Boas and his other liberal peers had just begun to do. His ideas clearly resonated with the increasing bitterness and disappointment many white northerners felt in the face of the falsity of Hoffman's predictions. The African American population continued not only to grow as the twentieth century unfolded, but also to spread northward, pressing for equality in America's modern metropolises against all odds—biological, cultural, and environmental.

In a 1910 essay, as both a personal and a figurative testament to black survival in spite of the white contempt facing black northerners, Du Bois described in bitter prose the "deep and passionate hatred," which he witnessed as a new arrival to New York City shortly before joining the national staff of the NAACP. "I sit and see the souls of the White Folk daily shriveling and dying in the fierce flame of this new fanaticism," he wrote. In lieu of an American tradition of moral greatness in the world, "whiteness" was becoming the new measure of the nation's "thought and soul":

> Are we not coming more and more day by day to making the statement, 'I am white,' the one fundamental tenet of our practical morality? Only when this basic iron rule is involved is our defense of right nationwide prompt. Murder may swagger, theft may rule and prostitution flourish, and the nation gives but spasmodic, intermittent and lukewarm attention. But let the murderer be black or the thief brown or the violator of womanhood have but a drop of Negro blood, and the righteousness of the indignation sweeps the world. Nor would this fact make the indignation less justifiable did not we all know that it was blackness that was condemned, and not crime.[224]

Here was a picture of modern urbanity in black and white strikingly at odds with Daniels's portrait of a color-blind urban America.

Daniels's work was made possible by the contradictions Boas and other racial liberals had failed to surmount. They pursued limited reforms for blacks in spite of their knowledge and their efforts to save whites from the disintegrating tendencies of modern capitalism that spawned crime everywhere in urban America. The examples were blatant and abundant: Corporations bribed city officials in exchange for their votes on the approval of new trolley lines; ward bosses owned or held interests in saloons where illegal gambling made them rich; political banquets were indistinguishable from black-tie events for organized criminals; judges, juries, bail bondsmen, and bailiffs sold protection to the well-to-do; police regulated prostitution and policy syndicates by controlling competition in exchange for middle-class incomes; lawyers and accountants negotiated

AMERICAN LOGIC.

THIS MAN is responsible for all that THIS MAN does because they belong to the same race.

THIS MAN is not responsible for THIS MAN even if they do belong to the same race.

and recorded the illegal transactions of well-paying clients; small business owners fenced the booty of petty thieves; pharmacists increased their profitability by selling over-the-counter cocaine; bellhops, bootblacks, cabdrivers, and waiters brought together buyers and sellers of illegal goods and services; and nearly all consumers favored the cheaper prices of stolen merchandise.[225] Nevertheless, more than any group in society, blacks were blamed for America's fundamental need to have winners and losers or haves and have nots.[226] Of the future to come in cities across the urban North, historian Thomas Sugrue has written that "Detroit's postwar urban crisis [in the 1940s] emerged as the consequence of two of the most important, interrelated, and unresolved problems in American history: that capitalism generates economic inequality and that African Americans have disproportionately borne the impact of that inequality."[227]

One of the lessons learned during the Progressive era was that on the white-side of the color line compassion was crucial to reform. It was a central theme in the work of muckraking journalists, liberal social scientists, and sympathetic settlement workers as they pooled their talents and fought against the ravages of economic, social, and political inequality in the industrial age. Because of the crisis of white crime and immorality in the urban North, these compassionate men and women called for citywide help and financial support. For sentimental and sympathetic progressives, white crime and poverty statistics signaled a call to action. In most instances, progressives used them to justify intervention against the ideology of social Darwinist neglect. With nationality so much a part of global industrialization, they looked beyond race, beyond the distinct histories of each group, whether Russian Jews escaping violence or southern Italians escaping economic subjugation. Liberal reformers did not call for parochial crime prevention to address the particular circumstances of each immigrant group's racial and cultural baggage. Settlement workers, for example, fought ecumenically against the social causes of native white and immigrant criminality. They fought, as Du Bois described in 1904, "by all the ways in which goodness and beauty and truth creep into the human heart."[228]

Figure 3-2 "American Logic" depicts the way that the NAACP's *Crisis* magazine began to explicitly identify a double standard in the crime discourse. The "logic" dictates that crime distinguishes class among whites but treats blacks as an undifferentiated racial group. *Crisis*, June 1913.

African American researchers and reformers during the Progressive era might have been known as progressive leaders in their own right had they had the resources and influence of their white liberal peers. As much as they were in the moment, they were not of it. They were so marginal as to be nearly invisible. The financial constraints they faced, the color of their skin, and the fact that they advocated for a group considered by most white liberals to be, at best, a "ward of civilization," as Lichtenberger put it, left them fighting for social work and crime prevention with one hand tied behind their backs. Even when money may have mattered most, the ineffectiveness of their short-lived organizations was not only a testament to the intractability of the economic and social problems impacting many black communities, but it also reinforced white liberal notions that incriminating black culture was the best approach to paving the way for civilization building. For those only recently brought into the light of civilization, the best way to improve their inherent resources for social control, to become assimilable, as Addams and Kelsey suggested, was to build cultural "capacity" by internally working out their own salvation.

The contradiction between racial liberals' soft pitch for self-segregation as the key to moral regeneration, and by extension racial advancement, and their hard line against racial terror and southern-style segregation was masked by their willingness to listen to and engage black writers and reformers.[229] Most other white reformers and social scientists of the Progressive era wrote off black experts for being too sentimental and hopelessly biased and for coddling their own criminals. Equally important, these few racial liberals also lent their support to the constitutional fight for racial equality. But the fragile nature of their arguments and their ambivalence cannot be ignored. Their ambivalence made it easier for more reactionary forces to simply ignore black suffering and to define most that was good in the world as "white."

Ida B. Wells's experiences with white club women in Chicago revealed the growing frustration of black researchers and reformers who exposed the cracked foundations of modern racial liberalism. Wells not only challenged the "tendency" of white liberals "to be condescending and self-congratulatory about their ventures into race-relations," in the words of her latest biographer Paula Giddings, but she also linked the double standards in the crime discourse to the realities of the deepening crisis of racial inequality and racial violence.[230] Her protestations were increasingly seconded by others. The mild-mannered George Edmund Haynes, who would become the first research director for the NUL in part because he was not a firebrand, wrote in 1913, "Professions of democratic justice in the North, and deeds of individual kindness in the South, have not" been enough to reverse the rising tide of segregation across the nation.[231] Du Bois had predicted in 1910 that if things continued on the same trajectory, trouble would appear on the horizon. "Eastward and westward storms are brewing—great, ugly whirlwinds of hatred and blood and cruelty," he wrote nearly a decade before the Red Summer of 1919. "I will not believe them inevitable. I will not believe that all the shameful drama of the past must be done again today before the sunlight sweeps the silver seas."[232]

In Philadelphia, where Du Bois first thrust himself into the "shameful drama of the past" and first studied from the inside out the modern matrix of race, crime, and inequality, storm clouds were indeed brewing. In the City of Brotherly Love where, Dr. Ball, the local prison doctor, had first debated Hoffman, the future of race relations was being shaped one random act of neglect, isolation, and violence at a time. A metropolis of the nation, the birthplace of modern democracy, and an iconic symbol of the American creed tied to a history of extending liberty to all who might seek it, Philadelphia was the perfect place to see on the ground how the future of race relations came to pass.

4

PREVENTING CRIME:

WHITE AND BLACK REFORMERS
IN PHILADELPHIA

Philadelphia's settlement house workers were positioned on the front lines of crime prevention during the Progressive era.[1] They dealt with the specter of crime and criminals every day, pursuing crime prevention as part of their efforts to improve immigrants' and, to a lesser extent, blacks' lives in northern cities. In addition to fighting the structural causes of crime, such as bad housing, political corruption, poor policing, and vice, they made moral reform a priority. By focusing on the moral character of the poor people they served, settlement house workers also stigmatized behavior. Because of their faith in their ability to change individuals' lives while also seeking reforms in public policy, their focus on individual behavior shifted some attention away from interpreting crime as symptomatic of structural inequalities. Where African Americans entered into this equation, individual moral reform of native-born whites and European immigrants gave way to limited racial reform or no reform at all.

Philadelphia was home to the largest population of African Americans in any northern city during the Progressive era, a major destination of southeastern migrants. In raw numbers, it fell to second in black population behind New York in 1920 and then to third behind Chicago in 1930. Through the 1930s, the proportion of African Americans in Philadelphia outpaced its big-city competitors on average by a factor of two to one.[2] As a city with a rich tradition of nineteenth-century Quaker liberalism and black elite institution-building, its northern-born black population was among the earliest targets of the sociological and statistical crime gaze as a baseline from which to measure what southern black migrants did with their freedom in the urban North. In Frederick L. Hoffman's work, in W. E. B. Du Bois's groundbreaking *The Philadelphia Negro*, and in numerous other studies, Philadelphia was one of the most important black-criminality research sites in the nation.

During Du Bois's eighteen-month stay while researching in a notoriously rough neighborhood at the College Settlement House beginning in 1897, he was never assaulted or robbed, although he noted that crime was all around him and his young bride, and he sounded almost surprised at their good fortune. Writing about the people among whom he lived, Du Bois vividly described the fluidity with which working-class life and crime melted together:

> The corners, night and day, are filled with Negro loafers—able-bodied young men and women, all cheerful, some with good natured, open faces, some with traces of crime and excess, a few pinched with poverty. They are mostly gamblers, thieves and prostitutes, and few have fixed and steady occupation of any kind. Some are stevedores, porters, laborers and laundresses. On its face this slum is noisy and dissipated, but not brutal, although now and then highway robberies and murderous assaults in other parts of the city are traced to its denizens. Nevertheless the stranger can usually walk about here day and night with little fear of being molested, if he be not too inquisitive.[3]

Du Bois's immersion in the haunts of criminals may have brought him close to danger, but his tame experience was more the rule than the exception for settlement house residents.

Susan Wharton, a board member at the College Settlement House, illustrates the sensitivity that some white settlement house reformers brought to the subject of crime among immigrants and blacks. In the opening paragraphs of the 1900 annual report of the Starr Centre, she described the situation in far more nuanced terms than did many writers like Hoffman, who were strictly on the outside looking in. That Wharton lived only a few blocks away from the people to whom she attended in South Philadelphia may have given her a discerning eye. "That many persons living in this neighborhood are criminals in the eye of the law cannot be denied," she wrote, "that many are not criminals, and are striving to lead a right life in the face of fearful conditions, is equally certain."[4]

South Philadelphia was home to a wide array of southern and eastern European immigrants, southern black migrants, and white and black old Philadelphians. Characteristic of preindustrial walking cities, Philadelphia's neighborhoods south of Market Street—the main dividing line between the northern and southern halves of the city—were separated by insurmountable class barriers no wider than a typical brick-laid street.

Pine Street, for example, was a visible border separating poverty from prosperity. Many of the homes beginning at Pine and proceeding north were built for the wealthy in the early nineteenth century. Wharton lived one-third of a block north of Pine on Clinton Street. Built in 1836, Clinton was a model street for wealthy families who wanted to escape the hustle and buzz of the downtown business district just four major blocks to the north at Market Street. The homes on Clinton, with their "carefully designed doorways and the contrast of white trim against red brick, enhanced by overhanging shade trees, made this one of the most charming streets in the city."[5]

Poverty had its model thoroughfares as well. To children especially, south of Pine Street was a world unto itself; Pine represented the end of the known universe.[6] Lombard Street extending from the Delaware River, the city's easternmost border, to Broad Street, where City Hall was built at the intersection with Market Street between 1870 and 1900, was a major corridor of dilapidated homes, disorderly houses, and charity experiments. At 7th and Lombard, the Starr Centre, established in 1897, stood at an intersection of municipal neglect, limited economic opportunity, and social isolation. It was home to some of Philadelphia's most troubled residents.

Through her daily work at the settlement house, where she transcended the enormous barriers of class, space, and time to help South Philadelphia's poor blacks and immigrants, Wharton noted in 1900 that the area surrounding the center had been a laboratory for social reform, a place where "literally all kinds of experiments ha[d] been tried" but without positive effect. Instead, the people here were "more dependent [and] more conscious of being objects of pity," which left them with less motivation and fewer reasons to be hopeful. "From the ineffectual raid of the police to the sentimental almsgiving of the visitor," Wharton wrote, seemingly exasperated, "everything seems to have had its day."[7] The 1907 annual report of the Starr Centre mocked the persistent poverty at its doors when it noted that the only luxury that could be found in this slum were the "abundant children."[8] Four years later little had changed; the center remained in "a district with a good deal of bad history, and an insistent present need for uplifting forces."[9]

The Starr Centre was not the only uplifting agency on Lombard Street. The venerable Mother Bethel church stood at 6th and Lombard as a beacon of hope and an outward sign to old black residents that things really did change, despite how much they appeared to stay the same. The men and women who supported the church had done more than survive; they had prospered to the extent that they were able to build a bigger and more charitable church.[10] Mother Bethel, built by Richard Allen in 1816, was the first church of the African Methodist Episcopal (A.M.E.) denomination. The country's first independent black denomination in the North, it had successfully severed all ties to the white Methodists of Philadelphia who had subjected their fellow black Christians to institutional racism.[11]

Almost perfectly centered between Mother Bethel and the Starr Centre, half a block south of Lombard on 7th Street, was the headquarters of the Octavia Hill Association (OHA). Neither a settlement house nor a church, the OHA, founded in 1896, was a housing renewal organization and another attempt to improve neighborhood conditions. On and around Lombard Street and deeper into South Philadelphia, the OHA targeted the most "insanitary, delapidated [sic], and over-crowded dwellings" for complete renovation through purchase or management.[12] Using its motto—"Philanthropy and 4 per cent"—the OHA set out to raise funds, buy property, renovate both the physical condition of the housing and the moral fiber of the tenants, and give its supporters a 4 percent return on their philanthropic investment. More than any other progressive reform organization in Philadelphia at the time, the OHA illustrated the extent to which poverty did not evoke passionate reform from private or public sources. In the context of limited local government attempts to fight poverty and social Darwinism, the OHA made charity an investment rather than a handout.[13] Noting in a 1902 pamphlet how important decent housing was to the health of a city and the "standard of the citizens toward their work and toward the city," an official wrote that it was "almost hopeless to expect a man who is living under bad conditions to do anything worth while [sic]."[14]

The Starr Centre and the OHA shared more than a common concern for inspiring impoverished South Philadelphians to respectable living through modest structural improvement and moral uplift; the Starr Centre also rented from the OHA. The director of the OHA, Mrs. William F. Jenks, resided on the 900 block of Clinton Street with Susan Wharton. These reformers and their agencies in particular were clearly cut from the same progressive cloth. Primarily as vehicles of neighborhood improvement, the agencies conducted a wide range of anticrime activities, if seen in the broadest light. That is, in the process of implementing standard progressive reforms such as social and moral training, industrial education, fiscal management, housing improvement, and political reform, neighborhood reformers attacked the root causes of crime. The Starr Centre, for example, offered classes in parenting, provided supervised recreation, and visited homes as three direct attempts at improving the moral environment of at-risk youth. Too many young children, reformers noted, were left at home alone or under the care of adolescents who could not properly behave themselves, let alone adequately supervise their younger siblings.

Wharton described the methods and goals of one of the Starr Centre's premier programs. Consisting entirely of black families, the Coal Club was a cooperative discount-buying program. Rather than having individuals buy coal by the bucket at the most expensive rates, the Starr Centre bought coal in bulk based on weekly collections from club members. Each member then received his or her share of coal at the discounted rate. Although the immediate goal of the Coal Club was member savings, visitors achieved the more significant objective through weekly collections. Wharton wrote, "Our visitors go nominally to collect savings, [but] really to influence the lives of the families among whom they visit."[15] Home visiting formed the centerpiece of the Starr Centre's work among "the submerged tenth."[16] In exchange for modest social service benefits through direct contact and influence, evil habits and conditions were literally checked at the front door.

The Octavia Hill Association's complement to the Starr Centre's Coal Club visitor was the friendly rent collector. As the owner or manager of a renovated property, the OHA sent trained female rent collectors to do social work and raise tenants' standard of living.[17] In many cases, the OHA limited its remodeled housing and direct contact to those who were apparently redeemable and "deserving." "All of our tenants are thoroughly investigated before they are accepted," announced an official.[18] In buildings whose tenants were identified as "lawless" or whose premises were used for "immoral purposes," renovations waited until the riffraff departed or were evicted. Property acquisitions might even be delayed where a negligent owner condoned bad tenants. OHA officials, for example, waited until a "well-to-do negro" died before buying his property in 1903. Then they evicted "a disreputable class" of his black tenants who riotously drank and gambled "often on the very steps of the houses." The OHA replaced the evicted tenants with "very poor Polish immigrants who . . . proved satisfactory and very appreciative of their homes."[19]

It comes as no surprise that the OHA drew a sharper line than did the Starr Centre between tenants considered likely criminals and the respectable poor. Money may have mattered most in OHA's case since it spent thousands of dollars to acquire and renovate its properties. It seems that from the association's perspective, it was one thing to make affordable, decent housing available to poor people by eliminating slumlords and absentee landlords; it was quite another to turn around and give the improved housing to misbehaving tenants who were unlikely to pay their rent on time or at all. In this way, crime prevention viewed broadly in the context of Progressive era reforms was often limited to "deserving" individuals, an action that simultaneously stigmatized the "undeserving," leading to further social isolation and inequality for a subgroup of the poor.[20]

In their public addresses and pamphlets, OHA reformers in particular highlighted criminality to the point that it sometimes overshadowed the miserable conditions that had caught their attention in the first place. Their rhetoric sometimes betrayed their stated concern for moral uplift through housing reform because it seemed to justify excluding the people who needed decent housing most. For example, in a 1902 pamphlet the OHA characterized the Irish tenants in one of its properties as "destructive." Citing individual examples, the writer gave the impression that Irish men and women were heavy drinkers. While the men worked as longshoremen during the day, the women trafficked in illegal liquor or rented space for gambling. Worse still, their children did not attend school, and many of the truant boys were in gangs that stole lead pipes to sell as scrap and that vandalized vacant houses.[21] A pamphlet titled "Distinctive Features of the Octavia Hill Association" mentioned the 1903 purchase and renovation of a disgraceful heap passing as a four-story brick house that had been occupied by a "low, shiftless class of negroes, living without supervision or control."[22] In a third case, at a 1913 meeting of the National Civic Federation in Washington, D.C., convened to discuss that city's alley housing situation—where the poorest of the poor lived—the OHA bragged of its successful housing reform in two predominately black courts behind Mother Bethel church. "These two courts were of large notoriety and harbored some of the worst elements of the neighborhood," noted the OHA speaker.[23]

This last statement fit with the overall conclusions drawn by experts on the alley housing problem in Washington, D.C., that the costs to the nation's capital of too few decent homes were disproportionately high rates of illegitimacy, mortality, and crime among blacks. Albeit in a small measure, the OHA had contributed to a national forum that emphasized improving bad housing as much as it did eliminating black criminals. To be sure, the district's housing reformers were on the side of the little people. They answered "nay" to the question of whether the people of the alleys, many of whom were "shiftless" and "some vicious," deserved capital punishment for their "shortcomings."[24] Yet their practices reflected the type of slippery thinking that shifted criminality from being considered a symptom of structural inequality to being considered the cause. The critical fact was that there was not enough adequate housing, regardless of people's overall respectability. That criminals could be found among the struggling black poor of D.C. or Philadelphia was not a legitimate justification for poor people's miserable housing conditions.

Reformers' judgments regarding crime among blacks as an excuse for inaction seem harsh, given the bleak social and economic conditions people faced, and considering that the reformers were intimately familiar with the almost conspiratorial neglect of politically impotent neighborhoods by city officials and the blatant exploitation by real estate owners and their agents. The OHA's carefully prepared investigations for local business leaders, regional conferences, and the Pennsylvania state legislature demonstrate its commitment to publicizing the need for housing reform, but at the cost to blacks of conflating slum conditions and criminality. In a 1916 summary of its latest research regarding the general area surrounding its headquarters, the OHA stated: "Densest negro population, dangerous for women to go into, surface drainage of the most flagrant and revolting kind, privy vaults almost universal."[25] As much as crime was a legitimate concern among reformers, the police, and residents in particular, there was no obvious connection between the need for indoor plumbing and the potential for harm to women in a crowded black neighborhood—unless, to mostly native white reformers, one ipso facto meant the other.

That was precisely the thinking of the University Settlement House of the University of Pennsylvania, which announced the near completion of a new settlement house at 26th and Lombard in May 1906. Just east of the university campus and across the Schuylkill River, the University Settlement stated proudly that it was "not doing slum work." "The boys and young men" whom it sought to uplift were of a distinctly better class than those found in a "low, filthy, quarter of a city or town, a street or place where debouched [sic] and criminal persons live or resort."[26] The reference was to an area like 7th and Lombard, where the Starr Centre and OHA were located—an area that in addition to its "filthy" conditions and crime also had a large, struggling black population. Consequently, for University of Pennsylvania students who "avail[ed] themselves of the opportunity to study human nature from every conceivable point [of] view," one view was not represented because poor blacks were not among the "young men and women on the east bank of the river."[27] If they had been, the area would have been considered a slum and therefore off limits, according to the University Settlement's own definition. "Slum development," an internal report noted, was "most characteristic in neighborhoods invaded by [a] low grade negro element."[28]

Whether they redlined these communities or not, many of Philadelphia's early settlement workers showed little reluctance to narrowly define black residential areas in terms of their crime. The Eighth Ward Settlement House, founded in 1897, the same year as the Starr Centre, and located about five blocks away, specialized in helping "low grade negro[es]." According to its head social worker, Francis R. Bartholomew, the surrounding community was almost entirely all black, with the Negro "at his worst." Here, she wrote, was a "degraded" community that was an embarrassment to its race. Bartholomew argued that because there were few exceptional blacks in the neighborhood, evildoing confirmed popular images of a crime-infested community. The combination of real crime in the neighborhood and the stereotype of innate black criminality was, in her opinion, "the most serious menace to the progress of the Negro race."[29]

To Bartholomew, as to so many other racialist writers of the post-Reconstruction period, crime had become a defining characteristic of the Negro Problem. Southerners used crime to justify disfranchisement, lynching, and Jim Crow segregation; northerners used it to justify municipal neglect, joblessness, and residential segregation. To an extent, race and crime experts at the national level were blind to the complexities of local causes and conditions. With a few exceptions like Jane Addams, Susan Wharton, and some of the contributors to the 1905 *Charities* report on black conditions in northern cities, many nationally recognized experts did not live among the people they studied. Instead, they relied heavily on Census Bureau statistics and recycled data from local experts that supported their interpretations.[30] Therefore, the characterizations of black neighborhoods by reformers like Bartholomew and officials at Octavia Hill and University Settlement traveled well beyond city limits.

Bartholomew's spirited concerns about crime, however, cannot be easily categorized as the product of her own racism. She blamed a "degraded white element"—corrupt white male politicians and white female prostitutes—for contributing to the bad moral condition of the neighborhood.[31] Wharton agreed entirely with this assessment of whites as contributors to the downward trajectory of the community, stating that in general whites took advantage of blacks. Through insurance schemes and below-market wages, whites worked blacks "for everything they are worth." Taking into consideration the "pessimistic attitude of the public," newspapers' negative portrayals of blacks as "dishonest and easily influenced," and a segregated housing market where many blacks are "fortunate if they find themselves in a decent alley," Wharton concluded that the "repressive policy of our cities is fast making criminals."[32] During the first decade of the twentieth century, in Manhattan's San Juan Hill district, a mixed black and immigrant community, settlement house reformer Mary White Ovington observed that even immigrant youths degraded black youths by way of fisticuffs and racial epithets.[33] Even though these local observers offered nuanced depictions of crime in black neighborhoods and often disagreed with national experts about who or what was ultimately to blame, they helped to cement black criminality as a foundational problem built into the very structure of urban black communities.

The extent to which this root crime problem represented a racial problem for blacks can also be measured by contrasting settlement workers' views of crime among immigrants and native whites in Philadelphia. Unlike black neighborhoods, poor white neighborhoods were not so easily characterized by the predominance of one foreign group. Although Philadelphia had mixed areas of blacks and immigrants prior to the Great Migration as did New York City and Chicago, blacks were still more segregated in the city than any one foreign group.[34] With the exception of Casa Ravello, opened for Italians in 1907 by the Starr Centre, no other settlement house studied here claimed to serve the needs of a single nonnative group.[35] Many settlement houses in Philadelphia were similar to Jane Addams's Hull House, which served all immigrants' needs on Chicago's polyglot West Side.[36] As long as the neighborhoods themselves were mixed, the settlement houses were also mixed. Therefore, because of their heterogeneous populations, immigrant communities were more difficult to stigmatize by the criminality of one group. Immigrant groups were occasionally singled out for their racial inferiority, as was the case in a 1910 memorandum by OHA officials describing Polish Catholics as a "race more ignorant than Jews and with much lower standards of living."[37] But by and large, and in comparison to African Americans, whole immigrant neighborhoods were almost never condemned because of an easily identifiable misbehaving foreign element.

The College Settlement House (CSH) was one of Philadelphia's oldest privately run social work agencies. Three branches were located deep in South Philadelphia, either on or near Christian Street (a half mile south of Lombard), which marked a corridor for social work primarily among immigrants. Head social worker Anna F. Davies referred to this inner-city area as the nation's new frontier with "perils more destructive than the western frontiersman ever knew."[38] The 1904 annual report of the CSH described the neighborhood conditions at its riverfront branch at 502 S. Front Street this way: "cheap lodging-houses, saloons and furnished-room houses, it stands against a background dark with economic and moral depression and depravity."[39] Although the annual report mentioned that native whites, Jews, Italians, and Irish lived in the area, no group was blamed for the "wharf rats" and "gutter rats" that "discredited" the neighborhood. The CSH pointed out that its volunteers stood guard at the branch, "letting in the right ones and keeping out the wrong ones," but there was no attempt to stigmatize the race, ethnicity, or nationality of troublemakers who were turned away more than others.[40]

Instead CSH officials emphasized troubled race relations between groups. A "drunken" Irish woman randomly mocked a Jew when she "pulled his beard." He attempted to cane her in response, but hit the wrong person, resulting in an exchange on the "relative merits of Jew and Christian." In another skirmish of epithets, an Irish vendor called a Jewish woman a "Christ Killer" because she offered him five cents rather than six for a box of strawberries. Native white children also showed flashes of anti-Semitism when they frequently threw things at Jewish peddlers.[41]

Police officials recognized the CSH's attempts to minimize intergroup confrontations through activities at the house, even if they could not agree on how effective the activities were at reducing crime. In one instance, a police lieutenant praised the CSH, noting that "we don't have nearly so many boys arrested since that house was opened."[42] But in another instance, a police officer jokingly commented, "Yes, you have 'em in there singing and things like that [but] then they come out and go through somebody's pockets."[43] CSH officials argued that this behavior was a

reflection of the need for "better grade Americans" to teach "good" Americanization rather than "bad."[44] Because of the impact of political corruption and vice, CSH officials believed that responsibility for street crime was "far more widely distributed throughout the community than [was] readily acknowledged."[45]

On the other side of Market Street, completely across town in North Philadelphia, the North House Association (NHA) had been helping its largely native white and immigrant neighbors find jobs and improve their moral character since the 1870s. The NHA described the people who used its facilities as the "stagnant backwater of humanity." Although the NHA was more explicit that the newest arrivals—Russian Jews and Polish Catholics—were "neither good neighbors nor good citizens," its staff could not decide whether the newcomers had "ruined the neighborhood, or conditions of life here [had] ruined them." Shifting attention away from the new immigrants, the NHA pointed out that the majority of the people in the neighborhood living in the worst housing were in fact "worn-out Americans." White men of few skills, without ambition or the desire for training, who lacked steady work but often drank their wages, these people were, according to the NHA, physically and mentally "stunted" and "entirely undeveloped morally." But as troubled as the men were, the NHA, unlike the OHA or University Settlement House, did not view their "immorality" as a justification for not trying to help them. Furthermore, they were not deemed a menace to the progress of the white race, nor were their Russian or Polish counterparts representative failures.[46]

White settlement houses chose not to define their work in racial terms. For example, the Friends Neighborhood Guild (FNG) defined its North Philadelphia "mission work" in terms of saving the children of the poor from the "classes of the indifferent poor and even criminals."[47] Despite working primarily among "ignorant and work-driven" foreign groups, the FNG identified its goals as "civic and social progress" rather than as racial progress.[48] Prior to the 1920s there were almost no blacks involved with the FNG, which may partly explain the absence of racial

Figure 4-1 Photo depicting the impoverished youth of the Friends Neighborhood Guild. Note that nearly every child is without shoes and without nationality. 1901 Annual Report of the Friends Neighborhood Guild, courtesy of the Friends Historical Library of Swarthmore College.

rhetoric. In that sense, downplaying racial characteristics was consistent with the Americanization goals of most settlement houses. The FNG envisioned its immigrant young people becoming full-blooded Americans. Through summer field trips to the Zoological Gardens, Atlantic City, and West Point Academy, offered as "reward[s] of merit" for good attendance and behavior, FNG officials broadened the horizons of their future fellow citizens. Some were even taken to the nation's capital. After completing a three-day trip to Washington, D.C., in June 1901, one of four teenagers who visited President William McKinley told his mother, "I'll be the better all my life for that trip."[49] The trip may or may not have changed the young man's life forever, but it certainly suggested to him and other native white and immigrant youth at the FNG how much was in store for the well behaved.

These small examples of positive reinforcement speak volumes about the optimistic attitude of many settlement workers toward wayward native white and immigrant youth, especially since, according to FNG records, so many of them were in trouble with the law. In response, the FNG obtained a probation officer in 1903 to investigate children's cases and advise them in court.[50] After more than a decade, young people were still getting in trouble with the law, according to an FNG report that indicated that the importance of the FNG as a crime-prevention agency was not to be understated, "witnessed by the number of boys of all ages who must report to the probation officers who have their evening office hours at the FNG." That same year, after "much debate," the FNG installed pool tables at its headquarters for boys to meet "night after night, rather than on street corners, or in commercial pool rooms."[51] Thirteen- and fourteen-year-old working girls were also targeted for crime prevention. Concerned that too many attended the "cheap dances and theaters of the neighborhood" with their "done-up hair," the FNG established a Department for the Older Girls, subjecting them to "moral and educational talks."[52] The "sex susceptibility" and "spirit of adventure" among Philadelphia's white female youth began to draw as much thoughtful attention as Addams was calling for in Chicago.[53] The FNG even did "rescue" work. Young women "found to be living an immoral life" were sent to the Society to Protect Children from Cruelty, where it was hoped, they would be placed in "good homes."[54] Considering the amount of time and energy the FNG devoted to crime prevention among immigrants, its reluctance to link race (or ethnicity) and crime is all the more striking when compared to organizations dealing with blacks.

Figure 4-2 "The Washington Party" captures the Americanization project among the older boys of the Friends Neighborhood Guild in real time. From the slum to the White House, their visit to President William McKinley demonstrates the powerful resources that settlement house workers marshaled to enrich the American dreams of European immigrants. 1901 Annual Report of the Friends Neighborhood Guild, courtesy of the Friends Historical Library of Swarthmore College.

The social workers and probation officers in the midst of the daily grind of crime prevention within settlements like the FNG may not have seen their good works as the building blocks of white privilege. Righting the wrongs of troubled teens by showing them that playing by the rules might lead them all the way to the White House was no minor demonstration of their humanity and worth as future law-abiding citizens. The message was that the sky was the limit. The same could hardly be said for African Americans, whether at-risk youths or the most respected black man in America. Four months after the FNG teens visited President McKinley, and one month after his assassination, Booker T. Washington dined with President Theodore Roosevelt at the White House. The "Dinner Incident," as it was billed by the press, was intended to be a gesture of goodwill by the new president and an opportunity to secure Washington's help in selecting a few conservative black Republicans for federal appointments in the South. It turned into a racial scandal. Southern journalists and politicians howled in outrage and described the dinner as an affront to white supremacy. So did some white northerners. In response to the incident, a New Jersey letter to the *New York Times* cautioned, "The Anglo Saxon race and the negro must reach their destinies in this country along parallel lines, let us trust, but with the lines never approaching to social unity." Washington never again dined at the White House, and a generation would pass before any other black man did. Although the national press buzz quieted after a few weeks, echoes of the event resounded for years. The *New York Times* reported in March 1905, for example, just as Roosevelt was about to be inaugurated for a second term, that a white high school student in a Washington, D.C., English class chose to demonstrate how to use the word *debased* in a sentence by writing "Roosevelt debased himself by eating with a nigger."[55] Whether at the level of presidential politics or local crime prevention, Progressive era racism was not an abstraction, even if the dots did not always connect clearly.

The complicated ways in which white progressive reformers responded to the needs of immigrants versus blacks were rarely as stark as the picture drawn by national race experts like Frederick Hoffman and John Daniels or as suggested by the "Dinner Incident."[56] Reformers did not necessarily go out of their way to stereotype and discriminate against poor blacks, though some obviously did. Instead, many paid no attention to a group of impoverished blacks that suffered greater isolation and inequality than immigrants. If poverty and social isolation were the only conditions for receiving social welfare assistance, African Americans would have been the overwhelming recipients in many city agencies, but even in the same neighborhoods, many organizations turned the other way.

The subtle ways in which broader notions of black inferiority widened the gap between white reformers' views of black criminality and their views of immigrant criminality may be understood in one sense as the difference between an instinctive thought process and a reflexive one. For example, in his 1907 study of race relations, journalist Ray Stannard Baker described being struck by the "greater prejudice against the coloured man" in regard to his criminality as compared to the immigrant. A Philadelphia grand jury presentment, he wrote, had called for "some measures" to be taken against a "crime wave" perpetrated by the "undesirable alien and the irresponsible coloured person." The newspaper reported the story under the headline "Negro Crime Abnormal" and made absolutely no mention of "the alien" at all. "When I inquired at the prosecutor's office about the presentment," Baker recalled, "I was told: 'Oh, the dagoes are just as bad as the Negroes.' "[57] When confronted face-to-face with such contradictions, many white progressives may have said the same, but in more ways than one—as writers and as reformers—their actions spoke louder than their words.

Consequently, there were clear differences in the way that settlement house workers defined black people's behavior as a racial problem in addition to a moral problem. The added element of racial thinking set blacks apart from immigrants and native whites, which intensified the stigmatization of black crime and made successful crime prevention among blacks appear more improbable and unlikely. This was so much the case that some settlement houses either avoided blacks altogether, like the University Settlement House, or deemed some blacks too unworthy for reform, like the Octavia Hill Association, or, in the case of the Eighth Ward Settlement, focused so heavily on the need for racial advancement that structural reform in a black neighborhood was barely on the agenda.

This third effect marked the clearest difference in crime prevention on behalf of immigrants and native whites compared to blacks. Despite the common strategy of rhetorically attacking the structural causes of crime but in reality pursuing goals that emphasized individual moral reform, organizations like the College Settlement House and Friends Neighborhood Guild still promoted avenues of opportunity for immigrants and native whites. Historian Thomas Philpott describes a similar situation in Chicago: "Among social workers and reformers, none were more conscious of Negro conditions than the leaders of the settlement movement. No other group of whites was so concerned about blacks nor so free of contempt for them. If the settlement workers were not ready to treat Negroes the same as other ethnic groups, then no white Chicagoans were."[58]

The racial thinking and rhetoric of progressive reformers that often accompanied crime prevention among blacks was a reflection of and a contribution to the growing racism and segregation that black Philadelphians increasingly faced during the first decade of the twentieth century. In other words, blacks' social and economic status in the urban North was on a downward trajectory compared to the status of new immigrants.[59] Blacks, therefore, could not afford to yield any ground to conservative

Figure 4-3 Staged charity photo of black children as pickaninnies, complete with protruding bright white eyes, eating watermelon in the yard of the Pennsylvania Society for Protecting Children from Cruelty. The racialized depiction of needy black youth draws on popular racist imagery as a stark reminder of the fundamental differences in black and white poverty. *Charities,* October 7, 1905.

interests who never doubted blacks' innate criminal tendencies and inability to survive in the industrial North, nor could struggling blacks avoid being victims of what Wharton observed was the "repressive policy of our cities [that] is fast making criminals."[60] Too many "friends of the Negro" in Philadelphia were ultimately too ambivalent about racial differences, as opposed to nationality differences, to stem the tide of black repression, thereby ineffectively preventing crime among blacks. Instead, they emphasized the need for racial progress, albeit through self-improvement rather than structural reform.[61]

Unlike several of their contemporaries in the local settlement house movement, some reformers in Philadelphia approached the twin evils of repression and crime with a much clearer understanding of their mutual dependence. During the Progressive era they emerged as part of a broader movement of interracial organizations on the national level, such as the National Association for the Advancement of Colored People (1910) and the National Urban League (1910), and of local organizations in Philadelphia, such as the Association for the Protection of Colored Women (1905), the Armstrong Association (1908), and the Association for Equalizing Industrial Opportunities and League of Civic and Political Reform (1910). Within the context of these national and local movements to stem the tide of repression against blacks, many reformers placed black criminality at the heart of their work.

When the leaders of what would become the National Association for the Advancement of Colored People decided to issue a call for a conference on racism in 1909, disfranchisement and racial violence had been sweeping through the South for over two decades.[62] Given that each southern state from Texas to North Carolina had adopted the equivalent of omnibus anti-black legislation, there was no end in sight to the South's white supremacy campaigns. From the North's perspective, the South had a monumental race problem, but most white northerners were inclined to do little about it. Since the Supreme Court had officially sanctioned segregation with its landmark "separate but equal" ruling in the 1896 case of *Plessy v. Ferguson,* the North had been justified in leaving the South to its own devices. There were, however, white northerners who were sympathetic to the plight of black southerners and who contributed time, money, or both to industrial education. Booker T. Washington, principal of Tuskegee Institute, had made his famous "Separation of the Races" speech in Atlanta, Georgia, the year before the highest law of the land codified second-class citizenship for African Americans. Washington's speech helped define the times, advising blacks to forsake their political rights and social freedoms by learning how to use their hands efficiently and profitably. Washington, Tuskegee, and industrial education in general became major targets for white northerners who turned away from the South's abrogation of the Constitution's Fourteenth and Fifteenth amendments to look toward the training of a vast pool of productive "free" black agricultural and industrial workers. Following in the wake of the Civil War's hideous devastation, many whites, northern and southern, thought that the nation finally appeared to be moving forward as one.

Whites were not mistaken. The most telling sign of this new national unity was an increase of racial violence in the North. The small minority of white northerners and infinitesimal number of blacks who signed the call for a race conference in Cooperstown, New York, had already seen much bloodshed in May 1908 with the "eighty injuries, six fatal shootings and two lynchings" from a race riot in Springfield, Illinois, home of Abraham Lincoln.[63] Naming their conference after Lincoln, they wrote in the conference call that the nation had failed to "live up to the obligation imposed upon it by the Emancipation proclamation" because of a "spread of lawless attacks upon the [N]egro, North, South and West." Recognizing widespread public apathy in the face of such violence, the call warned that "silence under these conditions, mean[t] tacit approval."[64] The call set out to reignite the fire of nineteenth-century abolitionism and marshal the advanced scientific guard of twentieth-century progressivism in order to uphold the civil and political rights of millions of Americans.

The list of signers was impressive, including Ida B. Wells, Jane Addams, and W. E. B. Du Bois. In addition to attending as Philadelphia's own national expert at the conference, Susan Wharton of the Starr Centre was a participant in this new movement. It probably came as no surprise to other Philadelphia reformers that Wharton identified with the nascent NAACP, given her exceptional commitment to blacks and their point of view.

By the time the NAACP became a formal organization in 1910, Wharton had begun to sever most ties with the Starr Centre after receiving lukewarm support for her proposal to open a new center for blacks in the Thirtieth Ward.[65] While pursuing her plans, the Starr Centre's board members expressed their unwillingness to broaden the organization's reach to accommodate the shifting population of blacks from the Seventh Ward to the neighboring Thirtieth Ward.[66] In 1912 board members voted to officially break all financial ties to Wharton's new branch, concluding that it was "unwise . . . to undertake at present so large a work for the Colored People."[67] Their decision appeared to be more than a practical matter of funding. It was consistent with the increasing segregation in Philadelphia that pushed blacks west and north from their historic home in the Seventh Ward. The Starr Centre's head social worker, Jane Rushmore, admitted in 1910 that economic conditions in Philadelphia were worsening for blacks while "race prejudice is always vigorously pushing them back." She also hinted that the Starr Centre would do even less for blacks who had not moved because experience had shown that working with the "slum negro" was not a "useful field."[68] Explaining Rushmore's comment, Lucy Barber, a student of white Philadelphia reformers, argues that the "spread of an ideology of racial segregation in Philadelphia" also contributed to the failure of "social services to distinguish between personal failures of individual blacks and group oppression."[69] Because Philadelphia's mixed immigrant and black neighborhoods were giving way to segregation, settlement houses and other social agencies in South Philadelphia were free to concentrate on a growing population of immigrants. The Starr Centre had already opened its Casa Revello branch for Italians in the winter of 1907, noting in an annual report that Italians were victims of "circumstance" and were "isolated among those with whom they ha[d] come to dwell."[70] Disdain for the "slum Negro" and uncertainty about whether blacks were victims of circumstance or agents of their own suffering led the Starr Centre to abandon them four years later. Wharton's experience as a former board member and worker at the Starr Centre, and now as head social worker of the newly opened Whittier Centre for the Study and Practical Solutions of Negro City Problems, gave the Lincoln Conference an updated perspective on Du Bois's findings of a decade before.

As a measure of the changing times among social workers, Du Bois noted in his Philadelphia research that charity work among blacks was fairly generous by comparison to job opportunities. By 1910 both were in short supply. In the late 1890's, he explained how shamelessly many Philadelphians barred blacks from good jobs, yet supported charity. "The same Philadelphian who would not let a Negro work in his store or mill will contribute handsomely to relieve Negroes in poverty and distress,"

Du Bois wrote. After citing dozens of specific examples of qualified blacks denied jobs because of their skin color, Du Bois made a convincing argument that most white Philadelphians preferred two kinds of blacks—the common laborer and the charity case. Barely hiding his outrage at this injustice, Du Bois strongly suggested that crime was the city's "penalty" for its prejudice: "How long can a city say to a part of its citizens, 'It is useless to work; it is fruitless to deserve well of men; education will gain you nothing but disappointment and humiliation?' How long can a city teach its black children that the road to success is to have a white face? How long can a city do this and escape the inevitable penalty?"[71] Similarly warning about the danger to northern cities resulting from the Negroes' "economic handicap," Kelly Miller, a Howard University sociologist, wrote in 1906 that "When these cities are threatened with such frightful death rate and crime rate among this neglected class they should remember that it is but the logical outcome of the hard industrial lot."[72] That Du Bois named this not-so-easily-detected paradox "contempt and pity" before the turn of the century reveals the quick pace of Philadelphia's embrace of black repression during the next decade.[73] Looking back from Wharton's perspective at the time of the conference, Philadelphia's overall feeling toward blacks might then have been more accurately described as contempt and loathing.

James Stemons, a Philadelphia postal clerk, writer, and reformer, also brought new evidence of northern repression to the Lincoln Conference. As Du Bois had done earlier, Stemons complained loudest about the failure of northern industries to open decent jobs to blacks. Besides work in domestic and personal service, "what opportunity," he asked, "has the average Negro for working to make an honest living in any northern locality?"[74] Even service work was disappearing for many blacks.[75] "Negro waiters" were no longer being employed in many "first class hotel[s] or restaurant[s]," according to Stemons. Choosing instead to take advantage of surplus labor from the new immigration, especially in New York and Philadelphia, these places often showed their contempt for blacks by displaying Jim Crow signs on menus and "conspicuous places" that read "None but white help employed in this establishment." The same movement was afoot in the employment of "colored domestics," Stemons continued. Newspaper classifieds revealed their shrinking job prospects: Blacks placed the majority of ads "asking for domestic positions, both males and females," while a "large percentage" of postings read "none but white need apply." Concluding his speech, Stemons said that elevating the industrial status of blacks to be equal to "other citizens" was a "problem which demands the immediate attention of this conference."[76]

As a local race man, Stemons spoke about what he knew. He had solicited local employers to hire qualified black workers; campaigned for Pennsylvania Democrats during the presidential election of 1908; written articles for newspapers; edited his own journal for a short time, for which he was featured in the 1908 *Colored Directory of Philadelphia;* and begun to network among black and white clergymen in order to bring his ideas to fruition. Stemons's credentials were all the more impressive because in 1897 he had come to Philadelphia, penniless and friendless, to seek financial support for his Industrial Rights League, which had failed the year before in Ohio. He left Cleveland, stopped a short time in Buffalo, New York, and eventually decided to make his mark in the City of Brotherly Love, where he hoped his would-be followers would be more generous. Originally a Midwestern migrant from Hutchison, Kansas, all he had when he arrived in Philadelphia, other than the clothes on his back, was a solution to the race problem, an earnest commitment to apply it, and a letter from a white clergyman vouching for his sincerity.[77]

Early on, Philadelphians proved as eager as others to hear his oratory, but as unwilling to bankroll his plans. To survive, Stemons worked as a janitor at a downtown theater and as a waiter at a first-class hotel, and he eventually became a full-time postal clerk in 1909, where he may have worked until retirement. To supplement his income and give voice to his ideas, Stemons attempted to publish an autobiographical novel that remains a 750-page manuscript to this day. He successfully published a book called *The Key* in 1916, an expansion of a 1907 pamphlet.[78] Otherwise, Stemons constantly struggled financially to become a full-time reformer. Lamenting another failed attempt to publish a manuscript, his sister wrote that she "long[ed]" to see him be rewarded "in a material way" for his "divinely inspired" commitment to solving the race problem. "I have never heard or read of such a life of sacrifice as yours," Mary Stemons wrote.[79]

Stemons was indeed exceptional as a working-class black intellectual. Few reformers of the day could match his experience at the end of a broomstick or at working overtime to be able to buy a "decent suit" for a conference. Few working-class blacks could say they had written books or discussed important matters with prominent national figures like Woodrow Wilson, William Jennings Bryan, and Booker T. Washington.[80]

At the Lincoln Conference, in addition to the problem of employment discrimination, Stemons also addressed Wharton's main concern that northern blacks were being abandoned or neglected by social service agencies. Stemons saw this problem in a broader context. He argued that the North and South had joined "upon a policy of submerging the race" based on the widespread belief that "the Negro must work out his own salvation." In an unpublished manuscript that Stemons wrote sometime before the conference, he attacked this policy by harshly criticizing one of its foremost architects, Booker T. Washington.[81] Washington had also acknowledged Stemons's criticisms in a letter to him.[82] The heart of Stemons's critique of Negro self-improvement and Washington's bootstrap philosophy was that it did not apply to millions of white workingmen for whom society had the "greatest concern." With no barriers placed on their ambitions, Stemons proclaimed, "no thought is ever suggested that the toiling white millions should work out their own salvation, except through the active aid and sympathy of every constructive element of society."[83]

Stemons exaggerated the generosity of American industrialists and philanthropists toward millions of "toiling" whites, but the spirit of progressivism could be deceptive. Stemons knew with certainty that it did not apply equally to blacks in places like Philadelphia. Even a decade before, when noting that charitable organizations preferred to help black dependents more than ambitious workers, Du Bois also noted that more than 90 percent of charity agencies discriminated to some degree against blacks.[84] Of the roughly 10 percent remaining, "protective, rescue and reformatory work" was "not applied to any great extent" among blacks. In other words, very few agencies in Philadelphia, including many settlement houses, were trying directly to save black children from becoming juvenile delinquents or adults from becoming criminals.

Outside of the limited crime prevention conducted by a small number of settlement houses, the best that could be said was that many liberal reformers supported industrial education in the South. Stemons considered this to be part of the problem. Since the early nineteenth century, Quakers had been among the most active supporters of abolition and were instrumental in making the Underground Railroad a safe passage to Philadelphia and beyond. Before the Civil War, Quakers established schools in Philadelphia, such as the Institute for Colored Youth founded in 1842, to help educate free blacks. Sixty years later, inspired by the example of Booker T. Washington—"a man sent of God," according to principal Hugh M. Browne—Quakers remade the institute into a normal school, called Cheyney, to train "colored teachers" for "Christian Industrial Tuskegee."[85] Before then, during the postbellum period, Quakers had turned their attention to the South, opening Christiansburg school in Cambria, Virginia, in 1865.

According to the Friends' Freedmen's Association, Christiansburg was a unique southern school because its "finances [were] entirely handled by a strong Board of Managers in Philadelphia." But the school's supporters became discouraged in 1896 because they felt that classical education for southern blacks had been squandered on "unworthy objects" who migrated north and "drifted into the slum life." Worse still, a few had committed "atrocious crimes."[86] Although there is no evidence that the school's managers were influenced by the publication of Hoffman's *Race Traits,* the timing of their concerns could not have been better. Suggestive too was their language stating that such "gloom[y]" conditions had raised one of the "greatest questions of this country": what to do to solve the "great Negro problem." To save the school and presumably the nation, Booker T. Washington was brought in to help. Based on his recommendations, one of his former assistants was hired to serve as principal, making half of the new teachers graduates of Hampton or Tuskegee. The newly staffed and retooled Christiansburg Industrial Institute had three educational goals: building character, teaching common English, and vocational training.[87]

The immediate success of Christiansburg's transformation heightened Washington's appeal among Philadelphia Quakers because it fed into the logic that liberal educators should no longer contribute to the creation of black criminals. Because of industrial education's focus on character building, "troublesome" blacks would have good reason to stay in the South. Those blacks in the North unwilling to go south to be properly educated would be left to work out their own salvation. In this sense, industrial education in the South was an anticrime solution, and for many white liberals in the North it represented the upper limit of reform among blacks. In 1906, several years before Wharton decided to leave the Starr Centre, she also supported the Hampton-Tuskegee model of race progress. She invited Washington to speak at the Starr Centre and at board meetings on several occasions. When she defended blacks against white prejudice, she argued that no Hampton or Tuskegee graduates could be found in jails or prisons. Seeing the Hampton-Tuskegee model as a panacea for blacks' problems at that time, she bemoaned, "Would that we had a Tuskegee in our midst."[88]

Not everyone agreed. One New York critic of Boston's Reform League summed it up this way: "These Boston people beat me. They will have mass meetings and raise money to help Mr. Washington educate the 'niggers' down South, but they will let a decent Northerner starve before they will give him a chance to earn an honest living."[89] Wharton herself had to deal with opposition to Tuskegee. During a Starr Centre board meeting in May 1905, Washington offered scholarships to Tuskegee to troubled young men from South Philadelphia as opportunities to get their lives together. Of the four recipients, three ran away from the industrial and agricultural training camp within weeks of the start of the fall semester.[90]

While Washington was canvassing Philadelphia, trading scholarships for financial support, Tuskegee's stock was soaring in some northern liberal circles. The preceding year's national debate over whether black crime rates increased with education, pitting Du Bois against Mississippi governor James K. Vardaman in a series of speeches and published articles, brought to light a significant body of research into the criminal records of the alumni of black colleges.[91] President Roosevelt, widely considered to be liberal on most race matters, added to the national media attention in a series of keynote addresses extolling the crime-fighting virtues of Hampton and Tuskegee. At Hampton's commencement on May 30, 1906, Roosevelt expressed his sincere appreciation for the school's "self-help mission" and its commitment to educating blacks on "how to conduct themselves with self-respect [as] hard working, intelligent, law-abiding citizens." The essence of this training, he emphasized, was the building of character in the entire race. Pointing to the outstanding achievements of the school's teachers and administrators, Roosevelt continued, "You have sent out from Hampton Institute in all something like 6,000 graduates, and, if I have remembered rightly, there are but two of whom you have record[ed] as criminals." Then he looked at the students and issued a stern warning to not let their school down: "The negro criminal, no matter at whose expense the particular crime may be committed, is a hundredfold more dangerous to the negro race than to the white race, because he tends to arouse the bitter prejudices for which, not he alone, but the whole race, will suffer. In the interest of the colored folks see to it, you colored men here, that you war against criminality in your own race with a particular zeal, because that criminality is in the ultimate analysis a greater danger to your race than any other thing can be." In a graduation speech at Tuskegee the year before, Roosevelt was even more frank in his repudiation of racism and his injunction to black college graduates to fight the criminality within: "[A]bove all, vice and criminality of every kind, are evils more potent for harm to the black race than all acts of oppression of white men put together." With these presidential ideas spreading around the country from the champion of the little guy, no wonder northern liberals were eager to see Hampton and Tuskegee as a solution to the black crime in their midst.[92]

Many of Philadelphia's liberal whites were huge supporters of industrial education in the South, in part because they believed it was an effective long-term solution to crime.[93] At a March 1907 meeting of the Society of Friends in the Germantown section of Philadelphia, Herbert Welsh, a Quaker education reformer, gave an address on "Some Present Aspects of the Negro Problem." Passionately arguing for Hampton and Tuskegee to be "multiplied" around the nation, Welsh began by praising Hampton's founder, General Samuel Chapman Armstrong, for seeing that "slavery was not all bad." According to Welsh, Armstrong built Hampton on slavery's good aspects: religious and mental training, "knowledge of handicrafts," and a "fair, practical education." What Armstrong did not believe in and what Hampton did not do was to treat the "negro" as an equal but recognized that as a "lower [and] ... weaker race," the "negro" needed character building from the start, according to Welsh.[94] But many in the North had not been as visionary as Armstrong, he continued, and had failed the Negro and the nation by educating him like a white man and granting him the right to vote.[95] Welsh told his northern audience that they had now become impatient with blacks and showed a "constant willingness to admit" that southerners had been correct. "In condemning the negro you may point to thousands of the ignorant, degraded, immoral negroes; you may say these people will not work; the proportion of crime among them is unduly large; you may give them, and with justice, an exceedingly bad name," Welsh proclaimed, but "on the other hand," Hampton and Tuskegee with their positive results have already shown the nation the way to eliminate its "heavy burden of negro ignorance and vice."[96]

A month before his address, Welsh sent a copy of his speech to Du Bois at Atlanta University and to H. B. Frissell, principal of Hampton, to get their feedback. Du Bois agreed with Welsh's main points and especially liked his idea of channeling more federal money into education, in spite of the fact that Welsh made this argument on the premise that educating blacks should be a national priority akin to national defense, defending against an "internal peril."[97] Du Bois's only disagreement with Welsh was his singular focus on the Hampton-Tuskegee model. He thought there should be funding for primary education, industrial high schools like Hampton and Tuskegee, and university training.[98] Perhaps out of respect to Du Bois, Welsh appears to have changed his speech by mentioning Atlanta University as an example of a successful school, despite the contradiction with his main point.[99]

Principal Frissell, General Armstrong's successor at Hampton and a prominent southern white paternalist, unequivocally supported industrial and agricultural schooling for blacks in the South but disagreed with Welsh's idea that the "general government" should become involved. He argued that too much work needed to be done by northern reformers before southern whites would accept broad federal intervention in the education of blacks. "Friends of the Negro" had done "comparatively little . . . for instance, in the city of Philadelphia," he wrote, "and yet crime is increasing at a tremendous rate and a feeling of bitterness is being engendered against the blacks." Philadelphians needed to start a "general movement toward the improvement of the conditions of the Negro race" before pursuing further support for industrial education in the South. The work in the South, Frissell continued, was indeed "being hindered more by the crime of the black man in the North, and the very unfortunate conditions under which he has to live there, than by any other cause."[100] Frissell had apparently been observant on his trips to Philadelphia to conduct Hampton meetings, but his conclusions were not popular among northerners, which may explain why he had no effect on Welsh's speech.

Frissell's willingness to hold northerners accountable for black repression and crime may also explain why Stemons, who made similar arguments, was almost shut out of the Lincoln Conference and was not allowed to make his entire speech.[101] Stemons believed that some northern leaders had read his work and had become determined to silence him.[102] William Walling, one of the main conference organizers and eventual founding member of the NAACP, who had promised to include Stemons on the program in the first place, suggested later that his associates had decided to limit "radical" speakers.[103]

About the same time that Frissell personally cautioned Welsh to tend to his own backyard, Stemons published a pamphlet, *The North Holds the Key*, that he called "the crowning article of my life"; it was his first opportunity for widespread exposure and in some ways his last.[104] Stemons argued provocatively that the North's failure to open industrial opportunities to blacks contributed directly to political disfranchisement and racial violence in the South. As long as the North continued to advise "the South [on] how to deal with the Negro" rather than providing fair opportunities, he wrote, the majority of blacks would remain in the South because of the abundance of work. White southerners would therefore continue to treat blacks with impunity because blacks had few employment options outside the South.[105]

Many race leaders may have balked at Stemons's words for two reasons. The most obvious reason was that he had insulted liberal whites like Welsh who had devoted considerable time and resources to the Negro Problem.[106] Even if they agreed that they had neglected their own black neighbors, they could still justify it because no more than 10 percent of the black population lived among them. Moreover, black leaders were more concerned about conditions in the South, as represented by followers of Washington. Those in the opposing camp represented by Du Bois's Niagara Movement agitated for civil and political rights to the exclusion of broaching the economic question.[107] Therefore, by the time Stemons enthusiastically advised Walling to put his ideas about "the question of the Negro's industrial disadvantages in the North" before the conference organizers, many leaders were probably already opposed to him. After being disappointed with his limited speaking time, Stemons huffed, "I have never seen the race in a worse light than at this conference—that is, I mean for arrogance and opposition to all who do not subscribe to all they say."[108]

By the spring of 1909, despite this disappointment, Stemons had become most successful at linking industrial repression and black criminality. Ostensibly, no other person in Philadelphia, following Du Bois's departure to Atlanta, was as committed to publicizing this dual problem. Stemons came into contact with people at all levels of the city, from black church members to the mayor. Although his direct influence on public policy is impossible to measure, he clearly brought together influential like-minded people to fight black crime and increase job opportunities. At the intersection of these two critical issues, Stemons and others helped to draw a line between those whom they defined as the ambitious and law-abiding and the shiftless and vicious, a line they felt would counter the negative portrayal of the race as criminal. With the discerning eye of an informed public, they believed the floodgates of industrial opportunity would open.

Beginning in the spring of 1907, Stemons noted that important people had begun to take a sincere interest in his anticrime work.[109] An editorial response to Stemons's article "Why Crime Increases among Negroes" in the Philadelphia *Public Ledger* praised him for describing "THE REAL 'NEGRO PROBLEM.'"[110] The editors were rightly seduced by Stemons's claim that as long as white employers refused to hire blacks and white employees refused to work beside them, crime among blacks would continue to rise. "With a feeling of hopelessness in the face of such odds, as well as of resentment against such treatment, many Negroes are turning against society with the reckless desperation born of despair."[111] Warning the city to take heed of Stemons's words, the editors wrote that the Negro "can afford to remain isolated and oppressed better than the community can afford to have him remain so, an unassimilated element of discord and danger."[112] Anything the editors had not gleaned from the actual article was clarified at a meeting with Stemons the day before the editorial's publication. Also in attendance were the editors of the Philadelphia *Press,* unnamed "prominent colored men," and the well-respected sociologist Alfred Holt Stone, who was at the time writing *Studies in the American Race Problem.*[113] Stone, a Mississippian, shared Stemons's opinion that northerners were as guilty as southerners of fomenting a "race problem" because they would not hire blacks for good jobs. Industrial opportunity was "the 'door of hope,'" Stone wrote, "upon whose cruel closing follow idleness and crime, vice and destitution, vagrancy and death, for the masses of the race."[114] Having Stone at the meeting certainly would have impressed the newspaper editors, making them more likely to take Stemons seriously.

Stemons also began to build a modicum of support among black clergymen. Charles Albert Tindley, pastor of East Calvary Methodist Episcopal, was moved by Stemons's crime article in the *Public Ledger.*[115] Tindley's church was among the most active black institutions in charity work, especially among poor southern migrants. His direct contact with struggling blacks in Philadelphia clearly exposed him to the need for expanding economic opportunities and crime prevention.[116] Tindley also drew people to him through his innovative music ministry. He is best known as the father of gospel music, having written several of the most popular gospel hymns of all times, including "We'll Understand It Better By and By," and directly influencing the late Thomas Dorsey.[117]

To be sure, many other black churches were surrounded by poverty, vice, and crime, but most of them appear to have avoided outright crime fighting. That had not always been the case, according to Du Bois. Black churches in Philadelphia had gained a reputation for crime fighting in the nineteenth century. As early as 1809, they had responded to an increase of crime when the gradual abolition laws began to take effect and too many freedmen along with immigrants began "to congregate." But a hundred years later, the situation churches faced was very different because of the growth of the black population through migration, the increased number of churches, and intensified competition for saving souls. A small but steady stream of migrants, primarily from Maryland and Virginia, also helped to intensify internal class and status divisions among blacks.[118] Ties that had bound together the small black communities of mostly native-born Philadelphians in the nineteenth century gave way to larger and more diverse communities in the twentieth. The result, historian Robert S. Gregg argues, was that churches felt greater pressure to hold on to their congregations for fear of losing them to other churches.[119]

Du Bois also observed that pastors feared losing their saints to new forms of entertainment and the most popular leisure activities in the city. Baseball, moving pictures, vaudeville, theater, and dancing increasingly competed for the attention of church members on late Saturday nights and Sunday afternoons. These amusements were often attacked by clergy, but their "precepts against specific amusements [were] often violated," Du Bois wrote.[120] Pastors may have sermonized against the evils of vice and unsupervised recreation, but they did not necessarily mount offensive weapons against them. Richard R. Wright, Jr., black sociologist and editor of the Philadelphia-based *Christian Recorder*, a journal of the A.M.E. denomination, also pointed out that most churches tended to avoid social work "chiefly because of lack of money."[121] Yet in 1912 Wright counted about six churches, including Tindley's East Calvary, that had sufficient resources to develop institutional features aimed at improving economic and social conditions in the communities they served. Two were exceptional, according to Wright. The Berean

Presbyterian Church, headed by Matthew Anderson, an Oberlin and Princeton graduate, featured a kindergarten, industrial training school, trades association, and building and loan association and sponsored conferences on educational, social, and economic issues. Henry L. Phillip's Protestant Episcopal Church of the Crucifixion was also unique because of its homeless shelter and novel approach to the "amusement question." To combat the evils awaiting blacks on the streets and in the dens of secular establishments, the Church of the Crucifixion went "against the general view of Negro Christians in establishing a poolroom and evenings for dancing."[122]

Aggressive crime fighting by black churches may have been counterproductive or at the very least may have produced limited results. The working-class Philadelphians who crowded into the storefront churches of the Baptists were especially vulnerable to being labeled criminals because of their proximity to crime in their daily lives.[123] To fend off the stigma of criminality based on the white public's racist assumptions, some church laymen wanted nothing to do with rescue and reform work. For others, physical closeness to criminals and vice may have implicated family members or even themselves, resulting in a passive attitude or ambivalence. Surely some members gambled on the "numbers" at the very least.[124] Although pastors may not have supported illegal lotteries and games of chance, they could understand the desperate desire of their members to take a shot at winning. The bottom line was that, on a practical level, many churches had to tolerate the complexities of urban poverty, where parables of good versus evil rang truer inside the sanctuary than outside.

Evelyn Brooks Higginbotham's research on the women's movement in the national organization of black Baptists provides some clues about what may have characterized the upper limit of anticrime work within Baptist churches in Philadelphia, and perhaps among other denominations. Following instructions of their national leaders, local Baptist women likely pushed for sports, music, and other recreational programs within their Philadelphia churches "as alternatives to the street's allurements," especially jazz music and public dance halls. Some local churches may have even punished members for "immoral" behavior committed outside the church. At Shiloh Baptist Church in Washington, D.C., for example, "individuals caught dancing, imbibing alcoholic beverages, or engaging in other 'improper' behavior were literally delivered a summons to come before the church for censure," according to Higginbotham.[125] Although all her examples of this type of direct intervention come from southern cities, where religious communities may have been stricter than those in Philadelphia, it is likely that some northern churches adopted southern practices as migration increased. The fact that in response to migration Baptists became the largest denomination in Philadelphia between 1900 and 1910 strongly suggests that local churches yielded some ground to the newcomers.[126]

Often overlooked by critics who claimed that black leaders coddled and protected criminals was the anticrime work of pastors and laymen outside of the church.[127] In fact, many church leaders wore multiple hats in their communities. Henry Phillips, rector of the Church of the Crucifixion, served on the board of the Starr Centre before the Wharton branch was formed; he later became the only black member of the city's first vice commission and was the first president of the Association for the Protection of Colored Women (APCW). The APCW's executive secretary, a black woman named Sadie W. Layten, served as the president of the Women's Convention of the National Baptist Convention. As part of a regional network of branches in Virginia, Maryland, and Pennsylvania and a national office in New York, the APCW's goal was to protect black women from being taken advantage of by labor agents who channeled unsuspecting southern migrants into vice work.[128] Layten's contacts with Baptist women were a valuable asset to the Philadelphia branch because the women frequently escorted newly arrived migrants to safe lodgings and found them jobs. If unsuccessful, APCW workers and church friends could take the migrants to headquarters in South Philadelphia for temporary shelter and domestic training. In 1905, the APCW was effectively the first and only black-run crime prevention agency in Philadelphia.[129]

Reverend Tindley of East Calvary M. E. was just beginning to establish another crime prevention agency separate from his church in 1907 when he came across Stemons's crime article and began to share ideas with Stemons.[130] Two years later Tindley launched his Beacon Light Institute for Civic and Moral Reforms. He described the institute as "undenominational [sic] or sectarian," open to "everybody white and colored," yet by scheduling the institute's mass meetings on Sunday afternoons at the Old Bainbridge Street M. E. church, he appealed directly to church laymen. "If you are good, come and help us to make others so," Tindley wrote. "Some bad person is waiting on the action of your goodness to make them better; don't talk about them, but help them. The newspapers

and the enemies of the race will do the talking." Tindley's distinction between helping and talking is an important indication of his discomfort
with the common practice of conflating crime issues and antiblack rhetoric as an excuse for inaction. At the first of four mass meetings, the
work ahead was clearly proposed: "What can be done to rid the street
corners, in this city, of the poorly dressed, ill mannerly, and objectionable peoples of our race?" The remaining meetings sought solutions to
the additional problems of morally corruptible leisure activities and domestic violence.[131]

When Stemons saw the institute's flyer announcing upcoming meetings, he wrote a note that the first meeting's topic was the "subject of my
paper." In the summer of 1909, shortly after Stemons had recovered from
his lackluster results at the founding conference of the NAACP and after
he had written another article, "The Influence upon the Race Situation of
the Venal and Vicious Element among Negroes," he and Tindley officially began to work together on a third crime prevention organization.[132]
Within a few weeks Stemons wrote to the members of the A.M.E. Preachers
Meeting, hoping for an invitation to speak in order to build support. In
the letter Stemons presented the usual evidence of blacks' losing ground
in domestic and personal services and being effectively locked out of industrial work, but this time to strengthen his appeal he encouraged the
preachers to consider the evidence in light of their own self-interests,
since their churches would "lose force and support" if job discrimination
worsened.[133] Curiously, Stemons made no mention of crime. He explained to his sister that he did not want to tell them his "plans or ideas"
until they invited him to speak.[134] More than likely, however, Stemons
took a page from Tindley's playbook and decided to tone down the crime
rhetoric while he was still seeking support. Apparently, hiding his trump
cards did not work: the A.M.E. ministers passed on him despite Tindley's
backing as a Methodist Episcopal preacher.

Stemons may have actually made a mistake when he decided to emphasize industrial repression without talking about crime. Du Bois's *The
Philadelphia Negro* had already shown that explaining black criminality
was critical to getting people's attention and helping them to fully understand that racism and discrimination had destructive consequences for
the city in general and black communities in particular. In the book's opening pages, Du Bois noted that most whites believed that crime defined the
Negro Problem, which explained blacks' low status or slum existence, but
he immediately instructed whites to reverse their thinking and recognize

their own prejudice as the problem. Much later in the book, he also pointed out the reluctance of middle-class blacks to do their part to uplift the "submerged tenth" for fear of losing their own respectability. But Du Bois rejected their apathy, arguing that they had an obligation to help the poor and criminal.[135]

Following in a direct line from Du Bois circa 1899, Stemons's used the same rhetorical approach, appealing to right-thinking people on the basis of fairness and the need for equal opportunity or to suffer the consequences. Stemons had in fact already begun to make this argument to influential whites by writing crime articles and holding meetings. He had recently obtained the endorsement of Temple University's president Russell H. Conwell, also the pastor of Baptist Temple, who, Stemons boasted, was "perhaps the wisest and most favorably known Baptist clergyman in the world."[136] But in one of his first attempts to gather support from influential blacks, he went only halfway. Du Bois had argued that the respectable status that the "Talented Tenth" attempted to preserve by keeping their distance from the "submerged tenth" could be strengthened through racial uplift. That is, black middle-class people could better define their class position and move the whole race forward by adopting the same attitude and behavior white progressives had shown toward their white-skinned social inferiors, which included modest attempts to improve economic conditions and crime prevention. Stemons got it right the next time and would never abandon this dual focus again.

In his opening statements to the Baptist Ministerial Conference on November 15, 1909, Stemons blamed economic discrimination for crime among young blacks: "I know, and you know, that there are countless thousands of Negro youth . . . who absolutely refuse to expend time and money in training and fitting themselves for the higher walks of life, and who are becoming depraved, and reckless and criminal, because of the persistent manner in which every door of opportunity is slammed in their faces." Du Bois could not have said it better. Stemons continued, "If you do not believe it, come with me to almost any community populated largely by colored people, or come with me on a public conveyance on which there chances to be a large number of Negroes, and I will show you enough in one day to almost make you ashamed of the fact that you are identified with the colored race." But "economic restrictions," he reiterated, were "directly responsible."[137]

In rhetoric alone, Stemons easily crossed the line into criminalizing jobless and underemployed blacks, diluting the strength of his attack on industrial repression. But Du Bois had done the same thing, according to his biographer. "When it came to African American morality Du Bois's measure was a rigid Calvinist ruler," David Levering Lewis writes. "The racially disproportionate crime rate that he deplored owed much to feeble group morality, but crime was at bottom symptomatic of systemic ills."[138] For black writers and reformers, then, highlighting black criminality was a double-edged sword.[139] At the same time that it carved out space to create a dialogue with liberal whites about racism's consequences and middle-class blacks about their duty to the race, it defended the conservative self-help solution that dominated the pace of racial reform before Washington's death in 1915 and the onset of the Great Migration. This conservative edge was not what Stemons or Du Bois had intended to use; nevertheless, historian Kevin Gaines is right to call the "discourse of uplift, the urban counterpart to industrial education."[140] In this sense, racial uplift discourse and black crime rhetoric made antidiscrimination complaints more palatable to northern audiences, at least to those willing to listen at all.

It is crucial to emphasize the distinction between direct complaints against economic discrimination and subtle appeals for expanded economic opportunity. The latter approach did not necessarily depend on a critique of black crime, nor did it explicitly recognize white racism as a major cause of the problem. Instead, it turned the presumption of prejudice as a cause into a subject for investigation and shifted attention toward blacks' industrial inefficiency and need for further education and training.

In contrast to Stemons's antidiscrimination complaints at the Baptist Conference, the Armstrong Association of Philadelphia (AAP) perhaps best illustrates the subtle approach to economic reform. The AAP, named for General Armstrong, was originally a group of local philanthropists like those in the New York Armstrong Association who raised money for Hampton and Tuskegee. After Carl Kelsey, a University of Pennsylvania sociologist, introduced his student Richard R. Wright, Jr., to John T. Emlen, a member of the AAP and a white teacher at Hampton, Wright convinced Emlen that the AAP should use its connections to help blacks "get skilled jobs." While working on his dissertation as a research fellow at the Eighth Ward Settlement, Wright had become aware of the need for such an organization after interviewing a large number of southern mechanics who could secure jobs as porters and menial workers only.[141]

Thus the new AAP was launched in May 1908. Emlen raised funds and Wright found jobs as treasurer and field secretary respectively. Since the AAP used its wealthy contacts and Wright himself as a sterling example of the race's "best" men, the association did not have to use fear tactics to get supporters as it sought to match highly qualified workers with sympathetic employers.[142] Besides, for the men the AAP identified and helped, crime presumably was not a paycheck away. The AAP also minimized the appearance of radical reform or the necessity for aggressive rhetorical strategies by relying on a conservative case-by-case approach rather than by seeking broad access for all types of black workers. When opportunity remained closed, there were no protests or mention of social consequences; the AAP simply determined whether "prejudice, improper supervision, or inefficiency" was the cause and whether it could be "remedied."[143]

Adding to the organization's conservative methods, its president, Carl E. Grammer, rector of St. Stephen Protestant Episcopal and a "very charming Southern gentleman," imposed his own ideas about the limits of economic reform. Wright wrote in his autobiography that Grammer preferred giving blacks charity rather than jobs on an equal basis with whites, and that he "condoned" unions that discriminated against blacks and counseled patience over action. Because of Grammer, the first three field secretaries of the AAP, all black, resigned after serving one-year terms. B. F. Lee, the third to resign in 1912, referred to Grammer as a "Southern missionary trying to covert the North to his Southern way of thinking about colored people."[144]

The AAP became part of a national movement as an affiliate of the National Urban League (NUL) shortly after its founding in 1910. During the Great Migration the NUL became the premier organization for the "adjustment" of southern migrants to northern cities, combining the ideas of the Association for the Protection of Colored Women and the Armstrong Association. Under the leadership of Columbia University sociologist George Edmund Haynes, the Urban League also commenced a major program of training black social workers to increase efforts on behalf of struggling blacks. But the NUL "floundered" before 1916, according to historian Nancy Weiss, who notes that during its earliest years the Philadelphia affiliate was in fact more successful at obtaining jobs. This is a testament to the extreme conservatism of the premigration NUL, whose membership was dominated by black educators allied with Booker T.

Washington. Their "dependence on white philanthropy, the influence of white churches, and the prevalent faith in industrial education all promoted a certain conservatism" among them.[145]

During the Great Migration and into the 1920s and 1930s, the NUL became much more successful at job placement, owing a great deal to the labor demands of wartime production and the cessation of immigration. Leadership also changed hands in 1917, from Haynes to the younger and less conservative Eugene Kinckle Jones.[146] As the NUL became more aggressive in its pursuit of jobs for skilled and unskilled black migrants, it also began conducting nationwide studies of black life, including crime surveys, sometimes with the financial support of corporate-sponsored philanthropy.[147] During this period the NUL also adopted racial uplift discourse. In a letter distributed to the black press at the height of the migration, Jones urged "right-thinking Negroes . . . to discourage the wholesale migration of shiftless people," since "indolent, inefficient men," quick to lose their jobs, would only "become a burden to the Northern communities and bring reproach and humiliation to thrifty colored citizens in communities where white people [had] not hitherto considered Negroes undesirables."[148] The organization also resorted to using crime rhetoric to stir its white supporters to greater involvement and largesse. A National Urban League Bulletin in 1917 portended the social consequences if migrants were "permitted to pack themselves into overcrowded colonies and drift into disease and crime through sheer ignorance of how to live and how to find work and hold a job in the North." Through the intervention of the NUL, the bulletin announced, migrants could be "taken hold of upon their arrival and . . . taught how to become independent, productive citizens at a time when effective labor is at a premium."[149] Throughout the 1920s and 1930s, the NUL continued its strategy of appealing to white philanthropists and businesses through depictions of blacks' desperate economic and social conditions in various northern cities, including Philadelphia. The cold facts presented in the organization's *Opportunity* magazine painted a clear picture to white readers: Pay now with jobs and structural improvements, or pay later with juvenile delinquency, crime, and disease. Yet during the Great Migration, the National Urban League and its affiliates shifted slightly to the left while adopting an increasing focus on crime at the expense of southern migrants.

Foreshadowing the AAP's eventual change in direction, important members began to publicly support Stemons at the time of the Baptist conference in late 1909. Tindley was already behind Stemons before the conference, while serving as one of two "colored" vice presidents of the Armstrong Association. The other black vice president, W. A. Creditt, introduced Stemons at the conference along with E. W. Moore, the Public Meetings committee chairman of the AAP.[150] In addition to Creditt and Moore's credibility as executives of the AAP, their support of Stemons was significant to black Baptists in Philadelphia. Creditt was pastor of the oldest Baptist church in the city, First African Baptist (established in 1809), which had the third-largest Baptist congregation, and Moore headed the fourth-largest congregation at Zion Baptist.[151]

Supporting Stemons's plans, Tindley, Moore, and Matthew Anderson, pastor of Berean Presbyterian and president of Berean Manual Training and Industrial School, signed their names to Stemons's published call for a "Negro Conference" to be held in the spring of 1910. They also issued a public statement in defense of Stemons's speech to the Baptists. Stemons's "solemn representations" of the race's economic and moral slide, they wrote, had caused some "colored clergymen" to withhold their endorsement of the "Race Conference." Feeling it their duty to take seriously their colleagues' objections, they investigated the evidence for themselves. "Being optimistically inclined, we could not, and would not believe his sweeping statement in this connection till he had confronted us with facts and figures, which are backed by the outspoken testimony of many of the most eminent, conservative and impartial sociologists of the country, white and colored alike. These facts have astounded and amazed us, and we feel that he minimized, rather than magnified, the true situation when he expressed grave apprehensions for the future of Negroes in this country, unless positive steps are taken to remedy the monstrous and depressing conditions which are being imposed upon the masses of the race."[152]

To corroborate Stemons's testimony, they could have consulted any one of the national black-crime experts, such as Frederick Hoffman, W. E. B. Du Bois, William H. Thomas, or Walter Willcox.[153] Whichever source they used, their official endorsement worked. Not only was the conference going forward as planned, but Washington had gotten wind of Stemons's rising influence. He may have even heard Stemons's address to the Baptists or read the public statement since he was in town around the same time and had spoken at Creditt's church.[154] Two days before his conference was to begin, Stemons received an invitation to the annual

OUR MISSION;

To Broaden the Opportunities of Colored Citizens for Honest Labor at Living Wages.

To suppress Corner-lounging, Public Indecency, Vicious Resorts and Political Crookedness among Colored Citizens.

THE JOINT ORGANIZATION

OF THE

ASSOCIATION FOR EQUALIZING INDUSTRIAL OPPORTUNITIES

AND THE

LEAGUE OF CIVIC AND POLITICAL REFORM

Figure 4-4 "Dual Mission" handbill of the Joint Organization of the Association for Equalizing Industrial Opportunities and the League of Civic and Political Reform, articulating Stemons's programmatic response to W. E. B. Du Bois's call for whites to police racism and for middle-class blacks to police their own criminals. The Historical Society of Pennsylvanian (HSP), James Samuel Stemons Papers.

Tuskegee conference. "We shall be very glad to offer you the hospitality of the school and to make your visit here pleasant and profitable," Washington wrote.[155]

Held at the "colored" YMCA on November 21–22, 1910, the race conference turned out to be the first public event of the Association for Equalizing Industrial Opportunities and League for Civic and Political Reform (AEIO-LCPR). Stemons's dream had finally come true: a dual-approach reform organization with major support from black and white heavyweights. Among white clergymen, the first day's proceedings were presided over by Alexander MacKay-Smith, the Protestant Episcopal Bishop of Pennsylvania, and the meeting was called to order by A. J. Rowland, the secretary of the American Baptist Publication Society. Speeches by Stemons, Tindley, and Carl Kelsey of the University of Pennsylvania focused on the problem of black criminality. Specifically, Stemons addressed the issue of political repression and the need for "civic virtue and political independence," calling blacks "politically dishonest." Tindley's address was titled "The Depraved and Rowdy Element among Negroes, and How They Aggravate the Race Situation." He argued that the paths to crime for blacks were far more numerous than the paths to legitimate opportunity. Finally, Kelsey added his perspective as a white progressive to the day's coverage of blacks' "shortcomings." "We must fill the [N]egroes with a profound dissatisfaction with themselves before a beginning toward their improvement is made," he said, because "there has been too much coddling" by "a certain class of whites" who "pitied" the freedmen. After the paradoxes of racial reform vis-à-vis racial condemnation had been shared for all to ponder, the first day closed with a discussion. The panelists included T. Thomas Fortune, editor of the *New York Age;* Francis Bartholomew, head social worker of the Eighth Ward Settlement and member of the AAP's education committee; and P. A. Wallace, pastor of Wesley A.M.E. Zion, the largest black church in Philadelphia.[156]

The second day shifted from crime and racial uplift to discrimination and industrial opportunity. The structure remained largely unchanged, but there were new dignitaries and speakers, such as Howard University's president Wilbur P. Thirkield and B. F. Lee, Jr., field secretary for the AAP.[157] Although the Tuesday evening speeches were no less significant than those of Monday afternoon, there was less press coverage.[158] Two Philadelphia dailies, the *Public Ledger* and *North American,* reported on the first day's events, highlighting portions of the main addresses and quoting from the anticrime resolution of the newly formed League of

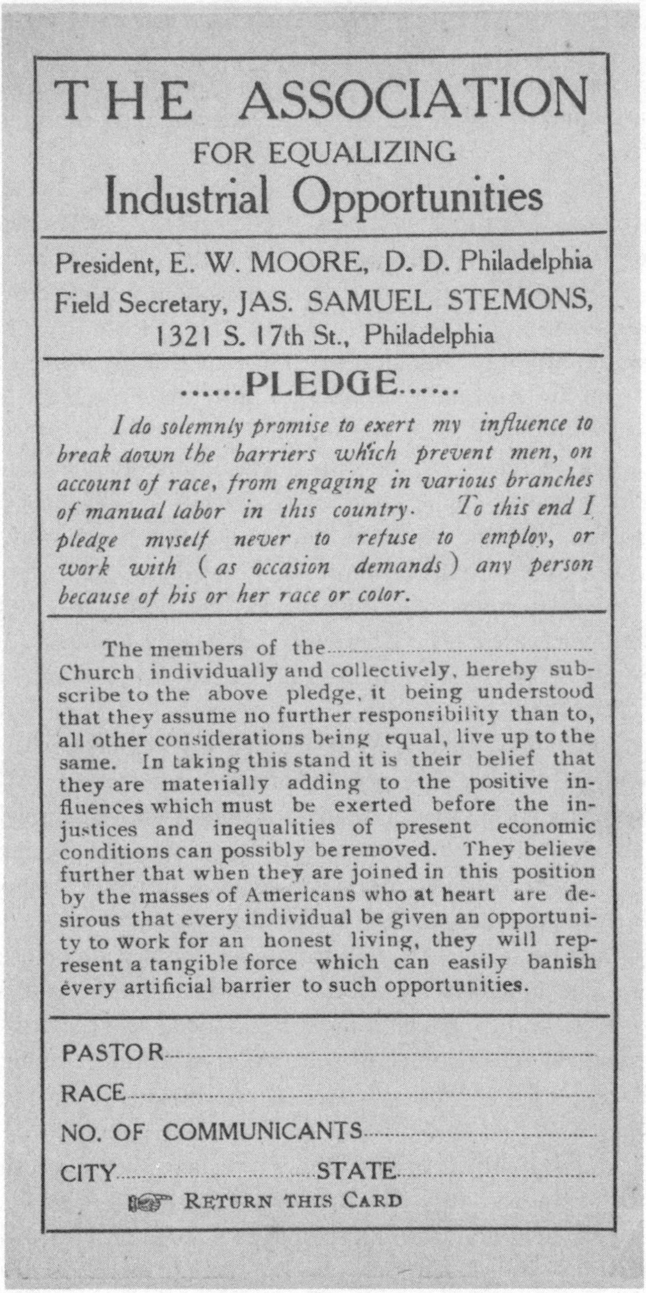

THE ASSOCIATION
FOR EQUALIZING
Industrial Opportunities

President, E. W. MOORE, D. D. Philadelphia

Field Secretary, JAS. SAMUEL STEMONS, 1321 S. 17th St., Philadelphia

......PLEDGE......

I do solemnly promise to exert my influence to break down the barriers which prevent men, on account of race, from engaging in various branches of manual labor in this country. To this end I pledge myself never to refuse to employ, or work with (as occasion demands) any person because of his or her race or color.

The members of the................ Church individually and collectively, hereby subscribe to the above pledge, it being understood that they assume no further responsibility than to, all other considerations being equal, live up to the same. In taking this stand it is their belief that they are materially adding to the positive influences which must be exerted before the injustices and inequalities of present economic conditions can possibly be removed. They believe further that when they are joined in this position by the masses of Americans who at heart are desirous that every individual be given an opportunity to work for an honest living, they will represent a tangible force which can easily banish every artificial barrier to such opportunities.

PASTOR................

RACE................

NO. OF COMMUNICANTS................

CITY................ STATE................

☞ RETURN THIS CARD

Figure 4-5 Pledge Card of the Association for Equalizing Industrial Opportunities distributed to members of white churches for the purposes of committing them to color-blind hiring practices and to ending economic discrimination. The Historical Society of Pennsylvanian (HSP), James Samuel Stemons Papers.

Civic and Political Reform (LCPR) adopted at the end of the panel discussion. The opportunity was ripe for both newspapers to trumpet anti-black crime rhetoric as stated by an obviously sympathetic crowd. White readers of these papers would also not miss the implicit admission of a black crime problem in the reporting of an interracial cast of prominent race leaders calling for "self-respecting negroes" to police their own communities by reporting crime to the "proper authorities."[159] By basically calling for community policing before it became a staple in the arsenal against inner-city crime, the League of Civic and Political Reform represented a practical response to Du Bois's earlier proposition that the "duty of the Negroes" in Philadelphia should "first be directed toward a lessening of Negro crime." True to his moral sensibility in 1899, Du Bois had suggested that Negroes start by making their homes incubators of self-respect that taught that "idleness and crime [were] beneath and not above the lowest work."[160]

In 1910 Stemons's LCPR merely changed the venue and broadened the scope of Du Bois's proposition. Taking its fight to the street, the LCPR distributed a handbill titled "To Self-Respecting Colored Citizens." The handbill addressed men and women of "refined sensibility" who were ashamed of the "rowdy, ruffianly, blatant, foul-mouthed, corner-lounging, dive-infested elements among them." To rid the race of "this stigma," they were instructed to "report every such crime against decency" to the LCPR. A pledge to show "moral support" for the organization was also required. Besides helping to "prosecute and penalize the dissolute and criminal elements among Negroes," pledge signers promised to hold city officials politically responsible for any dereliction of policing duty. No "administration of whatever party" would be allowed to ignore the LCPR's demands for the "suppression" of any activity "manifestly hurtful to the morals or good name" of the black community.[161]

The LCPR planned to alter the course of crime prevention among blacks nationwide, using the church as a source for recruitment and a sphere of influence. "It is purposed to get" the support of "every colored pastor in every community," an internal document noted, "to use his utmost influence to induce his entire congregation to do the same." Stemons, Tindley, and their influential supporters used the rhetoric of criminality to build a black army against it. Although they could draw rhetorical and practical examples from the anticrime work of settlement houses, institutional churches, the Association for the Protection of Colored Women, and the Women's Movement of the National Baptist Convention, there was no exact precedent for what they were attempting to do. They were not only engaging directly in crime prevention, but they were demanding better policing and by extension better accountability of municipal services as well. They were indirectly attacking the political support for mostly white-owned vice industries, such as speakeasies, brothels, and gambling dens. Most importantly, they were explicitly linking these battles to a broader war for economic and racial justice in the North.[162]

The LCPR was organized as an auxiliary of the Association for Equalizing Industrial Opportunities (AEIO), which planned to wage war against economic discrimination by whites. Using its influential white supporters, the AEIO would "appeal directly to the owners and employees" of businesses to "give merited recognition to coloured [sic] labor." They also expected to use employer surveys to research every angle of a company's "willingness or unwillingness to employ or work with Negroes, and why." In addition, the AEIO would ask white churches, starting with the congregations of the ministers involved with the organization, to take a collective pledge "when possible," and "individually when necessary," to actively broaden color-blind industrial opportunities.[163] Although the AEIO overlapped with the leadership, methods, and goals of the AAP, it planned to work on behalf of the masses *and* the mechanics. This is a further testament to the AEIO's serious desire to achieve immediate economic opportunity for blacks in the North when most interracial reform organizations were focused on industrial education or civil and political rights in the South.

Stemons's personal life deserves some credit for the AEIO's broader attack on economic discrimination. While the organization was building support, he was working twelve hours a day at the post office where, in his opinion, too many "brilliant" blacks found their best chance for respectable work.[164]

The freshly launched joint organization held two mass meetings during the next year and continued to recruit local leaders. For example, the very successful criminal defense attorney G. Edward Dickerson came onboard.[165] With popularity in the black press likened to the late Johnny Cochran's, Dickerson was the star personality in several major cases, some of which pitted his clients against the Philadelphia police, who were accused of being heavy-handed and quick-triggered. The *Public Ledger* also continued to show its support for Stemons, establishing a fund for donations in the organization's name. One of the fund's trustees was Henry Wilbur, the influential secretary of the Annual Conference of

Friends.[166] By the end of 1911, the AEIO-LCPR had enlisted the city's highest official, the newly elected head of the Keystone reform party, Mayor Rudolph J. Blankenburg.

But at this moment of greatest potential, the organization seemed to elevate its attack on crime above its war on economic injustice. Stemons had always insisted on linking the two, but because of his own need to become a recognized race leader, the personal jealousies and distrust of local leaders, the numerous competing agendas of other reform organizations, and the failure of too many whites to treat blacks as equals and to accept their responsibility for blacks' shortcomings, Stemons's rhetoric of black criminality quickly became the organization's passport to relevance. Writing to Blankenburg four days after his election, Stemons congratulated him, enclosed a copy of the "Appeal to Self-Respecting Colored Citizens," and wrote: "The colored people of this, and every other large city, furnish far too large a quota of venal [and] vicious . . . characters." He closed by expressing his desire to obtain the mayor's aid in the "suppression of this element."[167]

Less than two months later, on January 6, 1912, Stemons escorted an interracial delegation of some of his most prominent supporters to visit the mayor. Stemons made a "very brief address." In reply, Stemons told his sister, the mayor "assured" the delegation "of his most hearty sympathy with us and the colored race generally."[168] Although there is no complete record of what Stemons said to the mayor, the press account gave a strong indication of what the public wanted to hear. The Philadelphia *Inquirer* made no mention of economic discrimination or that the delegation included any white members. Instead, it highlighted little more than what was said regarding crime. "Reference was made by the speakers of the delegation and the Mayor to crimes to which the colored man is alleged to be addicted," announced the *Inquirer*.[169] Stemons also noted the one-sided press coverage in the *North American*, Pennsylvania's second-largest daily. "They left out the chief things I wrote about the Negro's disadvantages," he complained, "[and] . . . from the reports which I have seen they dwelt strongly on the side that related to criminality among Negroes."[170]

This watershed moment for his organization revealed the degree to which appeals to whites for racial reform depended on black leaders' willingness to traffic in the rhetorical currency of black inferiority. Stemons chose crime, as had Du Bois a decade before. Booker T. Washington testified to blacks' present incapacity for higher learning, political leadership, and in most cases social equality. Black Baptist women—Sadie Layten and clubwomen like Nannie Burroughs, president of the National Training School for Women and Girls—singled out sexual depravity among working-class black women. This is not to say that black leaders were not ambivalent about their social inferiors, as surely many white progressives were with respect to European immigrants. It is only to say that their public arguments in defense of their race hinged on conceding shortcomings in ways that white progressives' arguments in favor of immigrant advancement did not. The anticrime work of white settlement house workers examined at the beginning of this chapter illustrates the difference between their strategies and those of black reformers. White progressives helped to shape public knowledge about the need for structural change among immigrants, in contrast to racial change among blacks. Also, unlike black reformers, white progressives did not endure the personal pressure to define their respectability or right to middle-class standing as a negation of working-class culture and class, even though they accrued social status nevertheless. But the crucial point is that white progressives had access to money, power, and the ability to effect reform in ways that did not have to come at the expense of immigrants. The same cannot be said for black-organized reform in the North prior to the Great Migration.[171]

The benefits of Stemons's campaign for economic reform in 1912 were dubious, if not elusive. Although his supporters shared many of the same contacts as the successful Armstrong Association of Philadelphia, and the AAP made an offer to the AEIO-LCPR to join together, there is no evidence that the organization achieved any success in broadening industrial opportunities. Yet as a measure of the attractiveness of the organization's crime-prevention potential, the black branch of the Philadelphia YMCA offered to absorb it and to pay Stemons a full-time salary as a director.[172]

The costs seemed immediately apparent. Not more than a month after his meeting, Stemons anxiously informed his sister that he had read that Mayor Blankenburg and his director of public safety had "proposed among the white people the exact counterpart of my League—an association which should co-operate with the police, and report to them any disturbance, any law-breaking . . . any disorder of any kind." Stemons continued, "By good citizens and public officials thus acting together, the Director declared, almost perfect order in the city could soon be produced." Stemons could not believe what had happened. He was shocked that neither he nor any representatives of his organization had been invited to participate, except for one white clergyman who had left the organization on bad terms. Sounding exasperated, he wrote, "The whites have hitherto gone ahead with their meetings just as though no Negroes existed."[173] A month later the mayor officially announced the establishment of the first vice commission in Philadelphia. Just as Stemons had feared, no blacks were invited to serve on the commission.[174] Stemons believed that his penalty for highlighting black criminality was that his community policing idea had been stolen. Seeing himself as a proponent of reform rather than a source of contempt, Stemons did not see the obvious: that his efforts would contribute to the further stigmatization of blacks as criminals, regardless of whether blacks served on a vice commission or not.

Still, Stemons cannot be totally blamed for missing this point. He was not the only one who appeared at times to focus more on the need for black crime fighters than on seeking economic justice. A black columnist for the *Philadelphia Tribune,* for example, was also troubled by the absence of blacks on the commission and wondered whether prejudice was the cause. He contacted Mayor Blankenburg's office to investigate, only to be told a naked lie that "not a colored preacher had ever written a line on the matter or evidenced the slightest interest concerning vice." This was a self-serving misrepresentation for the mayor's benefit, though its meaning would not become clear until after the commission completed its work the following year. Without further question or apparent awareness of Stemons's mayoral visit, the columnist went on to blame blacks for not taking an active interest in crime. "I have tried to urge our folks to bestir themselves on this vice problem," he wrote, but to no avail.[175] Anticipating the worst in the coming year, the columnist cynically concluded, "Now our white friends will take the matter up, and as usual, they will lay all the blame of bad conditions at the door of colored people."[176]

5

FIGHTING CRIME:

POLITICS AND PREJUDICE IN THE
CITY OF BROTHERLY LOVE

The pace of crime prevention among progressives that began at the dawn of the twentieth century accelerated during the second decade. Social, moral, and political reform also continued to gain the lion's share of their attention. Although these reformers were sometimes fierce critics of industrialization's hunger for cheap labor and insensitivity to the quality of workers' lives, they mostly chose to wage battles outside the workplace. Soliciting the financial support of business owners and participating on the boards of various social agencies, progressives rarely challenged the inherent inequalities in the economic system. A conflicting story emerges when one compares what these liberals believed with what they were willing to fight against. They claimed that crime was more a function of economic forces than of individual moral failure, yet between 1911 and 1917 many of them initiated or supported vice crusades in major cities such as Chicago, New York, Philadelphia, and New Orleans. Their actions spoke louder than their words as they formed urban vice commissions to investigate and eliminate prostitution, gambling, and illegal drug use and trafficking. Like the settlement house movement, the movement to close red-light districts—the Tenderloin, as the district was called in Philadelphia—focused once again on the symptoms of inequality rather than on the causes, and this movement was as profoundly racialized.

Race mattered to city officials and reformers who hired former pimps and prostitutes to infiltrate the disorderly houses and gambling dens of Philadelphia in the spring of 1912. But proof of this claim is not necessarily revealed by the mistreatment of African Americans by Philadelphia's Vice Commission or its hired guns. Black reformer James Stemons had fought long and hard to bring black criminality to the attention of city authorities. Stemons had even credited himself for giving Mayor Rudolph J. Blankenburg the idea to commence a wide-scale assault on vice in Philadelphia with the help of ministers and reformers. That Stemons and the many supporters of the League of Civic and Political Reform (LCPR) demanded a coordinated response of concerned citizens and public officials to stamp out crime shows that blacks did not necessarily see aggressive crime fighting as inherently harmful to the race. For this reason, the work of the Vice Commission should have signaled a hopeful sign to black reformers that a broader effort was afoot to improve the quality of life for everyone: whites, immigrants, and blacks.

A major concern expressed by African Americans such as Du Bois, Stemons, and writers for the *Philadelphia Tribune* was that crime prevention among blacks had been too long ignored. There was also a booming body of evidence that anticrime forces that did descend on black communities acted with impunity and disregarded the individual rights of black citizens. In this thicket of paradoxical worries, blacks themselves contributed to the racialization of crime prevention by linking racial progress to crime fighting. In other words, although blacks needed the help of the city's mostly white police force to catch criminals regardless of race, blacks advocated crime fighting on the basis of what was good for the black community. They wanted to raise public awareness about crime among blacks in order to give their communities, particularly their vulnerable children, the same protection that white communities received. They also calculated that fewer black criminals would translate into better social treatment and more economic opportunity for the law-abiding. In 1912, however, Philadelphia city officials and reformers seemed to turn a deaf ear to the larger goals of black crime fighters. Instead, they accepted the premise that crime among blacks was a serious problem, but since less was at stake politically, white officials were unwilling to give it the same attention they gave crime among whites.

Vice raids against white members of the underworld were nothing new. All police districts in Philadelphia, most of which had majority white and immigrant populations, made vice arrests as part of their normal routine.[1] What was unique under the Blankenburg administration was an official policy of coordinated anti-vice efforts by the police, city officials, and citizens.[2] Upon taking office in December 1911, Blankenburg planned to keep a campaign promise to rid the city of vice.[3] As a political independent, he was beholden to neither the Republican machine that ruled Philadelphia and the state of Pennsylvania, nor the Democratic party, which had not run the city since the 1880s and would not run it again until the 1950s. Blankenburg was head of the Keystone party, a fusion party of anti-machine Republicans and Democrats who wanted to rid the city of political corruption.

To derail the Republican machine, Blankenburg attacked police corruption so that crooked politicians would no longer be able to pay for police protection. Police were the foot soldiers. Without their surveillance and strong-arm tactics at polling places, Republican candidates would be vulnerable to challenges by Democrats and reformers. The strength of the "Organization," as the machine was called, was its iron grip on the voters. Had the Republicans not been embroiled in an internal dispute between two warring machine factions, Blankenburg never would have had a chance to win the election. In the wake of the dispute, an unusual number of Organization loyalists failed to turn up at the polls, leaving room for Blankenburg to slip through. His winning margin of a paltry four thousand votes hardly qualified as a mandate by the voters.[4]

From the start of Blankenburg's administration, clear signals indicated that his new crime-fighting program would not be in the interest of color-blind law and order. The lack of results from the mayor's January 1912 meeting with Stemons's delegation of reformers and ministers to discuss better policing in black neighborhoods was the first clue that blacks' concerns would go unaddressed. By February the mayor had moved ahead with plans to assemble a committee of local anti-vice reformers, none of whom were black. In March Blankenburg met with U.S. Attorney General George B. Wickersham to coordinate local efforts to help the federal government combat white prostitution under the Mann Act.[5] Also known as the White Slave Law, the Mann Act made the transfer of white women across state lines for the purposes of prostitution illegal. Though mostly color-blind in its language (its popular moniker, an exception), the law was discriminatory in practice. Black women did not receive equal protection under the Mann Act, wherever it was applied.[6]

In the opening months of his administration, Blankenburg made it plain that he wanted to work with white moral reformers to save whites from becoming criminals. The Inasmuch Mission, for example, was located in "Hell's Half Acre," one of central Philadelphia's most notorious rough spots. At the center of a "district of vice," the mission was surrounded by as many as "65 houses being used for immoral purposes." Even the building owned by Inasmuch had a sordid past. It had once been known as a "get away house," complete with its own underground tunnel, and had also been the scene of a quadruple homicide. Crime flourished in this area, and the police were known to stand idly by—laughing, in some cases—while ownership of personal property was transferred via the force of arms. That was the situation the mission faced when it hired underworld investigators to tip off Blankenburg's policemen about criminal activity. By May 1912 the area was declared clean. One newspaper headline announced, "Hell's Half Acre Now Respectable."[7]

G. Grant Williams, an African American journalist and *Philadelphia Tribune* editor, called the crackdown an attempt to turn the area into a "white settlement." He observed that under the previous administration the area's black residents had not received any police protection. Now the area was swarming with police, but the beneficiaries of the mission's collaboration with the police, Williams charged, were the "white tramps and bums" who came from all over the city to use the mission.[8] Director of Public Safety George D. Porter had in fact praised the mission for its success. He compared it to Hull House, famous for its successful intervention in the lives of many impoverished whites and immigrants in a tough Chicago neighborhood.[9] Hull House offered limited services to its black neighbors.[10] The fact that Inasmuch Mission was following suit and becoming Philadelphia's model for a nearly whites-only, community-based policing mission did not bode well for the black residents of Hell's Half Acre. Williams complained, "What has the Inasmuch Mission done for the real residents of Hells [sic] Half Acre, who are colored people? Has it made any provisions for the colored children of the neighborhood to keep them away from the existing evils?" He concluded that Inasmuch was doing nothing to improve the conditions of black people.[11] The Inasmuch Mission became a major influence among local white moral reformers interested in redeeming the white underworld. In September, within four months of the mission's victory over crime, the Episcopal Church of Philadelphia absorbed Inasmuch, giving it the financial and institutional backing of a major religious organization.[12]

Episcopal churches were also beginning to take the lead in mission work among white prostitutes and pimps in North Philadelphia, an area with a much smaller population of blacks than South Philadelphia. Male evangelists inspired by the Social Service Committee of the Interchurch Federation visited the homes of residents in the Tenderloin with the "purpose of extending to men of the household an invitation to come to church." When they discovered a disorderly house, the evangelists notified the police, and raids were later conducted. "In this manner the men of the churches are engaged in what practically amounts to police work," the *Public Ledger* reported, "and are co-operating" with the police. Members of the Bible Class of Trinity Methodist Episcopal Church also conducted investigations to chart every disorderly house near the church building. To entice sinners, Trinity built a recreation room in the basement. James B. Ely, head of the Lemon Hill Association, also located in the Tenderloin, organized women missionaries from one hundred leading churches and synagogues to redeem "fallen women."[13]

The Inasmuch Mission likewise inspired individual white politicians. Former Thirty-third Ward councilman William Burke, who had recently revealed to the public that he was an ex-convict, announced plans to "devote the rest of [his] life to the uplift of the people of the underworld." Burke stated, "God knows they are the most miserable of all human beings. Almost every man's hand is against them, and those who have been behind the prison bars find it almost impossible to obtain employment. I know what they suffer. I have been through it. . . . I would like nothing better than to connect myself with that Inasmuch Mission which is doing such splendid work in their behalf."[14]

In an effort to draw attention to the absence of a "war on evils" in black communities, a column appeared in an October 5 issue of the weekly *Philadelphia Tribune*. Striking a cynical tone, the black columnist criticized the new administration's one-sided crusade: "Some people dreamed that with the coming of boasted Reform our street corners would be free of loafers; dens of vice would be closed, and a new condition of things would be seen. All, however, have been disappointed." Instead, the police in South Philadelphia continued to ignore the "corner loungers" who crowded the streets and harassed the innocent. According to the columnist, an especially "shameful sight" could be found on any Sunday afternoon near Allen A.M.E. church. Young children heading to Sunday School were "compelled to meet the insults of this motley throng, while the policeman jogs merrily on swinging his club."[15]

Arrest statistics strongly suggest that the *Tribune*'s criticism of the mayor's racially biased crime policy was accurate. By comparing arrest statistics for the year before Blankenburg took office—and the Philadelphia Vice Commission began—to those for the year the changes took effect, the immediate impact of the new crime policy can be measured. However, the statistics should be accepted cautiously as only one measure of change rather than as an accurate depiction of the amount of police activity or crime. Crime statistics were inherently flawed by political biases in

Philadelphia's criminal justice system and were as likely to exaggerate crime conditions as to underreport them, depending on the political climate. The Blankenburg reform years, 1912 to 1916, were exceptional, given Blankenburg's hard-line stance against police corruption and its ties to vice protection managed by Republican machine loyalists.[16] The city was also experiencing its first coordinated and sustained anti-vice crusade. Later in the 1920s, during Prohibition, anti-vice investigations would recur periodically, and police activity in white and black communities was grossly underrepresented by arrest statistics.[17] Police officers worked feverishly with suspected and known criminals to keep them from going to jail for most offenses short of murder. They were much more willing to accept payoffs to keep their pockets lined and criminals on the streets than to shut down a flush system of repeat offenders and repeat remittances.[18]

The sixth and eighth police districts, also the targeted areas of the Vice Commission's investigations, encompassed the main red-light district in Philadelphia. The Tenderloin extended directly north from the central business district into North Philadelphia. The population represented by these two police districts was overwhelmingly white and working class in 1912, with a small black population of similar economic status. The total number of arrests in these police districts was 12,523 in 1911 and 14,653 in 1912, a 17.0 percent increase. In the entire city over the same period, arrests rose only 9.7 percent. In South Philadelphia, the nineteenth district encompassed what could be called Philadelphia's Black Belt, although no ward in Philadelphia came close to having an all-black population. The nineteenth district had more black arrests than any other single district in the city, three times more than the next most active district among blacks, the adjacent second district. It also had the most black police officers in the city. Between 1911 and 1912, total arrests in the nineteenth district fell from 4,043 to 3,625, a 10.3 percent decline.[19] These statistics suggest how much more active the police were in the Tenderloin compared to the city as whole, and especially the predominately black area of South Philadelphia.

When the numbers are broken out by race, the results are even more dramatic.[20] White arrests in the Tenderloin districts rose 19.1 percent during 1912 compared to an 11.7 percent decline among blacks. Citywide, white arrests rose 11 percent, while black arrests fell 1 percent. Even juvenile arrests across the city followed the same pattern, with white youth arrests climbing a modest 0.1 percent, but black youth arrests falling

20.7 percent. The most striking change was seen in the nineteenth district of South Philadelphia, where black arrests fell sharply by as much as 21 percent, compared to a rise of 9.4 percent among whites.[21] Responding to the continued crisis facing black communities, the *Tribune* wrote, "[Public Safety] Director Porter may continue to praise policemen while thieves, robbers and bandits are holding a high carnival unmolested."[22]

The Vice Commission's final report confirmed the pattern of racial disparity suggested by the arrest statistics. White prostitution was the single most important issue raised by the commission. Over the course of several months the commission interviewed 3,311 women.[23] This number was not further disaggregated by race, but given the area of the city where the investigators did the bulk of their work there is no doubt that the overwhelming majority were white women.[24] The newspapers provided explicit clues as well when blotter-length articles mentioned that twenty white women were arrested in vice raids in the Tenderloin. Even when race was not mentioned in reports, as in the article about one hundred suspects arrested during raids of disorderly houses, the suspects were all white.[25] Integral to the main investigation of white prostitution, the commission also devoted considerable space to highlighting corruption among magistrates and policeman, the vast majority of whom were also white.[26] The only official acknowledgment of black participation in the mayor's anti-vice campaign was the delayed inclusion of the Reverend Henry L. Phillips on the commission.

In a context where crime fighting had become the mantra of the city's new reform mayor, whites looked after their own. The problem for black crime fighters was that saving their own meant working largely without the active support of the police, major city institutions, and influential politicians. The ultimate irrelevance of Stemons's League for Civic and Political Reform is a perfect case in point. The LCPR's program was basically identical to what white religious organizations and reformers were able to accomplish in the Tenderloin, but Mayor Blankenburg gave it no support, and the LCPR was thus unsuccessful. While it is impossible to know exactly why Blankenburg turned his back on the LCPR and denied the existence of black crime fighters like Stemons with whom he had agreed to work, more than likely he knew he could gain more political capital and success as a reform mayor by using the city's limited resources to clean up white areas.

The racially exclusive nature of Philadelphia's anti-vice movement echoed other incidents of racial discrimination involving Blankenburg's administration.[27] During the third week of January 1913, for example, the city held its first annual dinner for Public Works employees at Wanamaker's restaurant. Two black employees were refused admittance to the dinner. They were told by members of their own party that the white waiters refused to serve them. A Wanamaker spokesman challenged that claim, stating that the restaurant served everyone regardless of race. Given John Wanamaker's generous philanthropic support of southern black education, it seems unlikely that his restaurant would have been so blatantly racist.[28] A month later a *Tribune* investigator discovered that a southern white city employee who refused to be seated with his fellow black workers was behind the incident.[29] As a fusion party of independent Republicans and transplanted southern Democrats, Blankenburg's Keystone reform party was seemingly cut from the same progressive cloth as President Woodrow Wilson's administration. Suggesting that Blankenburg sponsored an unofficial policy of discrimination at City Hall, a *Tribune* columnist wrote that "an invisible sign hangs over the door in every department over which the Mayor presides." A more blatant example occurred when one of the city's highway commissioners was riding down a street in a carriage, commenting on how badly the streets needed repairing. Then he reportedly said, "We need not bother our heads about having this repaired because it is only occupied by niggers."[30]

Blankenburg's administration was evidently hostile to blacks. Although stricter civil service requirements were passed as part of Blankenburg's reform program, Benjamin E. Hinds, for example, was not given one of 150 jobs even though his exam score of 82.7 placed him fifty-fifth on the list of appointees. A score of 70 was the cutoff, and Hinds should have been a shoo-in for a civil service job. Director Porter did not acknowledge the injustice, but told Hinds to try again next time.[31] During the first several months of Blankenburg's term, at least nineteen black employees reportedly lost their jobs due to racism in city departments.[32] Heavily influenced by southerners, the reform administration had "no love for the Negro except it be as a servant or a menial," remarked a *Tribune* editorial.[33]

The administration's inimical attitude toward blacks was sometimes mirrored by violent confrontations between white citizens and police officers on one side and black citizens on the other. On September 21, 1912, Robert Henderson was escorting two women home from a party at about one o'clock in the morning. Although newspaper accounts differ as to exactly what happened next, for some reason Henderson began chasing three white young men. Henderson claimed that the men, two eighteen-year-olds and one nineteen-year-old, began "jeering" at him. The teenagers claimed that they were calling out to each other when Henderson mistook their yells as a personal affront. The young men threw two milk bottles in Henderson's direction, and Henderson drew a penknife. Upon noticing the "colored man" in hot pursuit of three white "boys," David Simpson, a white off-duty police officer, stepped in to block Henderson's path and was fatally stabbed. After fleeing the scene, Henderson was arrested. The teenagers were also picked up and held as material witnesses. Philadelphia's white press was unequivocal in its characterizations of Simpson as a hero: a loyal son, a young husband, and a father who died trying to protect white youths. Out of respect, the police station where Simpson had worked was "draped with black crepe" and had its flag "lowered to half staff." The *Evening Bulletin* even went a step further and characterized Henderson as a cold-blooded killer. The paper reported that at the moment of the stabbing Henderson had said, "I told you to keep away, so take this and you will learn better."[34]

Black men did not generally attack white youths or white police officers without provocation; the odds against them were simply too great.[35] However, the opposite scenario was not an unusual occurrence. In response to what happened, the *Philadelphia Tribune* regretted the death of Simpson but sympathized with Henderson's response, considering the danger he may have sensed from the teenagers. Henderson, the *Tribune* claimed, may have anticipated trouble, given the frequent attacks by white gangs on innocent blacks. "White roughs in the downtown district make it a practice to tantalize colored persons and frequently beat them unmercifully," the editorialist wrote. Worse still, if a policeman intervenes, "he invariably arrests the colored man who has been assaulted, and allows the white assailant to go scot free." Unlike the effort to improve crime control in North Philadelphia's most troublesome white areas, racial violence, wherever it occurred in Philadelphia, was not a priority among law enforcement officers. Many white policemen, the *Tribune* concluded, were simply not to be trusted because they usually sided with "white thugs" who made it a "night sport to assault one or more persons of color."[36]

The *Tribune* might have also mentioned that Henderson likely did not know that Simpson was a police officer since he was dressed in civilian clothes and standing on the corner with friends late at night. When

Simpson jumped out to subdue Henderson, Henderson probably panicked. Given that a black man had taken the life of a white police officer,
his defense attorney had to raise such questions in order to keep Henderson from going to the electric chair. At the trial during the first week
of December, Henderson's black attorney, G. Edward Dickerson, was
praised for winning the case with "strong" arguments.[37]

The same day as Henderson's acquittal, Dickerson was also recognized for representing a black physician, Thomas G. Coates, who had
been shot down a month before by two white police officers. Shortly after
midnight on November 1, 1912, Coates and his friend, D. Ogden, heard
a women "crying murder." When they rushed to her aid, they found two
white men beating an unarmed black man with blackjacks. Coates questioned the men, and one responded by swinging at him. Coates dodged
the blow, fell to the ground, and was shot twice at point-blank range. The
first bullet entered his "scalp behind the right ear and came out over the
temple." The second tore through his clothes but glanced off a button,
missing his flesh. Ogden was not harmed.[38]

When Coates and Ogden had come upon the scene, the two allegedly
drunk undercover police officers were brutalizing a black man, demanding to know to whom the man had paid police protection when he had
once owned a speakeasy. Ironically, police were willing to use illegal
means against blacks in the name of police reform. The facts that no one
was arrested and that Officers Martin Lyford and John Devinney made
no attempt to assist Coates added further proof of their unlawful intentions and deliberate "reckless[ness]." The *Tribune* did not hide its disgust
for what had happened, noting that "of late it is unsafe for a respectable
colored man to walk the streets after dark for fear of being assaulted."

Sometime between the attack on Henderson and the Coates shooting, Theodore Cuff was shot at twice by an officer while he was running to catch a trolley. He was unhurt but was then arrested for being a
"suspicious character." The charge was thrown out, and the officer was
reprimanded.[39]

Later in November yet another black man found himself in what he
perceived to be a life-or-death struggle with a white assailant. John Brown
was walking alone on November 28, 1912, when he was approached by
Steve McLaughlin. Based on witness accounts, McLaughlin asked Brown
for a match to light a cigarette. He also demanded a dime to buy a drink
at a nearby saloon. Without a match to give, Brown refused to hand over
any money. McLaughlin began beating Brown, sending him twice to the

ground. Upon rising the third time, according to a statement Brown made to the arresting officer, he shot McLaughlin three times. McLaughlin died at the hospital the following evening.[40]

According to half of the eight prosecutorial witnesses and six defense witnesses, McLaughlin was a very rough man. He drank regularly between sessions of corner lounging with his two friends, Albert Reilly and John Eagan, both known as "bums" by the local police. None of these three men held steady jobs, unlike John Brown who had worked at the water department for several years. Testifying for the prosecution, Officer Douglass said he had known McLaughlin for the past eleven years and had "never knowed [sic] him to work at any steady position." McLaughlin instead spent much of his free time building a "very bad" reputation, "always hunting for trouble." Officer Douglass testified that McLaughlin, a physically imposing figure, specialized in attacking black people: "His sole object was he had no use for colored men. If they walked up 20th street or 23rd street he would knock them down for nothing at all." On his deathbed, McLaughlin even admitted to Detective William Belshaw that he was as much to blame for being shot as was Brown for shooting him. "I was fighting with him," he added. True to form, the day McLaughlin was shot he had just been released from jail, having served a ten-day sentence for beating up a "colored" bootblack. Several police officers testified that McLaughlin had been arrested and served time on numerous other occasions. Detective John L. Porter stated that McLaughlin had been in the House of Correction "not less than fifteen or twenty times"; those convictions marked only the times when he had been caught.[41]

Brown's black coworker Russell Freeman testified for the defense that McLaughlin had also attacked him after demanding money for a drink. When Freeman told McLaughlin he did not have any money, McLaughlin "pulled out a pair of iron knuckles and he hit me over the eye and I will always have [a scar]." After a bystander pulled McLaughlin off Freeman, McLaughlin and "two of his buddies" followed Freeman home and began threatening him from the street. McLaughlin said, "What do you think, that black son-of-a-bitch comes all the way from the South with our money in his pocket and won't give us a dime. . . . Well we will lay for him and get him tonight." Freeman escaped further harm.[42]

In McLaughlin's North Philadelphia neighborhood, the increasing presence of black southern migrants, though still a small percentage of the population before the Great Migration, apparently touched off violent tendencies among some white men. African American men were the most underemployed and lowest-paid male workers in Philadelphia's prewar economy, and black city employees and civil service applicants were on notice that public jobs would go to white men first.[43] Complaints about blacks stealing whites' jobs thus had no basis in fact. McLaughlin's gang did not appear to be terribly interested in working anyway. Nevertheless, Brown and Freeman had been expected to pay a racial surcharge in either cash or blood for their hard work.

The fact that black men like John Brown and Robert Henderson armed themselves when walking Philadelphia's mean streets strongly suggests that they anticipated the kinds of racial attacks that the *Tribune* had noted were so common. Brown, characterized by his employer as a "quiet, peaceable man," had been attacked once before while working at the Water Department. Officer Douglass stated that he knew about the incident because a warrant had been sworn out for Brown's arrest. The officer testified that Brown was regularly harassed by his white coworkers. One of them went so far as to sodomize Brown by "putting his hand in his rectum and making a fool out of him." Brown "cut" the man in retaliation. Officer Douglass never served the warrant because the matter was "fixed up" and the "cutting didn't amount to anything." Brown was not so lucky the next time he used a weapon to defend himself.[44]

John Brown was tried twice for the death of Steve McLaughlin. The first trial occurred immediately after the shooting in the court of white popular justice. After hearing gunshots, several men ran from their houses in pursuit of Brown. John Feeney testified: "I came out to the door. I saw some boys running down the street and they hollered murder, and I ran out and followed this nigger up to 26th and Oxford, and then I caught him." The "big crowd" that caught Brown, which also included McLaughlin's buddies Reilly and Eagan, pummeled Brown to a pulp. "He was all beat up," Officer Douglass observed, "His eyes were swollen up and he was all marked up." Henderson narrowly escaped the same fate or worse after stabbing Officer Simpson, but the police managed to safely escort him to jail.[45]

Based on all the facts, Brown's defense attorney in the second trial could have argued self-defense or justifiable homicide. But on his attorney's advice, Brown did not make that claim in a courtroom. Sensing the anti-black mood of the community, and rather than taking the risk that a white jury might find Brown guilty of a more serious charge, Brown's attorney calculated that a judge, knowing the circumstances, would exercise greater reason after accepting a plea and would mete out a fair punishment. Before rendering his decision, Judge Norris S. Barratt, Jr., told the court that he did not agree with Brown's excessive use of force, but given McLaughlin's undeniably bad character, Brown's plea to manslaughter was appropriate. Judge Barratt rendered a relatively light sentence of eighteen months out of a possible twelve years, although a strong argument could be made that Brown should have walked, given that he had served six months awaiting trial.[46]

In the midst of Mayor Blankenburg's well-publicized anti-vice crusade, police reform and crime prevention among whites appeared to come at the expense of blacks' safety from assaults by white civilians and police officers. Within three months at least six black men and two black women (counting those accompanying Henderson) had been chased, beaten, or shot at without provocation at the same time that white reformers, ministers, and police officers were offering would-be white criminals a fresh start. Warning the city to take notice, the *Tribune* wrote, "It seems as though some of these white policemen have gone crazy, or else they are drunkards or dope fiends. Since the reformers have been in power, some of these crazy cops shoot at colored men as though they were squirrells [sic]."[47]

In December city officials took note by dismissing the officers involved in the Coates shooting. Police Superintendent James Robinson also issued a warning to all officers to stop using their guns unlawfully. His order read in part, "[A] police officer is not justified in using his revolver upon mere suspicion of a felony having been committed, much less a [mis]demeanor." The *Tribune* applauded the warning and, in response to the dismissal, expressed a sigh of relief that blacks would not have to go out and buy "firearms for self-protection."[48]

A few years later, southern blacks who migrated north in response to wartime labor shortages were singled out for carrying handguns in Philadelphia. For example, after sentencing several migrants from Greenwood, South Carolina, to jail terms, one judge said that he was going south to investigate "what caused all this meanness."[49] The judge did not need to leave town. Philadelphia played a significant part in encouraging blacks to arm themselves for self-defense, regardless of their native or migrant status.[50] Yet during this moment of increasing racial violence, it is very difficult to know just how many blacks who became violent offenders in the statistical record like John Brown or in the newspapers like Robert Henderson did so because they had to protect themselves. Incidents of racial violence contributed to the criminalization of African Americans.[51]

Philadelphia politics and the city administration played an instrumental role in the way crime was fought and was perceived by the public. Having gained public support, vice reform became a sympathetic movement to clean up predominately white neighborhoods and make new ones safe for whites, at the same time that vice reform largely ignored black neighborhoods. African American neighborhoods, however, could ill afford to be on the short end of a reform movement, given the structural handicaps that already plagued them. Low wages, unemployment, poor housing, and limited access to well-funded, politically popular social welfare agencies meant that, on the eve of the Great Migration, native black Philadelphians were already disproportionately suffering the social preconditions for crime.[52] The widespread belief that their inequality was linked to some racial or cultural fault of their own illustrates how profoundly critical the issue of crime was to defining black progress and potential. The stigma of criminality that in part defined the Negro Problem at the onset of the Progressive era was reinforced at the end of the period by the failure of white politicians and moral reformers to prioritize crime prevention among blacks as they had for whites. Because Progressive era moral reform was racially stratified and discriminatory, black criminality continued to be perceived as a racial problem and a reflection of black inferiority. Subsequent advances in racial reasoning that led to arguments about black cultural inferiority in the period just before and during the Great Migration were built on the assessment of crime as a persistent racial problem. There was little recognition that the black crime problem had been, and would continue to be, a truly collaborative project.

Putting 1912 behind but sensing the mood of the moment and the possibilities of renewal, the *Tribune* declared the "Future Is Promising" in a February 1913 editorial. It spoke to and for the optimism of black Philadelphians in spite of the crime problem:

> Some colored people, as well as some white people, appear to be somewhat discouraged because all our people are not saints, so to speak, forgetful of the fact that with centuries of freedom, civilization and education behind them, the white people themselves are guilty of committing all of the acts known in the calendar of crime. Taking it all in all, considering impartially, if possible, the depth

from which our folks have come, they are doing remarkably well, and were it not for the difficulties and discouragements in their path, they would have done infinitely more . . . The demand of the hour is that colored people themselves should strive to cultivate a stronger sense of faith and confidence in themselves. Of course, we have worthless ones among us. What people have not? But we have a number of worthy ones; let us pin our faith to the possibilities within them and not lose courage because it has been our luck to be disappointed in our transactions with others of the crooked sort. With all and in spite of all barriers, as a class, we can surmount them all, if we resolve to dare and do.[53]

The coming years would prove perhaps more difficult than the *Tribune* could have imagined.

The onset of wartime migration of African Americans to Philadelphia from southern farms and cities generated new discussions of black crime.[54] In part, this reaction was a simple calculation based on pure numbers: the more blacks who came to the city, the more crime that would follow. The link between black migration and crime had been firmly established at the end of the nineteenth century. But between 1900 and 1910, the highlighting of southern migrant criminality was all but muted in comparison to sweeping generalizations about the entire race. Prior to the wartime period, black migration to the North was largely born of individual motivations, which increased the population of newcomers but was not recognized as a mass movement or a coordinated one.

During the war, however, when labor agents, railroads, and black newspapers like the Chicago *Defender* became major proponents of migration, the movement became widely recognized, and criminality therefore gained broader attention.[55] Philadelphia's black population grew from 84,459 to 134,229 between 1910 and 1920, a sizable 58 percent gain, and blacks represented 7.4 percent of the 1920 population, compared to 5.5 percent in 1910 and 4.8 percent in 1900. New York City, home of the largest black population in the North, also witnessed a 66 percent increase during the decade of the teens. The Great Migration was a national phenomenon. Three Midwestern cities best illustrate the dramatic change. Cleveland's black population quadrupled in size, Detroit experienced a more than sevenfold increase, and the number of Chicago's black residents more than doubled between 1910 and 1920.

The wartime migration had such a big demographic impact that some contemporaries unwittingly distorted southern black criminality during the decade before. Looking to the immediate past, these observers virtually erased migrant crime from the historical record in order to emphasize it in the present.[56] The growth of the black middle class during the late teens throughout the twenties produced many black public intellectuals and reformers, some of whom tended to wax negatively about the roughness of black southern migrants, blaming them for the downturn in race relations. In their defense, the level of racial violence in the North had reached such a fever pitch by the bloody summer of 1919 that it may have been hard to imagine that white northerners could be so hateful on general principle alone. But this suddenly precipitous downturn had been gradually steepening since the turn of the century as measured by declining economic opportunity and residential immobility, as well as by increasing racial violence—the raison d'être of the NAACP in 1910. The debate about black southerners as a reason and justification for the increasing discrimination, segregation, and violence in the North was at least twenty years old by 1916, if one takes the publication of Frederick L. Hoffman's *Race Traits and Tendencies of the American Negro* in 1896 as the starting point. Blacks in Philadelphia, for example, had singled out southerners at least since Du Bois had famously done so in 1899. In 1914 the *Philadelphia Tribune* continued to do the same.[57]

The activist black newspaper began a series of editorials and articles in January that brought attention to a "number of corner loungers, idlers, [and] loafers" around the Thomas Durham elementary school. The school was a couple of blocks from the *Tribune* office in South Philadelphia, as well as near the black branch of the YMCA. According to the *Tribune,* "corner bums" harassed young black girls on their way to and from school, creating a serious threat to the girls' safety. The paper called for immediate action from concerned citizens, organizations, and the police. In the wake of the Vice Commission and the absence of police-assisted neighborhood watch groups, the *Tribune* did not hesitate to point out that the White Women's Christian Association had rallied crime fighters to break up a similar "corner assemblage" affecting a white school.[58] Within a week, the black female executive secretary of the Association for the Protection of Colored Women, Sadie W. Layten, and several teachers began an investigation. They then contacted the precinct lieutenant, who detailed officers to clear the streets. Police also raided a house that children had been seen entering. As a result of this investigation, a gang of young men and girls—one of them found "nearly" naked—was taken into custody. S. K. Whittle was singled out as the ringleader. It was his room in which, he claimed, the girls were being taught to become theatrical performers. Associating Whittle's crime with his southern roots, the *Tribune* wrote, "It is a great pity that he did not stay" in Norfolk, Virginia, because "he did not come here to better his condition and make of himself a good citizen."[59]

To the extent that black commentators had a hierarchy of blame for crime on the eve of wartime migration, blaming southerners did not rank at the top. Instead, they cast a much wider net, focusing on society's inequalities and inattention to black communities. J. R. Brock, principal of the Durham School, addressed the way to prevent such dangerous situations from reoccurring in the future. In addition to parents' taking greater responsibility for their children's safety, he wrote, "it is the duty of society . . . to make every highway safe, physically and morally. It is the duty of every place of business to keep its front free of loungers." Like Stemons and Du Bois, black commentators like Brock and the *Tribune* writers tried, if sometimes unsuccessfully, to strike a balance between blaming individuals and blaming society. That balance was echoed in their dual approach, summarized neatly by the *Tribune*'s response to the Durham School crackdown: a reignited commitment to fighting crime "from within" the race and "from without."[60]

Wartime migrants to Philadelphia were easy targets for intra-racial crime fighting because they suffered from not one but two social distinctions. Not only were many newcomers poor and desperate to take advantage of employment at shipbuilding yards and munitions plants, but they were also perceived to be distinctly backward in their social habits and culture. To the extent that class in the North had always distinguished between respectable, law-abiding blacks and the "submerged tenth," intra-racial southern culture became more meaningful and problematic to black northerners trying to minimize the stigma of criminality. What was new was the intensity of the rhetoric of blame toward southern migrants.

A representative example comes from the most authoritative study of the Great Migration in Philadelphia written by a contemporary, the first black woman to receive a doctorate from the University of Pennsylvania. Sadie T. Mossell's timely and well-received dissertation in economics was published in 1921 by the *Annals of the Academy of Political and Social Science*. Mossell analyzed the standard of living of one hundred migrant families, using household budget figures, to determine their degree of adjustment to life in Philadelphia. Concluding that most migrant families did not earn enough to meet the minimum standard of living to conduct decent lives, her research showed that the migrants had not only failed to adjust themselves to their new environment but were directly responsible for the downward turn in race relations. Mossell concluded:

> With few exceptions the migrants were untrained, often illiterate, and generally void of culture. On the other hand, there stood thousands of the native Negro population of Philadelphia, who had attained a high economic, intellectual and moral status. They found suddenly thrown into their midst about forty thousand migrants, whose presence in such large numbers crushed and stagnated the progress of Negro life. The process of assimilation which the colored citizens are carrying on cannot immediately bring back the pendulum which has swung to a position of depressed social, economic and moral life. Only gradually as the weights of ignorance, lack of culture, and increased racial prejudice aroused by the white people against the whole Negro citizenry as a result of the tremendous increase in the size of the Negro population, are removed, will the pendulum return to normal. The pessimist groans that it will never regain this position and points to the previous culture level of Philadelphia Negroes as if it had been permanently drowned by a torrent of migration. Certainly none of us can deny that the migration retarded the steady march of progress of the colored people in Philadelphia.[61]

Mossell's research is intriguing; had she not been primarily interested in blaming migrants for whites' stepping up their repression of black Philadelphians, she could have presented a stunning critique of structural inequality shaped by white racism. Two themes were particularly highlighted: segregation in housing and segregation in recreation. The housing shortage, as she noted, was the most critical issue affecting migrants. To make matters worse, whites violently resisted black expansion into predominately white areas, and landlords raised rents on already overcrowded and dilapidated housing.[62] The higher wages that brought the migrants north were canceled out by price gouging in the segregated black areas. Native blacks and migrants were underpaid and held the lowest-paying jobs despite the wartime flood of opportunity; they also paid the highest prices for essential goods and services, like food, clothing, rent, and insurance, relative to their white counterparts.

Despite such compelling evidence that migrants were not free to succeed or fail on their own individual and collective merits, Mossell saved her most passionate criticism for migrant criminality. "While crime and immorality among them never developed beyond control," she wrote, "many of their number were to be seen lounging on corners, frequenting dens of vice and saloons and arming themselves with razors and pistols, thereby increasing the number of court cases and greatly marring the records of the Negroes in Philadelphia and the peace of the city."[63] There is no doubt that corner lounging by whites and blacks was a problem in Philadelphia from the perspective of the middle class.[64] Moreover, the vice problem was endemic to the city's ruling Republican party. The saloon problem had reached such epic proportions in the entire country that the federal government would soon pass the Volstead Act to criminalize alcohol—America's favorite pastime. Finally, the possession of concealed weapons was arguably as much a reflection of criminal intent as it was a safety measure against random acts of racial violence.[65] None of these issues could be identified solely with southern blacks. Even without such nuances, Mossell's highlighting of migrant criminality was based on a false premise that, before the migrants arrived, the "Philadelphia Negro . . . had always enjoyed the same social and educational facilities as the whites and courteous treatment from them."[66]

Mossell was not the only observer to conflate white hostility and discrimination against blacks with some migrants' difficulty in quickly achieving middle-class social status and respectability. Life was rough in Philadelphia for many black newcomers despite the benefits of greater economic opportunity and social freedom relative to their southern communities. Emmett Scott, the first black assistant to the secretary of war, prepared a study of black migration during World War I. Scott argued that many migrants in Philadelphia had "used their liberty in their northern home as a stumbling block" by wasting their "high wages" in "saloons and dens of vice" to the "detriment" of themselves and the community.[67] Clearly, the idea of migrants' newly gained freedom in the North was used against them; Scott's characterization of liberty came with a built-in penalty. No matter how much migrants mirrored the behavior of their working-class white and northern-born black counterparts, they were resented for being strangers.[68] As outsiders, their behavior was a priori contemptible.

Forrester Washington, an African American researcher and head of the Armstrong Association of Philadelphia (a National Urban League affiliate), pointed this out in 1917: "Both the native colored and white people of our community have a feeling that the southern man is more criminal than the northern which creates a very unpleasant attitude towards the newcomers."[69] The contempt that black northerners felt toward southern strangers thus actually legitimized continued white prejudice against all blacks.

Other black reformers saw migrants' class status as a legitimate cause for alarm. "We need such Christian activities especially because of the class of colored people we are continually receiving from the South," wrote Henry Phillips of the Crucifixion Episcopal Church, a former member of the Vice Commission. "If we do not look after them in the right way, they are sure to look after us in the wrong way."[70] Phillips's use of an us-versus-them dichotomy as an argument for saving the black community mirrored the sentiment some whites had expressed throughout the Progressive era for stamping out black crime to save the city and/or the nation. Both uses obfuscated the reality of structural barriers and racist sentiment; the rhetoric implied that but for black migrants, there would have been no racial problems.

Critical to the idea of southern migrants as troublesome was the outbreak of race riots on an unprecedented scale in Philadelphia and surrounding areas in 1917 and 1918. The first outbreak occurred thirty-five miles south of Philadelphia in Chester, Pennsylvania. Chester's black population was in the process of doubling from forty thousand residents in 1914 to nearly eighty thousand by 1918. Migrant workers had flooded the small city to work at Baldwin Locomotive and the Sun Shipbuilding Company. White workers responded with uneasiness to the newcomers, especially by late July 1917 when ship workers went on strike. Chester's vice district was located in the Black Belt and became subject to public scrutiny during the migration. Given that it was a politically protected vice district, as was Philadelphia's under the new pro-vice leadership of Mayor Thomas B. Smith (1916–1920), blacks in general bore the brunt of public attacks on vice and crime. The conspicuous presence of so many strangers made blacks easy scapegoats for a system of political and police corruption that had been in place long before they arrived. Nevertheless, a series of robberies committed by blacks shortly before the riots played vividly in the racial imaginations of Chester's white residents.[71]

ADELLA BOND SHOOTS INTO MOB ATTEMPTING VIOLENCE

Police Disarm Colored Citizens and Then Help Mob Beat Them With Clubs.

OUR CITIZENS PRESENT A STRONG PROTEST

The mob rule spirit that made East St. Louis, Ill. and Chester, Pa., famous, has at last reached Philadelphia, and for the past week there have been a series of riots and disturbances which has resulted in several deaths.

The daily papers, as usual, came out with a statement that the riot was caused by two white girls being assaulted by colored men. Attorney G. Edward Dickerson, who has been the leader in the defense of the colored citizens, produced evidence to show that the trouble was caused by the white brutes, which aroused the citizens of color to such an extent that numerous committees have waited on the officials at city hall. The Mayor, however, has made it a point

Philadelphia's white citizens to resort to mob rule, after President Wilson has urged them to cease, it is a disgrace to this great commonwealth. How can a colored man go to France with a clear conscience? How can he willingly give his life for a country that will not protect his family during his absence?"

These are the questions Mr. Dickerson says many citizens are asking.

"What right," says he, "has an officer of the law to go into one's home without a warrant when that person has not committed any crime, search his home and take all weapons of defense away? There is no law in this commonwealth to back them up. But, like East St. Louis and Chester, these

ADELLA BOND

The plucky little probation officer, who shot to kill in defense of her honor and home and put a mob of white brutes and police sympathizers to flight, when Kelly fired a brick through her window.

2900 block on Ellsworth street, and colonize the same with colored, are the underlying causes of the race riots down town.

The white tenants put the blame on A. D. Morgan, a real estate agent, 1246 Real Estate Building, who resides at 1126 South Forty-seventh street, West Philadelphia. He is the representative of Charles E. Painter, the owner of the properties about which the battle has raged.

"They say I am to blame for it all," said Morgan. "Well, what of it? I guess we had a perfect right to dispose of our properties if we wanted to. These white tenants have been trying to 'run this block' for some time. We have had trouble with them for two years. They were always behind in their rent. There was much complaint of freight cars being looted from the tracks nearby.

"We got tired of dealing with these people. Yes, I employed a negro agent and sought to dispose of the eight house I owned there. We almost 'begged' the white tenants to buy the properties. They would not.

"A Mrs. Giddings, a colored woman, lived in the house that Mrs. Bond bought for a long time. Then she moved out and a white woman named Mrs. Ford moved in. When we got a chance to sell the house to Mrs. Bond we did so. We have sold six of the houses. Yes, all to colored people. We have two more houses on the market. I would like to see them go to colored tenants for they are far better tenants than the element which is now there.

"I don't know how far this will all go, but they'll have to get out as soon as their leases are up. And when they are all gone and the colored people take their places there will be no more trouble there.

"Did I make an especial attempt to dispose of the houses to colored people? No. Did I employ a colored man as agent? I did. We were glad, of course, to sell to the desirable colored people he found."

"What rents did you charge them, Mr. Morgan?"

"That is absolutely our affair," was the reply.

The white tenants say they formerly paid $11 a month. The houses are all alike architecturally.

They assert the rent was raised to $14 and then to $16. All now hold notices from Morgan to vacate since they refused to meet the raise.

The statement from Mr. Morgan corroborates the impression given by the mob, that they are nothing but roughs and undesirable citizens. Most undesirable they must be when one of their own race speaks so plainly. He speaks of them looting freight cars, well they have also looted the houses that they have broken into, taking clothing and jewelry and sometimes even furniture; this in spite of the fact that there are special details of policemen patrolling every block.

The police have disarmed all the colored men that they could, and the white roughs have been seen carrying blackjacks and revolvers openly and on one street where there were five policemen in a block they warned the colored residents to keep inside the houses as they couldn't give them any protection if the white roughs started something. One wonders what their clubs and revolvers were given them for, or how they would stop the mob if composed of colored men.

Prompt Action of Colored Committeemen

The rioting began after a white man was killed during a confrontation with two black teenage couples. The deceased had been drinking heavily. On his way home he allegedly insulted one of the black girls, and her date responded with a knife. Over the next three days, starting on July 26, 1917, white mobs roamed Chester's streets, assaulting blacks, dragging them from streetcars, and setting fire to their homes. By the end the death toll had reached five, with fifty seriously injured. Between the white press, Chester's white sheriff, and a "prominent [white] retired merchant," blame for the riot was attributed to black migrants and their "criminal element."[72]

According to historian Charles Hardy, city officials in Philadelphia responded to the Chester riot by taking notice of the "character of the southerners in their midst." The city also attempted to prevent its own racial conflagration by increasing the number of officers on patrol. On the last day of the Chester rioting, a Philadelphia police sweep of loitering black men netted some young men from Chester, a few of them armed. Meanwhile, the Philadelphia *Inquirer* reported that armed black Philadelphians were traveling to Chester, adding that there had been a run on firearms in South Philadelphia's pawnshops. It was also reported that fifteen hundred white residents of the Gray's Ferry section of southwest Philadelphia—a mixed area of Irish, Italians, and African Americans—came close to lynching a young black man accused of attacking a white boy.[73]

The near-lynching in the Gray's Ferry section was a glimpse of what was to come the following year. All hell broke loose in Philadelphia in the spring and summer of 1918. The immediate cause of the racial violence and rioting was the crisis of overcrowded housing due to migration into older black areas. Black population growth pushed the outer boundaries of black neighborhoods across previously settled lines of residential segregation. By the third year of wartime migration, many upwardly mobile blacks who could afford to move away from the most densely populated black neighborhoods began to do so. Many black homeowners and renters suffered fierce and violent opposition from their new white neighbors. For example, after Reginald Collender rented a house on Naudain Street above 28th, whites attacked him and his family, destroying

Figure 5-1 Adella Bond, a black homeowner who defended herself against a white mob at the start of the Philadelphia Race Riot. The Philadelphia Tribune, Philadelphia Penn., August 3, 1918.

their "household effects." Collender was then arrested, accused of assaulting a police officer who had been shot during the attack. Although no evidence was shown that Collender had possessed or used a gun or had done anything but attempt to protect his family, he was sentenced to serve two to five years in the Eastern State Penitentiary. Investigating Collender's conviction for improprieties, the Pennsylvania Prison Society successfully petitioned his release before the Board of Pardons on March 20, 1918. Collender was free from incarceration but had gained a felony conviction.[74]

More housing-related attacks followed at the end of June, when the contents of two black families' homes were set ablaze on the 2500 block of Pine Street. Keeping score of the growing list of black victims and sensing the potential for more attacks, *Tribune* editor G. Grant Williams instructed "law-abiding" blacks to defend themselves against the white criminals who attacked their homes. Respectable blacks—no longer in Dixie—had a right as American citizens, he insisted, to use arms against "the ragged rum-crazed hellion crew, prototypes of your old cracker enemies." Framing the confrontation over housing as a battle of good versus evil, Williams continued, "We stand for law and order, decency and cleanliness, but knowing as we do the facts, that our people are driven from pillar to post looking for houses to rent and that they pay more rent than whites for the same shacks, our patience runs out."[75]

Three weeks after Williams's editorial appeared, Adella Bond's patience ran out when a mob of white men came to remove her from her new house. After Joseph Kelly, a member of the mob, threw a brick through her parlor window, she fired a warning shot from her revolver. Not knowing what would happen next, Bond had used the gun to summon the police. Kelly ended up being shot in the leg, but in the commotion that followed once the police arrived it was not clear who the shooter was. Several white men, including Kelly, were arrested for inciting a riot. Later that same day groups of whites took to the streets, stoning blacks' homes and churches. The rioters also looted many homes that were abandoned.[76]

The events of July 26, 1918, were an undeniable demonstration of what Williams had observed in the preceding months—whites of questionable, if not criminal, backgrounds using violence to resist the residential encroachment of innocent, if not respectable, blacks. Bond was a probation officer with the Municipal Court. Kelly and his crew were well known to the neighborhood police as a gang of thieves who preyed on a nearby freight yard, peddling stolen goods to their neighbors. Lieutenant Myers of the Seventeenth Police District played up the criminality of the "gang of white hoodlums" who attacked Bond, arguing that the gang wanted to get rid of Bond "not because she bought the house," but because as a court officer she was a threat to their "thievery."[77] Although Myers's statements corroborated Williams's juxtaposition of white criminality versus black respectability, Myers's point was to deny the racist intent of the assault.

Believing that white criminality and police racism were the root problems, black leaders sharply criticized Lieutenant Myers's failure to stop the police in the riot areas from abdicating their responsibility to protect blacks' property in the several days of violence that followed. A little more than a week after the rioting began at the front lawn of Adella Bond's house, vandals and thieves returned, carted away her belongings, and distributed such items as shoes and silverware to the white neighbors. The police, who were supposed to be watching the house, instead allegedly cooperated with the looters. No one was arrested.[78] Some policemen's animosity toward blacks was starkly revealed by a white officer who received the complaint of Mrs. P. C. Williams, Bond's only black neighbor. Williams suffered property damage when a stone was thrown through the window of her grocery store on August 24. She reported the incident to an officer and said he replied, "What in the h[ell] have I got to do with that? It did not happen while I was on duty, and I don't give a d[amn] if they tear down the whole d[amn] building so long as I don't see them."[79] The veracity of Lieutenant Myers's statements in defense of his police officers seems suspect at best: "Every one of my men did his full duty and they treated every one alike . . . The policemen could not have done better than they did."[80]

Several police officers aided white mobs by disarming blacks, thereby limiting their ability to defend their homes. Policemen unlawfully entered homes looking for weapons to confiscate, without search warrants or a pretext for believing guns were owned illegally. Since Reconstruction black gun ownership and the right to keep firearms for self-protection had been subject to unlawful scrutiny and outright violent suppression by whites across the nation. After removing the weapons, white policemen told blacks to stay indoors; if a mob came, they were warned, the police would be unable to protect them.[81]

215

The homes of Joseph Bush and Henry Gillison, for example, were both "forcibly entered" by the police. The police took their arms, "turned them over to the mob who beat them up," and then arrested them. Bush and Gillison were both represented by defense attorney G. Edward Dickerson and later discharged by a judge. Along with Andrew F. Stevens, a highly respected black state-level politician, Dickerson complained bitterly about the illegal actions of the police. Stevens accused Director of Public Safety William H. Wilson of taking part in the drive to disarm blacks, stating that Wilson had issued an order to gun dealers to cease sales to blacks. Director Wilson denied any racial bias, but admitted that an order had been issued to stop all sales of firearms.[82]

If responsibility for the rioting was measured solely by the black-white ratio of arrests, blacks would have been overwhelmingly guilty. During the six days of rioting between July 26 and 31, not counting the several weeks of continued violence that followed, sixty blacks were arrested compared to three whites—a ratio of 20 to 1.[83] However, arrest statistics were misleading; in many cases blacks were arrested regardless of lack of evidence that they had started a confrontation. Whites were almost never arrested; if a white male was taken into custody, it was usually the chief suspect rather than all participants. The outcome of interracial confrontations often mirrored what happened when a mob in the Gray's Ferry section—the site of a near lynching the summer before—attacked two black men, Joseph Sherman and L. Sims, on August 11. Sherman was shot, and Sims was beaten with "clubs and fists." The only arrests were of Sherman and Sims.[84] The night before, John Lee, Walter Penn, and Edward Hinton were chased and beaten by a reported one hundred U.S. sailors who were training at the Philadelphia Naval Yards. Hinton died from the beating; Lee and Penn managed to escape into a black church where they were later arrested and charged with carrying concealed weapons. "Yet," the *Tribune* claimed, no weapons "were found on them."[85]

Some police officers did rescue blacks from mobs rather than simply arrest them after they were beaten. On July 29, J. A. Trotman was assaulted by a group of white men, one of whom threw "a large piece of iron" at him, striking him in the right shoulder. He managed to make it indoors and contact the police, who safely escorted him from the scene.[86] The following Saturday, two black motorists were dragged from their cars by several whites near 27th and South Street. With guns drawn and threatening to shoot, two policeman and several marines stopped the white mob in its tracks. The next day, however, military personnel were on the wrong side of the law when a white officer prevented thirty-five uniformed sailors from further beating a black man on North Uber Street.[87] Despite these uncommon acts of serving and protecting blacks, no whites were arrested.

An important factor in the disproportionate arrests of blacks during the summerlong rioting was the criminalization of black resistance to white violence. Black self-defense, especially with the aid of a weapon, was treated as a criminal offense regardless of the circumstances. Police not only entered blacks' homes without warrants to disarm them, but also repeatedly arrested them when they waged pitched battles against scores of white men, presumably to save their own lives. That the police may have profiled the combination of race and resistance rather than just the crime of "having a dark face"—unlike the unambiguous racial profiling done by many white civilians and military personnel—is suggested by those moments when white policemen intervened to protect blacks who reportedly did not fight back.[88] Police targeting of black resistance was clearly shown by the sharp contrast, obvious on the third day of the rioting, between blacks willing to fight to the death and those whose first instincts were to call for help.

On July 28 two black men arrested in separate incidents were responsible for the deaths of two white men. While being chased by a white mob, Jesse Butler opened fire, killing Hugh Lavery, one of his pursuers. Later that afternoon, Henry Huff purportedly "brandished" his gun while he "dared the crowd" to try to get him. When they did, he shot three white men, one of whom died. The deceased was Thomas McVay, an undercover patrolman attempting to disarm Huff.[89] For the remainder of the rioting, these early incidents may have justified criminalizing black resistance in the minds of white police officers who had long been accused of sympathizing with and assisting white mobs. The evidence is even stronger because white violence against blacks did not result in the unlawful disarmament of white men or police brutality and homicide against them.

Perhaps in retaliation, Preston Lewis was the first victim of police brutality the day after Thomas McVay was killed in the line of duty. In what appears to have been a random stop-and-frisk encounter, Lewis was detained on the street by Officers Ramsey and Schneider. Upon searching him and finding a "small pocket knife"—sufficient evidence to "justify" their behavior—the two white policemen beat him so severely that he was taken to a hospital. While Lewis lay on a cot receiving medical treatment, Officer Schneider decided that Lewis's twenty head wounds were not enough and again beat him over the head with a blackjack. Witnessing the beating, a black officer forced Schneider to stop by threatening to shoot him. A nurse summoned more police, who arrived shortly thereafter but refused to arrest the white officer.[90] Within a matter of minutes, Officer Schneider was back on the streets with his partner, looking to stop and frisk other black men.

Schneider and Ramsey found Riley Bullock, who fit the same profile as Lewis: black and in possession of a knife. Witness testimony later claimed that Bullock was arrested "while he was going on an errand and committing no crime." Subjected to what seemed to be the standard procedure of a curbside beating, Bullock was taken to the station house at 21st and Federal streets. Several whites gathered around the arresting officers while Bullock was escorted into the rear entrance. Officer Ramsey said that he and Schneider kept their guns drawn to protect Bullock because someone in the crowd yelled, "Let's lynch the coon." He then claimed that he slipped on a stair, his gun discharged, and Bullock received a lethal gunshot wound to his back. White press accounts initially reported that Bullock had been shot by an unknown "negro" who managed to elude the police. During a coroner's investigation, however, Officer Ramsey was recommended to the grand jury on a first-degree murder charge, and Officer Schneider was charged with second-degree murder. Schneider was also charged with aggravated assault and battery for his attack on Preston Lewis.[91]

Bullock's death and Lewis's beating on the morning and afternoon of July 29 represented two of the most extreme cases of police violence during the rioting. The response of black leaders was to hold a protest meeting the night of the attacks. The next day two delegations were selected to meet with Mayor Thomas B. Smith. The mayor, however, was unavailable for at least the next two weeks; he was reportedly playing golf.[92] Instead, the delegations, headed by B. G. Collier of the Knights of Pythias and Richard R. Wright, Jr., former field secretary of the Armstrong Association and editor of the *Christian Recorder*, met with Director Wilson. They presented a letter expressing their outrage at the total breakdown of law and order and the arresting of blacks "on any pretense." Their letter, reprinted in several newspapers, stated in part:

We desire you to understand that we put the whole blame upon your incompetent police force. But for the sympathy of the police, their hobnobbing with the mob, what has now become the disgrace of Philadelphia would have been nothing more than a petty row. Your police have for a long time winked at disorder, such as the beating up of negroes, the stoning of their homes and the attacking of their churches. . . . In nearly every part of this city peaceable and law-abiding negroes of the home-owning type have been set upon by irresponsible hoodlums, their property damaged and destroyed, while the police seem powerless to protect. It is not to be wondered at that the mob thought it could scare negroes from their homes with impunity. . . . We severely condemn mob rule, and we condemn negroes who disregard the law and we feel lawbreakers of all races should be treated alike.[93]

To achieve fair treatment of all lawbreakers, the protesters suggested the more effective use of black police officers. Many black policemen had been "kept out of the riot district" during the disturbances, and in more than one instance whites who were arrested by them were released by white policemen.[94] Their reasoning suggested that if, for example, the black officer had been allowed to take Officer Schneider into custody when he was beating Preston Lewis in the hospital, Riley Bullock might not have been killed. With such evidence in mind, Wright and others argued that black officers would have made prompt arrests and helped to prevent further violence, as, for example, in the case of John R. Evans. After several whites shot up Evans's home, they were arrested by a black officer but released almost immediately. Evans was a foreman in a federal department where war supplies and munitions were shipped to Europe, and his two sons-in-law were fighting in France, making the attack on him appear to blacks not only racist but treasonous. Adding insult to injury, Lieutenant Myers, who a week earlier was defending the police, had the black officer transferred to another district. Evans's house was then attacked a second time a week later, and an American flag hanging in his parlor window was shot to pieces—a tragic event bordering on the comic: a white neighbor had given Evans the flag following the first assault to protect his family from further harm. G. Grant Williams of the *Tribune* had seen enough of Myers's failure to serve and protect blacks and called for his removal from the Seventeenth Police District, where Officers Schneider and Ramsey had also worked.[95]

During the following week, a month after the rioting started, Myers and his entire staff were transferred from the Seventeenth, replaced by an interracial staff and a new lieutenant. The *Tribune* praised the change, noting that several whites had recently been arrested and given thirty-day sentences, and crediting the new staff with bringing peace to the riot's epicenter. Children were now seen playing on Ellsworth Street, where the riot had first begun.[96]

The pitch and scale of violence against blacks that summer would not soon be forgotten.[97] For black writers and reformers especially, answering the question of why the riots had happened led some to consider what blacks might have done to invite the worst manifestations of racial hatred that Philadelphia had ever witnessed. Looking back on the riots, it must have been hard for them to imagine that the pursuit of an authentic equality, expressed by the desire to live in a house and neighborhood of one's choosing, could alone illicit such venom against blacks. After all, hope was essential to progress. Rather than lay all the blame on white racism—an implicit acceptance that blacks had little control over their own futures—black race-relations experts blamed migrant criminality for legitimizing white contempt.

Sadie Mossell in her migrant study recalled the attack on Adella Bond, describing her as a "woman of refinement and training and old citizen of Philadelphia." To explain how a middle-class, native black Philadelphian was targeted by a white mob, Mossell argued that "colored people of every class received harsh treatment at the hands of the white public" because of the migrants.[98] Legitimizing the antiblack violence, Emmett Scott wrote that in reaction to the vice and crime among migrants, the white community, "unaccustomed to negro neighbors," showed its "displeasure" through a "number of fracases" leading to the riots.[99] These black writers must have also been aware of what some whites had said. While sentencing two black southern migrants convicted of rioting and carrying concealed weapons, a criminal court judge noted, "You and others like you who come here from other jurisdictions are the cause of three-fifths of the trouble we recently had."[100] To be sure, not everyone formulated unambiguous opinions about black migrant criminality in relation to the riots. William D. Fuller, a black lawyer who analyzed a second wave of black migration to Philadelphia from 1921 to 1923, argued that the first migration had "caused several problems to arise in relation to housing, crime and disease." Yet he also admitted that "an increase in crime" had not been "clearly proven."[101]

Although not in the way that many had argued, black criminality did lie beneath the battle over housing, of which the riots were the most violent manifestation. During the first three decades of the twentieth century, the issue of residential segregation in the North relied in part on the powerful racial imagery of black criminals.[102] Real and false evidence of black crime, such as stories in daily newspapers, reinforced the idea of blacks as a dangerous threat to white communities. Philadelphia's white dailies initially reported that the riots began because of an alleged attack on two white women by black men. No evidence existed to link that rumor with the riots.[103] Nevertheless, the idea of black criminality was a template that applied to all potential black renters and homeowners in predominately white areas, regardless of their class or birthplace. What makes the Philadelphia riot so instructive in this context is that the majority of blacks whose homes were attacked were, by black middle-class standards, "respectable" rather than "criminal." They were criminalized because of their willingness to fight back when whites resisted their demands for fair housing. Black resistance thus justified the initial assumption that blacks were a threat to white communities. The role of migrants in this cycle of racial criminalization was to increase the likelihood that more blacks would move into white areas and that more white violence would occur, resulting in more blacks adopting a militant stance and ending up arrested, beaten, or dead.

Much of black Philadelphia's leadership class expressed a defiant tone of militancy during and after the riots. The change was sudden and unmistakable. The outbreak of war in Europe had already heightened expectations among blacks that the fight to make the "world safe for democracy" would also make America safe for her twelve million black citizens. Ironically, on the same day that Adella Bond's house was attacked, President Woodrow Wilson condemned racial violence across the nation, calling it a "disgraceful evil." He reminded everyone from governors to local police officers to neighborhood residents that mob violence "can not live where the community does not countenance it."[104] Wilson's rhetoric belied his own segregationist leanings and hostility toward people who were not native white Protestants. Nevertheless, the blatant hypocrisy of racial violence during the war further inflamed the usually staid sensibilities of Philadelphia's black leaders. For instance, sixty-six-year-old Archdeacon Henry Phillips, the city's most respected black minister and public servant, spoke about blacks' response to mob violence: "The colored people should kill every one of the white people who molest them, that's all

I have to say as it is the only protection they will get," he told a reporter. Other ministers fully supported purchasing "guns and ammunition." G. Grant Williams agreed: "I would and will shoot any man who attempts to enter my home by force so long as I am peaceful and [a] law-abiding citizen." In a letter to Williams expressing his support for the *Tribune*'s coverage of the riot, Pastor R. J. Williams of the venerable Mother Bethel Church stopped short of calling for arms, but wrote, "Enough is enough, and it is time for the Negro to call a halt."[105]

State Republican committee member Andrew Stevens brought the issues of housing and militancy into full view when he used his fair complexion to buy a house at 3849 N. 16th Street on behalf of a client whose skin color had prevented him from making the purchase himself. After the deed was transferred to Martin Cowdery, "a representative of one of Philadelphia's oldest and most respected families of color," Joseph Sternberger, a lawyer representing Cowdery's future white neighbors, met with Cowdery to voice his "highly respectable" clients' displeasure and to present their counteroffer to buy back the property.[106] With the same goal in mind, the Sixtieth and Market Streets Business Men's Association adopted a resolution opposing the sale of real estate to blacks in "white residential sections."[107] Meanwhile rumors spread that violence would erupt if Cowdery refused the counteroffer. Stevens met with Director Wilson and warned that he would bring "two automatic revolvers" for protection to the move in.[108]

Sternberger and George Rote, an insurance agent, then arranged another meeting with Cowdery and Stevens. At that meeting Rote argued that his clients' only objection to Cowdery was that his presence in the neighborhood would depreciate their property values. Stevens apparently interpreted this second meeting as a veiled warning of what would happen if Cowdery insisted on moving in. He later threatened that if Cowdery was harmed, "organized" blacks would take revenge: "They will come to you and Mr. Sternberger and blow your families to ____." Sternberger and Rote submitted lengthy letters to the *Tribune* to "emphatically" deny Stevens's characterization of them as mob leaders, stating that they had "personally advised the white residents of the neighborhood to refrain from any act of opposition." Stevens replied that this advice was proof that violence had been threatened. On September 6, G. Grant Williams wrote to Director Wilson requesting police protection. In the end, Cowdery's move-in party was well armed and well attended, but uneventful. Several plainclothes officers joined extra patrolmen, along with Stevens's two guns and twenty black private guards, to ensure Cowdery's safety.[109]

The increased likelihood that black Philadelphians of all classes would own and use weapons in anticipation of racial violence strongly suggests that migrant criminality was not at the heart of the precipitous downturn in race relations in 1918. Rather, southern migrants were part of a demographic shift, beginning in the late nineteenth century but accelerating between 1916 and 1918, that brought structural barriers to black equality into sharper focus. White resistance to the demand for better housing by the black middle class amid heightened expectations born from the war was the primary cause of the riots.[110] Historian William Tuttle, Jr., came to the same conclusion about Chicago's race riot the following summer: "White antipathy and black aspirations mounted into an apex of racial antagonism in the summer of 1919."[111]

To the extent that southern migrants did assume an increasingly prominent place in Philadelphia's vice districts, their behavior mirrored that of their native white and black counterparts. Although he had studied vice in Pittsburgh as a student researcher at the University of Pittsburgh, Abraham Epstein spoke directly to the situation in Philadelphia: "That the Negro becomes a victim of the saloon and the vice elements is evidently more the fault of the community than of himself. He is often anxious to rid himself of these associations, but it can be done only by his white brother's realization of the social responsibility which he owes to the community."[112] Looking back more than a half century later, migration historian Florette Henri agrees with Epstein about the association of wide-scale vice and corruption with blacks in northern cities. "A less visible but more pernicious theme was corruption in politics, crooked politicians paid off by saloon, gambling, and prostitution interests to let vice flourish in the Negro sections of cities," Henri writes. "Where there were vice and crime in the black slums—and it was profitable to politicians that there should be—white people generalized that all blacks were vicious and criminal, which served as an excuse for mob action against the whole black community, not just the lawless element."[113]

By most accounts, Philadelphia was one of the most corrupt and crime-ridden cities in the country in 1918. Du Bois referred to the city's political corruption at an NAACP meeting in March 1918 as "worse probably than any other city in the world."[114] Interviewed by the press the same month, Public Safety Director Wilson admitted that the police were incapable of fighting a crime wave in the city because they were part of it. "Murders, robberies and crime of every description are of daily occurrence and in many cases the police are charged with these offenses," he stated. The scale of the city's corruption and crime was clearly shown by the city's own chief executive, Mayor Thomas B. Smith, who was under indictment for a campaign-related assassination. Even Smith's police superintendent, James Robinson, who had supervised the Tenderloin vice cleanup in 1912 under the Blankenburg administration, was now under criminal investigation for knowingly allowing police protection of vice. By the spring of 1918, fearing possible indictment, Robinson left office because the federal government moved in to clean up vice in Philadelphia.[115] Based on a report by Raymond Fosdick, chairman of the Commission on Training Camp Activities, which oversaw the social and moral welfare of sailors at military bases across the country, Philadelphia's vice was the worst in the nation: "Philadelphia, which perhaps gave us more trouble than any other city in the United States, was finally brought to terms only when Secretary [of the Navy, Josephus] Daniels put in a large squad of marines to patrol the streets."[116]

Blacks stood on both sides of Philadelphia's vice and crime problem. With the virus of political corruption that crippled the city in 1918, the need to continue to fight crime from "within the race" and from "without" was as important as ever. When the immensely popular black detective George L. Williams was gunned down on the street by four black men, who were labeled by the *Tribune* as a "band of drink and 'dope' crazed thugs," black crime fighters swung into action. But in a cruel reversal of the situation in 1912, when they could not rely on the police to assist their efforts, this time the police were in cahoots with the criminals. Complaining about this latest development, the *Tribune* wrote, "If our big political bosses, black and white, would devote less time in trying to get these bad colored thugs out of jail and give more protection to the law abiding colored citizens, this would be a much better place in which to live."[117]

A variation of that argument had been made before by James Stemons and his League for Civic and Political Reform, but the Great Migration changed the degree to which middle-class blacks would step up their commitment to crime fighting in the 1920s and 1930s, and more firmly ground the national debate over black criminality in terms of structural inequality and racial discrimination. The criminalization of the race because of white reformers' unwillingness to apply crime-prevention strategies in black communities, the intensification of racial violence among white citizens and police officers, and the more militant attitude of middle-class blacks toward achieving economic and social justice all converged during the next two decades to place black criminality near the forefront of an emerging civil rights agenda.

6

In the 1920s and 1930s the history of social scientific explanations and popular perceptions of crime among African Americans entered a new phase. The Great Migration, coupled with Prohibition, created wide-scale opportunities for white vice owners and corrupt politicians to hide their illegal activities under a cover of blackness. In the midst of successful Progressive era campaigns against white red-light districts across the nation, many observers noted that city officials had become more tolerant of crime in black communities than in white ones. As early as the 1910s in major northern cities like Philadelphia, New York, and Chicago, researchers and reformers had already begun to discern a pattern of discriminatory crime fighting.

The 1911 report of the Chicago Vice Commission observed, for example, that "whenever prostitutes, cadets and thugs were located among white people and had to be moved for commercial or other reasons, they were driven to undesirable parts of the city; the so-called colored residential sections."[1] Having witnessed firsthand the transformation of a white community, one Chicagoan observed, "A few years ago I could point out 100 joints right in this neighborhood. Now I don't know of one."[2] A decade later, the relocation of a significant portion of white organized crime into black communities had become an all-too-familiar phenomenon.[3] "White prostitutes and gamblers and vicious resorts" come into the "Black Belt," explained a black minister in Chicago, because "it is black; they operate with more safety than they do in the white belt. That is true of every American city that I know of personally."[4] According to historian Kenneth Kusmer, ineffective policing in black communities was good public policy from the standpoint of Cleveland's city officials. This race-based criminal justice policy worked to benefit white leaders and residents by making it less likely that "red-light districts might spring up again in white areas."[5]

City officials rarely acknowledged the reality that for vice districts to exist in black neighborhoods, the active support of politicians and police officers was required. Except for politically expedient moments when grand juries handed out indictments or when politicians made examples of a few ward leaders and beat cops by arresting them in the wake of public outrage over allegations of corruption, city officials ignored the truth.[6] Behind the borders of segregated black communities, many officials participated directly as patrons and protectors of illegal operations involving liquor, drugs, gambling, and prostitution. One white Philadelphia politician spelled out the situation as plainly as possible when he said to a white pimp, in front of a black female undercover vice agent posing as a prostitute, "You know, Frank, I've told you to go as far as you like, anything short of murder is alright with me and I'm at your back. If anything happens come to me and I'll see that everything is squared."[7]

The difference between the reality that vice districts in predominately black areas were mostly owned, partially operated, and unofficially regulated by a largely white power structure and the belief that blacks were at the root of these conditions can be traced to the rhetoric of black criminality and its long association with urban crime. Cleveland's mayor Harry L. Davis, for example, "implied in a speech in 1917 that the Central Avenue area had developed into a vice district because Negroes were naturally degenerate."[8] The stark contrast between the way the system actually worked, as revealed in the politician's private conversation with a pimp, and the image projected to the public, as conveyed in a speech by a big-city mayor, provides a rich example of how the vice problem became the starting point in the creation of new ideas about black criminality in the 1920s and 1930s.

As previous chapters have shown, since the late nineteenth century northern-born blacks and southern migrants in northern cities had to contend with a fluid set of racial attitudes and practices that defined them as members of a dangerous criminal population. Those attitudes and practices also aided or legitimized various forms of segregation and discrimination, particularly in relation to social agencies, employment, and housing. A small number of black reformers responded to inequality and the crime stigma by calling for a two-front war against both racial discrimination and black criminals, which they viewed as mutually dependent problems. In 1899 W. E. B. Du Bois pioneered this dual-approach strategy in the pages of *The Philadelphia Negro* by instructing his white readers to end discrimination and his black ones to help minimize "Negro crime."[9] A decade later a local black Philadelphia reformer named James S. Stemons formulated a programmatic response to Du Bois's recommendations. He launched a joint organization in which white members took an oath to uphold color-blind hiring practices and black members pledged to police their own communities.[10]

Thus for much of the first two decades of the twentieth century, a few black reformers in the urban North attempted to tackle the problem of black criminality by calling for more blacks to become involved in crime prevention and crime fighting. They did not ignore the broader, more fundamental problems of racism and structural inequality, but they did expect white reformers to handle what they considered a white problem or the failure of most whites to treat blacks fairly. In other words, black reformers reasoned that the best way to solve the black crime problem was if each race attacked its half of the problem. In the spirit of interracialism and racial progress during the Progressive era, blacks were expected to police their own criminals, while whites were expected to police their own racists.

Both groups had failed to achieve their goals by the 1920s. Neither rhetoric nor activism had stemmed the growing tide of segregation and discrimination affecting blacks before, during, and immediately after the Great Migration. Similarly, without institutional resources and political support from whites, no words or surveillance by blacks had proven adequate to the monumental task of crime prevention in black communities, especially when those communities were being inundated with southern migrants whose presence amplified racist sentiment and oppression.[11] As an explicit demonstration of an increasingly deteriorating situation, widespread outbreaks of racial violence occurred in many northern cities during this period, first in East St. Louis, Illinois, and Chester, Pennsylvania, in 1917, then in Philadelphia in 1918, culminating in the Red Summer of 1919.

In the 1920s a larger cohort of academically trained black reformers and local activists responded to this new era of racial conservatism by taking a greater role in the policing of white racism within black communities in the urban North.[12] In local and national interracial organizations, such as the Chicago Commission on Race Relations, the National Association for the Advancement of Colored People (NAACP), and the National Urban League (NUL), black researchers and reformers moved to the forefront of documenting and publicizing racism's toll on the quality of black lives across the urban North. Moving to the center of this intensification of antiracist activities among black reformers was a focus on racism in the criminal justice system, particularly in its most explicit forms. Clear and preponderant new evidence showed African American criminality, for example, to be a direct consequence of discriminatory policing.

By focusing on discriminatory policing in the 1920s and 1930s, particularly in the context of vice districts where numerous examples were easily observed, a growing number of black reformers and a small number of white liberals helped to transform the larger debate about black criminality. Ideologically, the entire debate shifted to the left in the sense that mounting evidence of police corruption, misconduct, and violence against blacks supported a powerful counterargument to the long-standing linkage of black crime rates and moral, cultural, or racial inferiority. Especially among black researchers and reformers, vice districts became the focal point for rewriting African American criminality in terms of its structural basis.

In the 1930s a black minister in Chicago recounted a conversation with city officials about increasing crime rates among black youth: "They told me that the Negro youth of Chicago were committing more crimes than ever in the history of Chicago. They wanted to know just what is the cause. I could only give this solution—wipe out vice and give my people jobs!"[13] In his thinking, vice was not a function of black degeneracy or even of southern migration, but of the city's failure to police black communities effectively, and to promote equal employment opportunities. Such formulations, which I call writing crime into class, represented a new paradigm shift: Structural inequality, or what Frederick Hoffman dismissed at the turn of the century as the "conditions of life," became the primary basis for explaining black criminality. Similiar explanations had existed in the context of and in opposition to earlier paradigms—the writing of crime into race and culture—but had never become the dominant argument among most liberals, black or white. That changed in the 1920s and 1930s. A 1930 editorial in the National Urban League's *Opportunity* magazine observed that the "problems of the Negro" had once been "considered purely racial in their origin." Because black social workers had now pursued "careful compilation, correlation, and interpretation of social materials as they related to the Negro," the "more significant social determinants" of the "so-called Negro problem" were no longer "obscur[ed]."[14] Policing racism in the northern criminal justice system became an effective counter-discourse—a statistical rebuttal—to the long-standing statistical discourse of black criminality and inferiority.

As a result of social surveys and crime studies conducted by NUL researchers, revelations about the role of politicians and the police in the administration of discriminatory criminal justice practices helped give way to these new structural understandings of black criminality.[15] Other researchers highlighted the direct connection between discrimination at recreation facilities (such as playgrounds and community centers) and higher rates of black juvenile delinquency.[16] In 1928 former Philadelphia Urban League official Forrester B. Washington wrote that the Negro migrant in major cities of the North and South "found the wholesome agencies of recreation either closed or closing to him, while at the same time the agencies of commercialized vice have welcomed him with open arms."[17]

During this period, growing concern about juvenile delinquency blended with an increased focus on vice and policing problems in black communities, demonstrating the devastating impact of institutional racism on what was considered the most vulnerable and least morally culpable population.[18] Describing the "threatened decadence" to blacks in North Philadelphia, for example, a high school principal wrote to officials of the Benezet House Association, a Philadelphia community center, that residents had been "abandoned to the exploiting ravages of a horde of vicious agencies which sprang up, multiplied and flourished until the district is now spotted with them. The effect, especially upon the children and young people, were at once apparent and have become steadily worse with each year."[19] In her 1925 study "A Survey of Crime among Negroes in Philadelphia," Anna J. Thompson, a black University of Pennsylvania graduate student and researcher for the NUL, wrote that "the case of the Juvenile delinquent is so much more hopeful than that of the adult criminal. The Juvenile delinquent is as a rule just beginning a life of delinquency which can, if taken in time and by the proper method, be nipped in the bud."[20]

Undergirding an increasing concern about black juvenile delinquency in the 1920s and 1930s were not only statistics tying higher rates of delinquency to majority white-owned and -regulated vice, but also a growing body of evidence of racial discrimination in the "proper method" of treating black delinquents.[21] In her examination of juvenile delinquency in 1920s New York City, historian Cheryl Lynn Greenburg found that black youths were twice as likely as white youths to be arraigned in Children's Court, more likely to be found guilty, twice as likely to be sentenced to over five years in an institution, and five times less likely to receive probation. White children also had "greater access to private services than blacks did," Greenburg writes. "Fewer white than black delinquent children ended up in Children's Court in the first place, because more were helped by private agencies before appearing there."[22] Researcher William I. Thomas, coauthor of *The Polish Peasant in Europe and America* (1918)—the first of many pathbreaking Chicago School of Sociology studies of immigrant life and settlement in the 1920s and 1930s—discovered in a subsequent study how important police discretion was in determining how white youth were treated and/or classified as juvenile delinquents. Out of 18,000 Chicago-area boys facing arrest in 1926, only 1,430 were actually arraigned in juvenile court.[23] A 1923 U.S. Children's Bureau report noted racial disparities in the distribution of black and white juveniles across various types of institutions. Of a total population of white youths among the Juvenile Court records analyzed by the study, 80.8 percent were sent to non-correctional facilities compared to 50.6 percent of black youths. Stated conversely, 19.2 percent of white children were sent to a prison, a reformatory, a jail, or a workhouse, compared to more than twice as many black children.[24] The mounting statistical evidence of bias in the juvenile justice system was in part a testament to, and a consequence of, the discriminatory nature of Progressive era crime prevention. Black juvenile delinquency became one of the most effective demonstrations that structural inequality was the primary cause of crime among blacks.

New concerns about vice, police misconduct, and juvenile delinquency led to an explosion of anticrime ideas and initiatives by middle-class blacks.[25] Black social workers became increasingly involved in recreation programs and probation work.[26] The National Association for Colored Women hired Ida B. Wells, the longtime antilynching activist and social welfare advocate, as a probation officer in Chicago.[27] In 1928 the head of the National Urban League, Eugene Kinckle Jones, announced that "the probation work movement has gained considerable headway, most of the larger cities having Negro probation officers for work with juveniles."[28] As a clear sign of black probation officers' growing importance, even adult prisoners like Clarence Brown began to seek their assistance. From a New York City jail in 1927, Brown wrote to the NAACP to "please send somebody down here to try and get me out on supened [sic] sentence or on probation . . . so I can start a new life. I have no father or mother . . . could you have a colored probation officer to look out for me."[29] From the standpoint of combating the stigma of crime, civil rights workers began to offer occasional legal assistance and frequent advice to men like Brown and others who claimed to be innocent or mistreated defendants. Civil rights workers also began to aggressively launch publicity campaigns against police brutality and de facto racial profiling.[30] The NAACP, for instance, stood out as a vocal opponent of northern urban police agencies that routinely profiled, arrested, and/or brutalized innocent blacks.

The growth of vice in black communities—resulting from the closing of white red-light districts, increased black migration, and the exigencies of Prohibition—made vice and discriminatory policing inescapable social problems for black reformers. How they and their white liberal allies responded to these challenges, in part by redefining African American criminality as a social rather than a moral and cultural problem is the focus of this chapter.

Racial violence swept across the nation beginning in East St. Louis in 1917; it erupted in Philadelphia the following year, and in twenty-two additional cities in the summer of 1919. Two differing views of black criminality emerged to explain the bloodshed and the chaos, especially with regard to southern migrants. The first view, advanced by writers such as Emmett Scott and Sadie T. Mossell, rationalized violence against black communities in part by blaming black southern migrants for their bad habits—for being culturally backward and thus overrepresented in the crime statistics.[31] In their analysis, southerners' inability to meet the demands of sophisticated urban living, coupled with the absence of overt forms of racial proscription in the urban North, had led to too much freedom, resulting in excessive crime rates.

Arriving at an entirely different assessment of migrant criminality and its root cause, Henderson H. Donald, a 1920 black graduate from Yale with an M.A. in sociology, instead underscored northern whites' treatment of migrants. Although Donald agreed that many migrants had committed "criminal acts" because of the "extremely difficult task" of adjusting to their new environment, especially given the absence of "the strict moral and religious checks of the southern communities," he completely rejected the "conclusion" that a "wave of crime" had been the result.[32] Rather than concluding that crime rates reflected cultural or moral inferiority, Donald instead focused on northern policing of public order violations and vice, what he called "minor" or "petty" offenses. Using Pittsburgh police court records from 1914 to 1917, he observed a "disproportionate increase in arrests" for "such offenses as suspicious characters, disorderly conduct, drunkenness, keeping and visiting disorderly houses, and violations of city ordinances." He repeated this analysis for other northern communities and noted similar findings. Cleveland's jail statistics were especially revealing: the black proportion of the jail population had grown from 13 percent in 1916 to 87 percent in 1917, settling at 60 percent in 1918. To drive his point home, Donald summarized the statements of a Cleveland superintendent of prisons. "These Negroes were not of the criminal type," the official exclaimed, but were instead victims of poor social conditions. "Often hatless on the streets, Negroes were summarily picked up by the police and sent to prison on the mere charge of suspicion." Police activity, in Donald's assessment, was therefore at the root of the "so-called 'Negro crime' in the United States." In Pittsburgh, where unemployment and inadequate housing were obviously the real problems needing official attention, Donald explained, "the situation . . . was all the more aggravated because [of] the attitude of the police department toward these newcomers. . . . With its usual lack of understanding, it permitted the police officers to arrest hundreds of these Negroes, many of whom were sent to the workhouses."[33]

Pointing out white police officers' negative attitudes toward blacks, whether southern migrants or native northerners, was not in itself a radical rhetorical move. Earlier writers had highlighted such attitudes while describing how police officers frequently aided or abetted mob attacks against blacks.[34] By this time, most urban reformers were well aware that racist thinking among police officers had real consequences for the development of northern black communities. The Chicago Vice Commission, for example, found in 1911 that police officers had, in the words of the *Nation*, "invariably driven the white prostitutes into the best Negro sections, where they are a demoralizing example and influence for the colored youth of both sexes."[35] Police violence and police misconduct in the black community had long been front-page news in local black newspapers such as the *Philadelphia Tribune*. But directly linking police officers' discriminatory attitudes and behavior to high crime rates among blacks was an entirely fresh approach.

233

Donald's novel approach interpreting of black crime statistics is illustrated by contrasting it to the way a major twentieth-century white criminologist stripped Donald's analysis of its context in order to highlight southern migrant criminality. Citing Donald's work in his 1924 edition of *Criminology,* one of the earliest American textbooks on the subject and a standard in the field for much of the twentieth century, white sociologist Edwin H. Sutherland wrote, "During the period of negro migrations to the North in the last decade there appears to have been a very great increase of crimes by negroes in many of the northern cities."[36] In one sentence, Sutherland readily accepted the veracity of the statistics cited by Donald while neglecting to mention Donald's conclusion that the numbers were flawed.[37] Sutherland, the specialist, may have been deliberately discrediting the nonspecialist's interpretation in his first textbook; however, in the second edition of his volume Sutherland would join Donald in questioning the reliability of racial crime statistics. He removed any mention of southern migrant criminality.[38]

Since the 1890s, disproportionately high crime rates among blacks had been the starting point and linchpin of modern discourse on black criminality. Neither racial liberals nor conservatives escaped that statistical "reality." In the world of numbers stripped of context, all black people were more likely to commit crimes against property and personhood. But context was everything for those writing in defense of blacks' humanity. Black social scientists of the postriot era did not shy away from numbers, but embraced the social scientific approach as a way to depict accurately the multifarious humanity of black people and as a way of documenting the impact of institutional and societal racism. As Marlon B. Ross points out in his literary analysis of "New Negro social science," black "sociologists were seeking an activist narrative that could contain an objective portrait of the race while motivating influential groups to act on behalf of the black masses."[39] These writers focused especially on the broader context of inequality that contributed to black crime rates. To be sure, white racial liberals also questioned the accuracy of the statistics, frequently calling for better and more comprehensive recording of black crime statistics. Black sociologist and Philadelphia race-relations reformer Richard R. Wright, Jr., for example, complained about "the difficulty of getting accurate information." Much "of what is written about Negro crime in large cities," he wrote, "is mere guess work, or impressions of observers, and cannot have any final scientific value for the sociologist."[40] Wright therefore attempted to expand the breadth of racial crime statistics beyond census prison data by soliciting unpublished racial arrest statistics from places like St. Louis, Boston, Pittsburgh, and Philadelphia.

In 1919, as part of the NAACP's initial efforts to discredit the black male rape myth and build a case for federal antilynching legislation, Herbert Seligman, director of publicity for the NAACP, sent letters to county officials across the country seeking black rape statistics.[41] One official answered that Hardin, Illinois, did not keep such statistics. He also explained why. "We have no colored people in this county, they are not allowed here," said the response signed by Clifford Plummer, county clerk.[42] In northern counties that did "allow" black residents and tracked their crimes, criminal justice officials could interpret the statistics in a discriminatory manner even when the data supported the NAACP's position. A New Jersey prosecutor answered Seligman's request by noting that his locale had not had any "complaints, indictments or convictions for rape against colored people . . . for the past ten years." In a revealing closing statement, Walter L. Hetfield, Jr., added, "Considering the large population of colored people we have in Union County, we have had very few criminal complaints against members of that race."[43] To many public officials, the association of blacks with crime was often a presumptive reality, even when the statistics showed otherwise.

Until the early 1920s racial liberals in the urban North countered such official thinking by focusing their energies on obtaining more accurate data or, more importantly, by presenting their own antiracist interpretations of how society shared some responsibility for why certain blacks, such as southern migrants, were admittedly criminally inclined. Donald's approach to statistics signaled a new trend. He shifted focus away from southern migrants as self-evident proof of criminality among a certain "class" of African Americans and instead turned the statistics on their head and stripped them of their prima facie value. Going forward, excessive crime rates among blacks in the race-relations literature of the postwar period represented a policing problem instead of a crime problem.

No other publication had as much influence on the rewriting of black criminality during this period than the 1922 report of the Chicago Commission on Race Relations, titled *The Negro in Chicago*. On July 27,

1919, shortly after whites stoned a black child to death at a public beach and a white police officer refused to arrest the white suspects identified by black witnesses, six days of rioting tore through Chicago, leaving 38 people dead and 537 injured, of whom 356 were black. To investigate the Chicago race riot of 1919, Illinois Governor Frank O. Lowden appointed a twelve-member commission, consisting of an equal number of prominent black and white civic reformers, to supervise an unprecedented eleven-month investigation into the causes and underlying conditions of one of America's worst and bloodiest race riots. The commission appointed Graham Romeyn Taylor, a white former settlement house worker and progressive journalist, and Charles S. Johnson, a black sociology graduate student at the University of Chicago, as the chief organizers of the project. Officially designated second in charge, Johnson took a leave of absence from serving as the director of research and investigation at the Chicago Urban League to assume principal authorship of *The Negro in Chicago*.[44]

Johnson was recommended for the position by his graduate advisor, Robert E. Park. The president of the Chicago branch of the Urban League, Park in 1921 was emerging as the most influential white sociologist of race-relations in the country. Until the mid 1930s Park and his career-long collaborator and fellow Chicago sociologist Ernest W. Burgess led a cohort of talented academics, including Louis Wirth, Clifford R. Shaw, Henry D. McKay, John Landesco, and E. Franklin Frazier in the systematic mapping and ethnographic study of community life among European immigrants and African Americans in the urban North.[45] Frazier, a black graduate student at the university from 1929 to 1932, was the only member of this cohort to focus on African Americans, writing a groundbreaking 1932 study of the black family, *The Negro Family in Chicago*.[46] As representatives of the Chicago School of Sociology, they established the field of urban ecology, sharing to varying degrees a scientific commitment to advancing environmental theories of poverty, crime, and delinquency, and carrying the intellectual temperament of Progressive era reformers and academics forward into the postwar period.[47]

The profound influence of these scholars in shaping a broader discourse of liberal environmentalism in the 1920s and 1930s came after publication of *The Negro in Chicago*. Nearly all of the Chicago School studies were published after 1921, with the notable exception of Thomas and Znaniecki's *The Polish Peasant in Europe and America* and Park and Burgess's *An Introduction to the Science of Sociology*. Among the social

Figure 6-1 Police arrive at the scene of a black man stoned to death by a white mob during the Chicago race riot. Note the presence of white civilians among the police and their proximity to the murder victim. Chicago Commission on Race Relations, *Negro in Chicago.*

workers and researchers hired by Taylor and Johnson to conduct field-work, and in the testimony of nearly two hundred local experts on various topics ranging from racial violence to real estate and crime and policing, the Chicago School sociologists are discernibly absent.[48]

In the immediate aftermath of the wartime riots, the work of the Chicago Commission on Race Relations was the latest and most influential study of African American life in the postwar urban North. Praising *The Negro in Chicago* for marking an "epoch" in the study of race relations, Walter White, assistant secretary of the NAACP and an eyewitness to the destruction left by the riot, wrote, "No student of racial problems or of the principal matters of concern to America can ignore this report."[49]

Although problems of police misconduct during the riot, or what White called "the actual connivance with the mob by the Chicago police force," were laced throughout *The Negro in Chicago,* the chapter called "Crime and Vicious Environment" was specifically devoted to an analysis of this phenomenon. The title is significant not only for the tenor of the discussion that followed, but also because, like Henderson's discussion the previous year, it signaled the shifting frame of analysis emerging in a postwar, postriot context, presaged by the changing mood of Philadelphia's black leaders during and after that city's riot. As principal author, Johnson played a major role in shaping not only the presentation of the commission's findings but also the tone of the book. As was the case with many New Negro intellectuals, one of his goals was to counter the racial conservatism of the era by being an "active publicist for liberal environmentalism." Historian Mia Bay writes that "the new generation of academically trained black social scientists that emerged during the 1920s employed their scientific training in research aimed at showing the primacy of environmental factors in determining human capacity."[50]

Johnson's training under Park certainly helped shape his structuralist views, as many scholars note. The roots of his analysis were planted in the fertile ground Park and Burgess were tilling at the University of Chicago, where there was an emerging sociological shift from focussing on ethnic and racial traits and individual pathology toward an urban ecological approach that explained inner-city criminality and juvenile delinquency. But Johnson was ahead of his time when it came to reinterpretating crime and policing. Not until nearly a decade later—when Shaw and McKay published cutting-edge scholarship on white juvenile delinquency and John Landesco on organized crime and police corruption—did the Chicago School have "its most concrete, transformative effect."[51] Landesco, for example, did not receive his undergraduate degree until the spring of 1924, nearly three years after *The Negro in Chicago* was published.[52] Instead, the two-decades-old epistemological and antiracist criticisms of the black crime discourse by Du Bois, Wells, and local black reformers (including James Stemons, Fannie Williams, and the *Philadelphia Tribune*'s G. Grant Williams) had helped to reframe, from the bottom-up the way Henderson and now Johnson would analyze the data. To that end, Johnson announced in the first sentence of the chapter that "The crime rate of Negroes is so largely controlled by a tangle of predisposing circumstances that it is hardly possible to isolate and measure its factors." Discrediting at the outset the use of racial crime statistics, Johnson argued that race was unimportant relative to the level of "general lawlessness, crime, and vice in the whole population."[53]

Figure 6-2 Police search African Americans for weapons during the Chicago Race Riot. Chicago Commission on Race Relations, *Negro in Chicago*.

Crime statistics were fundamentally flawed, according to Johnson. Striking discrepancies were found when Chicago police arrest data was compared with victims' surveys conducted by the Chicago City Council Crime Commission resulting in the considerable underreporting of crime for the entire city. The number of burglaries reported by victims in 1919, for instance, was found to be more than three times the number in the official police statistics. Other problems stemmed from the lack of the "systematic handling of criminal statistics" across various agencies, therefore limiting an accurate measure of "the prevalence of crime." Where race mattered, Johnson observed that blacks were more likely than the many "nationality" groups to be "debited" with their crimes because precinct desk sergeants more easily identified blacks by skin color. The fact that there were more blacks in the criminal age group (eighteen to thirty) compared to other groups, due to the recent influx of young single women and men from the South, also limited the comparability of racial crime statistics.[54]

Perhaps the most significant factor in a long list of problems with black crime data was revealed by the testimony of "judges and other authorities" that criminal justice officials were likely to "arrest Negroes more freely than whites, to book them on more serious charges, to convict them more readily, and to give them longer sentences." For example, one municipal court judge stated that he personally knew about "certain . . . police [who] were going into Negro clubs and arresting Negroes they found there, bringing them into court without a bit of evidence of any offense." Another judge discussed why large numbers of blacks were arrested on suspicion, attributing the practice to a lesser regard for "the rights" of black men compared to white men. "I think they hesitate a little longer when a white man is involved; I am certain that it is so." A former chief of police agreed, noting that southern migrants "naturally" attracted "greater suspicion than would attach to the white man who had lived for a greater length of time in the same district, and who also would be more easily identified and traced." Rather than arrest the white man, General Leroy T. Steward explained, the police would simply observe him, whereas they "would no doubt, feel if they permitted the colored man to pass on at the time, they would lose him completely."[55]

Such startling testimony coming from within Chicago's criminal justice community, clearly indicated the effectiveness of the commission's interracial makeup and attests to the members' prominence, legitimacy, and access to high-ranking officials. It was the strongest body of evidence yet to reveal the subjective nature of racial crime statistics, deeply influenced by the social, cultural, and political contexts in which they were created.[56] "These situations presented such obvious dangers," Johnson summarized, "that the [Chicago] Commission [on Race Relations] considered it best to avoid giving currency to figures which carried such clear evidence of their own inaccuracy and misrepresentation." Consequently, the commission abandoned its attempts to "work out comparative racial crime tables."[57]

At no point before 1922 had any published study argued that racial crime statistics were too unreliable to be usable. Since the end of the nineteenth century, such statistics, even if incomplete or subject to extreme antiblack interpretations, had been fundamental to assessing the progress and potential of African Americans. The unprecedented decision of the

Chicago Commission on Race Relations to disregard these figures influenced important members of the social scientific community.

Beginning in 1924 Edwin H. Sutherland, one of the greatest criminologist of the twentieth century, cited the Chicago Commission's conclusion that "there were no reliable [racial crime] statistics available."[58] He provided no additional commentary or evidence, but ten years later this somewhat tentative and ambivalent reference was transformed when he wrote that the "statistics were completely unreliable," then cited three studies corroborating *The Negro in Chicago*'s initial claims.[59] Sutherland's newly rekindled professional ties to the city and to the University of Chicago may have made him more receptive to the Commission's findings in the 1934 edition of his definitive textbook. Although he had received a doctorate in sociology from the University of Chicago in 1913, a year before Park's arrival, he left that year to teach elsewhere before returning to his alma mater in 1930, just as Shaw, McKay, Landesco, and Frazier were building a formidable body of statistical evidence that geography trumped nationality and race in explaining crime and delinquency.[60] In Burgess's preface to Frazier's 1932 study, for example, he wrote that "The rates of crime, delinquency, illegitimacy, poverty, and vice would seem from this study to be not a matter so much of race as of geography."[61] This latest research plus the Chicago Commission's earlier findings seemed to shake the very foundations of the statistical discourse on black criminality. Sutherland took note, especially since sociological research continued to show the potential for more racial violence in the nation's cities as a direct consequence of a perpetual cycle of bad data, bad policing, and bad treatment of black citizens.

One of the studies Sutherland cited revealed the potential of inaccurate racial crime statistics to inspire the kind of policing the Chicago Commission had called into question and to fuel popular perceptions about excessive crime among blacks. During a 1925 grand jury investigation of the Minneapolis crime scene, investigator Charles Davis noted that total black arrests documented in police records had grown from 470 in 1923 to 930 in 1924, leveling off to 890 in 1925. The doubling of arrests prompted Davis to write, "This condition is bad and is rapidly growing worse. Unless some method is devised to at least subdue the activities of these Negroes, there is certain to be a series of race riots in Minneapolis, followed by the usual lynchings and killings which always disgrace any civilized community when these outbursts occur."[62] Despite the level-headed cautions from Johnson's report in the aftermath of the Red

Summer of 1919 and a 1920 spectacle lynching of three black men in Duluth, Minnesota, 150 miles north of Minneapolis, some northern officials continued to single out black criminality rather than prevent or punish racist behavior among law enforcement officers and the public at large.[63] In 1928 Maurine Bois, a National Urban League researcher, reexamined the police records Davis had used and discovered that the numbers were incorrect and should have been recorded as 517, 389, and 478, respectively, for 1923 to 1925. Blaming the mistake on "printers and the system of record keeping," Minneapolis police accepted Bois's revised numbers as the "official" statistics. Thorsten Sellin, a nationally recognized crime statistics expert and a frequent collaborator with Sutherland, called the errors "an experience" that "makes one question all earlier totals for Minneapolis and creates a profound distrust of official records in general, even though there is no reason to regard the records of the city mentioned as typical."[64]

Sellin's critical eye for the shortcomings and inaccuracies of municipal arrest data had likely been honed by his initial interest in international comparative criminology. In a 1926 article he complained about the lack of uniformity in homicide statistics across European countries, warning researchers that only "trends" could be detected since "the statistics used have little or no value for comparative purposes."[65] Unlike many among the first generation of crime statisticians, Sellin benefited from a growing skepticism about the state of crime data among American criminologists.[66] Born the same year as Hoffman's *Race Traits* was published, Sellin was indeed a generation apart. As a Swedish-born immigrant to Canada and the United States, his initial experiences with race relations were very different from Hoffman's. He arrived in Philadelphia in 1915 and attended the University of Pennsylvania for graduate training, receiving his Ph.D. in sociology in 1922. Although there is nothing in Sellin's early published research or biographical record to explain his particular interest in racial crime statistics, he lived in Philadelphia through several of the tumultuous migration years including the Race Riot of 1918. The impressions made on the nineteen-year-old Sellin by daily headlines about racial violence in his newly adopted home, his early research into questions of comparative criminality, and his interest in the sociology of crime all suggest his openness to questioning the existing statistical discourse on black criminality. A short time after publication of "The Negro Criminal: A Statistical Note," in which Sellin repeatedly cited *The Negro in Chicago,* he and Sutherland collaborated as consultants to the U.S. Census

Bureau in the preparation of two federal prison reports covering the period 1929 to 1932.[67] Their official statement in the reports spoke directly to the way in which *The Negro in Chicago*'s unprecedented stance in 1922 influenced some of the most prominent white criminologists of the era: "The high commitment rate shown for Negroes is probably in some degree due to the combination of lower economic status, less frequent use of other forms of penal treatment for Negroes, and unfavorable race attitudes on the part of the white race. . . . It is hardly possible, therefore, to draw any conclusions from the data presented in this chapter, regarding the comparative criminality of race groups."[68]

At the intersection of mounting criticisms of racial crime statistics by white criminologists and by black scholars stood Nathaniel Cantor, a University of Buffalo criminologist. The title of his address at the 1930 annual meeting of the Association for the Study of Negro Life and History, "Crime and the Negro"—two of the most commonly-linked terms in race-relations titles by the 1930s—gave no clue that his was a fresh perspective coming from within the white social scientific community. Cantor wasted no time with the familiar recitation of blacks' disproportionate prison and arrest rates. Instead he completely rejected crime statistics in his opening lines: "There are few fields in social science where opinion readily passes for knowledge as in criminology. Perhaps in no other discipline are statistics as meaningless as in criminology and penology." The problem was, he explained, that racial interpretations were built on "unreliable statistics." National prison data, he noted, had become a "matter of deep suspicion" a year earlier when the director of the U.S. Census Bureau admitted that requests for data from local penal agencies had gone unanswered or had been haphazardly assembled. A recent Detroit survey, he continued, "showed that severer sentences were imposed on the Negroes than the whites for the same offenses." Clear evidence of police malpractice and judicial bias around the country made plain the fact "that our whole legal machinery tends to operate unfavorably toward the Negro criminal." For Cantor, a student of Franz Boas with a Columbia Ph.D. in anthropology, the whole situation starting with the old biological linking of "crime" and "negro"—the sleight of hand in his title finally revealed—was built on a flawed premise: "Unless one assumes a biological criminal type there is no more sense in speaking of the Negro criminal, than of referring to Presbyterian spaghetti." The racial signifier, in other words, made no sense when discussing a social problem.[69] Du Bois certainly agreed with Cantor, writing similarly from the helm of the NAACP's *Crisis* magazine, "It is senseless to regard crime as racial or characteristic of certain individuals. Crime is one of the best indices of social conditions."[70]

Cantor's speech and subsequent article made a lasting impression on at least one likely audience member: Carter G. Woodson, the Harvard-educated black historian who first created Black History Week (later Black History Month), the founder of the Association for the Study of Negro Life and History, and the editor of its *Journal of Negro History*. "Crime is not racial," he wrote in a 1938 review of Bernard Peyton Chamberlain's *The Negro and Crime in Virginia*. Borrowing Cantor's food analogy but spinning a tortured variation of his own, Woodson scolded the author, "To speak of 'Negro crime' is not less excusable than to speak of Irish salt or Malay bananas."[71]

Although an influential core of black and white researchers had begun the process of deconstructing and discrediting the statistical foundations of crime-as-race-and-culture arguments, other white writers proceeded more tentatively, seeking a balance between a bona fide police problem and a real crime issue among blacks. Thomas J. Woofter, Jr., a southern white liberal sociologist, race-relations expert, and member of the Commission on Interracial Cooperation, explained in 1925 that blacks were a "backward" group, "poorly adapted to the codes and institutions of the white civilization in which they live," but that "their [actual] criminality" was more a function of the environment than "racial tendencies." Blending old arguments with new insights, Woofter took crime off the table as the all-powerful symbol of a still-discernible black inferiority, emphasizing instead the "useless" practice of arresting large numbers of blacks in vice raids. As an example, Woofter described how police in an unnamed "large Northern city" had raided "every Negro pool room" in a single night, resulting in 160 arrests for vagrancy. Twenty of the arrests produced charges, sixty were thrown out upon proof of employment, and eighty individuals were forced to leave town or face indictment. "This high handed arrest of colored people is extremely galling to the law-abiding citizens," Woofter wrote indignantly. "It cannot be excused on any ground other than ignorance and inefficiency of police officers who engage in these practices, and indifference of the citizens who permit such officers to remain on the job."[72]

University of Iowa sociologist Edward B. Reuter, author of *The American Race Problem: A Study of the Negro*, saw the same underlying dynamics at work. "Some part of the apparent excessive criminality of the Negro people finds its explanation in police discrimination," Reuter argued, noting that police officers were "white men who share the general idea that Negroes are highly criminal." Yet police racism was only part of the story, he continued; "in very considerable part, [blacks] are still ill-adjusted to the secondary and highly individualistic nature of present-day American life."[73] Notwithstanding their opposition to discriminatory policing, these white sociologists remained quietly ambivalent about the link between black culture and crime.[74]

Part of their ambivalence is explained by their frame of reference. Beyond the debate about the inadequacies of crime statistics was the continuing effort among 1920s race-relations scholars to reinterpret the meaning of black criminality against the backdrop of a blatantly racist crime discourse. Speaking before a national audience at the annual meeting of the American Prison Association in 1921, G. Croft Williams, a white South Carolinian public welfare official, explained why the "proportion of Negro offenders is startlingly large." In addition to their present crisis of "maladjustment," "ignorance," "low mental power," and a "miserable environment," he stated, their African past had been decisive as well: "His dwelling for ages in tropical and semi-tropical forest and jungle life must have left vestiges in his physical constitution. These doubtless were strong factors in his behavior. Perhaps studies in glands, nerves, brains, and blood may some day give us a new conception of the Negro."[75] Among some influential public officials, the legacy of racial Darwinism continued into the third decade of the twentieth century as a legitimate ideological framework for explaining black criminality.

Chicago trial judge Marcus Kavanagh also clearly rejected 1920s liberal environmentalism. Unlike his judicial colleagues interviewed by the Chicago Commission, Kavanagh argued that whites had no responsibility for creating "negro criminal forces," one of the nation's "most perplexing and dangerous problems." "The worst enemy of the negro in America is the negro criminal. The white man is not an enemy of the negro, that is, he is not yet the negro's enemy," he warned. But he may become one unless "spokesmen for the dark race" mobilize against the "negro outlaw," who would otherwise "continue to ravage and destroy . . . and persist as a torment and a disgrace to his country."[76] Fully embracing racial crime statistics and police officers, both Williams's and Kavanagh's thinking better suited the public's general "impressions" of Negro criminality that liberals frequently criticized but rarely defined.[77] Within this larger constellation of antiblack ideas, black culture arguments were not so easily discarded by white liberal scholars in the 1920s.

Two rhetorical strategies helped white liberals to obfuscate the appearance of slipping into old racist discourses while simultaneously maintaining their credibility as objective scholars. First, they frequently juxtaposed black cultural inferiority in the urban North with racist police behavior. By linking the two issues, they distinguished themselves as moderate observers, since outside the boundaries of racial liberalism police officers were a protected class and southern migrants were otherwise still an unruly bunch. Also, by making the men in blue scapegoats for racism in the urban North, and by using code words for poor southern migrants such as "poorly adapted" or "ill-adjusted," they helped secure a space for interracial collaboration among well-intentioned northern whites and middle-class blacks. These were the men and women Woofter had referred to as "law-abiding citizens," presumably like himself and those participating in interracial commissions, conferences, and research projects, or representing the National Urban League or NAACP.

The second strategy practiced by white liberals was a corollary of the first: They presented their arguments in part as the product of legitimate black perspectives and research. Woofter, for example, began his discussion of discriminatory policing by framing it as "one of the most persistent complaints of Negroes."[78] Before doing the same, William T. Root, a white psychologist and lead researcher of a 1927 study of prisoners at Western Pennsylvania Penitentiary in Pittsburgh, told his readers point-blank that his findings presented such an "unfavorable comparison" of black criminality that he was "afraid of giving the impression of having a definite bias in the matter." To protect himself and his research from the taint of racial bias, Root put "negro case workers" in charge of dealing with black prisoners. In the processing of data such as the consideration "of extenuating circumstances," Root explained, "the most sympathetic help of his own race has been secured."[79] Root's disclaimers suggest that perhaps he and others had adopted the recommendation of the Johnson report that "white members of the public" seek "information from responsible and representative Negroes as the basis of the[ir] judgments about Negro traits, characteristics, and tendencies" so as to counter pejorative stereotypes.[80] Thus, new ideas about the structural basis of black criminality (for example, racism in the criminal justice system) were a reflection of a newly formed critical mass of black researchers who were demonstratively representative of a professional class of "law-abiding" citizens and, practically speaking, a potential bulwark against their fellow black criminals.

In the 1920s and 1930s a cohort of black women and men became authorities on black criminality. These sociologists, social workers, probation officers, criminal justice officials, journalists, and civil rights workers reshaped the continuing debate about crime as a measure of black progress and potential. Additionally, they called for and became increasingly engaged in crime fighting and crime prevention. Like their predecessors Ida B. Wells, W. E. B. Du Bois, Sadie Layten, and James Stemons, the new reformers were fierce defenders of the right of African Americans to be treated fairly under the law. As Kelly Miller put it in 1924, "[T]he inflexibility of law must be invoked to save order from anarchy." The breakdown he sought to redress was the arbitrary nature of law enforcement in black communities, frequently resulting in the harmful misapplication of criminal laws against African Americans.[81]

In her Urban League study of Philadelphia's criminal justice system using police and prison data and records of various social agencies for January to June 1924, black researcher Anna J. Thompson highlighted numerous examples of the capricious ways in which police officers and judges dealt with blacks. The fact that blacks made up only 7.4 percent of Philadelphia's population but comprised a quarter of the total arrests, according to Thompson's analysis, was due largely to frequent vice raids and "needless arrests." Thompson observed that police raids tended to inflate black arrest rates overall because of the high number of people arrested at one time, regardless of whether they were subsequently convicted of a petty offense or discharged. In one house raid, she noted, four black women and six black men had been arrested, all of them guilty of nothing more than being at home. The routine practice of arresting "suspicious characters" also proved to have a disproportionate impact on black arrest rates because these individuals should never have been arrested in the first place. Harry F., for example, was sent to the county prison for thirty days "on the charge of being a 'suspicious character'" after he informed a police officer that he was standing on the street because he was out of work and had been recently evicted by his landlady. Moses S. received an identical sentence for the same "crime," except he was picked up on the street while waiting for a friend. "No better proof of the many needless arrests," Thompson complained, was the fact that one-third of all blacks arrested were discharged. "The Negro is an easy prey for petty police officials who offer 'Tell it to the judge' as an explanation when arresting 'suspicious characters' and other ignorant as well as innocent victims of the law." Offhandedly she added that the "antagonism" between Irish police officers and blacks was the "basis for many jokes around City Hall."[82]

Ira De A. Reid, the National Urban League's director of research and publicity in the late 1920s and the 1930s, presented compelling evidence of poor policing in black communities in his several surveys of crime and policing. In a 1929 study of Denver, Colorado, for example, he found a pattern of "seeming recklessness" by the police when it came to arresting blacks because more than half had been booked on either "the all inclusive charge of 'Investigation' " or vagrancy.[83] In 1931 he came to a similar conclusion in Troy, New York, where 60 percent of the cases against blacks had been "offenses against the public order, probably the least criminal of all categories." Like Thompson, Reid looked at the extremely high number of cases—78 percent—that were "either suspended, discharged, or adjourned" as evidence of a problem. This situation, he reasoned, "bespeaks either indiscriminate arrests or extreme leniency on the part of the police."[84]

As Reid made his way across the country preparing NUL surveys in nine towns and cities in the West, Midwest, and Northeast, he stopped in Pittsburgh in 1930 and witnessed the total absence of law enforcement in the Hill district, a historic black neighborhood. "The amazing fact about the Hill," wrote Reid, "is that Pittsburgh has permitted intolerable, anti-social conditions to exist there for more than two decades and has done little to clean up."[85] To Reid, Pittsburgh's police officials may have seemed especially derelict in their duties because he had lived in the city while receiving his M.A. in sociology from the University of Pittsburgh in 1925 and while serving as one of the specially picked black research assistants in W. T. Root's local prison study.[86] By the time Reid had investigated five New Jersey municipalities in 1932—Trenton, Princeton, New Brunswick, Perth Amboy, and Plainfield—plus the beach towns of Monmouth County, he had seen enough ineffective policing and structural inequality to arrive at a rubber-stamp disclaimer about high black arrest rates: "That this is due to excessive criminality of the Negro is no longer a satisfactory answer to the problem."[87]

White municipal officials displayed a cavalier attitude about effectively policing black communities, according to Edward E. Wilson, a Howard

University Law School graduate and Illinois assistant state's attorney. "The whites who have the machinery of the law do not seem to care what crimes Negroes commit against each other," he wrote in 1929. "They are likely to take the attitude that 'this is a matter among niggers and why bother.'" Wilson's fifteen years as a black prosecutor afforded him a unique perspective as an insider, prompting him to focus on yet another form of discriminatory policing. Rather than highlight the problem of over-surveillance and excessive arrest activity, he focused on the problem of inadequate protection: "There is no greater cause for crime among Negroes than the contempt for law engendered by the conduct of certain police protecting and paltering with violations of the law."[88] By this reasoning, according to historian Kenneth Kusmer, what seemed an obvious contradiction was far from it: "As far as police protection was concerned, black people [in Cleveland] could without contradiction say that they received both too little and too much."[89] Likewise, criminologists Frankie Bailey and Alice Green state that "black urban communities such as Harlem were locations in which law enforcement was both too vigorous and too lax. Police brutality was accompanied by police corruption."[90]

As Philadelphia's black leaders had observed in the midst of the racial violence of 1918, police officers were often on the wrong side of the law, aiding and sometimes leading mob attacks against blacks. Updating the Chicago Commission's findings, the 1929 Illinois Crime Survey found that African Americans made up 30 percent of the recorded killings by police in 1926–1927, though they represented only 5 percent of the population.[91] Less than a year after the Crime Survey's publication, police shootings of black males in Chicago continued, according to Ida B. Wells. In the manhunt for a sixteen-year-old accused of breaking a restaurant window, she reported, the police entered his home without a warrant, guns blazing. He died in a hail of thirty-five bullets. Two others were killed in separate incidents. Continuing to speak truth to power, Wells expressed her outrage in the Chicago Daily News: "Perhaps if the city had recognized the above murders as a menace to her fair fame and public sentiment and then sternly demanded the removal of incompetent heads of the police department, Alfred Lingle [the sixteen-year-old] might not now be lying cold in death."[92] Police agencies across the urban North during the tumultuous migration years and beyond were, as scholars have noted, often involved directly in antiblack violence.[93]

Puzzle: Find the "Keepers of the Peace"

Figure 6-3 "Puzzle: Find the 'Keepers of the Peace,'" a cartoon depicting long standing criticisms of police indifference to white mob violence against black homeowners. The Philadelphia Tribune, Philadelphia Penn., May 10, 1928.

The consequence of this apparent paradox was that black communities were subjected to a hostile form of daily policing that was contrary to the criminal laws on which it was based and destructive to the communities it was supposed to serve and protect. In the broadest sense, however, "discretion was built into daily police work," according to crime historian Mark Haller. The system was overburdened by the fact that the number of violations within the entire population exceeded those that could be prosecuted. "Informal standards" were thus developed to help guide police work, resulting in a wide departure "from the impartial, due process model that was written into law and supported by civic reformers."[94] In this regard, blacks were the easiest targets of the police; their rights were the least respected, and they had only a modicum of political influence to hold officers accountable. "They are arrested more often and frequently receive longer sentences since they are not politically well known," noted A. A. Abraham in his study of black juvenile delinquency in Buffalo, New York. Worse still, Abraham added, was that state officials sometimes showed no remorse when they incarcerated innocent blacks. When Frank Harris was about to be released from a Pennsylvania prison after twenty-one years for a murder he did not commit, the state parole board delayed his departure until after its members were "assured Harris had a job and a home." Upon Harris's release, state officials gave him a "new suit and a $5 bill," announcing that "no great injury" had been done.[95]

Many law enforcement officials flouted the constitutional rights of black criminal suspects, posing a constant threat to innocent bystanders while simultaneously encouraging disrespect for law and order among everyone. Calling for a higher standard of policing as an anticrime solution, Kelly Miller wrote in 1935 that whites needed to "persuade and convince the Negro of the beneficent purpose and function of the law" rather than using it "as a means of humiliating and degrading them. Too often the policeman's club is the only instrument of the law with which the Negro comes into contact. This engenders in him a distrust and resentful attitude toward all public authorities and law officers. None can doubt that such a kindly attitude would go far to convince the Negro of the value to himself and advantage of law obedience and good citizenship."[96] Until that happened, indiscriminate and reckless policing remained, in state's attorney Wilson's opinion, "as responsible for criminality in Chicago as any other one agency."[97]

Black New Yorker George Fald expressed similar concerns about policing in Harlem in a 1922 letter to James Weldon Johnson, executive secretary of the NAACP. Identifying himself as a "law abiding citizen," Fald reported that numerous instances of police misconduct had "been going on for some time. Not only in the station house but on the street. I can recall several instances in which I have been an eye witness." Fald described one scene where a police officer searched a youth at gunpoint in the hallway of a building at West 137th Street, finding nothing on the "would be prisoner." Rather than stop there, the officer proceeded to question the "lad" about where he lived. When the youth responded, the officer cursed him and "struck the boy in the face." The subsequent action by the New York City police officer may have been a routine practice, but it was rarely described by witnesses. According to Fald, the officer "told the boy to run," then chased him while attempting "to strike him with his billie [sic]." The officer then "drew his revolver again to shoot but changed his mind." Puzzled and outraged, Fald asked Johnson, "How, if the officer had nothing on that boy, have he the right to molest him?" When questioned by Fald about his actions, the officer cursed him in the presence of "women and children" and said the boy was a "hold up man." Fald was not only unconvinced, but reasoned out loud that if the officer had probable cause to stop the youth, "he could arrest him on suspicious [sic] could he not?" Fald closed his letter by expressing hope that his testimony would deliver "justice to those who justice deserve."[98]

Brooklyn resident Rupert Clarke wanted the same justice when he conveyed the details of his own run-in with New York's finest while riding the subway on July 23, 1931. According to correspondence between Clarke and NAACP officials and an affidavit submitted to the New York City police commissioner, Clarke was sitting in a corner with two empty seats near him when "this man on entering [the subway car] promptly sat next to me[,] pushed my leg violently and ordered me to close them. I looked at him a little thought he was drunk or something of the kind and returned to my 'Times.' . . . A moment later he repeated the assault." As it turns out, the assailant was an undercover police officer, James E. Cleary, who arrested Clarke after he pushed back and they began to argue. "Of all the people in the world I would least expect an officer to do such a base thing: deliberately assault and provoke a man and then arrest him. Of course, I read about such things in newspapers but I never dreamed they applied to me." He said he refused to be arrested, but the officer pulled the emergency brake on the train and soon two additional officers assisted him. Clarke submitted. He was locked in two "dungeons" until he was taken before the judge, where he was found guilty and ordered to serve two days in jail or pay a fine. A white man witnessed the incident, but when asked by Clarke for his testimony, he replied, "I saw nothing." Frustrated by the eyewitness's lack of compassion, Clarke wrote, "Well it wasn't exactly a surprise but I shall always remember him." Without enough money for a lawyer, Clarke, a postal worker, unwillingly paid the fine instead of fighting it. Figuring that his case was closed, he wanted the "wonderful association" to know about Cleary because he suspected he would attempt "the base trick on other of my people." Clarke hoped his affidavit would help get Cleary fired. "I am sure the Commissioner doesn't want such men on his force."[99]

The professional standards and racial ethics of those in charge of police agencies could not be taken for granted in light of the racial scandal initiated by Raymond E. Gilyard, police chief in Seymour, Connecticut. Six weeks before Clarke's encounter, a small New England town only eighty miles northeast of New York City was rocked by the alleged gang-style murder of Chief Gilyard. The New Haven *Evening Register* reported on May 12, 1931, that moments before he died of a fatal gunshot Gilyard told a telephone operator, "I've been shot. . . . Three Negroes did it." A well-liked leader, Gilyard was "virtually [Seymour's] town manager" and had been "popular among the better element of the town as an anti-crime crusader." Recently he had been "prominent in the prosecution of Negro gangsters." Immediately following his death, with rumors suggesting that the murder was a retaliatory hit, as many as ten black suspects were rounded up and questioned by the police. The primary suspects were the brother and two associates of Harold Stanton, recently imprisoned by Gilyard for armed robbery. Town residents also joined in the manhunt for "the trio of Negro killers" by reporting the movements of suspicious blacks seen near Town Hall on the day of the shooting. Three "negroes . . . loitering," an impatient-looking Negro pacing outside a small sedan "parked just north of town hall," and four blacks driving away from the building at high speeds were all purportedly seen and suspected of foul play.[100]

While suspicious African Americans were being sought and arrested by Seymour police, some townspeople and journalists had begun to question the murder theory and speculate whether Gilyard had in fact taken his own life. The Manchester *Herald* stated that although it looked like blacks had killed him, "the nature of the crime . . . flies squarely in the face of the criminal history of the colored race." Not only were 90 percent of black murders intra-racial, according to the *Herald*, but they were never premeditated and were usually the outcome of a "sudden flaming of passion" due to "sex jealousy" and "gambling quarrels." Besides, the *Herald* concluded, "Feuds and considered revenges are completely foreign to the Negro psychology." Putting racial crime tendencies aside—the echoes of Hoffmanesque caricatures and Frances Kellor's claim that black criminals were incapable of executing "well laid plans or complicated schemings"—other observers began to analyze the facts of the case more closely, beginning with the improbability that Gilyard could have made a phone call after being shot through the heart.[101] Similarly odd was the ballistics report that all the bullets fired at the scene came from Gilyard's own guns. Although the coroner had initially discounted rumors of suicide, by the second day he changed his mind. The final ruling was that Gilyard "spent two months creating a fabrication of murder clews [sic] to escape his creditors"; he wanted his suicide to look like a murder in order to protect a large insurance policy. All suspects were immediately released.[102]

The Gilyard hoax was just one of many instances of racial scapegoating in the 1920s and 1930s. In New York City two white women, Mary Daly and Florence Kane, were murdered in separate incidents in 1925. In both cases, a flurry of press reports identified black men as the suspects until further investigation yielded white male perpetrators.[103] Two years later, in a slight variation, two white women falsely accused two black men in separate incidents of murder, when they themselves were the culprits.[104] Ida B. Wells had documented similar cases nearly a half-century before. More recently, the problem had become so noteworthy and widespread that the pioneering black sociologist Monroe N. Work continued Wells's work by compiling false accusations in an annual *Negro Year Book*.[105] In 1935, the Commission on Interracial Cooperation similarly released a report titled "Burnt Cork and Crime," where they highlighted not only false rape accusations by white women but also the "white man's trick of blackening his face before committing his crime." Taking note of the report and the scale of evidence, the white University of North Carolina sociologist Guy B. Johnson wrote that the full "incidence of the situations will probably never be known," except in the few cases where they "fail to work." But "to the extent that they succeed they are an absolute exaggeration of the Negro's *actual* criminality."[106]

Banking on the white public's readiness "to accept as fact the merest suspicion or accusation that a Negro is the perpetrator of a particular crime," Gilyard, it seems, hoped for his family's sake that his plan would succeed.[107] Although his suicide hoax proved that racist police behavior did not always originate with the rank and file, to many black observers like Walter White of the NAACP the scandal was simply another "instance of how Negroes are unjustly and with impunity accused of crime."[108] Claude McKay, a Caribbean-born poet and Harlem Renaissance writer, ostensibly agreed with White when he described in his autobiography how he had become an innocent victim of a "police dragnet." While working in Pittsburgh for the Pennsylvania Railroad, McKay was arrested and jailed overnight with a "motley gang of men, bums, vagrants, pimps, and honest fellows." The following day during his trial, McKay explained his employment situation and said that he had left his identification in New York. "The judge declared that I was doing indispensable work on the railroad, and he reprimanded the black detective who had pressed the charge and said the police should be more discriminate in making arrests and endeavor to ascertain the facts about their victims," McKay wrote. "My case was dismissed."[109]

Even when wrongful arrests were righted by judges—an arbitrary practice dependent on the appearance of respectability and likely concrete proof of employment—considerable damage had already been done. "The important fact . . . is the belief in the Negro's higher criminality," wrote Sellin in his influential 1928 article. "We are prone to judge ourselves by our best traits and strangers by their worst. In the case of the Negro, stranger in our midst, all beliefs prejudicial to him aid in intensifying the feeling of racial antipathy engendered by his color and his social status."[110] By the early 1930s Sellin's research had become its own source of inspiration for black researchers and crime fighters.[111] In a 1935 study, Sellin continued to uncover evidence of the ways in which "differential treatment" by criminal justice officials fueled the "apparent criminality" of blacks, finding that African American males in the North received harsher sentences overall than did native white or foreign-born males. He concluded that given the "great and relatively constant variations observed," racial prejudice is to blame and "equality before the law is a social fiction."[112]

Equality before the law was precisely the issue for many blacks in the segregated communities of the urban North. A 1927 *Philadelphia Tribune* editorial commented that "the best thinking element among our race group should not condone any wrong-doing on the part of any member of the group. We should insist, however, upon receiving fair treatment from those who are entrusted with the enforcement of the law; but they cannot afford us this equal treatment before the law if back in their minds they feel that we ought to be the recipients of treatment which is not only different, but unfair as well."[113] The bottom line for many residents of black communities was that police officers, white and black, needed to take seriously their duty to arrest the guilty and protect the innocent.

This was easier said than done within the white-controlled vice districts of black communities. Recorded observations of numerous black eyewitnesses ranging from undercover vice agents to NAACP informants and investigators showed that numerous entrenched interests were opposed to the effective policing of black communities. The rising influence of a critical mass of black crime fighters—middle-class women and men actively engaged in punishing criminals and preventing crime—helped to corroborate and enrich the claims of their social scientific counterparts that the "machinery of justice" was indeed discriminatory.[114] Their observations and efforts also reveal how so many individuals profited—politically, professionally, and/or financially—from perpetuating vice conditions in black communities.

Starting in January 1921 and lasting roughly four months, a black female undercover vice agent for the Philadelphia Police Department began recording daily entries in a journal.[115] Working alongside the "colored vice men" hired by the administration of Philadelphia Mayor J. Hampton Moore, she disguised herself as a prostitute in order to infiltrate the inner realms of a wide range of illegal enterprises. Without their knowledge or consent, she conducted daily interviews with dozens of white and black people directly engaged in prostitution, gambling, illegal liquor manufacturing and sales, drug dealing, and robbery. She also observed from close range numerous examples of blatant corruption and misconduct by police officers and high-ranking officials. Her journal entries are a unique and graphic description of a Prohibition era vice district, even more fascinating because they were written by a black woman who may have been a middle-class club woman turned crime fighter. Neither her name nor her identity were mentioned in the reports or in other documents examined in the Moore papers, but her condescending attitude toward and anxiety about some of what she witnessed reveals her social class.[116] After entering a room at the Royal Palace Hotel where a party was taking place, she wrote the following: "The place was packed with under-world characters and was dense with tobacco smoke and other odors so that it is really wonderful that I survived the ordeal. I doubt if in darkest Africa there was ever such ignorance displayed as went on here on this occasion. . . . They played a very low kind of jazz music. Most of them call it the slow drag. They shimied [sic] and acted in a manner beyond description. It was so vile."[117] Clearly unable to contain her personal disgust, she continued her entry: "There was plenty of gin and whiskey as well as beer, for all and most of the women present were dope users and also a number of the men. . . . I was offered both heroin and cocaine." Although most of her entries were quotations from the people she met and physical descriptions of the places, people, and things she witnessed, her middle-class sensibility occasionally crept through. At the first annual dance of the Claver Younger Set, a black social club, she described the auditorium as a "very nice hall." Although she had been invited by "a gambler" and knew other members of the "underworld" were present, she remarked that the guests were typically of "the better class of young men and women and all acted in an exemplary manner. There was neither loud talking nor bad language used, neither was anyone allowed to loiter in the halls."[118]

The black female undercover agent was apparently typical of her social peers when she disparaged storefront churches in South Philadelphia for a style of worship unacceptable to her kind. Among the majority of black middle-class people, public respectability and proper religious expression were one and the same, according to historian Evelyn Brooks Higginbotham.[119] "Conditions were terrible at a so called religious meeting," the agent wrote, indicating that she was repulsed by the playing of jazz-influenced gospel music, especially the use of a "trap drum and tamboreen [sic]." Given the lack of "decency" indicated by the dancing, shouting, and carrying-on, she called the place "ridiculous. It seems a pity that under the pretense of being religious any group should be allowed to practice such immorality and ignorance especially in neighborhoods in which there is already far too little inlightenment [sic]."[120] Her notions of respectability situate her as a person with little in common with those she was investigating. This suggests how easily she could have emphasized the "immorality and ignorance" of a different class of black people above and beyond the official corruption she witnessed. She, however, made only a single reference to southern migrant criminality.[121]

While documenting the movements of dozens of black "underworld" characters, the undercover agent paid considerable attention to the larger framework in which they existed. With housing, for example, she observed how many white landlords specialized in renting to "hardened criminal type[s]." Black tenants claimed that certain landlords marketed their rental units as safe havens for crime since they had personal connections with the police. J. Werner, for example, one of three brothers who shared a large real estate business, was also a police officer. According to a prostitute, one of the Werner buildings was a "fine house to live in as the landlord never bothers to see what is going on so long as he gets his rent." Morris Werner was even known to "boast . . . that he has sufficient pull in the district to prevent the arrest of anyone living in his houses if they are charged with anything short of murder, or that he can have anyone in bad with him picked up." Another property owner, Harry Levin, was reputed to lease his units to known drug dealers at rock-bottom prices.[122] The *Philadelphia Tribune* later complained that "something must be done to abolish those hellish tenement houses that enrich the landlord and breed criminals," accusing "city authorities" of being fully aware of such "dives."[123]

As shown by the agent's journal—page after page recording dozens of instances of corruption—the connection between law enforcement officers and vice operations was blatant and endemic. Her references are all the more revealing considering that the misconduct and unlawful behavior she described occurred among the people with whom she had a professional relationship. As fellow police officers they had sworn to uphold the law, but they routinely neglected to arrest suspects who committed crimes right before their eyes, collected protection money from vice operators, and frequently drank liquor in illegal establishments, sometimes while soliciting prostitutes. A few police officers ran their own shady places. J. Werner's Pool Hall was located near the corner of Broad and South streets. Here, the agent observed, "at almost any time police officers in uniform can be standing in this pool hall, in friendly conversation with tough characters." Although not owned by an officer, Kate's Resort was so popular among the police that it was called the "cops' retreat. Many cops come here for a good time during the time they are supposed to be on duty." Other police hangouts were the University Pool Room, Seegal's Pool Hall, and Vic Hamilton's Café, the largest and most popular cabaret in South Philadelphia. The "café" was the cream of the crop among police hangouts, given its VIP patrons. According to a waitress at the nightclub, "[t]he Chief of Detectives and other high officials often come [in] . . . to enjoy themselves and the proprietor is the leader in this ward, so you know that means nothing can happen here."[124]

At the opposite extreme of protected places was a "notorious thieving joint" run by a "colored man known as Jim." When prostitutes recruited him to help them rob their white clients, the police rarely interfered, Jim explained to the undercover agent. "Cops know everything and they'll just bluff the fellow and tell him to get to hellout [sic] of here, what's he doing hanging around niggers." The investigator agreed, adding that she had seen "uniformed police officers, prostitutes and the hold-up men divide the money between them in this court."[125]

Although there was considerable diversity among the beneficiaries of police corruption—Jewish landlords, Italian bootleggers, African American pimps, Chinese and native white drug dealers—whites dominated the ownership and management of vice.[126] In Harlem in 1928, for example, the Committee of Fourteen, a New York City Progressive era anti-vice agency reenergized to fight bootlegging during Prohibition, found eighty-five speakeasies, all but four of them owned by whites. Like many other black communities across the urban North, Harlem had become what one Committee of Fourteen investigator called "a convenient place in which to go on a moral vacation" for "certain classes of whites."[127] To the black poet Claude McKay, Harlem was the "paradise of bootleggers."[128] Estimates from Chicago and other cities suggest that from 80 to possibly 90 percent of vice businesses were owned by nonblacks.[129]

Ownership by whites also meant that they wielded greater political influence and received the bulk of protection from city officials, leaving black-run places more vulnerable to police raids that did occur. A December 22, 1927, *Philadelphia Tribune* headline, for example, announced that the police department had deliberately protected an exclusive white nightclub while "inconsequential houses of unsavory aspect maintained by Negroes are subjected to constant raids."[130] The scale of the problem in Philadelphia had become so great that the following year the *Tribune* launched its own investigation: "If you have been raided recently by the police, or if you know of anyone who has, without the proper presentation of a SEARCH AND SEIZURE warrant send your name, address, the date and time of the raid, and the police officers making the raid to the PHILADELPHIA TRIBUNE."[131] During a 1931 New York state legislative investigation of political and police corruption known as the Samuel Seabury Commission, witnesses testified that New York City police officers who did not make their arrest quotas "used to go to Harlem and in Harlem they go to any colored house or colored apartment and they make any arrests at all, just because they thought colored people had less chance in court."[132] An NAACP investigation of Harlem's vice conditions in 1932 discovered wide-scale police corruption and selective law enforcement to the benefit of the police and white vice operators. "[T]he field of money making in Harlem," a memo read, is "entirely in the hands of the white police and the white racketeer."[133] Knowing they were not alone, New York's black paper, the *Amsterdam News,* had years before editorialized about "Chicago Police Covering up Criminal Connections by Attacks on Negroes."[134] In his 1933 study, *Vice in Chicago,* white sociologist Walter Reckless observed that blacks were the primary targets of police activity in vice areas. Police were seven times more active in vice districts in 1928 than they had been in 1908, and based on 1931 police records, 87 percent of the cases were against the "obvious, cheap Negro resorts."[135] Detroit's prostitution scene was no different; "it is a noticeable policy of the Detroit police to arrest colored girls almost exclusively on week-ends, the days when business is most brisk."[136] Historian Irma Watkins-Owens concludes that "white racketeers operating in black communities were seldom pursued with the same rigor as black operators."[137]

Having the least political influence, black residents in vice districts were more likely to experience two extreme forms of policing: widespread corruption and frequent raids. The following conversation—between a black police officer and the undercover agent—about the racial politics of Philadelphia Mayor J. Hampton Moore gives a sense of the contradictions at work. The agent began:

> I noticed two white officers standing in the store doorway opposite the Green Dragon and one in the block. I said, "look at the law awatching us." He said, "no, they are watching Smithie Lucas's [a black man's] place. You know he is in bad with this city administration and the Mayor keeps cops there ready to pounce upon him and raid his place for the least thing that happens there. They are supposed to be watching it for liquor but if it is too long before something does happen they will raid him anyway, that's politics." Further said, "You know [Vic] Hamilton's [a white man's] is the only place in this ward that is supposed to run. He is Mayor Moore's man in the ward, the man he recognizes in [his fight against the machine politicians who] recognize decent colored people as well as the underworld. . . . When did you ever hear of Mayor Moore attending or coming to speak at a big colored affair. All those colored people who voted or worked for him are getting just what they deserve, a kick in the pants. Why he even turned [G. Edward] Dickerson [a popular black lawyer and civic reformer] down. Dickerson and his crowd really elected Moore, now Moore has as good as told him this is a white man's administration, no negroes need

apply and the town is on the bum, worse than ever, even the police are lying down, simply on duty for that $5.00 per [day]."[138]

Embedded in this insider's graphic description of the politics of race and crime fighting is a firsthand account of the arbitrary nature of law enforcement in black communities across the urban North. The fact that some blacks in these communities stood to gain from a contradictory pattern of ineffective policing did not change the overall dilemma faced by the majority of residents, particularly self-identified working- and middle-class citizens who demanded that the guilty be punished and the innocent be protected. For them, the degree to which the policing problem had become greater than the crime problem is demonstrated by their repeated references to it and by the fact that they saw it as clear evidence of racial inequality in American society.

Commenting on the need for reliable and effective police protection on Chicago's South Side in the 1930s, members of the Amethyst Girls, a black women's social club, complained about being the victims of a recent spate of robberies. Two of the women castigated the police, charging that "they are too busy wasting their time talking and drinking beer in such popular spots as the Apex Grill instead of keeping their eyes open and trying to do their duty as they should." Another woman chimed in that such neglect was not tolerated in white neighborhoods on the North Side. Across town, she stated, "cops . . . are more interested in the protection of their women and children."[139] A white scholar and contributor to *The Negro in Chicago* linked the disparity in the quality of policing on the South Side and the North Side to overall economic inequality among blacks. When it came to vice dens "in a territory upon the North Side," University of Chicago professor Charles Merriam explained, "where there are many lawyers and people of some means, if they found [such] a place . . . they would never rest until they got it out. They would just keep at it with time and money until they forced it out." Notwithstanding their lack of resources, he concluded, "Negroes ought to be protected."[140]

Civil rights activists agreed and increasingly used the media to highlight the need for police reform.[141] NAACP officials Walter White and James Weldon Johnson frequently issued press releases, for example, when they received complaints of police misconduct or read about it in newspapers. In the aftermath of Raymond E. Gilyard's conspiracy to frame blacks for his suicide, for example, White contacted a lawyer in New Haven, seeking accurate information for a press release. "We want to use this story," he wrote. "Please send us all details you can gather on the matter."[142] NAACP officials also publicized other instances of police misconduct, including "police indifference" to a mob attack in Chicago, the torture of an innocent mentally handicapped suspect in Pittsburgh, and unlawful police shootings in Cincinnati, Ohio, and Jersey City, New Jersey.[143]

In Jersey City, several allegations of police misconduct in the 1920s drew the attention of civil rights activists. On December 7, 1920, Police Chief R. T. Battersby issued an order "that members of the force were to arrest all Negroes found on the streets after nine o'clock." According to Chief Battersby, there had recently been three robberies by blacks, in his mind evidence of a black crime wave that threatened the city's public safety. Battersby stated that this "has got to stop." Before the curfew could be enforced, an Associated Press employee notified the national headquarters of the NAACP, which took immediate action by contacting the local branch of the organization and city officials. Walter White called the order "vicious and unjust" and demanded Battersby's immediate dismissal. James Weldon Johnson agreed and expressed his fear of the danger that could result from such an order. "It is likely to be stretched out too far by ignorant or wilful-minded [sic] policemen who will be ready to arrest Negroes for no causes at all." The potential for a race riot over something like this, A. L. Jackson of the National Urban League pointed out, was too real to be taken lightly.[144]

The fear that race riots would become a permanent feature of northern cities after the Red Summer of 1919 gave a sense of urgency to the swift backlash against Jersey City's chief law enforcement officer. In as close to an admission as he would make, Battersby denied that he had issued an order against the entire black community, but stated that he had in fact informed his officers to "pick up strange negroes." "Jersey City is pretty free from crime," he added, "and we intend to keep it so." Reminiscent of white southern journalist Clarence Poe, who along with Du Bois two decades earlier had attempted to debunk the statistical myth that education created black criminals, a Tennessee editorialist referred to the Battersby order as a "Jim Crow Curfew Law." With a touch of sarcasm and an appreciation for the racial double standard at work, he wrote, "Taking into account the enormous number of crimes committed by whites, not alone in Jersey City but in nearly all other centers of population, it would seem that if this director of public safety is right in his plan of solving the trouble, the thing to do is to establish a curfew law for whites."[145] Battersby kept his job but was publicly censured.[146]

In a letter Walter White sent to the editor of the New York *World*, thanking him for his "splended [sic] editorial" on the controversy in Jersey City, he made one of his clearest statements about the way in which he and arguably other civil rights activists viewed black criminality relative to police misconduct:

> There has been so much vicious propaganda which has later proven untrue, manufactured deliberately for the persecution of Negroes, that such action can do nothing but create a tremendous dissatisfaction among Negroes and an impressed oppression of the Negro by irresponsible elements. . . . Tactics of this sort can lead to but one thing and that is an aggravation of already acutely strained racial relations and the formenting [sic] of conditions which will result in race riots. We are glad that the *World* has taken so clean-cut a position on this matter. The fact that three crimes have been attributed to Negroes in three days has thus been used to case [sic] a stigma upon Jersey City's 3000 colored citizens and to brand all of them as criminals. If this is the kind of democracy for which the Negro fought, then his services indeed have been in vain.[147]

In the context of an emerging national civil rights struggle, White's statement can be seen as an early indication of the way in which other blacks would come to frame the problem over the next two decades. Stepping up their resistance to Jim Crow justice in the urban North, in 1929 Jersey City's civil rights activists returned to the streets to protest a suspicious shooting of a black man and the alleged attack on a "young colored woman" by a police lieutenant.[148] In the spirit of this new era, the *Philadelphia Tribune* put at the masthead of every issue of the paper the statement "Fighting Against: Segregated Schools; Police Brutality; Economic and Civic Discrimination; Racial Treachery."[149] The activist paper also increasingly brought local, regional, and national coverage of police brutality to its readers, accompanied by an occasional editorial cartoon.[150] Among the many new voices of protest, publicizing instances of racial injustice became a central civil rights strategy.

As the statistical discourse on black criminality underwent dramatic changes in the 1920s and 1930s, spurred by New Negro race-relations

writers and civil rights activists and assisted by some major white criminologists, broader calls for reform proceeded simultaneously in the nation's
criminal justice community. The national scene was a parallel universe,
and reform was only tangentially connected in most criminal justice officials' minds to the problems raised by African Americans in their communities. The situation was somewhat analogous to the Janus-faced approach to Progressive era crime prevention and crime fighting, given that
black communities contended with their own criminals and vice operators, and also carried a huge burden of white vice and criminality; the reverse did not hold true.

The standard discussions of Prohibition's failures over the decade of
its existence drew a color line through reform attempts to redress the impact of the underground economy. In 1926, as a result of Prohibition-
related crime and violence and sensational media reports of crime waves
sweeping the nation—with law-abiding white and immigrant citizens
wearing the face of victimization—prominent police and federal officials
began to collaborate on a national crime reporting system that would
standardize and improve the reliability of locally gathered crime statistics
to aid the police in crime control.[151] The collaborators were motivated by
a need to counter a groundswell of public criticism that the machinery of
law enforcement had completely failed. A 1930 *New York Times* editorial
remarked, "Predatory crime with homicidal incidentals seems never to
have been more prevalent in the country than it was at the close of last
year." Not only were there "no comprehensive trustworthy statistics . . .
available on the subject," the *Times* complained, but the "police service in
various cities" was "breaking down."[152] Bootlegging gang wars—framed
by images of high-priced lawyers and their smug clients, nattily dressed
white gangsters who never seemed to get caught or do time—played vividly in the white press. These criticisms accompanied further complaints

Figure 6-4 "Be First to Let Him Out," a cartoon depicting a disturbed Benjamin
Franklin looking at the Philadelphia Negro incarcerated behind the bars of "Ill
Will," "Prejudice," "Segregated Schools," and "Jim Crowism." The cartoon is an
editorial statement on the racist failures of American democracy in The City of
Brotherly Love. Note the ambiguity in Franklin's position. His face shows concern,
but his back is to the jail cell, casting a shadow onto it. It is not clear whether "Old
Man Phila" is upset with the Philadelphia Negro or with the criminalization of
blacks in his city—the birthplace of Liberty. The *Philadelphia Tribune*, Philadelphia
Penn., January 3, 1929.

of widespread police corruption and abusive third-degree tactics that as critics pointed out, fell heavily on "the poor and uninfluential."[153]

Leaders of the International Association of the Chiefs of Police (IACP), including former Berkeley chief August Vollmer and Detroit's police commissioner William P. Rutledge, along with U.S. Attorney General George B. Wickersham and FBI Director J. Edgar Hoover sought to create a uniform crime reporting system that would establish a scientific basis for judging police efficiency. Law enforcement personnel were, as Lawrence Rosen points out, "concerned about their image."[154] President Herbert Hoover convened a National Commission on Law Observance and Enforcement in 1929, appointing Wickersham as its chair. Building on the work of state crime commission surveys from the early 1920s, the Wickersham Commission examined every part of the system, from statistics to policing to parole, with the help of social science experts, including Shaw, McKay, Sutherland, and Sellin. Acknowledging the achievement of the FBI and the IACP, the commission signed off on the newly created *Uniform Crime Reports* of 1930.[155]

The nation's first comprehensive crime data system, authoritative to this day, was not an unqualified success.[156] The results were especially mixed regarding African American criminal justice experiences and their measurement. Standardized "reliable" statistics—properly recorded and tabulated—did not change the daily reality of racial bias among police officers. This problem was abetted by the fact that Report 11 of the Wickersham Commission, *Lawlessness in Law Enforcement,* was a "devastating indictment of police brutality and third degree," according to historian Marilynn Johnson, but made no mention of the "racial disparity in third-degree cases" among black urbanites in the ten northern cities examined.[157] In her own analysis, Johnson found that blacks were overrepresented by a factor of seven in New York's third-degree cases, topping the Illinois Crime Survey's findings that African Americans were overrepresented by a factor of six in Chicago police killings.[158]

The *Philadelphia Tribune* similarly noted the commission's under-reporting of cases in Philadelphia. The editors acknowledged that the investigation into police lawlessness was to "millions of Negro Americans" the "first tangible bit of good" that the commission had done. They then added, "we are tempted very strongly to tell you that somebody told a lie about the decrease in police brutality." They noted that sensational cases of brutality against blacks in the South, from Arkansas and the "uncivilized wilds of Mississippi," had received prominent coverage, but there was no mention of several local cases, including the beating of a sickly elderly black woman; the torture of a man "chocked, [sic] hung upside down, his joints twisted and told that Negroes should be treated like dogs"; and the "drag net" arrests of Negroes on the "steps of their own homes, beaten and in some cases sent home without a magistrate's hearing. Five hundred more cases even worse than these," they concluded, had gone unaccounted for.[159] Taking full stock of Wickersham's unfortunate omissions, the NAACP protested outside the White House to draw attention to the federal government's unwillingness to secure antilynching legislation in spite of its heightened interest in crime and crime fighting.[160]

To the commission's credit, one criticism of government crime data on African Americans came from within one of its own reports. The thirty-six-page "Notes on the Negro's Relation to Work and Law Observance," written by Ira De A. Reid, the NUL's director of research, appeared in the four-hundred-page first volume of the *Report on the Causes of Crime*.[161] Given the history of dominant nonstructuralist analyses of black criminality and the marginalization of black social scientists at the national level, this was an accomplishment in its own right. In the foreword to the study, Sellin was cited for taking a leading role in bringing the work of Charles S. Johnson, now at Fisk University, and Reid to the commission's attention. Sellin, the foreword also noted, had recently attended the National Interracial Conference organized by Johnson and Reid, where he warned against attributing racial characteristics to the disproportionate crime rates of blacks. The data only proved that "the Negro appears to be arrested, convicted, and committed to penal institutions more frequently than whites." Nothing more could be determined, he reiterated. Impressed by Sellin's advocacy and stature, the commissioners decided to "insure a more understanding interpretation of the disproportionate number of Negroes shown in our study of men at [New York's] Sing Sing."[162] Reid was then selected for his experience and because, as "an investigator of the Negro race," he could lift the veil of mystery regarding "his own racial group." In the study itself, Reid argued that his findings and those of many others had shown that economic discrimination and over-incarceration went hand in hand. Even with creditable crime data, he concluded, disproportionately high black crime rates were still unreliable as long as crime statistics could not properly account for economic discrimination and racism in the criminal justice system.[163] The impact of Reid's criticism and Sellin's warnings nevertheless remained in doubt.

Despite the likelihood that racial crime statistics would continue into the foreseeable future in light of the Wickersham commission's unwillingness to fully embrace evidence of racism in the criminal justice system, African Americans had made great strides in gaining a legitimate voice in the national black crime debate and in drawing attention to the need for police reform in black communities. Concerned blacks' vision of effective policing in the 1920s and 1930s had its roots in the Progressive era community policing initiatives of black crime fighters such as James S. Stemons. Like his New Negro counterparts, Stemons had sought to eliminate "vicious and ruffian characters" by attempting to make municipal authorities responsive to black communities. But in Stemons's day, talk of black criminality trumped discussion of the structural antecedents of crime. The rhetoric of black inferiority that characterized racial reform in an era of liberal backbiting and Booker T. Washington's accommodationist politics eventually dissolved in the wake of racial bloodletting and war-inspired militancy. A new antiracist crime discourse and civil rights activism emerged from the flames of race hatred and oppression in northern cities during the postwar period.

Thorsten Sellin's and Edwin H. Sutherland's cautions about the limits of racial crime statistics were a breakthrough accomplishment in the four-decades evolution of the national discourse on black criminality. By comparison to their Progressive era predecessors, the interracial collaborations of a new generation of social scientists proved to be far more responsive to the realities of racism in American society and to the voices of African American crime experts, crime fighters, and ordinary citizens. Nathaniel Cantor's colorful injunction against the linking of blackness and criminality, like those of M. V. Ball, W. E. B. Du Bois, and Ida B. Wells in the 1890s, revealed that the perspective had gained a level of unprecedented legitimacy within some circles of mainstream social science. None of these scholars and activists ignored the real crime in black communities or the toll that it took on law-abiding victims. But they resisted the condemnation of blackness. They resisted the racialization of crime among African Americans in the same way that progressives and later Chicago School sociologists opposed the racialization of immigrant crime and delinquency. "The problem of crime and colored groups," Cantor insisted, "does not differ from the general problem of crime causation."[1]

For the many researchers, journalists, crime fighters, and law-abiding citizens who were dedicated to the cause of civil rights, rewriting black criminality in terms of police misconduct was an attractive rhetorical weapon because it fundamentally undercut the use of black crime statistics to justify other forms of discrimination. Policing racism in the northern criminal justice system became an effective rebuttal to the statistical arguments of earlier white social scientists that the "numbers speak for themselves."[2] The many blacks and liberal white criminologists whose ideas were influenced by *The Negro in Chicago,* or whose work picked up where it left off, never again viewed racial crime statistics in quite the same way. Doubts were even raised within the pages of the *Journal of Criminal Law and Criminology,* a first-rate academic publication that merged with the *American Journal of Police Science* in 1932.

Hans Von Hentig's 1940 article, "The Criminality of the Negro," was rare in that it illustrated the unreliability of racial crime statistics in relation to policing in a periodical with no obvious sympathies for the black civil rights struggle. After showing evidence that white offenders were more likely to go undetected by the police than were black offenders, Hentig concluded:

> Many, many more than we think escape this formal judgment and remain in the category of law-abiding citizens. Others, in contrast, are subjected to another sort of error. They are not overlooked but are misjudged in the opposite way; they are, so to speak over-assessed. . . . Arrests are made by human beings; sentences are pronounced by human beings; statistics are compiled by the same unwise homosapiens [sic]. When, as it is in our case, minorities are the subject of judgment and treatment, it is more than ever important to turn our attention to these agencies which we would like to believe unbiased and evenhanded and which are the more liable to errors the less they feel free of them. Furthermore, the colored race is a minority of which we are in dread.[3]

By Hentig's reasoning, racism in the criminal justice system had become a central problem in the judgment and treatment of the "colored race." The gap separating Hentig's logic and reasoning from Frederic L. Hoffman's— the span of half a century of statistical discourse on black criminality— now seemed unbridgeable.

But it was not. Hoffman was still producing crime data and still shaping the statistical discourse on black criminality, much to Du Bois's frustration.[4] More importantly for the IACP and the FBI—creators of the *Uniform Crime Reports* (UCRs)—the cautions of Sellin, Cantor, and Ira De A. Reid seemed to fall on deaf ears. To the nation's top law enforcement officials, race tables continued to speak for themselves.

Three years after they were first published in 1930, the UCRs began, for the first time, to report arrest statistics by race, based on fingerprint cards sent by local police agencies to the Identification Division of the FBI. Sellin's and Sutherland's prison report warnings about the inappropriateness of using data to "draw any conclusions . . . regarding the comparative criminality of race groups" nowhere appeared in the new UCRs. Instead the following statement accompanied the first three annual racial tabulations of arrests by offense: "It is believed that figures pertaining to the number of Negroes and foreign-born whites who were arrested and fingerprinted can most fairly be presented by showing them in proportion to the number of such individuals in the general population of the country." After 1935 "foreign-born" was removed from the statement: "The significance of the figures showing the number of Negroes arrested as compared with the number of whites can best be indicated in terms of the number of each in the general population of the country." By 1941 the foreign-born had been completely absorbed in the race tables under the category "white," and the text simply read: "Most of the persons in this tabulation were members of the white and Negro races."[5]

On this statistical trajectory, the nation's most respected and authoritative crime source had simplified the racial crime calculus in 1930s America. Blackness now stood as the singular mark of a criminal. "Negro" became the only statistically significant category in the UCR tables upon which to measure "white" criminality, deviance, and pathology. It was a losing prospect for African Americans. "The machinery of justice" was after all, as many had long observed, "entirely in the hands of the white man."[6] So were democracy and the economy. The statistical gaze on European immigrant criminality was finally heading to extinction, a process that Jane Addams and other progressives had helped to spearhead decades before. The second generation of European immigrants was assimilated into white crime statistics, as revealed by the last mention of the foreign-born in the 1940 UCR: "[I]t is significant to point out that the figure for native whites includes the immediate descendants of foreign-born individuals."[7] In this latest chapter of ethnic succession in the urban North—the statistical equivalent of "white flight"—all European immigrants were securing their whiteness, as blacks hunkered down for the many civil rights battles yet to come.

As the first black expert on African American criminality, W. E. B. Du Bois demonstrated—more than any one individual, and perhaps like no other could—how far the debate about the use of crime to measure blacks' progress and potential in modern America had come since the late nineteenth century. In an era dominated by hereditarian and retrogressionist theories about black inferiority and savagery, Du Bois's stern warning in the 1890s that blacks needed to "conquer" their "present vices" and turn their homes into "incubators of self-respect" had the effect of legitimizing the prevailing discourse. Overshadowing his antiracist criticisms, his Victorian moralizing against the submerged tenth in *The Philadelphia Negro* perfectly fit a racist milieu that increasingly looked to the social sciences to justify racism and discrimination.[8]

But embedded in the academic discourse that Du Bois embraced was a framework for its undoing. As Du Bois had subtly shown in his early research, black criminality did not and could not exist apart from the reality of inequality. "How long can a city teach its black children that the road to success is to have a white face?" he asked indignantly, as if to suggest an inevitable expiration date on seeing black criminality only as black inferiority.[9] Over the next three decades, armed with increasing social scientific data about a growing black middle class and a panoptical view (as editor of the *Crisis*) of nearly every incident of racial violence and discrimination against blacks, Du Bois turned social science into civil rights activism and stood at the center of a major transformation.

By the late 1920s and early 1930s, Du Bois had seen enough. For him and for many others, police racism and judicial unfairness came to represent the height of hypocrisy in American society. It was bad enough that the most isolated, impoverished, and despised citizens in the country were further ridiculed and isolated for their crimes, but it was so much worse that agents of the criminal justice system seemed to be conspiratorial instigators. With a long view of history and little faith in his liberal white counterparts, Du Bois turned back to middle-class blacks, as he had in *The Philadelphia Negro,* demanding that they do something.[10]

Rather than simply reinvigorating calls for crime prevention, Du Bois demanded that middle-class blacks, like their Progressive era white predecessors be sympathetic to the plight of black suspects and criminals. Social uplift agencies "ought to . . . save these unfortunates from further debauchery once they are in the hands of the law," he told *Crisis* readers. "It is to the disgrace of the American Negro and particularly his religious and philanthropic organizations that they continually and systematically neglect Negroes who have been arrested, or who are accused of crime, or who have been convicted and incarcerated. . . . [E]very Negro knows that a frightful proportion of Negroes accused of crime are absolutely innocent. Nothing in the world is easier in the United States than to accuse a black man of crime."[11]

The idea of black criminality was crucial to the making of modern urban America. In nearly every sphere of life it impacted how people defined fundamental differences between native whites, immigrants, and blacks. It also impacted, by comparison, how people evaluated black people's presence—the Negro Problem, as it had once been called—in the urban North. In education, in housing, in jobs, in leisure and recreation, the idea shaped the "public transcript" of the modern urban world. Moreover, the various ways in which writers and reformers imagined black people as inferior to and fundamentally different from native whites and immigrants in the early twentieth century had a direct impact on the allocation of social resources for preventing crime in all communities, with the smallest amount flowing to black communities. Native whites and immigrants were much more likely to benefit directly from the most thoughtful and forward-thinking (or progressive) social work and social science during the early twentieth century. Regardless of whether one views Americanization programs as an attempt to strip European immigrants of their language, religion, and cultural institutions, the impetus grew out of a desire to eradicate differences rather than to accentuate them. Social workers and settlement house reformers were active agents in the effort to assimilate immigrants into American culture and society. They did not leave immigrants to work out their own salvation, though some immigrants tried mightily to disrupt these plans with their fierce attachment to cultural traditions and institutions derived from their homelands. Long before the late-model black drug dealer became public enemy number one, white bootleggers, drug pushers, pimps, common thieves, and thugs plied their trade in black communities alongside their black peers, but with the police on their side. Thoughtful, well funded crime prevention and politically accountable crime fighting secured immigrants' whiteness, in contrast to the experiences of blacks, who were often brutalized or left unprotected and were repeatedly told to conquer their own crime before others would help them.

The destructive consequences of the black crime discourse went beyond limited reform efforts in black communities; it also limited the application of pioneering sociological concepts to record and interpret the black experience. As much as progressives used statistical knowledge and social surveys as part of their arsenal of knowledge about immigrant inequality, they did not use data to shame immigrants into respectable behavior. Progressives used crime statistics to demonstrate the suffering of poor and working-class immigrants and native whites. They frequently rejected the data as "too statistical" because it submerged the humanity of the people and masked the "aggravating causes" of crime. The decriminalization of immigrants by progressives decades before the New Deal drew on immigrant crime statistics as an index of their assimilability—as "Americans in Process"—and of both their economic, social, and political oppression. This was the choice progressives made to bring immigrants into the fold of American life. For these reformers, immigrants' humanity trumped the scale of their crimes and the cultural expressions of their social resistance.[12]

By contrast, African American crime to many white race-relations experts stood as an almost singular reflection of black culture and humanity. For these writers, anything less than a full-throttle use of black crime statistics was deemed "too sentimental," too soft on crime. Downplaying the statistics, they often claimed, was no more than a biased attempt to conceal the dangerous criminal tendencies of the Negro stranger in America's midst. Even among white liberal social scientists and social workers who attached blacks to their broader pro-immigrant critiques of structural inequality in American society, ambivalence about the innate criminal tendencies of African Americans confounded their racial liberalism during the Progressive era. By the time liberals began to pay closer attention to the economic, political, and social factors that contributed to African American criminality in the 1920s and 1930s, larger numbers of second-generation immigrants were not only experiencing greater social mobility, but they were also increasingly less likely to be stigmatized by their criminality. Wide-scale lawbreaking and corruption during Prohibition actually helped to blur previously distinct lines between white immigrant groups, such as the Irish, Italians, and Jews, in part because of cross-ethnic alliances in the context of organized crime. As historian Humbert Nelli points out, "Ethnic diversity characterized many of the criminal syndicates that emerged during the Prohibition era."[13]

The irony that African American criminality stood out in the context of Prohibition as a result of the collusion of white ethnic groups with greater political power and economic resources was not lost on black researchers and crime fighters, leading them to shift their focus from targeting black criminals and the illicit pleasures of the working class to policing the criminal justice system. But paradoxically the antiracist rhetoric of civil rights activists contributed to sharpening the differences in how others viewed blacks' relationship to crime and policing compared to how they viewed nearly every other group.

Criminologists John Landesco and Sutherland perpetuated these differences in the 1930s as they began to explain second-generation immigrant criminality in terms of its likeness to native-white criminality. In the 1934 edition of his classic textbook *Principles of Criminology*, Sutherland wrote that "the second generation appears to approach the native-born of native parentage in regard to the kinds of crime committed."[14] Likewise, Landesco's contributions to the 1929 Illinois Crime Survey, a pioneering study of organized crime in Chicago, paved the way for viewing organized crime as an "intimate part of the total structure of urban life." His work, notes Mark Haller, "tended to minimize ethnic traits as explanatory factors" and became the basis for the work of Robert Merton and Daniel Bell in the 1950s. These modern proponents of Émile Durkheim's anomie theory explained criminality as a function of social strain produced when peoples' expectations do not match their level of legitimate access to material wealth and social status.[15] According to this theory, impoverished and isolated groups are more likely to experience greater social strain because the fewest legitimate options are available to them. Crime becomes a ready alternative and, in the words of Bell, an "American way of life."[16] Beginning with Hoffman, Durkheim's contemporary, at no point did any of the scholarship suggest that African Americans shared the same notions of success or that their crime could be similarly understood in these terms.[17] For white social scientists at midcentury, America's "great army of unfortunates" was still the white working class.

The trajectory of the discourse on white ethnic criminality and organized crime, on one hand, and African American criminality, on the other hand, had moved in two completely different directions since the arrival of new immigrant groups and a small number of early black migrants to the urban North in the 1890s. The gap in the discourse mirrored differences in reality, but more importantly the rhetorical disparity helped to shape those differences. Rhetorical celebrations of ethnic succession, even in the context of organized crime, were rooted in opposition to the stagnation or limited social mobility among African Americans, reinforcing the notion that there was something fundamentally wrong with blacks. Indeed, the dominant discourse on black criminality that emerged during the late nineteenth century established a framework for acknowledging racial inequality even among immigrants in modern American society, while simultaneously pathologizing African Americans. By the early 1940s the situation was compounded as a new wave of African American war-time migration three times larger than the Great Migration was underway in the major cities of the North.

As a window into the World War II period, an era marked by increasing national political influence among black civil rights activists, it is helpful to consider the most influential social science scholarship on race relations immediately following the period studied here. Just as Hoffman's *Race Traits and Tendencies* (1896), Du Bois's *The Philadelphia Negro* (1899), Franz Boas's *The Mind of Primitive Man* (1911), and Charles S. Johnson's *The Negro in Chicago* (1922) were pathbreaking studies that established new ways of defining the relationship between black criminality and racial liberalism, so too was Gunnar Myrdal's *An American Dilemma: The Negro Problem and Modern Democracy* (1944).[18]

Myrdal's analysis of African American criminality synthesized the arguments and findings of many of the major studies listed above. Myrdal also relied heavily on original research conducted by African Americans. This is significant because the studies were based on southern black conditions in 1940. The greater attention given to southern evidence fit within the liberal civil rights discourse emerging at the time, which highlighted the most extreme examples of southern racism and violence in order to stir the moral conscience of the nation. Myrdal devoted four chapters to racist and discriminatory criminal justice practices in the South. At the same time, he minimized racism and inequality in the urban North. "Northern Negroes are concentrated in big cities, where human relations are more formalized and where Negroes are a small minority of the total population," he explained. "The legal machinery in those cities might sometimes be tainted by the corruption of the city administration, but its size alone tends to objectify its operations and prevent its being influenced by the narrowest type of local prejudice. . . . In the North, for the most part, Negroes enjoy equitable justice." *An American Dilemma*, then, is the starting point for understanding why the historical scholarship after 1940 continued to neglect inner-city northern blacks' experiences with discriminatory policing and judicial practices until after the riots of the mid to late 1960s.[19]

Perhaps even more telling of the ways in which the post–World War II liberal discourse would shift its primary explanation for African American criminality back onto blacks themselves was Myrdal's statement that "in the North it is not so much discrimination which distorts the Negro's criminal record, as it is certain characteristics of the Negro population." Myrdal pointed to blacks' psychological deviance and maladjustment to racial inequality. Somewhat analogous to the ways in which racial liberals in the Progressive era incriminated black culture despite their knowledge of racism and discrimination, Myrdal's work signaled a renewed emphasis on culture defined as pathology: "*In practically all its divergences, American Negro culture is not something independent of general American culture. It is a distorted development, or a pathological condition, of the general American culture*" (Myrdal's italics). By the 1940s and 1950s social scientists were saying exactly the opposite regarding second- and third-generation immigrant criminality.[20] For all of Myrdal's insightful analysis of structural inequality and his strident criticism of racist treatment by southern police officers, African Americans in the urban North continued to be, in his estimate, their own worst enemies.[21] Despite the tremendous gains made by black crime researchers and civil rights activists in the 1920s and 1930s, racism in the northern criminal justice system was rendered nearly invisible by this latest formulation.

By illuminating the idea of black criminality in the making of modern urban America, it becomes clear that there are options in how we choose to use and interpret crime statistics. They may tell us something about the world we live in and about the people we label "criminals." But they cannot tell us everything. Far from it. For good or for bad, the numbers do not speak for themselves. They never have. They have always been interpreted, and made meaningful, in a broader political, economic, and social context in which race mattered. The falsity of past claims of race-neutral crime statistics and color-blind justice should caution us against the ubiquitous referencing of statistics about black criminality today, especially given the relative silence about white criminality. The invisible layers of racial ideology packed into the statistics, sociological theories, and the everyday stories we continue to tell about crime in modern urban America are a legacy of the past. The choice about which narratives we attach to the data in the future, however, is ours to make. Progressives rewrote white and immigrant criminality just as early civil rights activists rewrote, for a time, black criminality. The measure of crime, in both cases, was not racial inferiority but rather compassion towards the least among them. Sympathy and faith in humanity were chosen over scorn and contempt.

INDIVIDUALS

Alexander, Sadie Tanner Mossell. Papers. Collections of the University Archives, University of Pennsylvania, Philadelphia, Penn.

Buchanan, Alexander. Papers. Historical Society of Pennsylvania, Philadelphia, Penn.

Frazier, E. Franklin. Papers. Moorland-Spingarn Research Center, Howard University, Washington, D.C.

Haynes, George Edmund. Papers. Manuscripts, Archives and Rare Books Division, Schomberg Center for Research in Black Culture, The New York Public Library, New York, N.Y.

Miller, Kelly. Papers. Moorland-Spingarn Research Center, Howard University, Washington, D.C.

Moore, J. Hampton. "Report on Vice Conditions" and Correspondence. Historical Society of Pennsylvania, Philadelphia, Penn.

Reid, Ira De Augustine. Papers. Manuscripts, Archives and Rare Books Division, Schomberg Center for Research in Black Culture, The New York Public Library, New York, N.Y.

Stemons, James Samuel. Papers. Balch Institute for Ethnic Studies, Pennsylvania, Penn. (now at Historical Society of Pennsylvania, Philadelphia, Penn)

Welsh, Herbert. Papers. Historical Society of Pennsylvania, Philadelphia, Penn.

ORGANIZATIONS

Armstrong Association. Papers. Urban League of Philadelphia Papers. Urban Archives, Temple University, Philadelphia, Penn.

Benezet House Association. Records. Friends Historical Library of Swarthmore College, Swarthmore, Penn.

Big Brothers Association of Philadelphia. Papers. Urban Archives, Temple University, Pennsylvania, Penn.

Friends Neighborhood Guild. Papers. Friends Historical Library of Swarthmore, College, Swarthmore, Penn.

National Association for the Advancement of Colored People. Papers. Manuscript Division, Library of Congress, Washington, D.C.

National Urban League. Papers. Manuscript Division, Library of Congress, Washington, D.C.

Octavia Hill Association. Papers. Urban Archives, Temple University, Philadelphia, Penn.

Spring Street Mission. Annual Reports and Pamphlets. Friends Historical Library of Swarthmore College, Swarthmore, Penn.

Starr Centre Association. Papers. Center for the Historical Study of Nursing, University of Pennsylvania, Philadelphia, Penn.

University Settlements. Papers. Urban Archives, Temple University, Philadelphia, Penn.

Wharton Centre. Papers. Urban Archives, Temple University, Pennsylvania, Penn.

STATE AND LOCAL GOVERNMENT AGENCIES

Philadelphia Department of Public Safety. Report on Samuel Freeman. Historical Society of Pennsylvania, Philadelphia, Penn.

Philadelphia Juvenile Court. Reports on Black Juvenile Delinquents. Historical Society of Pennsylvania, Philadelphia, Penn.

Philadelphia Police Department. Records. City Archives of Philadelphia, Penn.

Philadelphia Quarter Sessions Court. Notes of Testimony, 1877–1915. City Archives of Philadelphia, Penn.

FEDERAL, STATE, AND LOCAL GOVERNMENT REPORTS

Criminal Research Bureau. *Older Boys and Crime in Philadelphia,* by Charles E. Fox. Philadelphia, 1932.

Criminal Research Bureau. *Older Boys and Crime in Philadelphia,* 2nd ed., by Charles E. Fox. Philadelphia, 1936.

Philadelphia Bureau of Police. *Annual Reports.* Philadelphia, 1900—1940.

Philadelphia Vice Commission. *A Report on Existing Conditions, with Recommendations.* Philadelphia: Commission, 1913.

Reid, Ira De A. "Notes on the Negro's Relation to Work and Law Observance." National Commission on Law Observance and Enforcement. Report on the Causes of Crime 13, no. 1. Washington: GPO, 1931.

U.S. Bureau of the Census. *Prisoners and Juvenile Delinquents in the United States.* Washington, D.C.: GPO, 1918.

U.S. Bureau of the Census. *Prisoners in State and Federal Prisons and Reformatories.* Washington, D.C.: GPO, 1930.

U.S. Bureau of the Census. *Prisoners in State and Federal Prisons and Reformatories.* Washington, D.C.: GPO, 1932.

U.S. Bureau of the Census. *Prisoners in State and Federal Prisons and Reformatories.* Washington, D.C.: GPO, 1933.

U.S. Department of Justice. *Uniform Crime Reports.* Washington, D.C.: GPO, 1930–1956.

NOTES

ABBREVIATIONS

The following abbreviations are used in the notes, unless otherwise noted.

AAAPSS   Annals of the American Academy of Political and Social Science
AJS   American Journal of Sociology

INTRODUCTION

1. The latest projection is that roughly one in three African American boys born in 2001 will eventually be incarcerated at some point in his life. By comparison, roughly one in five Hispanic boys and one in sixteen white boys of the same birth cohort will go to prison. See Doris Marie Provine, *Unequal under Law: Race in the War on Drugs* (Chicago: University of Chicago Press, 2007), 2; Beth Schwartzapfel, "A Nation of Jailers," *Brown Alumni Magazine,* March/April 2008, 32; Michael Jacobson, *Downsizing Prisons: How to Reduce and End Mass Incarceration* (New York: New York University Press, 2005); Marc Mauer and Meda Chesney-Lind, *Invisible Punishment: The Collateral Consequences of Mass Imprisonment* (New York: The New Press, 2002).

2. Statistics about black men going to prison were first tied to a national race relations discourse in the 1890s, particularly in the work of the racial Darwinist Frederick L. Hoffman, *Race Traits and Tendencies of the American Negro* (New York: American Economic Association, 1896). As recently as the 2008 Democratic presidential primary, Senator John Edwards remarked that "When you have young African-American men who are completely convinced that they're either going to die or go to prison and see absolutely no hope in their lives. . . . they don't see anything getting better" (Bob Herbert, "When Enough Is Enough?" *New York Times,* June 30, 2007). The use of the statistics on black male incarceration changed dramatically over the many decades between Hoffman's "scientific" discussion and Edwards's political rhetoric, demonstrating that black crime statistics have a long and rich history.

3. The underexamination of the historical roots of modern discourses on race and crime is also acknowledged in David J. Wilson's recent analysis of

"black-on-black violence" within statistical, media, and public policy discourses since the 1980s: "Most studies on this topic have examined it as a given reality and not as a racialized construct"; see Wilson, *Inventing Black-on-Black Violence: Discourse, Space, and Representation* (New York: Syracuse University Press, 2005), 13.

4. This book joins the work of other recent scholars such as Jeffrey S. Adler, Kali N. Gross, and Marilynn Johnson in its designation of the late nineteenth century as the starting point for modern racial criminalization; see Jeffrey S. Adler, *First in Violence, Deepest in Dirt: Homicide in Chicago, 1875–1920* (Cambridge: Harvard University Press, 2006), 120–158; Kali N. Gross, *Colored Amazons: Crime, Violence, and Black Women in the City of Brotherly Love, 1880–1910* (Durham: Duke University Press, 2006); Marilynn S. Johnson, *Street Justice: A History of Police Violence in New York City* (Boston: Beacon Press, 2003); also see Roger Lane, *Roots of Violence in Black Philadelphia, 1860–1900* (Cambridge: Harvard University Press, 1986). Drawing on Lane's work, Orlando Patterson situates his analysis in the late nineteenth century but argues that not until the early 1970s did black criminality become a "national problem," Patterson, *The Ordeal of Integration*, 39. Scholars of post-World War II race relations also tend to situate the politicization of race and crime in the 1960s and 1970s as the starting point for black criminality as a national discourse; see Michael Flamm, *Law and Order: Street Crime, Civil Unrest, and the Crisis of Liberalism in the 1960s* (New York: Columbia University Press, 2005), 14–16; Christian Parenti, *Lockdown America: Police and Prisons in the Age of Crisis* (New York: Verso, 1999), 3–45; David Garland, *The Culture of Control: Crime and Social Order in Contemporary Society* (Chicago: University of Chicago Press, 2001), 1–26, 53–74; Stephen Thernstrom and Abigail Thernstrom, *America in Black and White: One Nation, Indivisible* (New York: Simon and Schuster, 1997), 258–285; Marc Mauer, *Race to Incarcerate* (New York: The New Press, 1999), 1–68; Katherine Beckett, *Making Crime Pay: Law and Order in Contemporary American Politics* (New York: Oxford University Press, 1997), 28–43. Another body of influential research on contemporary racial criminalization by sociologists, legal scholars, and policy experts unintentionally dehistoricizes black criminality; see David Cole, *No Equal Justice: Race and Class in the American Criminal Justice System* (New York: The New Press, 1999); Elliott Currie, *Crime and Punishment in America: Why the Solutions to America's Most Stubborn Social Crisis Have Not Worked—and What Will* (New York: Henry Holt, 1998).

5. This study is not a comprehensive survey of every statement made by a race and crime expert. Although it notes a wide range of contributors to the discourse, it pays special attention to several key figures. Some were innovators, such as Frederick L. Hoffman, Ida B. Wells, W. E. B. Du Bois, Frances Kellor, Jane Addams, Franz Boas, Charles Johnson, and Thorsten Sellin. Others were influential representatives of schools of thought, such as Fannie B. Williams, Kelly Miller, G. Stanley Hall, John Daniels, and Edwin H. Sutherland. Still others wonderfully articulated the thinking of their contemporaries—for example Carl Kelsey, William Hannibal Thomas, and Sadie Mossell. Some local reformers found themselves in the middle of something, trying to make the best of a difficult situation, and they happened to leave records; they include Susan Wharton, James S. Stemons, Charles A. Tindley, Herbert Welsh, and an unidentified black female undercover vice agent.

6. Hinton Rowan Helper, *The Negroes in Negroland; the Negroes in America; and Negroes Generally. Also the Several Races of White Men, Considered as the Involuntary and Predestined Supplanters of the Black Races* (New York: Carleton, 1868); William Hannibal Thomas, *The American Negro: What He Was, What He Is, and What He May Become* (New York: Macmillan, 1901).

7. Porter argues that "numbers, graphs, and formulas [are] first of all . . . strategies of communication. They are intimately bound up with forms of community, and hence also with the social identity of the researchers." An important goal of this book is to caution historians and sociologists who turn to social surveys from earlier periods, often highlighting the work of the most recognizable white scholars, missing the voices of black experts, and totally unaware of the ideological forces bearing on the production and interpretation of racial statistics. Thus I share Porter's approach to reading statistical discourses as text and as identity construction. That is, in this book crime statistics are not used to reconstruct reality but are the problematic that is examined historically. They are a source of investigation into the discursive tactics of early-twentieth-century race-relations writers. They are off limits, by and large, as a way of defining the truth of any given matter, at any given moment. But readers will be swayed by certain statistical arguments and truth claims. In the end, this is the point. We cannot ignore seeing what we want to see. And when "we" are mostly white and privileged and use race and power to make claims to uncontested knowledge, the picture can (and often is) distorted. Black race and crime experts did not necessarily see the facts as they were either, but knowing what they claimed to see enriches our historical understanding of the enduring ideological currency of black criminality. See Theodore M. Porter, *Trust in Numbers: The Pursuit of Objectivity in Science and Public Life* (Princeton: Princeton University Press, 1995), viii–ix.

8. The historiography on racial thought and scientific racism has had a tremendous influence on my thinking. This study enriches the historiography in its explicit focus on early-twentieth-century crime rhetoric among northern writers and reformers: Richard Hofstadter, *Social Darwinism in American Thought* (Philadelphia: University of Pennsylvania Press, 1944); Rayford Logan, *Betrayal of the Negro* (1954, reprinted London: Collier, 1969); Thomas F. Gossett, *Race: The History of an Idea in America* (1963, reprinted New York: Oxford University Press, 1997); I. A. Newby, *Jim Crow's Defense: Anti-Negro Thought in America, 1900–1930* (Baton Rouge: Louisiana State University Press, 1965); George W. Stocking, Jr., *Race, Culture and Evolution: Essays in the History of Anthropology* (1968, reprinted Chicago: University of Chicago Press, 1982); George Frederickson, *The Black Image in the White Mind: The Debate on Afro-American Character and Destiny, 1817–1914,* 2nd ed.(Hanover, N.H.: Wesleyan University Press, 1987); John S. Haller, Jr., *Outcasts from Evolution: Scientific Attitudes of Racial Inferiority, 1859–1900* (Urbana: University of Illinois Press, 1971); Vernon J. Williams, Jr., *From a Caste to a Minority: Changing Attitudes of American Sociologists toward Afro-Americans, 1896–1945* (Westport, Conn.: Greenwood Press, 1989); William H. Tucker, *The Science and Politics of Racial Research* (Chicago: University of Illinois Press, 1994); Stephen J. Gould, *The Mismeasure of Man,* rev. and expanded (New York: Norton, 1996).

9. Thorsten Sellin, "The Negro Criminal: A Statistical Note," AAAPSS 140 (November 1928): 52–64.

10. In this article, the single most important source for Sellin's critique of racial criminalization and its statistical antecedents was the groundbreaking work of black sociologist Charles S. Johnson in the Chicago Commission on Race Relations, *The Negro in Chicago: A Study of Race Relations and a Race Riot* (Chicago: University of Chicago Press, 1922). Sellin also cited the findings of three National Urban League researchers: Anna J. Thompson, "A Survey of Crime among Negroes in Philadelphia," *Opportunity* 4 (July-September 1926); Forrester B. Washington, "A Race Emerging: A Survey Made for the Department of Welfare, Commonwealth of Pennsylvania" (Unpublished Manuscript, 1924); Maurine Boie, "An Analysis of Negro Crime Statistics for Minneapolis for 1923, 1924 and 1925," *Opportunity* 6 (June 1928): 171–173. Citations are found at Sellin, "The Negro Criminal," 52–56. For a significant moment when Sellin highlighted African American research to his white peers, see U.S. Wickersham Commission, "Work and Law Observance," *Report on the Causes of Crime*, vol. 1:1 (Washington, D.C.: GPO, 1931), 167.

11. Sellin, "The Negro Criminal," 52; see "unreliability" at p. 63.

12. Orlando Patterson, *The Ordeal of Integration: Progress and Resentment in America's "Racial" Crisis* (New York: Basic Civitas, 1997), 40. Patterson also raises the issue of real black criminals, writing that "A small hard core of dangerous people with multiple social problems does in fact exist" (38–39). Hard-core dangerous people live among all people and in all communities. (In the statistics used to define black criminality as exceptional in the 1890s, whites of all nationalities made up roughly 70 percent of the nation's prisoners.) The difference regarding blacks, as Glen Loury notes, is the legacy of "racial dishonor." The "specter of 'social otherness,'" Loury writes, "emerged with slavery and . . . has been shaped over the postemancipation decades by political, economic forces specific to American society, [and] remains yet to be fully eradicated"; Glen Loury, *The Anatomy of Racial Inequality* (Cambridge: Harvard University Press, 2002), 70. Defining black criminality through racial and cultural markers of inferiority was at the heart of post-emancipation race relations. Black Codes, Pig Laws, convict leasing, chain gangs, and lynching were direct consequences of inventing new ways of thinking about blacks and of using criminal laws, criminal justice practices, and violence to target them—all tracked by statistics, reifying racist presumptions that blacks were an exceptional and dangerous criminal population. Du Bois tried to parse the difference between the racialized context of the period and the real "hard core of dangerous people" by arguing that some black people turned to crime as a response to their oppression. For him, the solution was obvious: Law-abidingness and racial equality would minimize the number of dangerous black criminals. What he soon realized, however, was that this solution would not eliminate the *idea* of black criminality because too much was at stake. From Du Bois's point of view, racial inequality was tied directly to white supremacy and was justified by the idea of blacks as criminals. For a recent interview on Loury and his research, see Schwartzapfel, "A Nation of Jailers," 28–35. See also W. E. B. Du Bois, *The Philadelphia Negro* (1899, reprinted Millwood, N.Y.: Kraus-Thomson Organization Ltd, 1973), 387–397; Khalil G. Muhammad, "White May

Be Might, But It's Not Always Right," *Washington Post*, December 9, 2007, Sunday Outlook.

13. Du Bois, *The Philadelphia Negro*, 386–387; David Levering Lewis, *W. E. B. Du Bois: Biography of a Race, 1886–1919* (New York: Henry Holt, 1993), 224–225.

14. Thorsten Sellin, "Race Prejudice in the Administration of Justice," AJS 41:2 (1935): 212–217.

15. Antebellum racial scientists' failed attempts to prove the inferiority of African Americans inspired a new generation of scholars to try to succeed where they had failed; see Haller, *Outcasts from Evolution;* Lee D. Baker, *From Savage to Negro: Anthropology and the Construction of Race* (Berkeley: University of California Press, 1998).

16. John Roach Straton, "Will Education Save the Race Problem," *The North American Review* 170 (June 1900): 785–801; Booker T. Washington, "Education Will Save the Race Problem, A Reply," *The North American Review* 171 (August 1900): 221–232; W. E. B. Du Bois, "Notes on Negro Crime, Particularly in Georgia," *Atlanta University Studies* 9 (1904); James K. Vardaman, "A Governor Bitterly Opposes Negro Education," *Leslie's Weekly*, February 1904, 104.

17. For a sampling of important texts on late-nineteenth- and early-twentieth-century southern criminal justice history, see Edward L. Ayers, *Vengeance and Justice: Crime and Punishment in the 19th Century American South* (New York: Oxford University Press, 1984); Joel Williamson, *A Rage for Order: Black-White Relations in the American South since Emancipation* (New York: Oxford University Press, 1986); Stewart E. Tolnay and E. M. Beck, *A Festival of Violence: An Analysis of Southern Lynchings, 1882–1930* (Urbana: University of Illinois Press, 1995); W. Fitzhugh Brundage, ed., *Under Sentence of Death: Essays on Lynching in the South* (Chapel Hill: University of North Carolina Press, 1997); David Oshinsky, *Worse Than Slavery: Parchman Farm and the Ordeal of Jim Crow Justice* (New York: Free Press, 1996); Philip Dray, *At the Hands of Persons Unknown: The Lynching of Black America* (New York: Random House, 2002). For two exceptional works that emphasize racist southern criminal justice practices as crucial to the modernization of the New South, see Alex Lichtenstein, *Twice the Work of Free Labor: The Political Economy of Convict Labor in the New South* (New York: Verso, 1995), xix, 5; Mary Ellen Curtin, *Black Prisoners and Their World: Alabama, 1865–1900* (Charlottesville: University of Virginia Press, 2000), 62-80.

18. For a sampling of classic texts on late-nineteenth- and early-twentieth-century northern criminal justice history, see Anthony M. Platt, *The Child Savers: The Invention of Delinquency* (Chicago: University of Chicago Press, 1969); David Rothman, *The Discovery of the Asylum: Social Order and Disorder in the New Republic*, rev. ed. (New York: Aldine De Gruyter, 2002); Rothman, *Conscience and Convenience: The Asylum and Its Alternatives in Progressive America* (Boston: Little, Brown and Company, 1980); Eric H. Monkkonen, *The Dangerous Classes: Crime and Poverty in Columbus, Ohio, 1860–1935* (Cambridge: Harvard University Press, 1975); *Police in Urban America, 1860–1920* (New York: Cambridge University Press, 1981); Paul Boyer, *Urban Masses and Moral Order in America, 1820–1920* (Cambridge: Harvard University Press, 1978); David R. Johnson,

Policing the Urban Underworld: The Impact of Crime on the Development of the American Police, 1800–1887 (Philadelphia: Temple University Press, 1979); Estelle B. Freedman, *Their Sisters' Keepers: Women's Prison Reform in America, 1880–1930* (Ann Arbor: University of Michigan Press, 1981); Nicole Hahn Rafter, *Partial Justice: Women in State Prisons, 1800–1935* (Boston: Northeastern University Press, 1985); Allen Steinberg, *The Transformation of Criminal Justice: Philadelphia, 1800–1880* (Chapel Hill: University of North Carolina Press, 1989); Norval Morris and David J. Rothman, eds., *The Oxford History of the Prison: The Practice of Punishment in Western Society* (New York: Oxford University Press, 1998). A series of articles in 2003, "New Perspectives on Crime and Punishment in the American City," called attention to the "comparatively small historical literature on urban crime in the United States" in the early twentieth century as compared to other fields in social and urban history (519). The authors called for new scholarship on "the study of crime to national issues related to progressive reform, the rise of the New Deal, the evolution of urban criminal justice, and the rise of the modern carceral state," but their agenda-setting articles did not include race as a robust analytical category (versus a mention here and there) for examining the experiences of native-born whites, European immigrants, and northern blacks in relation to each other, nor for examining racial criminalization as a modern historical process. See Timothy Gilfoyle, "Introduction: New Perspectives on Crime and Punishment in the American City," *Journal of Urban History* 29:5 (2003): 521; "'America's Greatest Criminal Barracks': The Tombs and the Experiences of Criminal Justice in New York City, 1838–1897," *Journal of Urban History* 29:5 (2003): 525–554; Michael Willrich, "'Close that Place of Hell': Poor Women and the Cultural Politics of Prohibition," *Journal of Urban History* 29:5 (2003): 555–574; "The Racketeer's Progress: Commerce, Crime, and the Law in Chicago, 1900–1940," *Journal of Urban History* 29:5 (2003): 575–596; Rebecca McLennan, "Punishment's 'Square Deal': Prisoners and Their Keepers in 1920s New York," *Journal of Urban History* 29:5 (2003): 597–619; Gilfoyle, "Scorsese's Gangs of New York: Why Myth Matters," *Journal of Urban History* 29:5 (2003): 620–630.

19. David Courtwright's recent synthesis of the history of violence in America is a case in point. With the exception of a few scattered mentions over the century and a half covered in the first ten chapters of the book, African American violence is not examined until the final two chapters, which cover the 1960s forward: chapter 11, "Ghetto Violence," and chapter 12, "The Crack Era"; Courtwright, *Violent Land: Single Men and Social Disorder from the Frontier to the Inner City* (1996; reprinted Cambridge: Harvard University Press, 2001). Some notable exceptions to the periodization and regional biases of the dominant historiography include Richard Slotkin, "Narratives of Negro Crime in New England, 1675–1800," *American Quarterly* 25:1 (1973): 3–31; Lane, *Roots of Violence*; G. S. Rowe, "Black Offenders, Criminal Courts, and Philadelphia Society in the Late Eighteenth-Century," *Journal of Social History* 22 (Summer 1989): 704; Leslie C. Patrick-Stamp, "The Numbers That Are Not New: African Americans in the Country's First Prison, 1790–1835," *Pennsylvania Magazine of History and Biography* 119 (1995): 95–128; James H. Madison, *A Lynching in the Heartland: Race and Memory in*

America (New York: Palgrave, 2001); Cheryl D. Hicks, "'In Danger of Becoming Morally Depraved': Single Black Women, Working-Class Families, and New York State's Wayward Minor Laws, 1917–1928," *University of Pennsylvania Law Review* 151:6 (2003): 2007–2121; David B. Wolcott, "Shifting Priorities: Targeting Serious Crime and Minority Youth in Interwar Los Angeles," in *Cops and Kids: Policing Juvenile Delinquency in Urban America, 1890–1940* (Columbus: Ohio State University Press, 2005), 146–167; Johnson, *Street Justice;* Gross, *Colored Amazons;* and Adler, *First in Violence.*

20. Although Roger Lane's study stood as the only book-length historical analysis of nineteenth-century northern black criminality for the better part of two decades, his work furthered this perspective. Lane argued that "[t]here is no evidence of significant racial bias in Philadelphia's nineteenth-century court system, or indeed of those in any northern city in [the years 1860 to 1900]" (Lane, *Roots of Violence in Black Philadelphia,* 87). His explanation for black criminality was that a "criminal subculture . . . flourished in the later nineteenth century . . . [that is] still apparent late in the twentieth century (5)." On this score, Courtwright's post-1960s analysis echoes Lane's findings: "By the late 1960s and 1970s widespread alcoholism and drug abuse were established facts of ghetto life. They led to violence directly through intoxication, bad judgment, drug ripoffs, and other disputes; indirectly by compounding problems of marital and family stability, which were also being worsened by job loss and the steady growth of a self-contained, increasingly isolated, and deeply troubled urban 'underclass'. . . . What seems incontrovertible is that something like [Oscar] Lewis's culture of poverty . . . is indeed operating in the contemporary ghetto. That is, an oppositional lower-class subculture has taken root and has divided the black community along lines of value and class" (Courtwright, *Violent Land,* 219, 235). For a sampling of some of the most significant historical scholarship on black crime as a cultural way of life that discounts or ignores racial criminalization in the early-twentieth-century North, see Eugene Genovese, *Roll Jordan Roll: The World the Slaves Made* (New York: Vintage Books, 1972): 603–609; Williamson, *A Rage for Order,* 50; Oshinsky, *Worse Than Slavery,* 33; and Gilbert Osofsky, *Harlem: The Making of a Ghetto: Negro New York, 1890–1930* (New York: Harper Torchbooks, 1963), 139, 141, 148. For seminal critiques that call the uncritical use of statistical and sociological data by historians (such as Genovese and Osofsky) pathologizing, see Herbert G. Gutman, *The Black Family in Slavery and Freedom, 1750–1925* (New York: Vintage Books, 1976), 291, 293, 312, 314, 318, 455; Joe W. Trotter, "African Americans in the City: The Industrial Era, 1900–1950," in Kenneth W. Goings and Raymond A. Mohl, eds., *The New African American Urban History* (Thousand Oaks, Calif.: Sage Publications, 1996), 308–309; "Blacks in the Urban North: The 'Underclass Question' in Historical Perspective, in *The "Underclass" Debate: Views from History* (Princeton: Princeton University Press, 1993), 57, 61, 73; Curtin, *Black Prisoners,* 42–61.

21. The silences in the historical literature and the gaps in our historical knowledge are most obvious when crime policy researchers express surprise that the highest rates of black incarceration are in northern states and that police brutality and misconduct are most notable in cities outside the South. In a July 2007 report

by the Sentencing Project, researchers Marc Mauer and Ryan S. King emphasize, for example, that "states with the highest black-to-white [incarceration] ratio are located in the Northeast and Midwest, including the leading states of Iowa, Vermont, New Jersey, Connecticut, and Wisconsin"; see *Uneven Justice: State Rates of Incarceration by Race and Ethnicity* (Washington, D.C.: The Sentencing Project, 2007), 3. Also see New York Civil Liberties Union, *Criminalizing the Classroom: The Overpolicing of New York City Schools* (New York: American Civil Liberties Union, 2007); Robin L. Dahlberg, *Locking Up Our Children: The Secure Detention of Massachusetts Youth after Arraignment and before Adjudication* (New York: American Civil Liberties Union, 2008).

22. Higher levels of violence in Chicago's Black Belt, Adler explains, were due to racism; see Adler, *First in Violence*, 156–158, and "'The Negro Would be More Than an Angel to Withstand Such Treatment': African American Homicide in Chicago, 1875–1910," in *Lethal Imagination: Violence and Brutality in American History*, ed. Michael A. Bellesiles (New York: New York University Press, 1999), 298–299, 306–309.

23. Adler argues that "the character of African American violence did not reflect an alternative culture or an inverted value system"; Adler, "The Negro Would be More Than an Angel," 306. Some readers may be inclined to argue that African American crime was still worse than white crime, but this brings us back to the flawed assumption that early-twentieth-century statistical discourse was an objective measure of criminality. Rather, it was biased, incomplete, and no less a reflection of racial ideology and the political economy of the times than was the actual criminal behavior. Racial crime statistics were instrumental to white supremacist practices and policies at the dawn of their emergence in the postbellum period. It is impossible to disentangle the realities of racism from real patterns of criminal (or culturally adaptive) behavior. The "discount for prejudice," to use David Courtwright's term, has been underestimated by scholars, and its true value is likely unknowable. Ultimately, this was a numbers game to demonstrate racial inferiority for one group and class oppression for several others. For more on the flawed foundations of racial statistics, see Tukufu Zuberi, *Thicker Than Blood: How Racial Statistics Lie* (Minneapolis: University of Minnesota Press, 2001); Courtwright, *Violent Land*, 240. For a sample of scholarship on ethnic crime patterns and crime as culturally adaptive to economic, political, and social oppression, see Daniel Bell, "Crime as an American Way of Life," *The Antioch Review* (1953): 131–154; Robert K. Merton, *Social Theory and Social Structure* (New York: Free Press, 1957); Humbert S. Nelli, *Italians in Chicago, 1880–1930: A Study in Ethnic Mobility* (New York: Oxford University Press), 155; Nelli, *The Business of Crime: Italians and Syndicate Crime in the United States* (New York: Oxford University Press, 1976); Mark Haller, "Organized Crime in Urban Society: Chicago in the Twentieth Century," *Journal of Social History* 5:2 (1971–1972), 210–234; Haller, "Illegal Enterprise: A Theoretical and Historical Interpretation," *Criminology* 28:2 (1990): 207–229; Ivan Light, "The Ethnic Vice Industry, 1880–1944," *American Sociological Review* 42:3 (1977): 464–479; Light, "Numbers Gambling among Blacks: A Financial Institution," *American Sociological Review* 42 (December 1977): 892–1904; Jenna Weissman Joselit, *Our Gang: Jewish*

Crime and the New York Jewish Community, 1900–1940 (Bloomington: Indiana University Press, 1983); Robin D. G. Kelley, "The Black Poor and the Politics of Opposition in a New South City, 1929–1970," in Michael B. Katz, ed., *The "Underclass" Debate: Views from History* (Princeton: Princeton University Press, 1993), 300–302; Kelley, "We Are Not What We Seem," in *Race Rebels: Culture, Politics, and the Black Working Class* (New York: Free Press, 1996), 44–47; Irma Watkins-Owens, "The Underground Entrepreneur," in *Blood Relations: Caribbean Immigrants and the Harlem Community, 1900–1930* (Bloomington: Indiana University Press, 1996), 136–148; Tera Hunter, *To 'Joy My Freedom: Southern Black Women's Lives and Labors after the Civil War* (Cambridge: Harvard University Press, 1997), 60–61, 112–114, 132–134; Victoria W. Wolcott, "The Informal Economy, Leisure Workers, and Economic Nationalism," in *Remaking Respectability: African American Women in Interwar Detroit* (Chapel Hill: University of North Carolina, 2001), 93–126. For crime as banditry using the tools of folklore and cultural history, see also Eric Hobsbawm, *Bandits* (New York: Weidenfeld and Nicolson, 1969); Roger Abrahams, *Deep Down in the Jungle: Negro Narrative Folklore from the Streets of Philadelphia* (Chicago: Aldine Transaction, 1970); Lawrence Levine, *Black Culture and Black Consciousness: Afro American Folk Thought from Slavery to Freedom* (New York: Oxford University Press, 1977): 413–420; William Van Deburg, *Hoodlums: Black Villains and Social Bandits in American Life* (Chicago: University of Chicago Press, 2004), 76, 82–83, 116–135.

24. To borrow and reverse Robin D. G. Kelley's useful formulation, this book is about the "public transcript" of white *and* black criminality, not about the "hidden transcript" of either; Kelley, "We Are Not What We Seem," 53, and "The Black Poor," 295.

25. Matthew Pratt Guterl, *The Color of Race in America, 1900–1940* (Cambridge: Harvard University Press, 2001), 6.

26. Thomas Guglielmo, *White on Arrival: Italians, Race, Color, and Power in Chicago: 1890–1945* (New York: Oxford University Press, 2003), 77, 87.

27. Rothman, *The Discovery of the Asylum*, 254–256; *Conscience and Convenience*; Samuel Walker, *Popular Justice: A History of American Criminal Justice* (New York: Oxford University Press, 1998), 80–83,164–165.

28. On eugenics, see Nicole Hahn Rafter, *Creating Born Criminals* (Urbana: University of Illinois Press, 1997); for a general class-based analysis of Progressive era environmental views within the context of crime and criminal justice, see Michael Willrich, *City of Courts: Socializing Justice in Progressive-era Chicago* (Cambridge: Cambridge University Press, 2003); for discussions of the Chicago School of Sociology, see James B. McKee, *Sociology and the Race Problem: The Failure of a Perspective* (Urbana: University of Illinois Press, 1993); Alice P. O'Connor, *Poverty Knowledge: Social Science, Social Policy, and the Poor in Twentieth Century U.S. History* (Princeton: Princeton University Press, 2001).

29. Jane Addams, *The Spirit of Youth and the City Streets*, reprinted with a new introduction by Allen F. Davis (Urbana: University of Illinois, 1972; originally published 1909), and *A New Conscience and an Ancient Evil* (1912, reprinted New York: Arno Press and The New York Times, 1972).

30. Charles Richmond Henderson, *An Introduction to the Study of the Dependent, Defective and Delinquent Classes* (Boston: D.C. Heath and Company, 1901), 246–247.

31. This study pushes the periodization farther back in time than does Kelley, who says the discourse emerged "beginning with Robert Park and his protégés to the War on Poverty-inspired ethnographers"; see Robin D. G. Kelley, *Yo' Mama's Disfunktional! Fighting the Culture Wars in Urban America* (Boston: Beacon Press, 1997), 3, 16. For perceptive long-view essays on the historical origins of black pathology discourses, see Michael B. Katz, ed., *The 'Underclass' Debate: Views from History* (Princeton: Princeton University Press, 1993); Darryl Michael Scott, *Contempt and Pity: Social Policy and the Image of the Damaged Black Psyche, 1880–1996* (Chapel Hill: University of North Carolina Press, 1997).

32. I cautiously use "statistical ghetto" to signal the ways in which the emergence of racial crime statistics in the 1890s occurred precisely when northern segregation began to intensify. The term *ghetto* resonates with what Joe Trotter, Allison Isenberg, and others have criticized as the "ghetto synthesis" or the "ghetto framework" of earlier black urban historians such as Gilbert Osofsky, Allan Spear, Kenneth Kusmer, and David Gottlieb. These earlier historians tended to "cast African Americans as passive victims" of white racism, or "treated important facets of black life in pathological terms," or tended to minimize intra-racial differences (class, gender, sexuality, religion, birthplace, protest strategies, and so on) and how these differences changed over time. However, the term *statistical ghetto* still captures the intersecting processes at work in the 1890s. Northern segregation was *made* in part through the statistical discourse on black criminality and vice versa. The term therefore calls to mind the violence and dehumanization of racial quantification in the Progressive era. It is also a shorthand reminder of the tainted evidence used by urban historians and other scholars who rely uncritically on primary sociological evidence to draw their conclusions about African American urban life in the late nineteenth and the twentieth centuries. See Joe Trotter, "African Americans in the City," 308; "Appendix 7: Afro American Urban History: A Critique of the Literature" in *Black Milwaukee: The Making of an Industrial Proletariat, 1915–1945*, 2nd ed. (Urbana: University of Illinois Press, 2007), 264–282; Allison Isenberg, "Transcending Ghetto Boundaries," in *Black Milwaukee*, 327–337; Arnold R. Hirsch, "Second Thoughts on the Second Ghetto," *Journal of Urban History* 29:3 (2003): 289–309; Roger Biles, "*Black Milwaukee* and the Ghetto Synthesis," *Journal of Urban History* 33:4 (2007): 539–543; Osofsky, *Harlem: The Making of a Ghetto*; Allan H. Spear, *Black Chicago: The Making of a Negro Ghetto, 1890–1920* (Chicago: University of Chicago Press, 1967); David Katzman, *Before the Ghetto: Black Detroit in the Nineteenth Century* (Urbana: University of Illinois Press, 1973); Kenneth Kusmer, *A Ghetto Takes Shape: Black Cleveland, 1870–1930* (Urbana: University of Illinois Press, 1976).

33. Nikhil Pal Singh defines "color-blind universalism" as an antiracist ethos of the post-1960s civil rights era, where "biological arguments for black inferiority" have been discredited while "the belief that blacks are culturally deficient—less intelligent, less industrious, and less patriotic than whites—remains widespread." These color-blind attitudes toward blacks have been matched by the simultaneous

"rollback of federal civil rights enforcement . . . massive cutbacks in federal aid to cities, and the recoding of black existence in urban areas as a major threat to public safety and political virtue (that is, the moral panic over crime and welfare)"; see Singh, *Black Is a Country* (Cambridge: Harvard University Press, 2004), 12. For a similar critique, see Eduard Bonilla-Silva, *Racism without Racists: Color-Blind Racism and the Persistence of Racial Inequality in the United States* (Lanham, Md: Rowman and Littlefield, 2003).

34. Quoted in Frederick L. Hoffman, *Race Traits and Tendencies of the American Negro* (New York: American Economic Association, 1896), v, 310; "I am not a racist" is my paraphrase of John Daniels's statements in *In Freedom's Birthplace: A Study of the Boston Negroes* (Boston, Mass.: Houghton Mifflin Company, 1914; New York: Johnson Reprint Corporation, 1968), ix, 400–405, 410–411.

35. See, for example, more recent uses of the statement "I am not a racist" in Jonathan Rieder's ethnographic account of white ethnic backlash against black Brooklynites—described as "encroaching" black criminals and "ghetto dwellers"—in late-twentieth-century New York: *Carnesie: The Jews and Italians of Brooklyn against Liberalism* (Cambridge: Harvard University Press, 1985), 80, 93.

36. Rieder's ethnographic study of white ethnics in Brooklyn in the 1970s and 1980s documents the enduring and powerful resonance of late-twentieth-century attitudes about blacks as criminals: "Carnasians spoke about crime with more unanimity than they achieved on any other subject, and they spoke often and forcefully" (Ibid., 68, 69–79).

37. For examples of a progressive sociologist and a progressive U.S. president calling blacks their "own worst enemy," see F. W. Blackmar, "Review of *Studies in the American Race Problem* by Alfred H. Stone," *American Journal of Sociology* 14:6 (1909): 837–839, and Theodore Roosevelt's comments in "Roosevelt at Hampton," *New York Times,* May 31, 1906.

38. Early antiliberal sentiment tied to black criminality gave way to more measurable backlash movements in the 1960s and 1970s. According to Rieder's ethnographic research and survey data of the period, northern white urbanites "who were most nervous about crime . . . tended to oppose the civil rights movement"; see *Carnarsie,* 78. Similarly, post-World War II urban historians have observed the ubiquitous referencing of black criminality by 1940s and 1950s white homeowners who tirelessly resisted, often violently, upwardly mobile black home buyers; see Thomas J. Sugrue, *The Origins of the Urban Crisis: Race and Inequality in Postwar Detroit* (1996, reprinted with a new preface, Princeton: Princeton University Press, 2005); Heather Ann Thompson, *Whose Detroit? Politics, Labor, and Race in a Modern American* City (Ithaca: Cornell University Press, 2001), 17–18.

39. Allen F. Davis, *Spearheads for Reform: The Social Settlements and the Progressive Movement, 1880–1914* (New York: Oxford University Press, 1967), 94.

40. For a helpful guide to changing notions of (racial) liberalism in the nineteenth and twentieth centuries, see Cheryl Greenburg, "Twentieth-Century Liberalisms: Transformations of an Ideology," in *Perspectives on Modern America: Making Sense of the Twentieth Century,* ed. Harvard Sitkoff (New York: Oxford University Press, 2001), 55–66.

41. Franz Boas, *The Mind of Primitive Man* (New York: Macmillan, 1911).

42. The meaning of whiteness and blackness shifted, but their oppositional relationship remained stable.

43. For studies on how middle- and upper-class African Americans imagined themselves as racial representatives and/or showed contempt for their social inferiors, see Du Bois, *The Philadelphia Negro;* Evelyn Brooks Higginbotham, *Righteous Discontent: The Women's Movement in the Black Baptist Church, 1880–1920* (Cambridge: Harvard University Press, 1993); Kevin Gaines, *Uplifting the Race: Black Leadership, Politics, and Culture in the Twentieth Century* (Chapel Hill: University of North Carolina Press, 1996); Stephanie J. Shaw, *What a Woman Ought to Be and to Do: Black Professional Women Workers during the Jim Crow Era* (Chicago: University of Chicago Press, 1996); Glenda Elizabeth Gilmore, *Gender and Jim Crow: Women and the Politics of White Supremacy in North Carolina, 1896–1920* (Chapel Hill: University of North Carolina Press, 1996); Deborah Gray White, *Too Heavy a Load: Black Women in Defense of Themselves, 1894–1994* (New York: W. W. Norton, 1999); Victoria Wolcott, *Remaking Respectability: African American Women in Interwar Detroit* (Chapel Hill: University of North Carolina Press, 2001); Martin Summers, *Manliness and Its Discontents: The Black Middle Class and the Transformation of Masculinity, 1900–1930* (Chapel Hill: University of North Carolina Press, 2004); Marlon B. Ross, *Manning the Race: Reforming Black Men in the Jim Crow Era* (New York: New York University Press, 2004).

44. Thomas, *The American Negro.*

45. "Root cause solutions" is taken from Flamm, *Law and Order,* 179.

46. This book contributes to a recent trend in African American urban historiography focused on the limits of post–World War II racial liberalism. Heather Ann Thompson's recent study of Detroit's race and labor relations argues, for example, that "after the Second World War" the urban North "became embroiled in the same political tensions and battles that the South had experienced for generations in labor and civic relations"; see *Whose Detroit?* 8. This is true to a degree. But like many other excellent post–World War II studies of the urban North, much of this work underplays the impact of the Progressive era. The demographic smallness of northern black communities before the 1940s is one explanation. Also the expansion of the welfare state during the New Deal gave rise to a new order of rights consciousness that, as scholars rightly point out, did not exist in the earlier period. But progressives laid the groundwork and helped set the terms that later New Dealers would tweak and revise. From the 1890s through the interwar period, the limits of racial liberalism made legitimate the segregation of African Americans in both thought and practice. Black criminality was a core issue in this early debate about who was worth saving, why, and by what means. Mapping its significance is at the heart of this book. For a sample of post–World War II northern urban historiography on the limits of racial liberalism, see Sugrue, *Origins of the Urban Crisis;* Thompson, *Whose Detroit?;* Robert O. Self, *American Babylon: Race and the Struggle for Postwar Oakland* (Princeton: Princeton University Press, 2003); Matthew J. Countryman, *Up South: Civil Rights and Black Power in Philadelphia* (Philadelphia: University of Pennsylvania Press, 2006); Kevin Mum-

ford, *Newark: A History of Race, Rights, and Riots in America* (New York: New York University Press, 2007).

47. For a sampling of key works that emphasize African American agency, intra-racial cooperation and contestation, and institution-building during the Progressive era and the Great Migration, see Trotter, *Black Milwaukee;* Peter Gottlieb, *Making Their Own Way: Southern Blacks' Migration to Pittsburgh, 1916–1930* (Urbana: University of Illinois Press, 1987); James Grossman, *Land of Hope: Chicago, Black Southerners, and the Great Migration* (Chicago: University of Chicago Press, 1989); Earl Lewis, *In Their Own Interests: Race, Class, and Power in Twentieth-Century Norfolk, VA* (Berkeley: University of California Press, 1991); Elizabeth Clark-Lewis, *Living In, Living Out: African American Domestics in Washington, D.C., 1910–1940* (Washington, D.C.: Smithsonian Institution, 1994); Darlene Clark Hine, "Black Migration to the Urban Midwest: The Gender Dimension, 1915–1945," in Joe W. Trotter, ed. *The Great Migration in Historical Perspective: New Dimensions of Race, Class, and Gender* (Bloomington: Indiana University Press, 1991), 126–146; Kimberley L. Phillips, *Alabama North: African-American Migrants, Community, and Working-Class Activism in Cleveland, 1915–1945* (Urbana: University of Illinois Press, 1999); Andrew Wiese, *Places of Their Own: African American Suburbanization in the Twentieth Century* (Chicago: University of Chicago Press, 2004), 11–93; Jacqueline Najuma Stewart, *Migrating to the Movies: Cinema and Black Urban Modernity* (Berkeley: University of California Press, 2005), 114–188; Wallace D. Best, *Passionately Human, No Less Divine: Religion and Culture in Black Chicago, 1915–1952* (Chicago: University of Chicago Press, 2005); Davarian Baldwin, *Chicago's New Negroes: Modernity, The Great Migration, and Black Urban Life* (Chapel Hill: University of North Carolina Press, 2007).

48. The term *hidden costs* is borrowed from Thomas M. Shapiro, *The Hidden Cost of Being African American: How Wealth Perpetuates Inequality* (New York: Oxford University Press, 2004).

49. "Kelly Miller's Column: How To Restrain the Negro Criminal," February 9, 1935, Folder 80, Box 71–73, Kelly Miller Papers, Moorland-Spingarn Research Center, Howard University, Washington, D.C.

50. Recently, urban historians and others have begun to focus explicitly on the long-standing problem of police brutality and misconduct in black urban communities outside the South; see Martha Biondi, *To Stand and Fight: The Struggle for Civil Rights in Postwar New York City* (Cambridge: Harvard University Press, 2003), 2, 60, 61–66, 70–74, 148, 192–197, 286, especially chapter 2, "Lynching, Northern Style"; Johnson, *Street Justice.* For a recent treatment of the South, see Randall Kennedy, *Race, Crime, and the Law* (New York: Random House, 1997), 29–135, especially chapter 2, "History: Unequal Protection," and chapter 3, "History: Unequal Enforcement." Some new studies of the post-World War II urban North raise questions about historical patterns of police misconduct in understanding the causes of urban rebellions from 1964 to 1968. In Detroit, Heather Ann Thompson found survey data from the 1950s showing that the "abominable state of police-community relations is what most encouraged Detroiters to participate in the civil rights movement." She also argues that in 1960s Detroit white

police actions lit the powder keg of "deteriorated" race relations that exploded into a "full-blown urban crisis" (*Whose Detroit?* 21, 37, 38–47, 75–79, 82, 91–99); see also Sugrue, *Origins of the Urban Crisis,* 29, 255, 266; Flamm, *Law and Order;* Self, *American Babylon,* 78; Countryman, *Up South,* 2, 35, 154–155, 160, 166, 197, 249; Mumford, *Newark,* 94, 98, 114, 116–118, 125, 129, 131–135, 139–140, 147, 151–152, 156; Isenberg, "Transcending Ghetto Boundaries," 334.

51. For more on white ethnic succession in the urban North, see Stephen Thernstrom, *The Other Bostonians: Poverty and Progress in the American Metropolis, 1880–1970* (Cambridge: Harvard University Press, 1973); Thomas Philpott, *The Slum and the Ghetto: Immigrants, Blacks, and Reformers in Chicago, 1880–1930* (1978, reprinted Belmont, Calif.: Wadsworth Publishing, 1991); Stanley Lieberson, *A Piece of the Pie: Blacks and White Immigrants since 1980* (Berkeley: University of California Press, 1980); Theodore Hershberg, ed., *Philadelphia: Work, Space, Family, and Group Experience in the Nineteenth Century, Essays toward an Interdisciplinary History of the City* (New York: Oxford University Press, 1981); John Bodnar, Roger Simon, and Michael P. Weber, *Lives of Their Own: Blacks, Italians, and Poles in Pittsburgh, 1900–1960* (Urbana: University of Illinois Press, 1982); Kenneth Jackson, *Crabgrass Frontier: The Suburbanization of the United States* (New York: Oxford University Press, 1985); Oliver Zunz, *The Changing Face of Inequality: Urbanization, Industrial Development, and Immigrants in Detroit, 1880–1920* (Chicago: University of Chicago Press, 1988).

52. "The efforts of progressives to 'socialize' criminal justice in Chicago and other cities helped redefine American liberalism and the rule of law, laying an urban seedbed for the modern administrative welfare state" (Willrich, "'Close That Place of Hell,'" 564).

53. Ira Katznelson, *When Affirmative Action Was White: An Untold History of Racial Inequality in Twentieth-Century America* (New York: W. W. Norton and Company, 2005), 18, 23.

54. U.S. Department of Justice, *Uniform Crime Reports* (Washington, D.C.: GPO, 1930–1956). From 1935 to 1956, "Indian," "Chinese," "Japanese," "Mexican," and "All Others" appeared in the tables along with "White" and "Black," although the authors of the report emphasized only the latter two for comparative purposes.

55. Wilson, *Inventing Black-on-Black Violence,* 4.

1. SAVING THE NATION

1. Nathaniel S. Shaler, "The Negro Problem," *Atlantic Monthly* 54 (1884): 696–709. For Shaler's most influential race-relations articles, see "Science and the African Problem," *Atlantic Monthly* 66 (July 1890); "The African Element in America," *The Arena* 2 (1890): 660–673; "The Nature of the Negro," *The Arena,* December 1890, 23–35; "The Economic Future of the New South," *The Arena,* August 1890, 257–268; "European Peasants as Immigrants," *Atlantic Monthly* 71 (May 1893): 646–655; "The Negro since the Civil War," *Popular Science Monthly* 57 (1900): 29–39; "The Future of the Negro in the Southern States," *Popular Science Monthly* 57 (1900): 147–156.

2. For a sample of those who expressed fear of the "unimaginable" or strongly advised against it in the 1850s, see John Campbell, *Negro Mania, Being an Examination of the Falsely Assumed Equality of the Races of Mankind* (Philadelphia: Campbell & Power, 1851); Josiah Priest, *Bible Defense of Slavery and the Origin, Fortunes and History of the Negro Race* (Glasgow, Ky: Rev. W. S. Brown, M.D.,1852); George Fitzhugh, *Cannibals All! or Slaves without Masters!* (Richmond: A. Morris, 1857). For an analysis of this literature and the racial politics of the moment, see Charles H. Wesley, "The Concept of Negro Inferiority in American Thought," *Journal of Negro History* 25:4 (1940): 551–555; and Steven Hahn, *A Nation Under Our Feet: Black Political Struggles in the Rural South from Slavery to the Great Migration* (Cambridge: Belknap Press, 2003).

3. Lowercase "negro" has been preserved in original quotes throughout the book to maintain historical accuracy. Uppercase uses may be in the original or the author's use. Hinton Rowan Helper, *The Negroes in Negroland; the Negroes in America; and Negroes Generally. Also the Several Races of White Men, Considered as the Involuntary and Predestined Supplanters of the Black Races* (New York: Carleton, 1868), viii–xiv.

4. Shaler, "The Negro Problem," 697–698; Lawrence G. Friedman, *The White Savage: Racial Fantasies in the Post-Bellum South* (Englewood Cliffs, N.J.: Prentice-Hall, 1970); Wesley, "The Concept of Negro Inferiority," 554–557.

5. Shaler, "The Negro Problem," 696–697, 700, 703, 707.

6. Shaler, "Science and the African Problem," 42.

7. John S. Haller, Jr., *Outcasts from Evolution: Scientific Attitudes of Racial Inferiority, 1859–1900* (Urbana: University of Illinois Press, 1971), 187.

8. Shaler, "Future of the Negro."

9. Other scholars, Lee Baker in particular, do not see Shaler as a racial liberal. There is plenty of evidence to support Baker, but my interpretation is different. Shaler's liberalism was characteristic of a core contradiction among turn-of-the-century liberals, including some black liberals. They believed in an activist education program to uplift black people while simultaneously believing in black inferiority. Black criminality was the most commonly used example among liberals for this temporary defect, which education was supposed to help eradicate. See Lee D. Baker, *From Savage to Negro: Anthropology and the Construction of Race, 1896–1954* (Berkley: University of California Press, 1998), 47–48.

10. Ibid.

11. Haller, *Outcasts from Evolution*, 167. Haller adds that Shaler's "racial thinking" along with the ideas of Joseph Leconte, a University of California evolutionary idealist, and Edward Drinker Cope, a University of Pennsylvania paleontologist, "epitomized in many ways the most 'scientifically' accepted attitudes of the late nineteenth century on the Negro, the immigrant, and the so-called 'inferior races'" (153).

12. Shaler, "Science and the African Problem," 41–44.

13. Shaler, "The Future of the Negro in the Southern States," 153; Haller, *Outcasts from Evolution*, 173, 178. For more on Shaler's southern sympathies, see Baker, *From Savage to Negro*, 48.

14. James B. McKee, *Sociology and the Race Problem: The Failure of a Perspective* (Urbana: University of Illinois Press, 1993), 23. For a first-rate analysis of

the changing attitudes of northerners towards African Americans in this period, see Heather Cox Richardson, "The Un-American Negro, 1880–1900," in *The Death of Reconstruction: Race, Labor, and Politics in the Post-Civil War North, 1865– 1901* (Cambridge: Harvard University Press, 2004), 225–246.

15. Winthrop Jordan, *White over Black: American Attitudes toward the Negro, 1550–1812* (Chapel Hill: University of North Carolina Press, 1968); Thomas F. Gossett, *Race: The History of an Idea in America* (1963, reprinted New York: Oxford University Press, 1997); William L. Van Deburg, *Hoodlums: Black Villains and Social Bandits in American Life* (Chicago: University of Chicago Press, 2004).

16. Shaler, "The Negro Problem," 697, 703.

17. Ibid., 703.

18. Tukufu Zuberi, *Thicker Than Blood: How Racial Statistics Lie* (Minneapolis: University of Minnesota Press, 2001), 81.

19. Van DeBurg, *Hoodlums: Black Villains and Social Bandits*, 42–49.

20. Carl Linnaeus, *Systemae Naturae* (1735); Johann Friedrich Blumenbach, *On the Natural Variety of Mankind* (1795); Gossett, *Race*, 35–38.

21. William Drayton, *The South Vindicated from the Treason and Fanaticism of Northern Abolitionists* (Philadelphia: H. Manley, 1836), quoted in George M. Frederickson, *The Black Image in the White Mind: The Debate on Afro-American Character and Destiny, 1817–1914* (1971, reprinted with a new introduction, Hanover, N.H.: Wesleyan University Press, 1987), 47.

22. Shaler, "The Negro Problem," 700–702; Charles Richmond Henderson, *Introduction to the Study of the Dependent, Defective, and Delinquent Classes and of Their Social Treatment*, 2nd ed. (Boston: D.C. Heath & Co., 1901), 3–4; Frederickson, *The Black Image in the White Mind*, 50, 63, 70.

23. Darwin argued that human beings, like all species, naturally varied over time in their endowed capabilities, which could be measured. "Races" whose innate characteristics, such as bigger brains, allowed them to excel would by nature's plan be the superior organisms destined to survive and dominate. See Stephen J. Gould, *Mismeasure of Man*, rev. and expanded (New York: W. W. Norton & Company, 1996); G. Stanley Hall, "The Negro in Africa and America," *Pedagogical Seminary* 12 (1905): 358; Gossett, *Race*, 68; William H. Tucker, *The Science and Politics of Racial Research* (Chicago: University of Illinois Press, 1994), 22–25.

24. Wesley, "The Concept of Negro Inferiority," 548; Tera W. Hunter, "Tuberculosis as the 'Negro Servants' Disease'" in *To 'Joy My Freedom, Southern Black Women's Lives and Labors after the Civil War* (Cambridge: Harvard University Press, 1997), 192–195.

25. Among scientists, polygenesis was discredited by Darwin's influential theory of evolution, placing all human beings within the same species, even with the evolution of differences among them.

26. Gossett, *Race*, 65; Frederickson, *The Black Image in the White Mind*, 78–79.

27. Gossett, *Race*, 83.

28. Thomas Dyer, *Theodore Roosevelt and the Idea of Race* (Baton Rouge: Louisiana State University Press, 1980), 89–90; Frederickson, *The Black Image in*

the White Mind, 70–89; Haller, *Outcasts from Evolution*, x, 40–68; Charles Johnson and Horace Bond, "The Investigation of Racial Differences before 1910," *Journal of Negro Education*, 1934, 329.

29. Gossett, *Race*, 77, 79, 83; W. I Thomas, "The Mind of Woman and the Lower Races," *American Journal of Sociology* 12 (March 1904): 442; quoted in McKee, *Sociology and the Race Problem*, 30, 32.

30. McKee, *Sociology and the Race Problem*, 28; Rayford Logan, *Betrayal of the Negro* (1954, reprinted London: Collier, 1969), 165–174, 218–275, 359–370; Gail Bederman, *Manliness and Civilization: A Cultural History of Gender and Race in the United States, 1880–1917* (Chicago: University of Chicago Press, 1995), 50.

31. Herbert Shapiro, *White Violence and Black Response: From Reconstruction to Montgomery* (Amherst: University of Massachusetts Press, 1988); Hunter, *To 'Joy My Freedom*, 31–35.

32. Dorothy Ross, *The Origins of American Social Science* (New York: Cambridge University Press, 1991), 17; Haller, *Outcasts from Evolution*, 164–165; W. E. B. Du Bois, *Dusk of Dawn: An Essay toward an Autobiography of Race Concept* (New York: Harcourt, Brace & World, 1940; reprinted New Brunswick: Transaction Books, 1984), 51.

33. Gossett, *Race*, 101–122.

34. Shaler, "European Peasants as Immigrants," 648–653.

35. Edward A. Ross, "The Causes of Race Superiority," AAAPSS 18 (July 1901): 67–89.

36. David Levering Lewis, *W. E. B. Du Bois: Biography of a Race, 1886–1919* (New York: Henry Holt, 1993), 182.

37. Ibid., 184; Zuberi, *Thicker Than Blood*, 19.

38. Baker, *From Savage to Negro*, 26–27; Lewis, *Du Bois*, 184.

39. Ross, *Origins of American Social Science*, 36.

40. Gossett, *Race*, 146–153; Tucker, *Science and Politics of Racial Research*, 27; Davarian L. Baldwin, "Black Belts and Ivory Towers: The Place of Race in U.S. Social Thought, 1892–1948," *Critical Sociology* 30 (2004): 403.

41. Ross, "The Causes of Race Superiority," 85; Tucker, *Science and Politics of Racial Research*, 30–33.

42. Baldwin, "Black Belts and Ivory Towers," 407.

43. Shaler, "Science and the African Problem," 37.

44. W. E. B. Du Bois, *The Philadelphia Negro: A Social Study* (1899, reprinted Philadelphia: University of Pennsylvania Press, 1996), 386–387; Lewis, *Du Bois*, 224–225.

45. Lewis, *Du Bois*, 276.

46. W. E. B. Du Bois, *Black Reconstruction in America, 1860–1880* (1935, reprinted New York: Free Press, 1998); Stephen Thernstrom, *The Other Bostonians: Poverty and Progress in the American Metropolis, 1880–1970* (Cambridge: Harvard University Press, 1973), 186, 194; Thomas Philpott, *The Slum and the Ghetto: Immigrants, Blacks, and Reformers in Chicago, 1880–1930* (Belmont, Calif.: Wadsworth, 1991), xiv–xv; Theodore Hershberg, ed., *Philadelphia: Work, Space, Family, and Group Experience in the Nineteenth Century: Essays toward an*

Interdisciplinary History of the City (New York: Oxford University Press, 1981), 469–470, 476, 489; Stanley Lieberson, *A Piece of the Pie: Blacks and White Immigrants since 1880* (Berkeley, University of California Press, 1980); David Roediger, *The Wages of Whiteness: Race and the Making of the American Working Class* (London: Verso, 1991); Matthew Frye Jacobson, *Whiteness of a Different Color: European Immigrants and the Alchemy of Race* (Cambridge: Harvard University Press, 1998); Matthew Pratt Guterl, *The Color of Race in America, 1900–1940* (Cambridge: Harvard University Press, 2001); Richard Slotkin, *Gunfighter Nation: The Myth of the Frontier in Twentieth-Century America* (New York: Harper Collins, 1992); Thomas C. Leonard, "'More Merciful and Not Less Effective': Eugenics and American Economics in the Progressive Era," *History of Political Economy* 35:4 (2003): 687–712; William Z. Ripley, "Race Progress and Immigration" AAAPSS 34:1 (1909): 130–138. Thomas A. Guglielmo has recently described the settlement experience of Italian immigrants: "Even within the broader contours of nativism, xenophobia, and anti-Italian violence in particular, Italian immigrants were still on the right side of the color-line"; see *White on Arrival: Italians, Race, Color, and Power in Chicago, 1890–1945* (Oxford University Press, 2003).

47. John Higham, *Strangers in the Land: Patterns of American Nativism, 1860–1925* (New Brunswick, N.J.: Rutgers University Press, 1953).

48. Racism and discrimination were also directed at Asian immigrants but often occurred in places and circumstances quite distinct from European immigrants. Yet by comparison to blacks, some viewed Asians as "white." "We make every effort to keep the Chinese from becoming citizens of the United States, yet they are superior to the negro and much nearer our own race than the negro. Now, does it not strike any reasonable man that we should take greater precautions against the increase of the negro race in our midst," wrote William P. Calhoun, *The Caucasian and the Negro in the United States: They Must Separate. If Not, Then Extermination. A Proposed Solution: Colonization* (Columbia, S.C.: R. L. Bryan Company, 1902). For more on ideas about the relative labor advantages of Chinese immigrants as compared to African Americans, see Matthew Pratt Guterl, *American Mediterranean: Southern Slaveholders in the Age of Emancipation* (Cambridge: Harvard University Press, 2008), esp. chapter 4, "The Labor Problem," 114–146.

49. Logan, *Betrayal of the Negro*, 165.

50. *Frederick Douglass's Paper,* January 20, 1854, quoted in Jay Rubin, "Black Nativism: The European Immigrant in Negro Thought, 1830–1860," *Phylon* 39:3 (1978): 199.

51. Guglielmo, *White on Arrival*, 6.

52. McKee, *Sociology and the Race Problem*, 22.

53. G. W. F. Hegel, *Philosophy of Right,* trans. T. M. Knox (London: Oxford University Press, 1965).

54. One historian writes, "The new immigrants colonized the US urban frontier of the late nineteenth and early twentieth centuries and, in turn, the urban spaces changed the new immigrants"; see Thomas C. Mackey, *Pursuing Johns: Criminal Law Reform, Defending Character, and New York City's Committee of Fourteen, 1920–1930* (Columbus: Ohio State University Press, 2005), 50.

55. Cheryl Greenburg, "Twentieth-Century Liberalisms: Transformations of an Ideology," in *Perspectives on Modern America: Making Sense of the Twentieth Century*, ed. Harvard Sitkoff (New York: Oxford University Press, 2001), 59–62.

56. On southern progressivism, see Hunter, *To 'Joy My Freedom*, 124; Joel Williamson, *A Rage for Order: Black-White Relations in the American South since Emancipation* (New York: Oxford University Press, 1986); Michael McGerr, *A Fierce Discontent, The Rise and Fall of the Progressive Movement in America, 1870–1920* (New York: Oxford University Press, 2003).

57. Bederman, *Manliness and Civilization*, 47, 51.

58. Elisabeth Lasch-Quinn, *Black Neighbors: Race and the Limits of Reform in the American Settlement House Movement, 1890–1945* (Chapel Hill: University of North Carolina Press, 1993); Glenda Elizabeth Gilmore, ed., *Who Were the Progressives?* (Boston and New York: Bedford/St. Martin's, 2002).

59. Ray Stannard Baker, *Following the Color Line: American Negro Citizenship in the Progressive Era* (1908, reprinted New York: Torchbooks, 1964), 118.

60. T. Thomas Fortune, *Black and White* (Chicago: Johnson Publishing Company, 1970), 4.

61. Gossett, *Race*, 160.

62. Ray Stannard Baker, quoted in Bederman, *Manliness and Civilization*, 52. Also see Friedman, *The White Savage*; Lewis, *Du Bois*, 364.

63. Daryl Michael Scott, *Contempt and Pity: Social Policy and the Image of the Damaged Black Psyche, 1880–1996* (Chapel Hill: University of North Carolina Press, 1997).

64. Richard Hofstadter, *Social Darwinism in American Thought* (1944, reprinted New York: George Braziller, 1955); *The Age of Reform: From Bryan to F. D. R* (New York: Vintage Books,1955); Lewis, *Du Bois*, 185.

65. Allen F. Davis, *Spearheads for Reform: The Social Settlements and the Progressive Movement, 1880–1914* (New York: Oxford University Press, 1967); Nancy Weiss, *The National Urban League, 1910–1940* (New York: Oxford University Press, 1974); David Levering Lewis and Khalil G. Muhammad, "The NAACP and Violence," in Ronald Gottesman, ed., *Violence in America: An Encyclopedia* (New York: Charles Scribner's Sons, 1999).

66. John H. Stanfield, *Philanthropy and Jim Crow in American Social Science* (Westport, Conn.: Greenwood Press, 1985), 21, 25, 27–28.

67. Frank Blackmar, "Review of *Studies in the American Race Problem* by Alfred H. Stone," *American Journal of Sociology* 14:6 (1909): 837–839.

68. McKee, *Sociology and the Race Problem*, 28, 38.

69. Lewis, *Biography of a Race*, 98-99.

70. Philip Dray, *At the Hands of Persons Unknown: The Lynching of Black America* (New York: Random House, 2002); W. Fitzhugh Brundage, *Lynching in the New South, Georgia and Virginia, 1880–1930* (Urbana: University of Illinois Press, 1993); Mary Ellen Curtin, *Black Prisoners and Their World, Alabama, 1865–1900* (Charlottesville: University Press of Virginia, 2000).

71. Shaler, "European Peasants," 648.

72. Baker, *From Savage to Negro*, 26–46; Frederickson, *The Black Image in the White Mind*, 246–255; Laura M. Westhoff, *A Fatal Drifting Apart: Democratic*

Social Knowledge and Chicago Reform (Columbus: Ohio State University Press, 2007), 188–189.

73. Shaler, "The African Element in America," 670.

74. Francis A. Walker, "The Colored Race in the United States," *Forum* 11 (September 1891): 502, 504, 506; Frederickson, *The Black Image in the White Mind,* 245–246; William Darity, Jr., "Many Roads to Extinction: Early AEA Economists and the Black Disappearance Hypothesis," *History of Economics Review* 21 (1994): 48.

75. Frederickson, *The Black Image in the White Mind,* 246–255.

76. Shaler "The African Element," 670, and "The Negro Problem," 698; Emory R. Johnson, ed., "The Negro's Progress in Fifty Years," AAAPSS 49 (September 1913): 1–266.

77. Walker, "The Colored Race in the United States," 502–503.

78. The 1870 and 1890 figures were "partly estimated" (Ibid., 503).

79. Ibid., 504, 506.

80. Darity, "Many Roads to Extinction," 48.

81. Walker, "The Colored Race in the United States," 507–508, 509.

82. Vernon J. Williams, *From a Caste to a Minority: Changing Attitudes of American Sociologists toward Afro-Americans, 1896–1945* (Westport, Conn.: Greenwood Press, 1989); Mia Bay, *The White Image in the Black Mind, African American Ideas about White People, 1830–1925* (New York: Oxford University Press, 2000); John David Smith, "A Different View of Slavery: Black Historians Attack the Proslavery Argument, 1890–1920," *The Journal of Negro History* 65:4 (1980): 298–311.

83. Shaler, "Science and the African Problem," 41–43.

84. By the 1890s, there was a clarion call for greater use of the statistical method in explaining rates of birth, death, disease, suicide, and crime. Though many scholars across different fields embraced the new positivism, there were radical differences in the interpretation and application of statistical findings. The French sociologist Émile Durkheim helped to establish the sociological approach, creating a vision of suicide as a social problem rather than as a "highly individual and personal one"; see *Suicide: A Study in Sociology,* trans. John A. Spaulding and George Simpson (1897, reprinted New York: Routledge, 1952). Twentieth-century American sociologists promoted progressive reform measures to alleviate social problems caused by economic and political friction. The British statistician Francis Galton established the eugenic approach, looking at the same problems through statistics, but attributing them to the inferiority of various population groups. Since their inferiority was inheritable, their diseases and crimes were symptoms of their racial inferiority. The eugenics solution was the better breeding of better types of mankind. Eugenicists promoted policies that gave a reproductive advantage to so-called superior races, such as the Anglo-Saxon. In the hands of a progressive or a eugenicist or a racial Darwinist, the same statistics were defined very differently as either a social or a racial problem, and they were used to promote very different solutions (Zuberi, *Thicker Than Blood,* 81–82). On Galton's statistical innovations, see Stephen M. Stigler, *The History of Statistics: The Measurement of Uncertainty before 1900* (Cambridge: Harvard University Press, 1986).

85. Richard Mayo-Smith, "Statistics as an Instrument of Investigation in Sociology," *Publications of the American Economic Association,* 10:3 (1895):103–104; Darity, "Many Roads to Extinction," 47.

86. Richard Mayo-Smith, "Statistical Data for the Study of the Assimilation of Races and Nationalities in the United States," *Publications of the American Association of the American Statistical Association* 3 (1893): 429–449. Unlike Shaler, Mayo-Smith was calling for more statistical research on the assimilation of the foreign-born, which he tentatively concluded seemed to be going well: "The process of assimilation is going . . . on very effectually and rapidly" (449). The "colored population," however, was "a peculiar element in the American population," in "many respects an inferior race," and its future prospects were not so clear(433).

87. Zuberi, *Thicker Than Blood,* 81.

88. Ross, *Origins of American Social Science;* Theodore M. Porter, *The Rise of Statistical Thinking, 1820–1900* (Princeton: Princeton University Press, 1986).

89. Michael B. Katz and Thomas J. Sugrue, eds., *W. E. B. Du Bois, Race, and the City: The Philadelphia Negro and Its Legacy* (Philadelphia: University of Pennsylvania Press, 1998), 24.

90. Curtin, *Black Prisoners and Their World,* 1–61; David M. Oshinsky, *"Worse than Slavery": Parchman Farm and the Ordeal of Jim Crow Justice* (New York: The Free Press, 1996), 31–54.

91. Shaler, "Negro since Civil War," 38.

92. Shaler, "Science and the African Problem," 44.

2. WRITING CRIME INTO RACE

1. Frederick L. Hoffman, *Race Traits and Tendencies of the American Negro* (New York: American Economic Association, 1896), 217–234.

2. Francis A. Walker, "The Colored Race in the United States," *Forum* 11 (September 1891): 501–509.

3. George M. Fredrickson, *The Black Image in the White Mind: The Debate on Afro-American Character and Destiny, 1817–1914* (1971, reprinted with a new introduction, Hanover: Wesleyan University Press, 1987); Lee D. Baker, *From Savage to Negro: Anthropology and the Construction of Race, 1896–1954* (Berkley: University of California Press, 1998).

4. *Race Traits* was also published by Macmillan in the United States and by Swan Sonnenschein in Britain; see, F. J. Sypher, ed., *Frederick L. Hoffman, His Life and Works* (Philadelphia: Xlibris, 2002), 90.

5. Hoffman, *Race Traits,* v, 310.

6. On Hoffman's determination, see Sypher, *Frederick L. Hoffman, His Life and Works,* 68.

7. Ibid., 39, 42, 43. Sypher makes no comment on the apparent inconsistency between Hoffman's apparent sympathy with the black ship workers and his later beliefs. This seems to be Hoffman's earliest encounter with the color line.

8. As a white immigrant in the South, the exploitation of black workers helped make his own *passage* possible. I italicize *passage* here to mark Hoffman's journey as an instance of passing as a white immigrant with extremely limited finances and

even less social standing in a way that even the most prosperous black person typically could not. Fares were affordable for poor white travelers like Hoffman because of the underpaid, brutalized black workers aboard riverboats such as the *City of New Orleans*. And white immigrants in the South escaped most of the nativist violence found in the North, given the stakes of hyper-polarization of whiteness and blackness in the postbellum South. Hoffman could easily identify with being a worker aboard a ship; he frequently worked aboard various water vessels as a means of getting by and traveling the country. He never mentioned being brutalized. For more on southern travel on riverboats, see Howard N. Rabinowitz, *Race Relations in the Urban South, 1865–1900* (New York: Oxford University Press, 1978), 191; Andrew Karhl, "The Cultural Currency of Leisure: African American Beaches and Resorts in the Jim Crow South" (Ph.D. diss., Indiana University, 2008), 84–87.

9. Corson received his education from Cornell University (Fredrickson, *The Black Image in the White Mind*, 248).

10. This recollection comes from Hoffman's unpublished autobiography, "Life Story of a Statistician," written around 1919. Hoffman added, "In a large measure it [Corson's lecture] formed the basis of all my subsequent interest in statistics, medicine, and related sciences." This is a surprising claim given that Hoffman went on to have a forty-year career at Prudential as a highly respected national and international health expert on cancer and tuberculosis. He was also known for his expertise in occupational hazards, homicide, and suicide, garnering the reputation as the "dean" of American statisticians; see Sypher, *Frederick L. Hoffman, His Life and Works*, 7. Sypher adds that Hoffman's comment on Corson's influence was an "overstatement, since his diaries and correspondence show unmistakably that his interests in 'statistics, medicine and related sciences' antedate this event" (86). That Hoffman credited his earliest work on black criminality and mortality for launching his career demonstrates how much professional success and acclaim he achieved early-on as a result of *Race Traits*.

11. Until her marriage to Hoffman, Ella had never lived without black "servants"; see Sypher, *Frederick L. Hoffman, His Life and Works*, 49, 69.

12. Ibid., 70–71, 86–87.

13. Ibid., 87.

14. Frederick and Frances quickly became lifelong friends and "maintained an extensive correspondence" for many years. In late 1893 the Hoffmans named their second-born child Frances Armstrong Hoffman; she died before reaching six months of age. Three years later, their third child was born in Newark, New Jersey, and was also given the name Francis Armstrong Hoffman. See Sypher, *Frederick L. Hoffman, His Life and Works*, 70–71, 74, 76, 87.

15. Ibid., 65.

16. Frederick L. Hoffman, "Vital Statistics of the Negro," *The Arena*, April 1892, 539–542. N. S. Shaler, "The Economic Future of the New South," *The Arena*, August 1890, 257–268; "The African Element in America," *The Arena*, November 1890, 660–673; "The Nature of the Negro," *The Arena*, December 1890, 23–35.

17. Hoffman claimed that he could not "secure reliable [birth] data from a *single* State or city." Mortuary reports, on the other hand, were abundant and reliable,

yielding "considerable statistical material of great value"; see Hoffman, "Vital Statistics of the Negro," 532–533.

18. Ibid., 537.

19. M. V. Ball, "Correspondence: Vital Statistics of the Negro," *The Medical News*, October 1894, 392–393; "Correspondence: The Mortality of the Negro," *The Medical News*, April 1894, 389–390.

20. Hoffman, "Vital Statistics of the Negro," 534, 537, 538–540.

21. Frederick L. Hoffman, "Suicide and Modern Civilization," *The Arena* 7 (1893): 680–695. To Hoffman's credit, Émile Durkheim's pathbreaking study of suicide in Europe did not appear until 1897, even after *Race Traits*. Hoffman went on to have a long publication record, spanning decades, on American suicides.

22. Ibid., 687. The rising trend coincided with the Second Industrial Revolution. In most cases the suicide rate increase outstripped the rise in the general mortality rate and the overall population rate.

23. Ibid., 683, 686–691, 694.

24. The term "emergency measures" comes from *The Arena* editor, B. W. Flower, in an editorial that appeared a few months after Hoffman's suicide article, "Emergency Measures Which Would Have Maintained Self Respecting Manhood," *The Arena* 3 (1894): 822–826. Flower's editorial was a response to the 1893 economic depression, as well as a critique of the nation's growing military budget alongside massive unemployment. "The unheeded cry for work . . . has resulted in driving numbers of men, women and children to drink, crime, suicide, and immorality. And these irreparable calamities might have been averted had our nation appreciated the importance of maintaining the manhood of her citizens and holding their loyalty by bands woven of love and wisdom" (823). Hoffman's article and Flower's editorial were linked by a shared reformist agenda on behalf of the white "masses" to correct the imbalances of laissez-faire capitalism at the end of the Gilded Age and the dawn of the Progressive era.

25. Lundy Braun, "Spirometry, Measurement, and Race in the Nineteenth Century," *Journal of the History of Medicine and Allied Sciences* 60:2 (2005): 167. According to some scholars, Hoffman was a social Darwinist rather than a progressive in his views of the government's role in assisting the struggling white masses. Paul Finkleman writes that Hoffman "was no progressive, at least in the modern sense of the word." Finkleman argues that Hoffman rejected government regulation of health care for American workers, believing instead that "Americans should rely on private enterprises"; see Finkleman, "Introduction: On Reading and Understanding Scientific Racism: A Brief Introduction of the Work and World of Frederick L. Hoffman," in Frederick L. Hoffman, *Race Traits and Tendencies of the American Negro* (1896, reprinted Clark, New Jersey: The Lawbook Exchange, 2003), iii. In his early writings such a view is not clearly supported and was probably not yet set in stone. Hoffman's biographer writes that Hoffman "campaigned ardently for governmental regulation of health conditions," though his mature ideas "oscillated" between "self-reliance" and regulation; see Sypher, *Frederick L. Hoffman, His Life and Works*, 72. Both Sypher and Finkleman seem to agree that Hoffman "believed in the fundamental inferiority" of blacks (Sypher, *Frederick L. Hoffman, His Life and Works*, 72; Finkleman, "Introduction"). On

Hoffman as a racial Darwinist, see, Fredrickson, *The Black Image in the White Mind,* 251; Joel Williamson, *A Rage for Order: Black-White Relations in the American South since Emancipation* (New York: Oxford University Press, 1986), 86–90; Vernon J. Williams, *Rethinking Race: Franz Boas and His Contemporaries* (Louisville: University of Kentucky Press, 1996), 37–38. Haller writes that his work "reflected a summation of the century's medical and anthropological accumulations concerning racial relations in America"; John S. Haller, Jr., *Outcasts from Evolution: Scientific Attitudes of Racial Inferiority, 1859–1900* (Urbana: University of Illinois Press, 1971), 62. Though I agree with Haller's statement I think he and others miss the innovative dimensions of Hoffman's work. Its broadest dimensions were most certainly grounded in the standards of racial Darwinist thought; his evocation of the Negro Problem and his focus on mortality certainly attest to this. But his emphatic use of his foreign identity to transcend the sectionalism of the period, his amazing ability to compile statistical data from far-ranging sources (comparable to Durkheim's accomplishment the following year), his coupling of northern statistics with southern ones, a real first among race-relations experts, and finally his attention to black crime statistics in particular, when all put together, were a show of real genius and innovation for someone who truly wanted northerners to be sympathetic to southerners' racial worldview.

26. Frederick L. Hoffman, "Correspondence: Vital Statistics of Negro," *The Medical News* 65:12 (1894): 323.

27. Megan J. Wolff, "The Myth of the Actuary: Life Insurance and Frederick L. Hoffman's *Race Traits and Tendencies of the American Negro,*" *Public Health Reports* 121 (January–February 2006): 91.

28. William Darity, Jr., "Many Roads to Extinction: Early AEA Economists and the Black Disappearance Hypothesis," *History of Economics Review* 21 (1994): 50–54.

29. R. M. Cunningham, "The Morbidity and Mortality of Negro Convicts," *The Medical News* 64:5 (1894): 113.

30. Ibid., 115. For a comparison of Cunningham's claim of Alabama's race-neutral prisons to a recent historian's assessment, see Mary Ellen Curtin, *Black Prisoners and Their World, Alabama, 1865–1900* (Charlottesville: University Press of Virginia, 2000), 113, 116.

31. Ball, "The Mortality of the Negro," 389, 390.

32. Hoffman, "Vital Statistics of Negro," 320, 321.

33. Ibid., 321. For the third straight time, Hoffman claimed to present original data on mortality, first with black health statistics in 1892, then with white suicide in 1893, and now with the "first attempt to present in tabular form the mortality for a number of West Indian colonies."

34. Ibid., 322–323. Hoffman came closest to directly engaging Ball's analysis when he showed that native and foreign whites in Boston, Massachusetts, Providence, Rhode Island, and Washington, D.C., lived on average ten years longer than Boston's blacks. The data were limited, uneven, and awkwardly presented, since he had no "Colored" data for Providence and Washington, and no "Foreign" data for Boston. He also admitted that "the Irish population shows some similarity in its

mortality to the negro population," but not enough data were available, so "a consideration of this point would be inadvisable."

35. Wolff, "The Myth of the Actuary," 6.

36. Mark Aldrich, "Progressive Economists and Scientific Racism: Walter Willcox and Black Americans, 1895–1910," *Phylon* 40:1 (1979):1–14; Thomas Gossett, *Race: The History of an Idea in America* (1963, reprinted New York: Oxford University Press, 1997); Fredrickson, *The Black Image in the White Mind*; Baker, *From Savage to Negro*; Rayford Logan, *Betrayal of the Negro* (1954, reprinted London: Collier, 1969).

37. Dorothy Ross, *The Origins of American Social Science* (New York: Cambridge University Press, 1991); Theodore M. Porter, *The Rise of Statistical Thinking, 1820–1900* (Princeton: Princeton University Press, 1986).

38. Author's italics, Dr. A. Corre, "Le Crime en Pays Creoles," (Paris, 1889), quoted in Hoffman, "Vital Statistics of Negro," 323.

39. Ibid.

40. Prior to the late 1860s, the vast majority of black people, as enslaved men, women, and children, were generally subjected to plantation punishment for their real or perceived transgressions rather than being punished according to the policies and practices of criminal justice agencies. As David Oshinsky observes for antebellum Mississippi, criminal justice "was meant for white folk alone. Slaves 'had no rights to respect,' wrote one authority, 'no civic virtue or character to restore, no freedom to abridge.' Slaves were the property of their master, and the state did not normally intervene. In the words of one Natchez slaveholder, 'Each plantation was a law unto itself' "; Oshinsky, *"Worse Than Slavery": Parchman Farm and the Ordeal of Jim Crow Justice* (New York: Free Press, 1996), 6. For more evidence on the absence of blacks in prisons of the antebellum South, see Curtin, *Black Prisoners and Their World,* 6; Edward L. Ayers, *Crime and Punishment in the 19th Century American South* (New York: Oxford University Press, 1984), 61.

41. Kali N. Gross, *Colored Amazons: Crime, Violence, and the Black Women in the City of Brotherly Love, 1880–1910* (Durham: Duke University Press, 2006).

42. Leslie Patrick-Stamp, "Numbers That Are Not New: African Americans in the Country's First Prison, 1790–1835," *Pennsylvania Magazine of History and Biography* 119 (1995): 95–128; Mary Frances Berry, *The Pig Farmer's Daughter and Other Tales of American Justice: Episodes of Racism and Sexism in the Courts from 1865 to the Present* (New York: Vintage Books, 1999).

43. H. H. Powers's AAAPSS review noted that a textbook of this nature anticipated a large audience that did not yet exist. Yet he expected one was "certain to develop rapidly in the near future"; see H. H. Powers, "Review of *An Introduction to the Study of the Dependent, Defective and Delinquent Classes* by Charles R. Henderson," AAAPSS 4 (January 1894): 174. Powers's prediction was right; a reviewer of the second edition (1901) referred to the first edition as a "pioneer work"; see Samuel W. Dike, "Review of *An Introduction to the Study of the Dependent, Defective and Delinquent Classes,* by Charles R. Henderson," *American Journal of Theology* 6:3 (1902): 640. Another reviewer of the second edition called the text "comprehensive" and "the only work in English covering the entire field"; see J. E. Hagerty, "Review of *An Introduction to the Study of the Dependent, Defective and*

Delinquent Classes by Charles R. Henderson," AAAPSS 19 (January 1902): 136–137. Slavery had, of course, minimized the need for thinking criminologically about the vast majority of blacks, even though free blacks in the colonial and antebellum eras were often defined as a race of dangerous criminals. The real need arrived with emancipation, and the tools to statistically track black criminality arrived with the 1890 census, the first clear picture of blacks born outside of slavery.

44. To Henderson's credit, he did not take Hoffman's 1896 interpretation as the last word on the matter, though like Hoffman he did emphasize that the primary causes of black criminality were "racial inheritance, physical and mental inferiority, barbarian and slave ancestry and culture"; Charles R. Henderson, *An Introduction to the Study of the Dependent, Defective and Delinquent Classes,* 2nd ed. (Boston: D.C. Heath and Co, 1901), 247. Henderson added that social factors had contributed to black criminality, especially in the North, noting economic discrimination, trade union exclusion, and racial prejudice. Henderson credited the earliest work of two pioneering black social scientists, W. E. B. Du Bois and Monroe N. Work, whose statistical research on northern black criminality had been published in 1899 and 1900 respectively, following the path blazed by Hoffman's *Race Traits;* W. E. B. Du Bois, *The Philadelphia Negro* (1899, reprinted Millwood, New York: Kraus-Thomson Organization Ltd, 1973); Monroe N. Work, "Crime among the Negroes of Chicago: A Social Study," AJS 6 (September 1900): 204–212.

45. Hoffman continued to consult Wright for unpublished census data, which he used in *Race Traits,* 43.

46. Carroll D. Wright, "The Relation of Economic Conditions to the Causes of Crime," AAAPSS 3 (May 1893): 100.

47. Cesare Lombroso, *Criminal Man,* ed. and trans. Mary Gibson and Nicole Hahn Rafter (1876, reprinted with a new introduction, Durham: Duke University Press, 2006); Stephen J. Gould, *The Mismeasure of Man,* rev. ed.(New York: Norton, 1996), 151–175; Nicole Hahn Rafter, *Creating Born Criminals* (Urbana and Chicago: University of Illinois Press, 1997); Gross, *Colored Amazons.*

48. Wright "kindly furnished" Hoffman with data again as he wrote *Race Traits.* By then, Wright had become acting U.S. census superintendent; see Hoffman, *Race Traits,* 43.

49. Harry Vrooman, "Crime and the Enforcement of Law," *The Arena* 65 (April 1895): 263–274. On Vrooman, see Ross E. Paulson, *Radicalism and Reform: The Vrooman Family and American Social Thought, 1837–1937* (Lexington: University of Kentucky Press, 1968).

50. Ball, "Vital Statistics of the Negro," 392.

51. Ibid.

52. Ibid. So did the fact that small white ethnic enclaves of poor people lived in a variety of housing from dilapidated buildings to tenements "conducted on sanitary principles." In Philadelphia, Ball observed that a model tenement occupied by blacks returned mortality rates of 10 per 1,000 compared to rates of 40 per 1,000 among blacks and whites who resided in a "court" behind the same tenement. Italians on a nearby street in the "rag-pickers district" died at a rate of 45 per 1,000.

53. Ibid., 393.

54. Marilynn S. Johnson, *Street Justice, A History of Police Violence in New York City* (Boston: Beacon Press, 2003), 52, 55.

55. Ball, "Vital Statistics of the Negro," 393.

56. Hoffman, *Race Traits,* 37, 49, 50, 59, 60, 85, 310.

57. For a pioneering gendered analysis of the crimes of violence committed by black women, see Gross, *Colored Amazons.* For a seminal discussion of violence among blacks during the late nineteenth century, see Roger Lane's *Roots of Violence in Black Philadelphia* (Cambridge: Harvard University Press, 1986). Although Gross pays far greater attention to the interplay between real and imagined crimes committed by black women (particularly in press accounts), both she and Lane are primarily interested in describing and analyzing real crime and its consequences. Gross states, "Ultimately, this book seeks to understand how black female crime functioned in the lives of the perpetrators as well as in that of the society" (3).

58. Hoffman, *Race Traits,* 221. For more on the actuarial implications of Hoffman's book and the ways in which Prudential "and other insurers" used statistical explanations as a cover for excluding black clients because "to sell insurance policies at equal rates or for equal benefits across racial lines would offend" whites, not because they were too great a financial risk, see Wolff, "The Myth of the Actuary," 3.

59. Hoffman, *Race Traits,* 229.

60. Philip A. Bruce, *The Plantation Negro as a Freeman, Observations on His Character, Condition, and Prospects in Virginia* (1889, reprinted Williamstown, Mass.: Corner House Publishers, 1970), 84; Hoffman, *Race Traits,* 231.

61. Bruce, v, vi, 77–92.

62. Hoffman, *Race Traits,* 228, 234.

63. Ibid., 140–141. The evidence amounted to eighteen cases of black suicide about which Hoffman claimed to have personally "collected the facts."

64. Ibid., 238, 311.

65. Ibid., 236. The logic of this followed from the frequent references Hoffman and many others made to the West Indies as a signpost for what black people did with freedom.

66. John Roach Straton, "Will Education Save the Race Problem," *The North American Review* 170 (June 1900): 785–801; Booker T. Washington, "Education Will Save the Race Problem, A Reply," *The North American Review* 171 (August 1900): 221–232; W. E. B. Du Bois, "Notes on Negro Crime, Particularly in Georgia," *Atlanta University Studies* 9 (1904); James K. Vardaman, "A Governor Bitterly Opposes Negro Education," *Leslie's Weekly,* February 1904, 104.

67. The views of Hoffman and Morgan also mark a generational shift toward a less hopeful view of the Negro Problem emblematic of the late 1890s, in contrast to Nathaniel Shaler and his support of Morgan's father-in-law and Hampton's founder, General Samuel Chapman Armstrong.

68. Straton, "Will Education Save the Race Problem"; Gary Calkins, "Review of *Race Traits and Tendencies of the American Negro* by Frederick L. Hoffman," *Political Science Quarterly* 11:4 (1896): 754–757.

69. Kelly Miller, "Review of *Race Traits and Tendencies of the American Negro,* by Frederick L. Hoffman," *The American Negro Academy Occasional Papers* 1 (1897); Frederick S. Starr, "Review of *Race Traits and Tendencies of the American Negro,* by Frederick L. Hoffman," *The Dial* 22 (January 1897); Miles M. Dawson, "Review of *Race Traits and Tendencies of the American Negro* by Frederick L. Hoffman," AAAPSS 5 (September-December 1896); Calkins, "Review of *Race Traits*"; Du Bois, "Notes on Negro Crime"; Fredrickson, *The Black Image in the White Mind*; Baker, *From Savage to Negro*; Wolff, "The Myth of the Actuary"; David Levering Lewis, *W. E. B. Du Bois: Biography of a Race, 1886–1919* (New York: Henry Holt, 1993), 368.

70. Lewis, *Biography of a Race,* 276.

71. Fredrickson, *The Black Image in the White Mind,* 249.

72. Hoffman, *Race Traits,* 311.

73. Ibid., 217, 285.

74. Ibid., 1, 13–15, 17, 31, 319, 329.

75. Jacob A. Riis, *How the Other Half Lives: Studies among the Tenements of New York* (1890, reprinted Boston: Bedford Books, 1996), 162. See also Adler, *First in Violence,* 121, who indicated that "some observers blamed immigrants or hoboes" for the city's violence, but most Chicagoans blamed blacks for "much of the city's violence." The newspapers Adler cites, however, are all from or after 1906, a decade after publication of Hoffman's book. In those ten years, dozens and dozens of major studies on black criminality in the urban North were written.

76. Hoffman, *Race Traits,* 225.

77. Fredrickson, *The Black Image in the White Mind,* 255.

78. Adler, *First in Violence.* 122, 124, 318 fn. 10.

79. That the race of the reviewer mattered was not a new development. Throughout the nineteenth century, African American religious leaders, educators, and journalists had wielded their pens mightily in defense of the race against slavery's defenders and scientific racists. In the 1890s a new but small cohort of black scholars and leaders emerged; see Mia Bay, *The White Image in the Black Mind, African American Ideas about White People, 1830–1925* (New York: Oxford University Press, 2000); Wilson Jeremiah Moses, *The Golden Age of Black Nationalism, 1850–1925* (Hamden, Conn.: Archon Book, 1978); T. Thomas Fortune, *Black and White* (1884, reprinted Chicago: Johnson Publishing Company Inc., 1970); Alfred A. Moss, Jr., *The American Negro Academy: Voice of the Talented Tenth* (Baton Rouge: Louisiana State University Press, 1981); Ida B. Wells, *Southern Horrors. Lynch Law in All Its Phases* (New York: New York Age Print, 1892), reprinted in *Southern Horrors and Other Writings: The Anti-Lynching Campaign of Ida B. Wells, 1892–1900,* ed. Jacqueline Jones Royster (Boston: Bedford Books, 1997); *A Red Record: Tabulated Statistics and Alleged Causes of Lynchings in the United States: 1892–1893–1894* (Chicago, 1894), reprinted in *Southern Horrors and Other Writings: The Anti-Lynching Campaign of Ida B. Wells, 1892–1900,* ed. Jacqueline Jones Royster (Boston: Bedford Books, 1997).

80. Dawson, "Review of *Race Traits*"; Starr, "Review of *Race Traits*"; Wolff, "The Myth of the Actuary"; Braun, "Spirometry, Measurement, and Race."

81. Dawson, "Review of *Race Traits,*" 142, 147, 148.

82. Starr, "Review of *Race Traits*," 17. For his views on the application of Cesare Lombroso's criminal anthropology in North America, see "Study of the Criminal in Mexico," AJS 3:1 (1897): 13–17.

83. Starr, "Review of *Race Traits*," 18.

84. Shaler, "The Negro Problem," *Atlantic Monthly* 54 (1884): 709.

85. Davarian L. Baldwin, "Black Belts and Ivory Towers: The Place of Race in U.S. Social Thought, 1892–1948," *Critical Sociology* 30 (2004): 406.

86. Calkins, "Review of *Race Traits*," 754–755, 756.

87. Wolff, "The Myth of the Actuary," 2; Beatrix Hoffman (no relation), "Scientific Racism, Insurance, and Opposition to the Welfare State: Frederick L. Hoffman's Transatlantic Journey," *Journal of the Gilded Age and Progressive Era* 2:2 (April 2003): 150–190.

88. Willard B. Gatewood, *Aristocrats of Color: The Black Elite, 1880–1920* (Bloomington: Indiana University Press, 1993).

89. One response of the scientific racists, including Hoffman, was to attribute black elites' educational accomplishments to the fact that many had white blood in their veins. They also discredited the achievements of these men and women, mocking their academic success. During a series of lectures in France in the 1860s, anthropologist Carl Vogt, known as "the Darwin of Germany," for example, said of Lille Geoffroy, the celebrated black engineer and mathematician and member of the French Academy, that his talent would be totally unremarkable if he were white. Among anti-Darwinians, Vogt noted, Geoffroy was commonly cited as "proof" of the Negro's intellectual capability. "The fact is that the mathematical performances of . . . [Geoffroy] were of such a nature that, had he been born in Germany of white parents, he might perhaps, have been qualified to be a mathematical teacher in a middle class school or engineer of a railway; but having been born in Martinique, of colored parents, he shone like a one-eyed man among the totally blind . . . Besides [he] was not a pure black but a mulatto"; see Hoffman, *Race Traits*, 187. Biographical background on Vogt from J. MacGregor Allan, "Review of *Lectures of Man: His Place in Creation and in the History of the Earth* by Carl Vogt," *Anthropological Review* 7:25 (1869): 177. For a recent spin on attributing black's "unremarkable" success to skin color rather than merit, see Geraldine Ferraro's comments about Senator Barack Obama at Katherine Q. Seeyle and Julie Bosman, "Ferraro's Obama Remarks Become Talk of Campaign," *New York Times*, March 12, 2008.

90. Glenda Elizabeth Gilmore, *Gender and Jim Crow: Women and the Politics of White Supremacy in North Carolina, 1896–1920* (Chapel Hill: University of North Carolina Press, 1996).

91. Deborah Gray White, *Too Heavy a Load: Black Women in Defense of Themselves, 1894–1994* (New York: W. W. Norton & Company, 1999), 87–109.

92. Ibid., 7–8 (manuscript version of *Too Heavy a Load*); Moss, *The American Negro Academy*; Alford A. Young and Donald R. Duskins, "Early Traditions of African American Sociological Thought," *Annual Review of Sociology* 27 (2001): 447; Lewis, *Biography of a Race*, 168–169.

93. For more on the direct tie of Washington's leadership to white support, see Louis R. Harlan, *Booker T. Washington: The Making of a Black Leader, 1856–1901*

(New York: Oxford University Press, 1972), 324, and *The Wizard of Tuskegee, 1901–1915* (New York: Oxford University Press, 1983), 5.

94. W. S. Scarborough, "The Race Problem," *The Arena*, October 1890, 560. For more of Scarborough's writing along these lines, see "The Negro Question from the Negro's Point of View," *The Arena*, July 1891, 219–22; and "Lawlessness vs. Lawlessness," *The Arena*, November 1900, 478–483. For biographical information, see Michele Valerie Ronnick, "William Sanders Scarborough: The First African American Member of the Modern Language Association," *Publication of the Modern Language Association* 115: 7 (2000): 1787–1793. Scarborough was also a member of the American Negro Academy, "delivering ten papers before the society between 1884 and 1896" (Moss, *The American Negro Academy*, 17).

95. Kevin K. Gaines, *Uplifting the Race: Black Leadership and Culture in Twentieth-Century America* (Chapel Hill: University of North Carolina Press, 1996) xiv; S. P. Fullinwider, *The Mind and Mood of Black America* (Homewood, Ill.: Dorsey Press, 1969), 3–5. For an excellent discussion of the initial conflict between black elite women and men, and between club women and the masses of women, in response to the new discourse of criminality and sexual immorality, see White, *Too Heavy a Load*, 1–43.

96. It is impossible to prove that Hoffman knew of Wells's publications, but she drew international attention from British dignitaries and reformers and journalists of international repute, many of whom accepted her brilliant claims that white Americans were perverting their Anglo-Saxon heritage and expressed their outrage to American officials, conducted their own independent investigations, and threatened to divest from American businesses in lynching states. By 1894, after her second tour abroad and before she published her second pamphlet, while Hoffman still remained in the South, white journalists across the South were condemning her. The *Memphis Commercial*, for example, wrote that her campaign "had 'done more to intensify the bitterness of race-prejudice' among whites than any other event in the past ten years"; Patricia A. Schechter, *Ida B. Wells-Barnett and American Reform, 1880–1930* (Chapter Hill: University of North Carolina Press, 2001), 105, 84–120; Gail Bederman, *Manliness and Civilization, A Cultural History of Gender and Race in the United States, 1880–1917* (Chicago: University of Chicago Press, 1995), 53–76.

97. Schechter, *Ida B. Wells-Barnett and American Reform*, 75–79.

98. Royster, *Southern Horrors and Other Writings*, 50.

99. Bederman, *Manliness and Civilization*, 56; Schechter, *Ida B. Wells-Barnett and American Reform*, 85.

100. Bederman, *Manliness and Civilization*, 58, 61.

101. Schechter, *Ida B. Wells-Barnett and American Reform*; Bederman, *Manliness and Civilization*, 74–75.

102. Marlon B. Ross, *Manning the Race: Reforming Black Men in the Jim Crow Era* (New York: New York University Press, 2004).

103. The *Colored American Magazine* stated in 1902 that Wells was "without doubt the first authority among Afro-Americans on lynching and mob violence" (quoted in Schechter, *Ida B. Wells-Barnett and American Reform*, 124). For more on Wells's pioneering use of statistics, see Laura M. Westhoff, *A Fatal Drifting*

Apart: Democratic Social Knowledge and Chicago Reform (Columbus: Ohio State University Press, 2007), 196–207.

104. Lynching data from Williamson, *A Rage for Order*, 84; for more on the origins of anti-black lynching, see Herbert Shapiro, *White Violence and Black Response: From Reconstruction to Montgomery* (Amherst, Mass.: University of Massachusetts Press, 1988); Philip Dray, *At the Hands of Persons Unknown: The Lynching of Black America* (New York: Random House, 2002), vii–viii.

105. Royster, *Southern Horrors and Other Writings*, 82, 120.

106. Hoffman, *Race Traits*, 231. On the same page, Hoffman also wrote that "the rate of increase in lynchings may be accepted as representing fairly the increasing tendency of colored men to commit this most frightful of crime."

107. Royster, *Southern Horrors and Other Writings*, 126–128. Wells's pioneering research exposed a hidden pattern and practice among whites who covered their crimes by corking their faces or falsely accusing black men. Black sociologist Monroe N. Work would systematically detail such instances in his annual almanac of black facts; see Monroe N. Work, ed., *Negro Year Book: An Encyclopedia of the Negro* (Tuskegee: Negro Year Book Publishing Co., 1931), 289-292, and *Negro Year Book* (1938), 147. Katheryn K. Russell, Barry Glassner, and Michael Moore in his award-winning documentary *Bowling for Columbine* (MGM, 2002) have also examined the political and cultural significance of black scapegoating in the late twentieth century; Katheryn K. Russell, *The Color of Crime: Racial Hoaxes, White Fear, Black Protectionism, Police Harassment, and Other Macroaggressions* (New York: New York University Press, 1997); Barry Glassner, *The Culture of Fear: Why Americans Are Afraid of the Wrong Things: Crime, Drugs, Minorities, Teen Moms, Killer Kids, Mutant Microbes, Plane Crashes, Road Rage, and So Much More* (New York: Basic Books, 1999). As recently as May 2009, a white Philadelphia suburban mother Bonnie Sweeten, faked her and her daughters kidnapping by accusing two black men of carjacking them, see "Abduction Hoax Ends at Disney World; Girl Safe," *Philadelphia Inquirer*, May 28, 2009; "The Big Black Lie," and "Mother in Bogus Kidnap Probed for Theft," Ibid., May 29, 2009.

108. Royster, *Southern Horrors and Other Writings*, 126–130.

109. Tera W. Hunter, *To 'Joy My Freedom, Southern Black Women's Lives and Labors after the Civil War* (Cambridge: Harvard University Press, 1997), 33–34.

110. Schechter, *Ida B. Wells-Barnett and American Reform*, 114–119.

111. U.S. Census Bureau, *Census Bulletin: Convicts in Penitentiaries: 1890*, no. 31 (Washington, D.C.: GPO, 1891), 1.

112. Schechter, *Ida B. Wells-Barnett and American Reform*, 104–110, 118–120. Her most recent biographer notes that Wells was "more militant than all of the reform figures" who were prominent in the early twentieth century; Paula J. Giddings, *Ida: A Sword among Lions* (New York: Amistad, 2008), 6–7.

113. Williams B. Thomas, "Black Intellectuals' Critique of Early Mental Testing: A Little Known Saga of the 1920s," *Journal of American Education* 90:3 (1982). Davarian Baldwin states that "Reformers rejected the idea that the race was inherently devoid of virtue but also worried that perhaps some behaviors ascribed to the entire race did actually exist within the 'lower classes'"; Davarian Baldwin, *Chicago's New Negroes: Modernity, The Great Migration, and Black*

Urban Life (Chapel Hill: University of North Carolina Press, 2007), 59; Tukufu Zuberi, "Deracializing Social Statistics: Problems in the Quantification of Race," AAAPSS 568 (March 2000): 184.

114. Ross, *Manning the Race*, 408 fn. 2; Jacquelyne Johnson Jackson, "Black Female Sociologists," in *Black Sociologists: Historical and Contemporary Perspectives*, ed. James E. Blackwell and Morris Janowitz (Chicago: University of Chicago Press, 1974), 267–295.

115. Moss, *The American Negro Academy*; Gaines, *Uplifting the Race*, xiv; on their growth in the 1920s, see Thomas, "Black Intellectuals," 258–292.

116. Lewis, *Biography of a Race*, 169.

117. Vernon Williams, Jr., *The Social Sciences and Theories of Race* (Chicago: University of Illinois Press, 2006), 26.

118. Baldwin, "Black Belts," 405.

119. Lewis, *Biography of a Race*; Young and Duskins, "Early Traditions of African American Sociological Thought."

120. W. E. B. Du Bois," Review of *Race Traits and Tendencies*, by Frederick L. Hoffman," AAAPSS (January 1897): 132–133.

121. Kelly Miller, "Review of *Race Traits and Tendencies of the American Negro*, by Frederick L. Hoffman," *American Negro Academy Occasional Papers*, no. 1 (Washington, D.C., 1897).

122. Ibid. With reference to the South, Miller did raise the issue of discrimination as a factor that exaggerated incarceration and arrest rates among southern blacks. To avoid the "charge of slander," he quoted a "distinguished [white] Virginian" who found pervasive racial discrimination in courtrooms, particularly among white juries.

123. Ibid. Miller applies the laws of large and small numbers, saying smaller population distorts true criminality. "It is hard to see how 'race traits' could account for this discrepancy."

124. Ibid.

125. W. E. B. Du Bois, "Review of *Race Traits*," 132.

126. Editorial note in *Writings by W. E. B. Du Bois in Periodicals Edited by Others, vol. 1, 1891–1909*, ed. Herbert Aptheker (Millwood, N.Y.: Kraus-Thomson Organization Limited, 1982), 279.

127. Du Bois, "Review of *Race Traits*," 130–132.

128. Lewis, *Biography of a Race*, 193.

129. Ibid., 202; Matthew Pratt Guterl, *The Color of Race in America, 1900–1940* (Cambridge: Harvard University Press, 2001), 103; Zuberi, "Deracializing Social Statistics," 86; Ira Katznelson, "Presidents' Address: Du Bois's Century," *Social Science History* 23:4 (1999): 459–474; W. E. B. Du Bois, "The Black North: A Social Study," *New York Times*, December 1, 1901.

130. W. E. B. Du Bois, *Dusk of Dawn: An Essay toward an Autobiography of a Race Concept* (New York: Harcourt, Brace & World, 1940, reprinted New Brunswick, N.J.: Transaction Books, 1984), 57–58.

131. Lewis, *Biography of a Race*, 190–191; W. E. B. Du Bois, "The Study of the Negro Problems," AAAPSS 11 (1898): 10.

132. Du Bois, "The Study of the Negro Problems," 19.

312

133. Ibid., 15.

134. Ibid., 16.

135. W. E. B. Du Bois, "The Conservation of the Races," *Occasional Papers* 2 (American Negro Academy, 1897), reprinted in David Levering Lewis, ed., *W. E. B. Du Bois: A Reader* (New York: Henry Holt, 1995), 25–26.

136. Ibid. It is not known whether Hoffman's study and language shaped Du Bois's speech or slipped into his subconscious. But even beyond the influences of his own independent research, by his choice of words if nothing more, an infectious temptation to conflate ideas about black mortality, criminality, and morality seems to have been spreading.

137. Lewis, *Biography of a Race*, 174, Guterl, *The Color of Race*; Thomas C. Holt, "The Political Uses of Alienation: W. E. B. Du Bois on Politics, Race, and Culture, 1903–1940," *American Quarterly* 42 (June 1990): 301–323; Bay, *The White Image in the Black Mind*.

138. DuBois, "Conservation," 26–27. Sociologists, criminal justice, and black studies scholars have paid closer attention to Du Bois's crime research; see Shaun L. Gabbidon, "W. E. B. Du Bois: Pioneering American Criminologist," *Journal of Black Studies* 31:5 (2001): 581–599; Zuberi, "Deracializing Social Statistics"; Lawrence D. Bobo, "Reclaiming a Du Boisian Perspective on Racial Attitudes," AAAPSS 568 (March 2000): 186–202. See also the article by philosopher Lucius T. Outlaw, "W. E. B. Du Bois on the Study of Social Problems," *Annals* 568 (March 2000): 281–297; Marlon B. Ross, *Manning the Race: Reforming Black Men in the Jim Crow Era* (New York: New York University Press, 2004): 149–162.

139. Thomas C. Holt, "W. E. B. Du Bois's Archaeology of Race: Re-Reading 'The Conservation of Races,'" in *W. E. B. Du Bois, Race, and the City: The Philadelphia Negro and Its Legacy,* ed. Michael B. Katz and Thomas J. Sugrue (Philadelphia: University of Pennsylvania Press, 1998), 62.

140. W. E. B. Du Bois, "The Negroes of Farmville, Virginia: A Social Study," *Bulletin of the Department of Labor* 14 (January 1898): 1–38. In his letter to Wright, Du Bois also noted that "both the preliminary and the main work must of course be strictly limited in scope; great care must be taken to avoid giving offence to white or black, to raise no suspicions and at the same time to get definite accurate information"; see W. E. B. Du Bois to Carroll D. Wright Esq., May 5, 1897, in *The Correspondence of W. E. B. Du Bois, vol. 1, 1877–1934,* ed. Herbert Aptheker (1973, reprinted Amherst: University of Massachusetts Press, 1997), 41–43.

141. "Convictions on all great matters of human interest one must have to a greater or less degree, and they will enter to some extent into the most cold-blooded scientific research as a disturbing factor" (Du Bois, *The Philadelphia Negro,* 3).

142. Lane, *Roots of Violence in Black Philadelphia*, 148–161; Holt, "Archaeology of Race"; Lewis, *Biography of a Race;* Gaines, *Uplifting the Race*, 164–169; Young and Duskins, "Early Traditions of African American Sociological Thought," 460.

143. Gaines, *Uplifting the Race;* Victoria W. Wolcott, *Remaking Respectability: African American Women in Interwar Detroit* (Chapel Hill: University of North Carolina Press, 2001); White, *Too Heavy a Load.*

144. Hoffman, *Race Traits,* 181. Hoffman provided no citation for this statement and presented no statistics on black prostitution. Instead he measured non-marital sex and prostitution by illegitimacy. And illegitimacy, he claimed, was yet another "inadequately treated [area] by those who have written on the subject of negro morality" (235). According to the "health office" of Washington, D.C., between 1879 and 1894 the average rate of illegitimate childbirths was 2.92 for white women and 22.49 for black women. "That under a civilized government," Hoffman wrote, "one-fourth of the children of one race should bear '*the bar* sinister' is a fact which is fraught with far-reaching consequences" (236).

145. Jane Addams, *Twenty Years at Hull House* (1910, reprinted New York: New American Library, 1981), 101–102; Hoffman, *Race Traits*, 223–224.

146. Du Bois, *Dusk of Dawn,* 58.

147. Du Bois, *The Philadelphia Negro,* 282–283.

148. Ibid., 236–268, 282–286, 387, 392–397.

149. Lewis, *Biography of a Race,* 148–149, 173. Thomas Holt briefly mentions Du Bois's critique of the criminal in "Political Uses," 303.

150. Du Bois, *The Philadelphia Negro,* 389–394, 396–397.

151. David Levering Lewis writes, "Behind the moralizing and the stern admonitions to black people to behave like lending-library patrons, the book would speak calmly yet devastatingly of the history and logic of poverty and racism" (Lewis, *Biography of a Race,* 189–190). Roger Lane agrees that Du Bois emphasized racism as a major factor in crime and immorality, but criticizes him for it. He writes that Du Bois "shrank from the dismal implications of his own findings" and "systematically, if unconsciously, minimized the relative extent of black crime in the city." Du Bois, he explains, was unprepared by his elitism and his European training to confront the reality before him. "The ominous suggestion that criminal behavior was actually on the rise was perhaps too bleak for Philadelphia's black leaders [including Du Bois] to face, certainly to admit or discuss openly. The situation was especially acute in the fearful 1890s" (Lane, *Roots of Violence in Black Philadelphia,* 149). According to Lane, all the indicators of black pathology in the late twentieth century were in operation by this moment: overcrowded and female-headed households, domestic violence, ownership of weapons, juvenile delinquency, prostitution, and epidemic vice. Had Philadelphia's black elite, "who advised Du Bois," faced up to and fought these "conditions in the city itself," Lane writes, the "fear and hatreds" that followed might have been averted (153–160). "The late twentieth century, moreover, has greatly intensified not only the traditional white contempt for black," he writes in the epilogue, "but also the kind of racial fear first felt in Philadelphia during the late 1890s" (171).

152. In *The Philadelphia Negro,* Du Bois uses "unconscious prejudice" and the "half-conscious actions of men and women" as references to the state of mind of "white people" (396–397).

153. Du Bois described this article as his "national debut" (Lewis, *Biography of a Race,* 198).

154. W. E. B. Du Bois, "Strivings of the Negro People," *The Atlantic Monthly,* August 1897.

155. Herbert Aptheker, ed., *Writings by W. E. B. Du Bois in Periodicals Edited by Others, vol. 1, 1891–1909* (Millwood, N.Y.: Kraus-Thomson Organization Limited, 1982), 57.

156. Aptheker, ed., *Writings, vol. 1,* 67–68. As a southern sequel to *The Philadelphia Negro,* Du Bois's clearest, dual-sided statement on black criminality is found at W. E. B. Du Bois, "The Relation of the Negroes to the Whites in the South," AAAPSS 18 (July 1901): 121–140. With an increasing focus on racism, variations on his crime discourse are notable in several additional publications (with a heavy emphasis on the South) until 1910, when as editor of the NAACP's *Crisis* magazine, he put down his scholarly pen for an activist sword; see W. E. B. Du Bois, "To Solve the Negro Problem," *Collier's Weekly,* June 18, 1904, 14, reprinted in Aptheker, ed., *Writings, vol. 1,* 223.

157. David Levering Lewis, "Review of *W. E. B. Du Bois, Race and the City: The Philadelphia Negro and Its Legacy,* by Michael B. Katz and Thomas J. Sugrue, eds.," *Journal of American History* 88:1 (2001): 227.

158. The two favorable reviews by the *Academy of American Social and Political Science* and *The Journal of Political Economy* had little measurable impact on Du Bois's academic stature; see Percy N. Booth, "Review of *The Philadelphia Negro: A Social Study* by W. E. B. Du Bois," AAAPSS 15 (January 1900): 100–102; Katherine B. Davis, "The Condition of the Negro in Philadelphia," *The Journal of Political Economy* 8:2 (1900): 248–260.

159. Of the many universities surveyed, Hampton is the only one that listed Du Bois's book in its curriculum; see Frank L. Tolman, "The Study of Sociology in Institutions of Leaning in the United States, IV," AJS 8:4 (1903): 531–558.

160. W. I Thomas, "The Mind of Woman and the Lower Races," *American Journal of Sociology* 12 (March 1904): 442.

161. Michael B. Katz and Thomas J. Sugrue, eds., *W. E. B. Du Bois, Race, and the City: "The Philadelphia Negro" and Its Legacy* (Philadelphia: University of Pennsylvania Press, 1998), 19.

162. Lewis, *Biography of a Race,* 343–385.

163. Thomas D. Boston, "W. E. B. Du Bois and the Historical School of Economics," *The American Economic Review* 81:2 (1991): 305.

164. Katznelson, "Presidents' Address," 467–469.

165. "Review of *The Philadelphia Negro,* by W. E. B. Du Bois," *American Historical Review* 6:1 (1900): 162–164.

166. Mark Aldrich states that Willcox was "the most important economic demographer of the Progressive era," a leading figure in the American Economic Association and the American Statistical Association. He had been a student of Richard Mayo-Smith at Columbia University, a pioneering force in the adoption of statistical analysis in the United States. Willcox's reach crossed the color line and included a broad spectrum of those with varying racial views, including Carroll D. Wright, Alfred Stone, Frederick Hoffman, Mississippi Governor James K. Vardaman, Booker T. Washington, and W. E. B. Du Bois. Aldrich argues, along with John Stanfield and William Darity, that Willcox produced and supported "ostensibly objective statistical studies . . . to justify and rationalize the oppression of

black Americans" (Aldrich, "Progressive Economists and Scientific Racism," 1–14); see Walter Darity, Jr., "Many Roads to Extinction: Early AEA Economists and the Black Disappearance Hypothesis," *History of Economics Review* 21 (1994): 47–64; Williamson, *A Rage for Order*, 89–90; John H. Stanfield, *Philanthropy and Jim Crow in American Social Science* (Westport, Conn.: Greenwood Press, 1967), 23.

167. Walter F. Willcox, "Negro Criminality," in Alfred Stone, *Studies in the American Race Problem* (New York: Doubleday, Page & Co., 1908), 444.

168. Among the other "faults" discussed, one participant corroborated the "health and high rate of mortality" problems presented in Hoffman's book and another spoke of the "spread of vicious tendencies" in the "crowded tenements" of New York; see "Colored Man's Chances: Lessons from the Convention of Representative Negroes at Hampton, Virginia," *New York Times*, July 25, 1898.

169. Willcox, "Negro Criminality," 444, 446.

170. G. Stanley Hall, "The Negro in Africa and America," *Pedagogical Seminary* 12 (1905): 358, 363, 368. Also see Gossett, *Race*, 154.

171. Du Bois, "Black North."

172. Illustrative are papers from the panel on the "The Race Problem at the South" during the America's Race Problems conference at the fifth annual meeting of the American Academy of Political and Social Sciences, April 12–13, 1901. The panel participants were Hilary A. Herbert, former secretary of the Navy, George T. Winston, the white president of North Carolina College of Agriculture and Mechanic Arts, and W. E. B. Du Bois. In his introductory remarks, Herbert said, "The Negro's prospects for improvement, his development since emancipation, his industrial conditions, his relation to crime, the scanty results of the system of education that has been pursued, how that system can be bettered—all these questions as they exist to-day are before you for debate"; see "America's Race Problems," AAAPSS 18 (July 1901): 100. The speeches were published consecutively in the same journal issue by author's name, under separate subtitles (95–140). See also Du Bois, "To Solve the Negro Problem."

173. Ronald P. Falkner, "Crime and the Census," AAAPSS 9 (January 1897): 43, 44, 62–66. According to Michael Katz and Thomas Sugrue, *W. E. B. Du Bois, Race, and the City*, Falkner was the first to teach statistics at Penn (19).

174. Lawrence Rosen, "The Creation of the Uniform Crime Report," *Social Science History* 19:2 (1995): 220. While sociologists and statisticians in more recent decades may all uniformly recognize the logical and/or mathematical mistakes of their predecessors, they can not change the past. The real-time consequences of these past errors shaped what was possible for African Americans as the subjects of sociological investigations and the objects of social welfare reform.

175. Daryl Michael Scott, *Contempt and Pity: Social Policy and the Image of the Damaged Black Psyche, 1880–1996* (Chapel Hill: University of North Carolina Press, 1997), 42.

176. Rosen, "The Creation of the Uniform Crime Report," 215–238; Edwin H. Sutherland and C. C. Van Vechten, Jr., "The Reliability of Criminal Statistics," *Journal of Criminal Law and Criminology* 25 (1934): 10–20; Khalil G. Muhammad, "Policing Racial Crime Statistics: *Uniform Crime Reports,* 1930–1940." Paper pre-

sented at the annual Warren Susman Graduate History conference, Rutgers University, New Brunswick, N.J., April 1998.

177. Willcox, "Negro Criminality," 446–447.

178. All of them followed after Wells and Du Bois with the exception of Monroe N. Work and Fannie Williams. Along with Franz Boas they were part of the process of shifting the discourse toward emphasizing cultural inferiority rather than race; see Work, "Crime among the Negroes of Chicago"; James S. Stemons, "Increase of Crime among Negroes," *Colored American Magazine* 13 (July 1907): 66.

179. Williams, *Social Science and Theories of Race,* especially chapter 7.

180. Work computed the ratio of black arrests to the black population in Chicago to assess the relative criminality of blacks in the North versus the South. At a ratio of 1:3 in 1897, Chicago topped the list with a far higher ratio than the southern cities he examined: Washington, D.C. (1:6.3), Richmond (1:9.7), and Charleston (1:13.5 for the year 1890). Chicago also trumped New York (1:7). Work did not include Philadelphia. Work, "Crime among the Negroes of Chicago," 211, 222.

181. Work, "Crime among the Negroes of Chicago," 223. By his ambiguous use of "race characteristics peculiar to him," it is not clear whether he meant innate criminal tendencies or racism. The ambiguity may have been a deliberate effort to satisfy the editorial demands of the journal.

182. J. Shadrach Shirley, "The Growth of the Social Evil among All Classes and Races in America," *Colored American Magazine* 6 (February 1903): 259–263; Fredrickson, *The Black Image in the White Mind,* 256.

183. William Hannibal Thomas, *The American Negro: What He Was, What He Is, and What He May Become* (New York: Macmillan, 1901), x–xix.

184. John David Smith, *Black Judas: William Hannibal Thomas and The American Negro* (Athens, Ga.: University of Georgia Press, 2000), 181.

185. Thomas, *The American Negro,* 109–116, 120, 129, 134, 139. Thomas's book was part of the cultural and intellectual landscape that made it possible for a Zaire man named Ota Benga to be exhibited in a cage at the Bronx Zoo in 1905 as an "African Pygmy" who proved the human evolutionary link to primates, see Baker, *From Savage to Negro,* 72.

186. For a discussion of the controversy and backlash surrounding the work, particularly among African American leaders such as Booker T. Washington and Francis Grimke, see Smith, *Black Judas,* 191–234. Also see Richard R. Wright, Jr., "Review of 'The American Negro,'" *AJS* 6:6 (1901): 850–852; W. E. B. Du Bois, "The Storm and Stress in the Black World," *The Dial* 30 (April 16, 1901): 262–264.

187. Franklin H. Giddings to Macmillan Company, October 10, 1899, Macmillan Papers, quoted in Smith, *Black Judas,* 167. Smith notes that Giddings's review was the only one of three that was positive and recommended publication. One reviewer, William Z. Ripley, was himself the author of a standard text of scientific racism, *The Races of Europe: A Sociological Study* (New York: D. Appleton and Co., 1899). His complaints and those of the third in-house reviewer were largely about style and the total lack of scientific evidence. The publisher, however, moved forward with publication after insisting on revisions (167–173).

188. *New York Times,* January 12, 1901, BR1.

189. "The Negro Arraigned," *New York Times,* February 23, 1901.

190. William Patrick Calhoun, *The Caucasian and the Negro: They Must Separate. If Not, Then Extermination* (Columbia, S.C.: R. L. Bryan, 1902), 6; Guterl, *The Color of Race*; Matthew Frye Jacobson, *Whiteness of a Different Color: European Immigrants and the Alchemy of Race* (Cambridge: Harvard University Press, 1998).

191. With Thomas's success, even the actual statistics did not matter. Du Bois offered a comment in his review of Thomas's *The American Negro* that is suggestive of the pressure some black writers may have succumbed to when trying to get their antiracist ideas noticed. Du Bois wrote that Thomas's book was first published in 1890 as a pamphlet. "The pamphlet was a defense of the Negro, with severe criticisms on the whites, and laid down the thesis that land owning and education—both industrial and higher—would solve the Negro problem." In the rewrite, according to Du Bois, there was "added a denunciation of the Negro in America unparalleled in vindictiveness and exaggeration" (Du Bois, "The Storm and Stress in the Black World," 263). Of course, Thomas may have simply revised his interpretations in light of the new crime and immorality discourse. Whatever the cause, his book became a widely quoted source for many white writers.

192. C. C. Closson, "Review of *The American Negro* by William Hannibal Thomas," *Journal of Political Economy* 10:2 (1902): 316.

193. Influenced by the Social Gospel movement of the late nineteenth and early twentieth centuries while working closely with the African Methodist Episcopal minister Reverdy C. Ransom, Wright applied Christian principles of serving the needs of the least of God's children before leaving Chicago. By 1905, Wright was a doctoral sociology student at the University of Pennsylvania. He would eventually become a major force in the African Methodist Episcopal church, editing the *Christian Recorder* and becoming president of Wilberforce University; see Terrell Dale Goddard, "The Black Social Gospel in Chicago, 1896–1906: The Ministries of Reverdy C. Ransom and Richard R. Wright, Jr.," *The Journal of Negro History* 84:3 (1999): 227–246.

194. "Book Notes," *Political Science Quarterly* 17:3 (1902): 547.

195. Du Bois, "The Storm and Stress in the Black World," 262–264.

196. Frances Kellor, "The Criminal Negro: A Sociological Study," *The Arena* 25:1–5 (January–May 1901): 59–68, 190–197, 419–128, 510–520.

197. Thomas Nelson Page, *The Negro: The Southerner's Problem* (New York: Charles Scribner's Sons, 1904), 102. Describing Page, I. A. Newby writes: "As much as any individual he contributed to the crystallization of Southern mythology concerning the Old South and the Negro"; see I. A. Newby, *Jim Crow's Defense: Anti-Negro Thought in America, 1900–1930* (Baton Rouge: Louisiana State University Press, 1965), 68.

198. Willcox, "Negro Criminality," 445.

199. Page, *The Negro*, 82–83, 84.

200. Ibid., 296; Florette Henri, *Black Migration: Movement North, 1900–1920* (Garden City, N.Y.: Doubleday, 1975), 263.

201. Henri, *Black Migration*, 228.

202. W. H. Johnson, "The Case of the Negro," *The Dial* 34 (May 1, 1903): 301. Thomas Dixon, Jr., *The Leopard's Spots: A Romance of the White Man's Burden, 1875–1900* (New York: Doubleday Page, 1902).

203. Johnson, "The Case of the Negro," 301.

204. Williamson, *A Rage for Order*, 106.

205. Michael P. Rogin," 'The Sword Became a Flashing Vision': D. W. Griffith's *The Birth of a Nation,*" in *Ronald Reagan, the Movie: And Other Episodes in Political Demonology* (Berkeley: University of California Press, 1988), 191–197; Jacqueline Najuma Stewart, *Migrating to the Movies: Cinema and Black Urban Modernity* (Berkeley: University of California Press, 2005), 33, 230.

206. Lewis, *Biography of a Race*, 367.

207. Alfred Holt Stone, "Is Race Friction between Blacks and Whites in the United States Growing and Inevitable?" AJS 13:5 (1908): 678, 687, 693.

208. W. F. Willcox, "Discussion of the Paper by Alfred H. Stone, 'Is Race Friction between Blacks and Whites in the United States Growing and Inevitable?'" *American Journal of Sociology* 13:6 (1908): 820, 824, 828, 833; Lewis, *Biography of a Race*, 372.

209. F. W. Blackmar, "Review of *Studies in the American Race Problem* by Alfred H. Stone," *American Journal of Sociology* 14:6 (1909): 837–839; James B. McKee, *Sociology and the Race Problem: The Failure of a Perspective* (Urbana: University of Illinois Press, 1993), 30.

210. Lewis, *Biography of a Race*, 373–374.

211. Charlotte Perkins Gilman, "A Suggestion on the Negro Problem," AJS 14:1 (1908): 79–81.

212. Hoffman, *Race Traits*, 217, 285; Willcox, 448–449; Du Bois, "The Black North," 11; Thomas, *The American Negro*, 213; Page, *The Negro*, 57, 96; Williamson, *A Rage for Order* 98.

213. Shaler, "The Negro since the Civil War," *Popular Science Monthly* 57 (1900): 36–39.

214. N. S. Shaler, "The Future of the Negro in the Southern States," *Popular Science Monthly* 57 (1900): 154, 155.

215. Ibid., 156. With his call for historical research, Shaler seemed to be backpedaling on his earlier faith in statistical data as an unproblematic method of racial science.

3. INCRIMINATING CULTURE

1. Kellor was also the first American criminologist to study white female criminality in a series of articles published in the *American Journal of Sociology*; Frances A. Kellor, "Psychological and Environmental Study of Women Criminals, I," AJS 5 (January 1900): 527–543; "Psychological and Environmental Study of Women Criminals, II," AJS 5 (March 1900): 671–682.

2. Frances Kellor, "The Criminal Negro: A Sociological Study," *The Arena* 25: 1–5 (January-May 1901): 59–68, 190–197, 419–128, 510–520, and *Experimental Sociology: Descriptive and Analytic: Delinquents* (New York: The Macmillan Co., 1901).

3. E. Fitzpatrick, *Endless Crusade: Women Social Scientists and Progressive Reform* (New York: Oxford University Press, 1990), 58–66.

4. All were cited in her bibliography. Jane Addams, *Hull House Maps and Papers* (New York: T. W. Crowell & Co., 1895).

5. Kellor, "The Criminal Negro," 61, 313.

6. Ibid., 62–63. The results of her research seem not to have been published. The year before, however, she published the results of similar studies among northern white female college students. Kellor, "Psychological and Environmental Study of Women Criminals, I and II."

7. Charles Richmond Henderson, *An Introduction to the Study of the Dependent, Defective and Delinquent Classes* (Boston: Heath & Co., 1893).

8. Kellor, "The Criminal Negro," 512–520.

9. Although Kellor studied black women prisoners in particular, she wrote of their experiences and black men's in racial rather than gendered terms. She also frequently drew attention to conditions facing northern blacks and tended to argue her evidence in national terms.

10. Kellor, "The Criminal Negro," 60, 61. Kellor cited estimates of prison profits ranging from $30,000 to $150,000 per state.

11. Ibid., 65–67, 190–191, 527; Kellor, *Experimental Sociology,* 32, 34, 143–144, 153.

12. Kellor, "The Criminal Negro," 313; W. E. B. Du Bois, "The Black North: A Social Study," *New York Times,* December 1, 1901.

13. Kellor, *Experimental Sociology,* 34.

14. Franz Boas, *The Mind of Primitive Man* (New York: Macmillan, 1911); George Stocking, *Race, Culture and Evolution: Essays in the History of Anthropology* (1968, reprinted Chicago: University of Chicago Press, 1982); Vernon J. Williams, *Rethinking Race: Franz Boas and his Contemporaries* (Louisville: University of Kentucky Press, 1996); Christopher Shannon, *A World Made Safe for Differences: Cold War Intellectuals and the Politics of Identity* (Lanham, Md.: Rowman and Littlefield, 2001); David Steigerwald, *Culture's Vanities: The Paradox of Cultural Diversity in a Globalized World* (Lanham, Md.: Rowman and Littlefield, 2004).

15. The following are a sample of the variety of works that demonstrate Hoffman's "authority" in some way: Marcus Kavanagh, *The Criminal and His Allies* (Indianapolis: Bobbs-Merrill Co., 1928); H. C. Brearley, "The Negro and Homicide," *Social Forces* 9 (1930); Raymond B. Fosdick, "Review of *The Homicide Record of American Cities for 1915,* by Frederick L. Hoffman," *Spectator,* December 21, 1916, and published by *Publications of the American Statistical Association* 15 (March 1917): 559–561; George Edmund Haynes, *The Negro at Work in New York City: A Study in Economic Progress* (New York: Arno Press, 1912); Charles H. McCord, *The American Negro as Dependent, Defective and Delinquent* (Nashville: Benson, 1914), 213; "National Urban League Conference," *Opportunity,* March 1926, 96; W. E. B. Du Bois, "Crime," *Crisis,* March 1922, 200–201; Henry Lee Moon, "Harlemite Has One Chance of Being Murdered to Two at 'Hitting the Numbers': Negro Homicide Rate Rises to Serious Total for City," *New York Amsterdam News,* April 20, 1932, 1.

16. Fosdick, "Review of *The Homicide Record of American Cities for 1915,*" 559; Louis N. Robinson, "History of Criminal Statistics," *Journal of Criminal Law and Criminology* 24 (May-June 1933): 125–139.

17. Kevin Gaines, *Uplifting the Race* (Chapel Hill: University of North Carolina Press, 1996); Glenda Gilmore, *Gender and Jim Crow: Women and the Politics*

of *White Supremacy in North Carolina, 1896–1920* (Chapel Hill: University of North Carolina Press, 1996); Deborah Gray White, *Too Heavy a Load: Black Women in Defense of Themselves, 1894–1994* (New York: W. W. Norton & Co., 1999).

18. Richard R. Wright, Jr., "The Economic Condition of Negroes in the North, Tendencies Downward: Negro Criminal Statistics," *Southern Workman* 40 (May 1911): 306; Ida Joyce Jackson, "Do Negroes Constitute a Race of Criminals?" *Colored American Magazine* 12 (April 1907): 252–255; J. Shadrach Shirley, "The Growth of the Social Evil among All Classes and Races in America," *Colored American Magazine* 6 (February 1903): 259–263; Du Bois, "The Black North," 11; R. Henri Herbert, "Our Problems and Our Burdens," *Colored American Magazine* 12:5 (May 1907): 346.

19. Race Conference Program, November 21, 1910, Box 3, Folder 7, Stemons Papers, Balch Institute for Ethnic Studies, Philadelphia, Penn.

20. Carl Kelsey, "Review of *The Souls of Black Folk*, by W. E. B. Du Bois," *AAAPSS* 22 (July 1903): 230–232.

21. Thomas Nelson Page, *The Negro: The Southerner's Problem* (New York: Charles Scribner's Sons, 1904), 74–75.

22. Gilbert Stephenson, "Education and Crime among Negroes," *South Atlantic Quarterly* 16 (January 1917): 15.

23. W. E. B. Du Bois, ed., *Some Notes on Negro Crime: Particularly in Georgia* (Atlanta: Atlanta University Press, 1904): 16.

24. W. E. B. Du Bois, "Crime and Our Colored Population," *The Nation*, December 25, 1902, 499.

25. Guichard Parris and Lester Brooks, *Blacks in the City: A History of the National Urban League* (Boston: Little, Brown and Company, 1971): 8–10; McCord, *The American Negro as Dependent, Defective and Delinquent*, 206.

26. Ida B. Wells, *Southern Horrors. Lynch Law in All Its Phases* (New York: New York Age Print, 1892), reprinted in *Southern Horrors and Other Writings: The Anti-Lynching Campaign of Ida B. Wells, 1892–1900*, ed. Jacqueline Jones Royster (Boston: Bedford Books, 1997).

27. Du Bois, *Notes on Negro Crime*, 16–17.

28. Frederick L. Hoffman, *Race Traits and Tendencies of the American Negro* (New York: American Economic Association, 1896), 228–229.

29. Statistics by Poe in Du Bois, *Notes on Negro*, 17; Du Bois, "Crime and Our Colored Population," 499.

30. Kelly Miller, *Race Adjustment: Essays on the Negro in America*, 2nd ed. (New York: Neale Publishing, 1909), 100.

31. Ibid.

32. Miller, quoted in Stephenson, "Education and Crime among Negroes," 17.

33. Washington, quoted in ibid., 19.

34. Stephenson, "Education and Crime among Negroes," 17, 19.

35. Ray Stannard Baker, *Following the Color Line: American Negro Citizenship in the Progressive Era* (1908, reprinted New York: Torchbooks, 1964), 123.

36. James K. Vardaman, "A Governor Bitterly Opposes Negro Education," *Leslie's Weekly*, February 4, 1904.

37. Mary White Ovington, "The Negro Home in New York," *Charities* 15:1 (October 7, 1905): 30; David Levering Lewis, *W. E. B. Du Bois: Biography of a Race, 1886–1919* (New York: Henry Holt, 1993), 223.

38. Lewis, *Biography of a Race*, 347–349.

39. Kellor, *Experimental Sociology*, 34, 143–147, 192.

40. Gilbert Osofsky, *Harlem: The Making of the Ghetto, Negro New York 1890–1930*, 2nd ed. (New York: Harper Torchbooks, 1971), 54.

41. Franz Boas, "The Negro and the Demands of Modern Life: Ethnic and Anatomic Considerations," *Charities* 15:1 (October 7, 1905): 87.

42. Editors, "The Negro in the Cities of the North," *Charities* 15:1 (October 7, 1905): 2.

43. Katherine B. Davis, "The Condition of the Negro in Philadelphia," *The Journal of Political Economy* 8:2 (1900): 248–260; Judith Ann Trolander, *Professionalism and Social Change: From the Settlement Houses Movement to Neighborhood Centers, 1886 to the Present* (New York: Columbia University Press, 1987).

44. Boas, *The Mind of Primitive Man*. George Stocking, a historian of anthropology, similarly describes Boas as a "transitional figure in the development of a concept that only gradually emerged from the conditioning of its 'inherited name.'" Stocking writes that Boas was the "first to use the term [*culture*] in the plural prior to 1895," establishing it as a reference point to the cultures of individual human groups. The long-term consequence was to explode the racial hierarchy upon which human groups had been previously organized in the nineteenth century. Stocking adds that beginning around 1910 the term became popular among a "first generation" of students (Stocking, *Race, Culture and Evolution*, 202–203, 202–267). Vernon Williams, a historian of social science and race, similarly shows that even before *The Mind of Primitive Man*, Boas was influential among white progressives and African Americans, including W. E. B. Du Bois and Booker T. Washington (Williams, *Rethinking Race*, 16, 29–30).

45. Tukufu Zuberi, *Thicker Than Blood: How Racial Statistics Lie* (Minneapolis: University of Minnesota Press, 2001), 88.

46. Kellor, *Experimental Sociology*, 31.

47. Kellor would by 1905 be among the first white liberals to lead an effort to protect black migrant woman from these very dangers; see Frances Kellor, "Assisted Emigration from the South: The Women," *Charities* 15:1 (October 7, 1905): 11–14.

48. Kellor, "The Criminal Negro," 191, 194.

49. According to Phillip A. Bruce, the Virginia planter turned professional historian who was a major source in Hoffman's crime analysis, the "aspect of a pistol is still more formidable; it is prudently eschewed for that reason, and properly so; for the negroes, being thoughtless and heedless, are in far more danger of shooting themselves accidentally when they carry such firearms than of implanting a bullet in their adversary"; see Philip A. Bruce, *The Plantation Negro as a Freeman, Observations on His Character, Condition, and Prospects in Virginia* (1889, reprinted Williamstown, Mass.: Corner House Publishers, 1970), 82.

50. Frederick A. Bushee, "Ethnic Factors in the Population of Boston," *Publications of the American Economic Association*, 3rd Series 4:2 (May 1903): 1–171;

William Z. Ripley, *The Races of Europe: A Sociological Study* (New York: D. Appleton and Co., 1899); Kelsey, "Review of *The Soul of Black Folks*"; William S. Bennet, "Immigrants and Crime," AAAPSS 34:1 (July 1909): 117–124.

51. Bushee, "Ethnic Factors in the Population of Boston," 103, 113.

52. William Z. Ripley, "Race Progress and Immigration," AAAPSS 34:1 (1909): 130. For more on Ripley's nativist views, see John Higham, *Strangers in the Land: Patterns of American Nativism, 1860–1925* (New Brunswick, N.J.: Rutgers University Press, 1953), 154–156.

53. Bushee, "Ethnic Factors in the Population of Boston," 152, 158.

54. Ripley, "Race Progress," 136.

55. Bennet, "Immigrants and Crime," 123.

56. Allen F. Davis, *Spearheads for Reform: The Social Settlements and the Progressive Movement, 1880–1914* (New York, Oxford University Press, 1967); Trolander, *Professionalism and Social Change*; Mina Carson, *Settlement Folk: Social Thought and the American Settlement Movement, 1885–1930* (Chicago: University of Chicago Press, 1990).

57. Bushee, "Ethnic Factors in the Population of Boston," 115, 160.

58. Davis, *Spearheads for Reform*, 94.

59. Carson, *Settlement Folk*, 195. The page on which this quotation appears has the only mention of African Americans in the entire book.

60. The term "becoming Caucasian" is borrowed from Matthew Frye Jacobson, *Whiteness of a Different Color: European Immigrants and the Alchemy of Race* (Cambridge: Harvard University Press, 1998). On immigrant upward mobility by way of settlements, see Trolander, *Professionalism and Social Change*, 20. For general discussions of the limits of Progressive era reform by comparing the experiences of immigrants and blacks, see Thomas J. Philpott, *The Slum and the Ghetto: Immigrants, Blacks, and Reformers in Chicago, 1880–1930* (Belmont, Calif.: Wadsworth Publishing, 1991); Stanley Lieberson, *A Piece of the Pie: Blacks and White Immigrants since 1880* (Berkeley: University of California Press, 1980). Thomas Guglielmo challenges Jacobson's premise that immigrants experienced a whitening process. In light of the upward mobility of all European immigrants relative to African Americans, he argues that they were "white on arrival" despite being the targets of anti-immigrant racism; Thomas A. Guglielmo, *White on Arrival: Italians, Race, Color, and Power in Chicago, 1890–1945* (New York: Oxford University Press, 2003).

61. Ovington, "The Negro Home in New York," 30.

62. See, for example, how skin color accounted for the advantages experienced by white Appalachian migrants to northern cities during the post-World War II period in Jacqueline Jones, "Southern Diaspora: Origins of the Northern 'Underclass,'" in *The "Underclass" Debate: Views from History*, ed. Michael B. Katz (Princeton: University of Princeton Press, 1993), 52.

63. Thomas Philpott counted nine settlements for black Chicagoans that opened between 1900 and 1916. None survived into the 1920s (Philpott, *The Slum and the Ghetto*, 317). Allan Spear counted "perhaps about a dozen" over the same period: *Black Chicago: The Making of a Negro Ghetto, 1890–1920* (Chicago: University of Chicago Press, 1967), 97. In a more recent investigation of African

American settlements, Anne Meis Knupfer looked closely at the records of five settlements that most resembled Hull House. Following Philpott's count of white settlements opened over the same period, she notes that there were at least sixty-seven white settlements, but there were "undoubtedly more" based on the statements of officials of the National Federation of Settlements; *Toward a Tenderer Humanity and a Nobler Womanhood* (New York, NYU Press, 1996), 91, 98. For more on the failure of white settlements to address the needs of blacks, see Trolander, *Professionalism and Social Change* who notes that "as late as the 1930s, most settlement workers still thought of their movement as being primarily for whites. Before World War II, only a handful of settlements [in the nation] made more than a token attempt at integration" (93–94).

64. White, *Too Heavy a Load:* "The practice of self-help was buttressed by an ideology of economic and social uplift that was as heartening as it was crippling. On the one hand, uplift stressed racial solidarity, where those with means helped those without it. . . . However, as heroic as was this emphasis on self-reliance, uplift also marked a capitulation to racism. When black people picked up the burden that white racism, violence, and negative stereotypes thrust upon them, they accommodated white exclusionary practices. They tacitly, and perhaps unwittingly, surrendered not only those basic civil and political rights enjoyed by white Americans but rights that were needed to maintain economic self-sufficiency" (270, note 11).

65. Trolander, *Professionalism and Social Change,* 94.

66. Philpott, *The Slum and the Ghetto,* 325; Knupfer, *Toward a Tenderer Humanity and a Nobler Womanhood,* 91.

67. Kelsey, "Review of *The Souls of Black Folk,*" 231.

68. Even though the NAACP was far more committed to an antiracist agenda embodied in its major focus on putting a stop to southern mob violence in its earliest years, it was not until after the post-World War I race riots that it began to seriously target racism and inequality in the urban North. It would never pursue an aggressive economic attack on northern job discrimination, focusing instead on equalizing teacher pay in the South in the 1940s.

69. Editors, "The Negro in the Cities of the North," *Charities* 15:1 (October 7, 1905): 1.

70. Fannie Barrier Williams, "Social Bonds in the 'Black Belt' of Chicago: Negro Organizations and the New Spirit Pervading Them," *Charities* 15:1 (October 7, 1905): 40–44, and "Growth of Social Settlement Idea," *New York Age,* August 5, 1905.

71. For biographical information, see Domenica M. Barbuto, *American Settlement Houses, and Progressive Social Reform: An Encyclopedia of the American Settlement Movement* (Phoenix, Ariz.: Oryx Press, 1999), 63–64, 111–112. For another summary, see Alvin B. Kogut, "The Negro and the Charity Organization Society in the Progressive Era," *Social Service Review* 44:1 (1970): 11–21.

72. New York and Philadelphia dominated as research sites and as cities in which the editors and the contributors were based. Chicago, Baltimore, Washington, D.C., and Boston were also well represented.

73. Richard R. Wright, Jr., "The Negro in Times of Industrial Unrest," *Charities* 15:1 (October 7, 1905): 67–73; John Daniels, "Industrial Conditions among

Negro Men in Boston," *Charities* 15:1 (October 7, 1905): 35–38; Lilian Brandt, "The Make-up of Negro City Groups," *Charities* 15:1 (October 7, 1905): 11; Carl Kelsey, "Some Causes of Negro Emigration: The Men" *Charities* 15:1 (October 7, 1905): 17.

74. Kellor, "Assisted Emigration from the South," 11–12. According to Hazel Carby, Kellor's article "provides important evidence that as early as 1905 the major discursive elements were already in place that would define black female urban behavior throughout the teens and twenties as pathological"; Hazel V. Carby, "Policing the Black Woman's Body in an Urban Context," *Critical Inquiry* 18 (Summer 1992): 739–740.

75. Barbuto, *American Settlement Houses*, 239, Fitzpatrick, *Endless Crusade*, 55–68; Steven J. Diner, "Chicago Social Workers and Blacks in the Progressive Era," *Social Service Review* 44 (December 1970): 403–406. Diner notes that Woolley's primary concern was with "educated middle-class blacks." In contrast to Ovington, she "had little interest in the conditions of poor blacks" (404). See also Ida B. Wells, *Crusade for Justice: An Autobiography of Ida B. Wells,* ed. Alfreda M. Duster (Chicago: University of Chicago Press, 1970); Spear, *Black Chicago*, 105.

76. Elisabeth Lasch-Quinn, *Black Neighbors: Race and the Limits of Reform in the American Settlement House Movement, 1890–1945* (Chapel Hill: University of North Carolina Press, 1993).

77. Editors, "The Negro in the Cities of the North," 2.

78. Booker T. Washington, "Why Should Negro Business Men Go South?" *Charities* 15:1 (October 7, 1905): 19.

79. J. H. N. Waring, "Some Causes of Criminality among Colored People," *Charities* 15:1 (October 7, 1905): 44–47; for more on how police treated white juvenile delinquents by comparison to African Americans and Mexican Americans, see David B. Wolcott, *Cops and Kids: Policing Juvenile Delinquency in Urban America, 1890–1940* (Columbus: Ohio State University Press, 2005).

80. William L. Bulkley, "The School as a Social Center," *Charities* 15:1 (October 7, 1905): 76.

81. Washington, "Why Should Negro Business Men Go South," 17.

82. Williams, "Social Bonds in the 'Black Belt," 40–44.

83. Fannie B. Williams, "The Need for Social Settlement Work for the City Negro," *Southern Workman* 33 (September 1904): 504.

84. Taking a slightly more complicated view of Boas, Stocking writes that Thomas Gossett, author of *Race: The History of an Idea* (Dallas: Southern Methodist University Press, 1963) describes Boas as "a kind of mythical hero figure carrying the torch of reason into an irrational racial darkness"; see Stocking, *Race, Culture and Evolution,* 133; Williams, *Rethinking the Race,* 2, 4; Mia Bay, *The White Image in the Black Mind, African American Ideas about White People, 1830–1925* (New York: Oxford University Press, 2000), 187–188, 195–196; James B. McKee, *Sociology and the Race Problem: The Failure of a Perspective* (Urbana: University of Illinois Press, 1993), 31–33; Jacobson, *Whiteness of a Different Color,* 33, 81.

85. Stocking, *Race, Culture and Evolution,* 149–150.

86. John Stanfield notes, however, that the kind of critical rethinking about the "status of blacks in society" that Boas represented was equally present among

black researchers, but their work had been largely "ignored or ridiculed" since it was published in black newspapers and journals; see John H. Stanfield, *Philanthropy and Jim Crow in American Social Science* (Westport, Conn.: Greenwood Press, 1967), 22.

87. Boas, *The Mind of Primitive Man,* 33, 94, 272.

88. Matthew P. Guterl, *The Color of Race in America, 1900–1940* (Cambridge: Harvard University Press, 2001).

89. Higham, *Strangers in the Land,* 151.

90. Jacobson, *Whiteness of a Different Color,* 78–184; David A. Orebaugh, *Crime, Degeneracy and Immigration: Their Interrelations and Interreactions* (Boston: Gorham Press, 1929).

91. Boas, *The Mind of Primitive Man,* 127, 196, 272–273.

92. Ibid., 271.

93. W. E. B. Du Bois, *The Philadelphia Negro, A Social Study* (1899, reprinted with a new introduction by Elijah Anderson, Philadelphia: University of Pennsylvania Press, 1996); "The Negroes of Farmville, Virginia: A Social Study," *Bulletin of the Department of Labor* 14 (January 1898): 1–38.

94. Boas, *The Mind of Primitive Man,* 271. This statement was removed from the 1938 edition.

95. While conducting physical anthropological research on immigrants for the Dillingham Commission between 1908 and 1909, Boas collected over 18,000 head-form measurements of mostly southern and eastern Europeans and their descendants in New York City. The bulk of his findings indicated to him that the social conditions in America had significantly altered the cephalic index of the children of immigrants for the better (Stocking, *Race, Culture and Evolution,* 177). As early as 1894 and included in *The Mind of Primitive Man,* Boas used skull capacity measurements from the work of Paul Topinard, the most prominent scholar of European anthropology in the late nineteenth century, to argue that the normal range between 1,450 and 1,650 cubic centimeters was roughly the same for whites and blacks. The implication was that the great mass of blacks would be able to hold their own intellectually against the great mass of whites, even though at the largest skull capacities (greater than 1,550) fewer blacks measured up and therefore could "anticipate a lack of high men of genius"; see Stocking, *Race, Culture and Evolution,* 193; Williams, *Rethinking the Race,* 12. Vernon Williams adds that beginning in 1904, Boas began to use anthropological and historical research on African populations, such as observations of fully developed African political systems and highly impressive metallurgical skills, to demonstrate the "true capacity of blacks" (Williams, *Rethinking the Race,* 27–30).

96. For discussions of Boas's influence on these scholars, see Lewis, *Biography of a Race,* 351–352, 414; Williams, *Rethinking the Race,* 2–85; Stocking, *Race, Culture and Evolution,* 300; Melville J. Herskovits, *The Myth of the Negro Past* (Boston: Beacon Press, 1958). For his influence on Ruth Benedict and Margaret Mead, see Shannon, *A World Made Safe for Differences.* On the long-term consequences of his cultural concept on identity politics and the culture wars of the mid- to late twentieth century, see Shannon, *A World Made Safe for Differences*; Steigerwald, *Culture's Vanities.*

97. Stocking, *Race, Culture and Evolution,* 189–190.

98. Williams, *Rethinking the Race,* 5–7; Stanfield, *Philanthropy and Jim Crow in American Social Science,* 33 fn. 18.

99. Osofsky, *Harlem,* 18.

100. Nancy Weiss, *The National Urban League, 1910–1940* (New York: Oxford University Press, 1974).

101. Mary White Ovington, *Half a Man: The Status of the Negro in New York,* with a foreword by Franz Boas (New York: Longmans, Green & Co., 1911), vii–ix.

102. Ovington, *Half a Man,* 36–39, 40, 65, 68.

103. Ibid., 72–73.

104. Ibid., 198.

105. Helena Titus Emerson, "Children of the Circle," *Charities* 15:1 (October 7, 1905): 83.

106. Ovington, *Half a Man,* 197–201. For more on the riots, see Marilynn Johnson, "Riots and the Racialization of Police Brutality, 1900–1911," in *Street Justice: A History of Police Violence in New York City* (Boston: Beacon Press, 2003).

107. W. E. B. Du Bois, "Crime," *Crisis* (November 1911).

108. Crime folders, 1921–1933, Box 264 and 265, NAACP Papers, Manuscript Division, Library of Congress, Washington, D.C. Joel Williamson's graphic account of the "Robert Charles Riot in New Orleans" is a suggestive portrait of the kind of violence that could erupt when blacks attempted to defend themselves against random assaults by white police officers, see Joel Williamson, *A Rage for Order: Black-White Relations in the American South since Emancipation* (New York: Oxford University Press, 1986), 131–141; Edward L. Ayers, *Crime and Punishment in the 19th Century American South* (New York: Oxford University Press, 1984).

109. David Nielson, *Black Ethos: Northern Urban Negro Life and Thought, 1890–1930* (Westport, Conn.: Greenwood Press, 1977), 130.

110. Ovington, *Half a Man,* 200.

111. Florette Henri, *Black Migration: Movement North, 1900–1920* (Garden City, N.Y.: Doubleday, 1975), 120–121.

112. Ovington, *Half a Man,* 218–224.

113. Ibid., 67–68, 190.

114. S. P. Breckenridge, "Review of *Half a Man: The Status of the Negro in New York* by Mary White Ovington," *American Journal of Sociology* 17:3 (1911): 416–417.

115. Bowen donated several buildings for the expansion of Hull House; see Allen F. Davis, "Introduction to Jane Addams, *The Spirit of Youth and the City Streets*" (1909, reprinted with a new introduction by Allen F. Davis, Urbana: University of Illinois, 1972), viii, xvii–xviii. Louise de Koven Bowen, "Colored People of Chicago," *Survey* 31 (November 1, 1913): 117, 119.

116. Jane Addams, *A New Conscience and an Ancient Evil* (1912, reprinted New York: Arno Press and The New York Times, 1972), 119; Addams, *Spirit of Youth,* 34, 77, 91, 93, 114, 158.

117. Addams, *Spirit of Youth.*

118. Addams, *Spirit of Youth*, 13, 16, 20, 26. She echoed this point in Jane Addams, "Recreation as a Public Function in Urban Communities," AJS (March 1912): 615–619.

119. Addams, *Spirit of Youth*, 15, 47.

120. Eric C. Schneider, *In The Web of Class: Delinquents and Reformers in Boston, 1810s–1930s* (New York: New York University Press, 1992), 153; Wolcott, *Cops and Kids*, 102–107, 127.

121. Davis, "Introduction," xiii.

122. Sympathy was a core tenet of Addams's reformism, as it was for many other settlement workers, according to historian Laura M. Westhoff in her recent study of Progressive era Chicago reformers. "Without sympathetic understanding," Westhoff writes, Addams believed "democratic reform was impossible"; *A Fatal Drifting Apart: Democratic Social Knowledge* (Columbus: Ohio State University Press, 2007), 105.

123. J. P. Lichtenberger, "Review of *The Spirit of Youth and the City Streets*, by Jane Addams," AAAPSS 35:2 (1910): 247; Harriet Park Thomas and William James, "Review of *The Spirit of Youth and the City Streets*, by Jane Addams," AJS 15:4 (1910): 551. Also see Mary Kinsbury Simkhovitch, "Review of *The Spirit of Youth and the City Streets*, by Jane Addams," *Political Science Quarterly* 25:3 (1910): 555–556.

124. Addams, *The Spirit of Youth*, 55–59, 61–62.

125. Ibid., 65–66. All were sent to drug rehabilitation at a local hospital, and all but one seemed to be on the road to recovery. He was sent to an Iowa farm and was still "struggling with the appetite."

126. Ibid., 69, 93–95.

127. Ibid., 117–119.

128. Addams made one mention in the entire book of a black child, a "little colored [school] girl" whose industrial training was cited as a model of culturally relevant industrial work because she had the opportunity to embroider an Egyptian design. "Of course, I like it awfully well," Addams quoted her, "because it was first used by people living in Africa where the colored folks come from" (ibid., 122–123).

129. Ovington, *Half a Man*, 162.

130. Teresa Amott and Julie Matthaei, *Race, Gender and Work: A Multicultural Economic History of Work in the United States* (Boston: South End Press, 1996), 141–192.

131. Based on the 1900 census; Ovington, *Half a Man*, 146.

132. Addams, *The Spirit of Youth*, 170.

133. Elizabeth Clark-Lewis, *Living In, Living Out: African American Domestics in Washington, D.C., 1910–1940* (Washington, D.C.: Smithsonian Institution Press, 1994), 83–84. For more discussion of the limited choices facing black women migrants in the urban North, see Darlene Clark Hine, "Black Migration to the Urban Midwest: The Gender Dimension, 1915–1945," in *The Great Migration in Historical Perspective: New Dimensions of Race, Class, and Gender*, ed. Joe Trotter (Bloomington: University of Indiana Press, 1991).

134. Bowen, "Colored People of Chicago," 117, 119; Addams, *The Spirit of Youth*, 119; Ovington, *Half a Man*, 154; Chicago Commission on Race Relations,

The Negro in Chicago: A Study of Race Relations and a Race Riot (Chicago: University of Chicago Press, 1922), 343; hereafter cited as CCRR, *Negro in Chicago*; Kevin Mumford, *Black/White Sex Districts in Chicago and New York in the Early Twentieth Century* (New York: Columbia University Press, 1997), 96; Roger Lane, *The Roots of Violence in Black Philadelphia, 1860–1900* (Cambridge: Harvard University Press, 1986), 131.

135. Chicago Vice Commission, *The Social Evil: A Study of Existing Conditions* (Chicago: Gunthorp-Warren Printing Co., 1911), 39.

136. Lane, *The Roots of Violence in Black Philadelphia*, 131. Much of the primary evidence in Lane's discussion of black women's prostitution is an uncritical restatement of contemporary newspaper articles or reformer's observations without an adequate appreciation for the ways in which both sources were seriously handicapped by racial assumptions. Furthermore, his admiration for the fact that black prostitutes could "assert control" over their "bodies and their labor," in addition to making rational economic decisions, is a straw man that he waylays in the final two chapters, "The Price of Sin" and "Crime and Culture," where he concludes that black women's participation in vice as a response to persistent social exclusion as well as blacks' criminality in general became a self-generating subculture of pathology in which blacks themselves bore most of the responsibility for their hard times and white prejudice (131, 134–143, 144–161).

137. Mumford, *Black/White Sex Districts*, 98–104, 116. Mumford states that in addition to being forced to the bottom rung of the commercial sex industry, black women also performed the most deviant sexual acts (104). In an otherwise nuanced, though exceedingly complicated, discussion, he imputes the sexual deviance that white reformers so easily associated with black sexuality without questioning their underlying racial assumptions about blacks' natural inferiority.

138. For additional perspectives on the degree to which black women sought economic autonomy in prostitution, see Tera W. Hunter, *To 'Joy My Freedom, Southern Black Women's Lives and Labors after the Civil War* (Cambridge: Harvard University Press, 1997), 112–114, and "The 'Brotherly Love' for Which This City Is Proverbial Should Extend to All: The Everyday Lives of Working-Class Women in Philadelphia and Atlanta in the 1890s," in *W. E. B. Du Bois, Race, and the City: The Philadelphia Negro and Its Legacy,* ed. Michael B. Katz and Thomas J. Sugrue (Philadelphia: University of Pennsylvania Press, 1998), 139–140, which includes additional critiques of Lane on 147 fn. 7, 149–150 fn. 42; Carby, "Policing the Black Woman's Body"; Victoria W. Wolcott, *Remaking Respectability: African American Women in Interwar Detroit* (Chapel Hill: University of North Carolina Press, 2001), 106–113; Kali N. Gross, "The Dismembered Body of Wakefield Gaines and Other Tales of African American Female Criminality, 1880–1910" (Ph.D. diss., University of Pennsylvania, 1999).

139. Eleanor Tayleur, "The Negro Woman: Social and Moral Decadence," *Outlook* 76 (January 30, 1904): 270.

140. Ovington, *Half a Man,* 190–191; Lasch-Quinn, *Black Neighbors,* 10.

141. Addams, *The Spirit of Youth,* 119, 176.

142. Jane Addams, "Social Control," *The Crisis* 1 (1911): 22.

143. Addams, *The Spirit of Youth*, 65. She also mentions another drug dealer by the name of "Army George" (64). Presumably, he was white.

144. "The Wreaked Foundations of Domesticity" is the title of chapter 2 in *The Spirit of the Youth*.

145. Also see Jane Addams, "Has the Emancipation Act Been Nullified by National Indifference," *Survey* 29:13 (February 1, 1913): 566. This article and "Social Control" appear to be among the few non-press articles Addams wrote specifically about African Americans; see Diner, "Chicago Social Workers and Blacks in the Progressive Era."

146. Wells, *Crusade for Justice*, 276-278; Paula J. Giddings, *Ida: A Sword among Lions* (New York: Amistad, 2008), 444–445; Mary Jo Deegan, *Race, Hull-House, and the University of Chicago: A New Conscience against Ancient Evils* (Westport, Conn.: Praeger, 2002): 77–89.

147. Addams, "Recreation as a Public Function in Urban Communities," 615–619.

148. Davis, "Introduction to Jane Addams, *The Spirit of Youth*," xii-xiv.

149. G. Stanley Hall, "The Negro in Africa and America," *Pedagogical Seminary* 12 (1905): 358, 363, 368. Also see Gossett, *Race*, 154. The influence of intellectual peers and confidantes mattered among race-relations writers. Muckraking journalist Ray Stannard Baker, for example, was like Ovington directly advised by Du Bois to tone down his black crime rhetoric. "Of course, I think you exaggerate somewhat the influence of crime upon the race problem," Du Bois instructed him. Du Bois was critiquing previously published articles by Baker that were being revised for *Following the Color Line*, Baker's 1907 book about race-relations in the Progressive era; Lewis, *Biography of a Race*, 363–365.

150. White, *Too Heavy a Load*, 21–55.

151. Carl Kelsey, "Review of *Following the Color Line*, by Ray Stannard Baker," *Annals* 33:2 (1909): 243.

152. All whites were by definition neither African nor former slaves. European peasants were far from being treated as the equivalents of Anglo-Saxons, but in the civilizationist discourse they were still far above African Americans.

153. Mabel Carter Rhoades, "A Case Study of Delinquent Boys in the Juvenile Court of Chicago," *American Journal of Sociology* 13:1 (1907): 78; Wolcott, *Cops and Kids*, 105.

154. Philpott, *The Slum and the Ghetto*, 344.

155. Ibid., 304, 334; Knupfer, *Toward a Tenderer Humanity and a Nobler Womanhood*, 90–91, 94.

156. Children's Aid Society, *The CAS 77th Annual Report*, 1929 (New York: 1930), 19; quoted in Cheryl Lynn Greenburg, *"Or Does It Explode": Black Harlem in the Great Depression* (New York: Oxford University Press, 1991), 35.

157. Haynes, *The Negro at Work*, 14; George Edmund Haynes, "Conditions among Negroes in the Cities," AAAPSS 49 (September 1913): 116–117; *Negro Newcomers in Detroit, Michigan: A Challenge to Christian Statesmanship, A Preliminary Survey* (New York: Home Missions Council, 1918), 35; Abraham Epstein, *The Negro Migrant in Pittsburgh* (Pittsburgh: 1918), 50; McCord, *The American Negro as Dependent, Defective and Delinquent*, 325; Knupfer, *Toward a*

Tenderer Humanity and a Nobler Womanhood, 26; Anne Firor Scott, "Most Invisible of All: Black Women's Voluntary Associations," *The Journal of Southern History* 56:1 (1990): 13.

158. Haynes, *The Negro at Work*, 14.

159. Haynes, "Conditions among Negroes in the Cities," 116–119.

160. CCRR, *The Negro in Chicago*, 5–7; Darvarian L. Baldwin, *Chicago's New Negroes: Modernity, The Great Migration, and Black Urban Life* (Chapel Hill: University of North Carolina Press, 2007), 206–207.

161. Bowen, "Colored People of Chicago," 119.

162. Ibid.

163. Quoted in Diner, "Chicago Social Workers and Blacks in the Progressive Era," 398.

164. McCord, *The American Negro as Dependent, Defective and Delinquent*, 300, 327.

165. Included in C. V. Roman, *American Civilization and the Negro: The Afro-American in Relation to National Progress* (1916, reprinted Northbrook, Ill.: Metro Books, 1972), 213. For a similar statement by a southern white reformer, see Stephenson, "Education and Crime among Negroes," 15.

166. Studies of racial discrimination on northern playgrounds began after the Great Migration with a study presented in the Chicago Commission on Race Relation report. T. J. Szmergalski of the West Chicago Park Commission found that "the establishment of a supervised park or playground tends to decrease complaints of delinquency from 30 to 40 percent within the range of its usefulness—a radius of about three-quarters of a mile . . . With these facts as a background it is significant that there is no recreation center and only a few small playgrounds freely available for Negro children within the congested Negro district" (CCRR, *The Negro in Chicago*, 341).

167. Lasch-Quinn, *Black Neighbors*, 10–11; Knupfer, *Toward a Tenderer Humanity and a Nobler Womanhood*, 26.

168. Dorothy Salem, *To Better Our World: Black Women in Organized Reform, 1890–1920* (Brooklyn, N.Y.: Carlson Publishing Inc, 1990), 126; Scott, "Most Invisible of All," 12, 21; Trolander, *Professionalism and Social Change*, 20, 173.

169. Philpott counted nine black settlements opened between 1900 and 1916. According to Domenica Barbuto, in addition to donating Bowen Hall for women's activities, Bowen purchased a five-story building for men and boys and, after being widowed, established a seventy-two-acre, ten-building summer camp for Hull House called the Bowen Country Club. Barbuto, *American Settlement Houses*, 31.

170. Giddings, *Ida: A Sword among Lions*, 499. The calculation was based on a conversion factor of 21.5758 using a historical cost-of-living calculator for 1913, the earliest year available, which coincides with the time Bowen was treasurer of Hull House; see the American Institute for Economic Research calculator at www.aier.org/research/cost-of-living-calculator (accessed August 28, 2008).

171. For more on the influence of progressives, see Davis, *Spearheads for Reform;* Wolcott, *Cops and Kids;* Michael McGerr, *A Fierce Discontent, The Rise and Fall of the Progressive Movement in America, 1870–1920* (New York: Oxford University Press, 2003).

172. Lewis, *Biography of a Race,* 378–383.

173. Darlene Clark Hine, Stanley Harrold, William C. Hine, eds., *The African American Odyssey, Volume Two: Since 1865,* 3rd ed. (Upper Saddle River, N.J.: Pearson Prentice Hall, 2006), 415; Herbert Shapiro, *White Violence and Black Response, from Reconstruction to Montgomery* (Amherst: University of Massachusetts Press, 1988), 121–122.

174. She also supported the organizing conferences of the NAACP in 1909 and 1910, which were called in response to the violence in Illinois.

175. Wells, *Crusade for Justice,* 299–301.

176. Ibid., 301.

177. Another influential member of the audience, Judge Jesse A. Baldwin, chief justice of Chicago's criminal court, was brought to tears upon hearing her remarks. He admitted not knowing that the YMCA had drawn the color line even though he was a member of the board of directors. "I never knew before that they were refused. But now that you mention it, although I am a director, I remember now that I have never seen a colored man there." Baldwin became a supporter of some of Wells's initiatives, including the League (ibid., 307).

178. Spear, *Black Chicago,* 106. In the wake of revelations about racism at the YMCA, Chicago's civic-minded elites, most prominently, Julius Rosenwald of Sears and Roebuck, pledged matching dollars (as much as $25,000) for the opening of a "colored branch" of the YMCA. The color line would remain at the main branch. Allan Spear says the fundraising initiative was perceived by many as an "experiment in Negro self-help." Black Chicagoans rose to the occasion, raising $65,000 to be matched by $125,000 more from others, including Cyrus McCormick of International Harvester. As the Progressive era was entering its final years, the Wabash Avenue YMCA opened in 1913. It became a major institution in Chicago's expanding Black Belt and was stretched to the hilt during the Great Migration period.

179. Philpott, *The Slum and the Ghetto,* 325.

180. Stanfield, *Philanthropy and Jim Crow in American Social Science*; White, *Too Heavy a Load*; Scott, "Most Invisible of All"; Salem, *To Better Our World.*

181. White, *Too Heavy a Load,* 103.

182. "Color Line at Luncheon: White Club Women Asked to Meet National Leader," *Chicago Tribune,* March 19, 1902; "Obituary: George W. Plummer," *New York Times,* July 12, 1936.

183. Giddings, *Ida: A Sword among Lions,* 446–447, 454–455; Westhoff, *A Fatal Drifting Apart,* 221–229.

184. Hine, et al., *The African American Odyssey,* 415; Shapiro, *White Violence and Black Response,* 97–98; Hunter, *To 'Joy My Freedom,* 126–127.

185. Wells, *Crusade for Justice,* 283–285; White, *Too Heavy a Load,* 104.

186. White, *Too Heavy a Load,* 104; Westhoff similarly sees the Plummer affair as an indication of the limits of white reformers "to confront their own prejudice, to be reflective about their practices, and to be willing to suspend their own habits of mind and carefully listen to the Other" (*A Fatal Drifting Apart,* 230–231); Knupfer, *Toward a Tenderer Humanity and a Nobler Womanhood,* 97–99.

187. Michael Katz, *Poverty and Policy in American History* (New York: Academic Press, 1983), 187. "Great crusade" are Katz's words, paraphrasing Paul

Boyer in *Urban Masses and Moral Order in America, 1820–1920* (Cambridge: Harvard University Press, 1978), 233–274.

188. Section 2, *White Slave Traffic Act [Mann] Act,* reprinted in David Langum, *Crossing over the Line: Legislating Morality and the Mann Act* (Chicago: University of Chicago Press, 1994), 261. Prosecutors' racial motivations of "targeted defendants," writes legal scholar Langum, were sometimes plainly obvious, as in the 1912 conviction of Jack Johnson, the flamboyant, transgressive first black heavyweight champion boxer who openly slept with, lived among, and married white prostitutes (188). For more on the cultural and political significance of Johnson's reinvention of black masculinity and the challenge he posed to Progressive era white supremacy, see Gail Bederman, *Manliness and Civilization: A Cultural History of Gender and Race in the United States, 1880–1917* (Chicago: University of Chicago Press, 1995), 1–10; Baldwin, *Chicago's New Negroes,* 2–7, 194–204.

189. Mara L. Keire, "The Vice Trust: A Reinterpretation of the White Slavery Scare in the United States, 1907–1917, *Journal of Social History* 35:1 (2001): 7.

190. A letter written by the French novelist Victor Hugo in 1870 is instructive: "The slavery of black women is abolished in America, but the slavery of white women continues in Europe and laws are still made by men in order to tyrannize women" (quoted in Keire, "The Vice Trust," 7).

191. Mark Thomas Connelly, *The Response to Prostitution in the Progressive Era* (Chapel Hill: University of North Carolina Press, 1980), 114–118. Another historian interprets white slavery to apply to "young, white, middle-class women forced into prostitution by unscrupulous, usually foreign, men and syndicates"; Thomas C. Mackey, *Pursuing Johns: Criminal Law Reform, Defending Character, and New York City's Committee of Fourteen, 1920–1930* (Columbus: Ohio State University Press, 2005), 39.

192. Jean Turner Zimmermann, *America's Black Traffic in White Girls* (1912), 29, quoted in Connelly, *The Response to Prostitution,* 118.

193. Connelly, *The Response to Prostitution,* 202 fn. 6.

194. Section 6, *White Slave Traffic [Mann] Act,* in Langum, *Crossing over the Line,* 263.

195. Mumford, *Black/White Sex Districts,* 17–18.

196. Quoted in W. E. B. Du Bois, "Negro Crime," *Crisis* (June 1911), 56–57; also see Chicago Vice Commission, *The Social Evil,* 38–39.

197. The best measure of Kellor's efforts on behalf of black women is found in Fitzpatrick's discussion of her broader fight for immigrants and their rights. In *Endless Crusade,* Fitzpatrick writes that Kellor's influence reached all the way to the White House, where President Theodore Roosevelt followed her research findings closely. In 1906 he instructed his cabinet to "receive Kellor with courtesy" and to listen to her counsel on immigration matters. "After reviewing the accounts Kellor submitted to them, Roosevelt requested his staff to 'report to me the results of your investigation and action thereon.' When a bulletin on Kellor's research entitled 'The State and the Immigrant' was published in 1907, Roosevelt requested the first available issue" (140). "The most striking aspect of Kellor's approach to immigration was her direct appeal for a government 'system' to 'protect' the foreign-born. This was essential she said, 'not for dependents or for those needing charity—not

for rescue work, for most immigrants do not need this upon arrival, but for the average normal healthy immigrant who wants to work and to be a citizen' "(140). She "called for a national immigration policy that addressed social welfare concerns." (141) "She pressured [New York] Governor Charles Evans Hughes to appoint a special investigative committee on New York immigration in 1908. Hughes readily acceded to her demands and those of fellow lobbyists, including Lillian Wald. Within months he had won the legislature's approval to appoint the 'Commission to Inquire into the Conditions, Welfare, and Industrial Opportunities of Aliens' "(142).

198. Carby, "Policing the Black Woman's Body," 740–741.

199. Lasch-Quinn, *Black Neighbors*, 19.

200. Mark Schneider, *Boston Confronts Jim Crow, 1890-1920* (Boston: Northeastern University Press, 1997), 22, 31–37, 45–50.

201. William O. Scroggs, "Review of *The Color Line in Ohio* by Frank U. Quillin," *Mississippi Valley Historical Review* 2:3 (1915): 444.

202. John Daniels, *In Freedom's Birthplace: A Study of the Boston Negroes* (Boston: Houghton Mifflin Company, 1914; New York: Johnson Reprint Corporation, 1968), 36, 54, 80, 96, 105.

203. Ibid., 106–113, 218–219. Daniels's dismissal of the necessity for citing black crime statistics illuminates how pervasive they had become by this time.

204. Ibid., 193. One exception, of course, was his own Shaw House, for it stood "for justice and equal opportunity for all" (195).

205. Ibid., 212.

206. Ibid., 404. "Moral stamina" was a term Frederic Bushee had used in 1903 to denote what immigrants, unlike blacks, possessed in sufficient quantity for assimilation (Bushee, "Ethnic Factors in the Population of Boston," 110).

207. Daniels, *In Freedom's Birthplace*, 406–408, 420.

208. Ibid., 408, 409, 420. Clearly, Daniels dismissed the experiences of racial oppression and violence directed at a small, but manifest and overeducated, black elite in the North—segregated by racists on all sides, and whose physical or material lives were shaped in profound ways by the real threat of death at the end of a noose, an assassin's bullet, or a neighbor's Molotov cocktail because their superior credentials still didn't qualify "niggers" to live next door.

209. Ibid., 405, 426.

210. Boas, "The Negro and the Demands of Modern Life," 86–87.

211. Daniels, *In Freedom's Birthplace*, ix, 400–405, 410–411, 416, 421, 430–431.

212. U. G. Weatherly, "Review of *In Freedom's Birthplace* by John Daniels," AJS 20:1 (1914): 122.

213. J. P. Lichtenberger, "Review of *In Freedom's Birthplace* by John Daniels," AAAPS 54 (1914): 330–331.

214. Ibid., 331.

215. Bushee, "Ethnic Factors in the Population of Boston," 115, 160.

216. Daniels, *In Freedom's Birthplace*, 432.

217. American Sociological Association, "Presidents by Date," www.asanet .org/cs/root/leftnav/governance/past_officers/presidents_by_date (accessed May 7, 2008).

218. J. P. Lichtenberger, "The Negro's Progress in Fifty Years," AAAPSS 49 (September 1913): 177–185.

219. Boas, *The Mind of Primitive Man*, 20.

220. Ovington, *Half a Man*, 219–220.

221. Bowen, "Colored People of Chicago," 120; Du Bois, "Some Headlines," *Crisis* 3 (December 1911).

222. Du Bois, "Some Headlines."

223. Lasch-Quinn, *Black Neighbors*, 20.

224. W. E. B. Du Bois, "The Souls of White Folks," *The Independent* 69 (August 10, 1910): 339–342, reprinted in Herbert Aptheker, ed., *Writings by W. E. B. Du Bois in Periodicals Edited by Others, vol. 2, 1910–1934* (Millwood, N.Y.: Kraus-Thomson Organization Limited, 1982), 26–27, 28.

225. Kenneth Jackson, *Crabgrass Frontier: The Suburbanization of the United States* (New York: Oxford University Press, 1985); Mark H. Haller, "Illegal Enterprise: A Theoretical and Historical Interpretation," *Criminology* 28:2 (1990): 207–229, and "Urban Vice and Civic Reform: Chicago in the Early Twentieth Century," in *Cities in American History*, ed. Kenneth T. Jackson and Stanley Schultz (New York: Alfred A. Knopf, 1972); Allen F. Davis and Mark H. Haller, *The Peoples of Philadelphia: A History of Ethnic Groups and Lower-Class Life, 1790–1940* (Philadelphia: Temple University Press, 1973), 284; Rufus Schatzberg, *Black Organized Crime in Harlem: 1920–1930* (New York: Garland Publishing, 1993).

226. Crime was one of the "city's poverty statistics," Joe Trotter argued, that proved that "black workers paid disproportionate costs of capitalist development in the urban North"; Joe Trotter, "Blacks in the Urban North," in *The Great Migration in Historical Perspective: New Dimensions of Race, Class, and Gender* (Bloomington: University of Indiana Press, 1991), 61, 73.

227. Thomas J. Sugrue, *The Origins of the Urban Crisis: Race and Inequality in Postwar Detroit* (1996, reprinted with a new preface Princeton: Princeton University Press, 2005), 5.

228. W. E. B. Du Bois, "To Solve the Negro Problem," *Collier's Weekly*, June 18, 1904, 14; reprinted in Herbert Aptheker, ed., *Writings by W. E. B. Du Bois in Periodicals Edited by Others, vol. 1, 1891–1909* (Millwood, N.Y.: Kraus-Thomson Organization Limited, 1982), 223.

229. Deegan, *Race, Hull-House, and the University of Chicago*, especially "Fighting Jim Crow in Chicago's Public Schools: The Color Line at Wendell Phillips High School, 1912–1915," 77–89.

230. Giddings, *Ida: A Sword among Lions*, 480.

231. Haynes, "Conditions among Negroes in the Cities," 109–110.

232. Du Bois, "The Souls of White Folks."

4. PREVENTING CRIME

1. For more on settlement houses as exemplary crime-prevention agencies during the Progressive era, see David J. Rothman, *Conscience and Convenience: The Asylum and Its Alternatives in Progressive America* (Boston: Little, Brown and Company, 1980), 46–47, 51–53.

2. U.S. Fifteenth Census, 1930 (Washington: GPO, 1933), 67–73.

3. W. E. B. Du Bois, *The Philadelphia Negro* (1899, reprinted with an introduction by Herbert Aptheker, New York: Schocken Books, 1967), 60.

4. "The Situation" by Susan Wharton, Annual Report of the Starr Centre, 1900, Series 1, Box 4, Folder 40, Starr Centre Association Papers, Center for the Study of the History of Nursing, Philadelphia, Penn. (hereafter cited as Starr Papers).

5. Federal Writers Project, *Philadelphia: A Guide to the Nation's Birthplace* (Philadelphia: William Penn Association of Philadelphia, 1937), 422.

6. Manager's Report by Jane P. Rushmore, Annual Report of Starr Centre, 1907, Series 1, Box 4, Folder 41, Starr Papers.

7. "The Situation," Starr Papers.

8. Manager's Report, Starr Papers.

9. Secretary's Report, Annual Report of Starr Centre, 1911, Series 1, Box 4, Folder 42, Starr Papers.

10. Du Bois, *The Philadelphia Negro*, 204.

11. Robert S. Gregg, *Sparks from the Anvil of Oppression: Philadelphia's African Methodists and Southern Migrants, 1890–1940* (Philadelphia: Temple University Press, 1993), 2.

12. "The Improvement of a Street," Pamphlet of the Octavia Hill Association, 1902, Box 46, Series II, Folder 9, Octavia Hill Association Papers, Urban Archives, Temple University Library, Philadelphia, Penn. (hereafter cited as OHA Papers).

13. For general discussions of poverty and social Darwinism during the Progressive era, see James T. Patterson, *America's Struggle against Poverty, 1900–1980* (Cambridge: Harvard University Press, 1981), 3–36; Richard Hofstadter, *Social Darwinism in American Thought* (1944, reprinted with an introduction by Eric Foner, Boston: Beacon Press, 1992).

14. "Improvement of a Street," OHA Papers.

15. Manager's Report, Starr Papers.

16. Annual Report of Starr Centre, 1904; "What Is Thrift" by Susan Wharton, Annual Report of Starr Centre, 1906, Series 1, Box 4, Folder 41, Starr Papers.

17. "Improvement of a Street," OHA Papers.

18. Newspaper Clipping, "On Improving Housing Conditions" by H. J. Baringer, n.p., n.d., OHA Papers.

19. "Distinctive Features of the Octavia Hill Association," Pamphlet of the Octavia Hill Association, 1906, Box 46, Series II, Folder 9, OHA Papers.

20. Michael Katz notes that the idea of criminality as a marker of individual failure (the "undeserving poor") rather than of social conditions (the "deserving poor") goes back to the poor laws in the late eighteenth and early nineteenth centuries; "The Urban 'Underclass' as a Metaphor of Social Transformation," in *The "Underclass" Debate: Views from History*, ed. Michael B. Katz (Princeton: Princeton University Press, 1993), 6–10. By the late nineteenth century, however, with the arrival of Herbert Spencer's social Darwinism and massive immigration of southern and eastern European immigrants to industrial cities, these distinctions writ large became more "powerful and frightening." Also see Michael B. Katz, *Poverty and Policy in American History* (New York: Academic Press, 1981); Patterson, *America's Struggle against Poverty*, 20–36.

21. "Improvement of a Street," OHA Papers.

22. "Distinctive Features," OHA Papers.

23. Octavia Hill Address before the Civic Federation in Washington, D.C., January 1913, Box 46, Series II, Folder 13, OHA Papers.

24. Edith Elmer Wood, "Four Washington Alleys: Some Phases of Life in Fenton Place, Madison Alley, Essex Court and Naylor's Court as Brought out in a Recent Survey," reprint from *The Survey,* December 6, 1913, 2–3, Box 46, Series II, Folder 11, OHA Papers.

25. "Negro Tenants," Memo of the OHA, November 1916, Box 46, Series II, Folder 14, OHA Papers.

26. "The Settlement House Not Doing Slum Work," Press Release of the University Settlement House, May 19, 1906, Box 20, Series III, Folder 244, University Settlements Papers, Urban Archives, Temple University Library, Philadelphia, Penn. (hereafter cited as US Papers).

27. Press Release, January 20, 1907, Box 20, Series III, Folder 244, US Papers.

28. Datasheet, December 26, 1911, Box 20, Series III, Folder 244, US Papers.

29. Francis Bartholomew, "A Northern Social Settlement for Negroes," *Southern Workman* 35 (February 1906): 99–102.

30. The following works also deal broadly with the limitations of scientific research based on preconceived notions of blacks' racial inferiority: Stephen Jay Gould, *The Mismeasure of Man,* rev. ed. (New York: W. W. Norton, 1996); Daryl Michael Scott, *Contempt and Pity: Social Policy and the Image of the Damaged Black Psyche, 1880–1996* (Chapel Hill: University of North Carolina Press, 1997); James B. McKee, *Sociology and the Race Problem: The Failure of a Perspective* (Urbana: University of Illinois Press, 1993).

31. Bartholomew, "A Northern Social Settlement for Negroes," 101.

32. Annual Report, 1906, 14, Starr Papers. Compare Wharton's comment to Du Bois's: The "environment in this city makes it easier for [blacks] to live by crime or the results of crime than by work" (*The Philadelphia Negro,* 313).

33. Mary White Ovington, *Half a Man: The Status of the Negro in New York* (New York: Longmans, Green, and Co., 1911), 72–73.

34. Theodore Hershberg, ed., *Philadelphia: Work, Space, Family, and Group Experience in the Nineteenth Century, Essays toward an Interdisciplinary History of the City* (New York: Oxford University Press, 1981), 479; Thomas J. Philpott, *The Slum and the Ghetto: Immigrants, Blacks, and Reformers in Chicago, 1880–1930* (Belmont, Calif.: Wadsworth Publishing, 1991), xiv–xv, passim; Gilbert Osofsky, *Harlem: The Making of a Ghetto: Negro New York, 1890–1930,* 2nd ed. (New York: Harper Torchbooks, 1971), 130–131.

35. "Casa Ravello Branch," Annual Report of Starr Centre, 1908, 23, Starr Papers.

36. Jane Addams, *Twenty Years at Hull House* (1910, reprinted New York: New American Library, 1981).

37. Recent Acquisitions Memo, 1910, Box 46, Series II, Folder 10, OHA Papers.

38. "The Philadelphia Settlement: Report of the Headworker," *Eighteenth Annual Report of the College Settlements Association,* (New York: Sherwood, 1907),

62; General Collection, Van Pelt Library, University of Pennsylvania, Philadelphia, Penn. (hereafter cited as CSA/VPL).

39. "The Philadelphia Settlement," *Sixteenth Annual Report of the College Settlements Association* (New York: Sherwood, 1905), 64; CSA/VPL.

40. "The Philadelphia Settlement: Report of the Headworker," *Seventeenth Annual Report of the College Settlements Association* (New York: Sherwood, 1906), 62; CSA/VPL.

41. *Seventeenth Annual Report,* 59–60.

42. *Sixteenth Annual Report,* 66.

43. *Eighteenth Annual Report,* 61.

44. *Seventeenth Annual Report,* 60.

45. *Sixteenth Annual Report,* 65.

46. "Neighborhood Conditions," Annual Report of the North House Association, 1911, 3, 5–6, North House Association Papers, Friends Historical Library of Swarthmore College, Swarthmore, Penn.

47. Annual Report of the Friends Neighborhood Guild, 1901, 7, Box 5, Series 6, Friends Neighborhood Guild Papers, Friends Library of Swarthmore College, Swarthmore, Penn. (hereafter cited as FNG Papers).

48. Annual Report, 1916, 14; Annual Report, 1917, 8, FNG Papers.

49. Annual Report, 1901, 26.

50. Annual Report, 1903, 25–27, FNG Papers.

51. Annual Report, 1917, 8, 17.

52. Annual Report, 1907, 12, 9, FNG Papers.

53. Jane Addams, *The Spirit of Youth and the City Streets"* (1909, reprinted with a new introduction by Allen F. Davis, Urbana: University of Illinois, 1972), 13, 16, 20, 26.

54. "Instances of the Guild's Work," Pamphlet of the Friends Neighborhood Guild, 1910, Box 5, Series 8, FNG Papers.

55. Louis R. Harlan, *Booker T. Washington: The Making of a Black Leader, 1856–1901* (New York: Oxford University Press, 1972), 313–322; "Mr Roosevelt Explains the Dinner Incident," *New York Times,* October 20, 1901, 1; "The President's Dinner to Booker T. Washington," *New York Times,* October 27, 1901, 11; *New York Times,* March 11, 1905. For a sample of white northerners' positive reactions to the affair, see "The President Commended," *New York Times,* October 21, 1901, 1.

56. Frederick L. Hoffman, *Race Traits and Tendencies of the American Negro* (New York: American Economic Association, 1896); John Daniels, *In Freedom's Birthplace: A Study of the Boston Negroes* (Boston: Houghton Mifflin Company, 1914; New York: Johnson Reprint Corporation, 1968).

57. Ray Stannard Baker, *Following the Color Line: American Negro Citizenship in the Progressive Era* (1908, reprinted New York: Harper Torchbooks, 1964), 296.

58. Philpott, *The Slum and the Ghetto,* 295.

59. Michael Katz and Thomas J. Sugrue, eds., *W. E. B. Du Bois, Race, and the City: The Philadelphia Negro and Its Legacy* (Philadelphia: University of Pennsylvania Press, 1998), 164–165; Hershberg, *Philadelphia,* 469–470, 476, 489; Stephen

Thernstrom, *The Other Bostonians: Poverty and Progress in the American Metropolis, 1880–1970* (Cambridge: Harvard University Press, 1973), 186, 194.

60. Annual Report, 1906, 14, Starr Papers.

61. Elisabeth Lasch-Quinn, *Black Neighbors: Race and the Limits of Reform in the American Settlement House Movement, 1890–1945* (Chapel Hill: University of North Carolina Press, 1993), 10–11; Evelyn Brooks Higginbotham, *Righteous Discontent: The Women's Movement in the Black Baptist Church, 1880–1920* (Cambridge: Harvard University Press, 1993), 197.

62. Robert L. Zangrando, *The NAACP Crusade against Lynching, 1909–1950* (Philadelphia: Temple University Press, 1980).

63. David Levering Lewis, *W. E. B. Du Bois: Biography of a Race* (New York: Henry Holt, 1993), 389–390.

64. Newspaper Clipping, February 12, 1909, Box 1, Folder 13, James Stemons Papers, part of the Balch Institute for Ethnic Studies Collection at the Historical Society Philadelphia, Penn. (hereafter cited as Stemons Papers).

65. Lucy Barber, "'Even Numbers of White and Colored': White Philanthropy and Blacks in South Philadelphia, 1884–1914" (Urban Archives, Temple University Library, Philadelphia, Penn., photocopy), 55.

66. John T Emlen, "The Movement for the Betterment of the Negro in Philadelphia" AAAPSS 49 (September 1913): 84.

67. Board Minutes, May 28 and June 11, 1912, Series 1, Box 2, Folder 15, Starr Papers.

68. Annual Report, 1910, 7–9, Series 1, Box 4, Folder 42, Starr Papers.

69. Barber, "'Even Numbers of White and Colored,'" 61.

70. Annual Report, 1908, 23, Starr Papers.

71. Du Bois, *The Philadelphia Negro*, 351, 352, 355.

72. Kelly Miller, "The Economic Handicap of the Negro in the North," AAAPSS 27 (January 1906): 85.

73. Daryl Michael Scott builds on this theme with an examination of the social scientific construction of black psychology and pathology throughout the twentieth century; see *Contempt and Pity* (Chapel Hill: University of North Carolina Press, 1997).

74. Lincoln Conference Speech, n.d., Box 4, Folder 13, Stemons Papers.

75. Miller, "The Economic Handicap of the Negro," 84.

76. Lincoln Conference Speech, Stemons Papers.

77. This summary of Stemons's life is drawn from several letters to his sister and a manuscript of a semi-autobiographical novel, "Jay Ess," Box 3, Stemons Papers; and Richard R. Wright, comp., *The Philadelphia Colored Directory: A Handbook of the Religious, Social, Political, Professional, Business and Other Activities of the Negroes of Philadelphia* (Philadelphia: Philadelphia Colored Directory, Co., 1907), 50.

78. James S. Stemons, *The Key: A Tangible Solution to the Negro Problem* (New York: Neale Publishing Co., 1916), Box 2, Folder 1; *The North Holds the Key* (Philadelphia: Sumner Press, 1907), Stemons Papers.

79. Mary Stemons to James, September 3, 1907, Box 1, Folder 11, Stemons Papers.

80. William J. Bryan to Stemons, June 11, 1908; Woodrow Wilson to Stemons, March 16, 1911; Box 1, Folder 16, Stemons Papers.

81. James Stemons to his sister, June 4, 1911, Box 1, Folder 16, Stemons Papers.

82. Booker T. Washington to Stemons, June 6, 1908, Box 1, Folder 12, Stemons Papers.

83. Lincoln Conference Speech, Stemons Papers. For a similar recent historical analysis, see Ira Katznelson, *When Affirmative Action Was White: An Untold History of Racial Inequality in Twentieth-Century America* (New York: W. W. Norton, 2005).

84. Du Bois, *The Philadelphia Negro,* 357.

85. Hugh M. Browne, "The Training of the Negro Laborer in the North," AAAPSS 27 (January 1906): 127; Emlen, "The Movement for the Betterment of the Negro," 89.

86. "Work of the Friends' Freedmen's Association and Christiansburg Industrial Institute," by J. Henry Scattergood; reprint from *The Westonian,* March 1907, 16, 8–9, Box 14, Series 20, Friends' Freedmen's Association Papers, Friends Historical Library of Swarthmore College, Swarthmore, Penn. (hereafter cited as FFA Papers).

87. Scattergood, "Work of the Friends' Freedmen's Association and Christiansburg Industrial Institute," 9–13.

88. Annual Report, 1906, 14, Starr Papers.

89. *Bulletin of the Inter-Municipal Committee on Household Research* (New York, May 1905), 15, quoted in Alfred H. Stone, *Studies in the American Race Problem* (New York: Doubleday, Page, & Co., 1908), 161.

90. Board Minutes, May 9 and October 19, 1905, Series 1, Box 1, Folder 1, Starr Papers.

91. W. E. B. Du Bois, "Notes on Negro Crime, Particularly in Georgia," *Atlanta University Studies* 9 (1904); James K. Vardaman, "A Governor Bitterly Opposes Negro Education," *Leslie's Weekly.* February 1904, 104.

92. "Roosevelt at Hampton," *New York Times,* May 31, 1906; the Tuskegee speech can be found at Theodore Roosevelt, *The Works of Theodore Roosevelt,* vol. 18 (New York: C. Scribner's Sons, 1923–1926), 465. Roosevelt was also on the record as stating that rape was the *single* cause of lynching; see *The Works,* vol. 17, 411–412. For more on Roosevelt's attitudes toward African Americans, see Thomas Dyer, *Theodore Roosevelt and the Idea of Race* (Baton Rouge: Louisiana State University Press, 1980), 89–92, 99, 109.

93. Philadelphia *Public Ledger,* March 23 and December 5, 1912. According to historian Vernon A. Williams, Jr., most southern sociologists, like their northern counterparts, "backed" industrial education because it was "purportedly an antidote to the transplanted Africans [sic] retrogressive propensities," *From a Caste to a Minority: Changing Attitudes of American Sociologists toward Afro-Americans, 1896–1945* (Westport, Conn.: Greenwood Press, 1989), 39.

94. "Some Present Aspects of the Negro Problem," by Herbert Welsh, Address Delivered in the Coulter Street Meeting House, Germantown, Philadelphia, March 18, 1907, 2–3, 6, Afro-Americana Collection at the Historical Society of Pennsylvania, Philadelphia, Penn. (hereafter cited as Welsh/HSP).

95. For more information on General Armstrong's "vision" of industrial education for blacks, see James D. Anderson, *The Education of Blacks in the South, 1860–1935* (Chapel Hill: University of North Carolina Press, 1988), 31, 33–78.

96. Welsh, "Some Present Aspects of the Negro Problem," 4–6.

97. Ibid., 7.

98. W. E. B. Du Bois to Herbert Welsh, March 8, 1907, Welsh/HSP.

99. Welsh, "Some Present Aspects of the Negro Problem," 11.

100. H. B. Frissell to Welsh, February 14, 1907, Welsh/HSP.

101. Stemons to his sister, June 1, 1909, Box 1, Folder 13, Stemons Papers.

102. Stemons to his sister, May 21 and 29, 1909, Box 1, Folder 13, Stemons Papers.

103. William E. Walling to Stemons, May 6, 1909, Box 1, Folder 13, Stemons Papers.

104. Stemons, *The North Holds the Key*; Stemons to his sister, May 24, 1907, Box 1, Folder 10, Stemons Papers.

105. Stemons, *The North Holds the Key*, 6–7.

106. Herbert Welsh, Diary Entries Related to Blacks, Boxes 57, 94, 106, in Welsh/HSP.

107. Kelly Miller also broached the economic question in 1906 in terms of its direct effect on the South: "So long as the North treats the negro workman with blighting discrimination it is left little moral ground for complaint against the South where a like spirit assumes a different form of manifestation" (Miller, "The Economic Handicap of the Negro," 88).

108. Stemons to his sister, March 13, 1909; Stemons to his sister, June 1, 1909, Box 1, Folder 13, Stemons Papers.

109. Stemons to his sister, May 12, 1907, Box 1, Folder 10, Stemons Papers.

110. Editorial, Philadelphia *Public Ledger*, May 12, 1907 (caps. in original).

111. James Stemons, "Why Crime Increases among Negroes," Philadelphia *Public Ledger*, May 10, 1907, reprinted in *Colored American Magazine*, July 1907, 65–68.

112. Editorial, Philadelphia *Public Ledger*.

113. Stemons to his sister, May 6 and December 7, 1907, Box 1, Folder 11, Stemons Papers.

114. Stone, *Studies in the American Race Problem*, 18–21, 161–163.

115. Stemons to his sister, May 24, 1906, Box 1, Folder 10, Stemons Papers.

116. Gregg, *Sparks from the Anvil of Oppression*, 60, 211.

117. Horace Clarence Boyer, "Charles Albert Tindley: Progenitor of Black-American Gospel Music," *The Black Perspective in Music* 11:2 (Autumn 1983): 103–132.

118. Du Bois, *The Philadelphia Negro*, 74–75.

119. Gregg, *Sparks from the Anvil of Oppression*, 48–50, 57–58, 65–66.

120. Du Bois, *The Philadelphia Negro*, 206; Gregg, *Sparks from the Anvil of Oppression*, 48. Statistics prepared by the University Settlement House on most popular leisure activities are available in Datasheet, December 26, 1911, US Papers.

121. Richard R. Wright, Jr., *The Negro in Pennsylvania: A Study in Economic History.* (1912, reprinted New York: Arno Press, 1969), 116; Emlen, "The Movement for the Betterment of the Negro," 85.

122. Wright, *Negro in Pennsylvania*, 117–118; Gregg, *Sparks from the Anvil of Oppression*, 58.

123. Wright observed that "only of late years has it been possible to interest the best class of Negro women in active philanthropic work which took them among the lower element, because they feared they might be considered by the outside world as members of the group they went to help. Still these groups shade almost imperceptibly into one another" (*Negro in Pennsylvania*, 178).

124. Charles A. Hardy III, "Race and Opportunity: Black Philadelphia during the Era of the Great Migration, 1916–1930," vol. 2 (Ph.D. Diss., Temple University, 1989), 436; Roger Lane, *Roots of Violence in Black Philadelphia, 1860–1900* (Cambridge: Harvard University Press, 1986), 116; Rufus Schatzberg and Robert J. Kelley, *African-American Organized Crime: A Social History* (New York: Garland Publishing, 1996); St. Clair Drake and Horace R. Cayton, *Black Metropolis: A Study of Negro Life in a Northern City* (New York: Harcourt, Brace and Co., 1945).

125. Higginbotham, *Righteous Discontent*, 199, 201.

126. Wright, *Negro in Pennsylvania*, 112; Emlen, "The Movement for the Betterment of the Negro," 84; Gregg, *Sparks from the Anvil of Oppression*, 65.

127. For example, one critic wrote, "One of the most discouraging aspects of the problem appears in the well known sympathy a guilty negro receives from his brothers, simply because of the black man's color"; Marcus Kavanagh, *The Criminal and His Allies* (Indianapolis: Bobbs-Merrill Co., 1928), 144. Also see Charles H. McCord, *The American Negro as a Dependent, Defective, and Delinquent* (Nashville: Benson, 1914), 279, 318.

128. Wright, *Colored Directory*, 43–44.

129. Hardy, "Race and Opportunity," 461; Higginbotham, *Righteous Discontent*, 180; B. F. Lee, "Negro Organizations," AAAPSS 49 (September 1913): 135; Wright, *Negro in Pennsylvania*, 74; Emlen, "The Movement for the Betterment of the Negro," 85.

130. Stemons to his sister, December 21, 1907, Box 1, Folder 12, Stemons Papers.

131. Beacon Institute Flyer, Box 1, Folder 13, Stemons Papers.

132. Stemons to his sister, July 29, 1909, Box, 1, Folder 13, Stemons Papers.

133. Stemons to A.M.E. Preachers Meeting, September 4, 1909, Box 1, Folder 14, Stemons Papers.

134. Stemons to his sister, September 4, 1909, Box 1, Folder 14, Stemons Papers.

135. Du Bois, *The Philadelphia Negro*, 6, 389–390.

136. Stemons to Walling, February 15, 1909, Box 1, Folder 13, Stemons Papers.

137. Baptist Address, November 15, 1909, Box 4, Folder 12, Stemons Papers.

138. Lewis, *Du Bois*, 196, 208. For a similar statement, see Kevin Gaines, *Uplifting the Race: Black Leadership, Politics, and Culture in the Twentieth Century* (Chapel Hill: University of North Carolina Press, 1996), 176.

139. In order for Du Bois to "gain the widest and most respectable hearing possible," according to David Levering Lewis, and to simultaneously present a subtle

critique of northern racism and economic discrimination, "much of the monograph calculatedly lent itself to one-sided, unthreatening interpretations" (Lewis, *Du Bois*, 206).

140. Gaines, *Uplifting the Race*, 177.

141. Richard R Wright, Jr., *87 Years behind the Black Curtain: An Autobiography* (Philadelphia, Penn.: Rare Book Company, 1965), 151, 156–159, in Charles Blockson Collection, Temple University Library, Philadelphia, Penn. Although Wright's reform efforts focused almost exclusively on improving opportunities for skilled black laborers, he had published extensively on Philadelphia crime based on his dissertation research. His views matched Du Bois's, except his publications were met with near total silence and were almost never cited; see Richard R. Wright, Jr., "Negroes in the North, I: The Northern Negro and Crime," *Southern Workman* 39 (March 1910): 137–142; "The Economic Condition of Negroes in the North: Tendencies Downward, Second Paper: Negro Criminal Statistics," *Southern Workman* 40 (May 1911): 291–307; *The Negro in Pennsylvania*; and two lectures in 1911 published as *The Negro Problem: A Sociological Treatment, Being Extracts from Two Lectures on "The Sociological Point of View in The Study of Race Problems," and "The Negro Problem; What It Is Not, and What It Is"* (Philadelphia, Penn.: A.M.E. Book Concern, 1911), a copy of which can be found at the Library Company of Philadelphia in Center City, Philadelphia.

142. For additional examples of professional blacks using their own image as a defense of the race, see Deborah Gray White, *Too Heavy a Load: Black Women in Defense of Themselves, 1894–1994* (New York: W. W. Norton & Co., 1999); Glenda E. Gilmore, *Gender and Jim Crow: Women and the Politics of White Supremacy in North Carolina, 1896–1920* (Chapel Hill: University of North Carolina, 1996).

143. Emlen, "The Movement for the Betterment of the Negro," 92.

144. Wright, *87 Years behind the Black Curtain*, 160–162.

145. Nancy J. Weiss, *The National Urban League, 1910–1940* (New York: Oxford University Press, 1974), 55, 59–60, 79, 91, 131.

146. Ibid., 104, 131.

147. Anna J. Thompson, "A Survey of Crime among Negroes in Philadelphia," *Opportunity* 4 (July-September 1926): 217–219, 251–254, 285–286; Maurine Boie, "An Analysis of Negro Crime Statistics for Minneapolis for 1923, 1924 and 1925," *Opportunity* 6 (June 1928): 171–173; Ira De A. Reid, *The Negro Population of Denver Colorado: A Survey of Its Economic and Social Status* (New York: Lincoln Press, 1929); *The Negro Population of Elizabeth, New Jersey: A Survey of Its Economic and Social Conditions* (Newark: New Jersey Conference of Social Work, 1930); *Social Conditions of the Negro in the Hill District of Pittsburgh* (Pittsburgh: General Committee on the Hill Survey, 1930); *Trojans of Color: A Social Survey of the Negro Population of Troy, New York* (New York: National Urban League, 1931); *The Negro in New Jersey* (Newark: New Jersey Conference of Social Work, 1932).

148. Norfolk *Journal and Guide*, December 2, 1916; quoted in Weiss, *The National Urban League*, 111.

149. National Urban League Bulletin, 1917; quoted in Weiss, *The National Urban League,* 108.

150. Baptist Address; B. F. Lee to unknown, October 13, 1910, Box 1, Folder 15, Stemons Papers.

151. Wright, *Colored Directory,* 19–29.

152. Public Statement, n.d., Box 3, Folder 7, Stemons Papers.

153. Hoffman, *Race Traits;* Du Bois, *The Philadelphia Negro;* William Hannibal Thomas, *The American Negro: What He Was, What He Is, and What He May Become, A Critical and Practical Discussion* (New York: MacMillan Co., 1901); Walter F. Willcox, "Negro Criminality," in Alfred Stone, *Studies in the American Race Problem* (New York: Doubleday, Page & Co., 1908), 443–475.

154. Hardy, "Race and Opportunity," 448.

155. Washington to Stemons, November 19, 1910, Box 1, Folder 15, Stemons Papers.

156. Conference Program, November 21, 1910, Box 3, Folder 7, Stemons Papers; Philadelphia *Public Ledger,* November 22, 1910.

157. Stemons bragged to his sister about Thirkield's support; November 26, 1910, Box 1, Folder 15, Stemons Papers.

158. Conference Program, Stemons Papers.

159. Philadelphia *Public Ledger* and *North American,* November 22, 1910.

160. Du Bois, *The Philadelphia Negro,* 390–392.

161. "Appeal to Self-Respecting Colored Citizens," n.d., Box 3, Folder 3, Stemons Papers.

162. Plans and Purposes Document, Box 3, Folder 3, Stemons Paper.

163. Ibid.

164. Stemons to his sister, October 5, 1911, Box 1, Folder 16, Stemons Papers. Wright also noted the high number of blacks in civil service jobs, especially at the post office (*Negro in Pennsylvania,* 82).

165. Philadelphia *Record,* November 23, 1911.

166. "To Curb the Vicious Elements among Negroes," Press Release, n.d., Box 4, Folder 1; Stemons to his sister, May 6, 1912, Box 1, Folder 17, Stemons Papers.

167. Stemons to Mayor Rudolph J. Blankenburg, November 11, 1911, Box 1, Folder 16, Stemons Papers.

168. Stemons to his sister, January 6, 1912, Box 1, Folder 16, Stemons Paper.

169. Philadelphia *Inquirer,* January 6, 1912.

170. Stemons to his sister, January 6, 1912, Stemons Papers.

171. If one considers the NAACP as exceptional in this light—as a defender of blacks' civil and political rights—prior to the 1920s, it cannot be considered analogous for two reasons. First, the NAACP was initiated and led, for the most part, by white progressives, not by blacks; Lewis, *Du Bois,* 387; Allen F. Davis, *Spearheads for Reform: The Social Settlements and the Progressive Movement, 1890–1914* (New Brunswick, N.J.: Rutgers University Press, 1984), 102. Second, the early NAACP attacked the most explicit and illegal examples of racism and unconstitutional behavior in the country on the primary basis of legal principle and with secondary appeals for basic human rights. Appeals for economic justice, by contrast, relied far too heavily on penetrating the decentralized, impersonal

market forces of an inherently unequal capitalist economy and the individual preferences of its agents.

172. Stemons to his sister, March 2, 1912, Box 1, Folder 17, Stemons Papers. There is no clear evidence in his papers about why the YMCA position did not work out. Stemons remained a postal employee until his retirement. Through the 1920s, Stemons organized black postal workers in Philadelphia's main branch to fight against workplace discrimination.

173. Stemons to his sister, February 6, 1912, Box 1, Folder 17, Stemons Papers.

174. Philadelphia *Public Ledger,* March 16 and 17, 1912; *Philadelphia Tribune,* June 8, 1912.

175. There is no evidence explaining why the *Tribune* columnist did not acknowledge the efforts of Stemons and his colleagues; nor did any letters to the editor challenge the columnist's remarks.

176. *Philadelphia Tribune,* June 8, 1912.

5. FIGHTING CRIME

1. Bureau of Police Annual Report, 1911, 1912, 1913, 1914, 1915.

2. In a family biography, the mayor's wife, Lucretia Blankenburg, later called the Vice Commission a "tremendous innovation for Philadelphia"; Lucretia L. Blankenburg, *The Blankenburgs of Philadelphia* (Philadelphia: John C. Winston Co., 1928), 63.

3. Bureau of Police Annual Report, 1911, 36.

4. Peter McCaffrey, *When Bosses Ruled Philadelphia: The Emergence of the Republican Machine, 1867–1933* (University Park: Pennsylvania State University, 1993); Donald W. Distrow, "Reform in Philadelphia under Mayor Blankenburg, 1912–1916," *Pennsylvania History* 27:4 (October 1960): 381.

5. *Public Ledger,* March 17, 1912.

6. The racial bias and consequences of the Mann Act have been discussed by Kevin J. Mumford, *Interzones: Black/White Sex Districts in Chicago and New York in the Early Twentieth Century* (New York: Columbia University Press, 1997), 14–21. For a reprint of the law, see David Langum, *Crossing over the Line: Legislating Morality and the Mann Act* (Chicago: University of Chicago Press, 1994), 188, 261–264. Though Langum does not discuss any cases of black women as victims, he discusses Jack Johnson's and Chuck Berry's convictions, indications of black men becoming "targeted defendants" under the law.

7. "Hell's Half Acre Now Respectable," *Public Ledger,* May 7, 1912.

8. *Philadelphia Tribune,* May 8, 1912.

9. *Public Ledger,* May 7, 1912.

10. Thomas Philpott, *The Slum and the Ghetto: Immigrants, Blacks, and Reformers in Chicago, 1880–1930* (Belmont, Calif.: Wadsworth Publishing, 1991), 294–295, 315, 332.

11. *Philadelphia Tribune,* May 8, 1912.

12. *Public Ledger,* September 27, 28, 1912.

13. *Public Ledger,* November 11, 1912.

14. *Public Ledger,* September 23, 1912.

15. *Philadelphia Tribune,* October 5, 1912.

16. Bureau of Police Annual Report, 1912, 1913, 1914; George Morgan, *The History of Philadelphia, The City from Its Founding in 1682 to the Present Time* (Philadelphia: Historical Publication Society, 1926), 447–448; *Public Ledger,* March 3, 15–17, 21, 1912; *Philadelphia Tribune,* April 6, 1912; McCaffrey, *When Bosses Ruled Philadelphia,* 178.

17. As a further illustration of the difficulty of using arrest statistics to measure actual crime, police activity during periods of vice reform also inflated arrests because of raids. When whole establishments were taken into custody, the innocent and guilty alike showed up in the arrest statistics, but most of those arrested were often subsequently discharged. Therefore, even when police corruption was at its height and police allowed crime to go unpunished, other methods, such as raids, simultaneously had the effect of inflating arrest data.

18. For a journal-style, typewritten, unpublished report of an investigator's daily observations of vice conditions and police corruption in Philadelphia during the entire year of 1921, see "Report on Vice Conditions," Box 273, Folder January 6–April 7, 1921, and Folder June 6–January 29, 1922, J. Hampton Moore Papers, Historical Society of Pennsylvania. For additional evidence of widespread police graft in Philadelphia, see the Report of the Special August Grand Jury of 1928, photocopy, Urban Archives, Temple University.

19. Bureau of Police Annual Report, 1911, 1912.

20. As early as the first decade of the twentieth century, Philadelphia, like Chicago and New York, was exceptional in recording arrest statistics by race. Most places, including major northern cities such as St. Louis, Boston, and Pittsburgh, did not yet do the same; see Richard R. Wright, Jr., "The Economic Condition of Negroes in the North: Tendencies Downward; Second Paper: Negro Criminal Statistics," *Southern Workman* 40 (May 1911): 292.

21. Bureau of Police Annual Report, 1911, 1912.

22. *Philadelphia Tribune,* January 18, 1913.

23. Vice Commission of Philadelphia, *A Report on Existing Conditions with Recommendations to the Honorable Rudolph Blankenburg, Mayor of Philadelphia* (Philadelphia, Penn.: Vice Commission of Philadelphia, 1913), 10, available at the Historical Society of Pennsylvania in Philadelphia.

24. Putting aside the limits of crime statistics, no data on the actual number of black prostitutes in Progressive-era Philadelphia exists, see Tera W. Hunter, "'The 'Brotherly Love' for Which This City Is Proverbial Should Extend to All': The Everyday Lives of Working-Class Women in Philadelphia and Atlanta in the 1890s," in Michael B. Katz and Thomas J. Sugrue, eds., *W. E. B. Du Bois, Race, and the City: The Philadelphia Negro and Its Legacy* (Philadelphia: University of Pennsylvania Press, 1998), 140, 149–150n42. Controversial estimates of the number of Philadelphia's black prostitutes by historians, however, range as high as 25 percent, see Roger Lane, *Roots of Violence in Black Philadelphia, 1860–1900* (Cambridge: Harvard University Press, 1986), 159, and Kali N. Gross, *Colored Amazons: Crime, Violence, and Black Women in The City of Brotherly Love, 1880–1910* (Durham: Duke University Press, 2006), 81, 205n. 52.

25. *Public Ledger,* March 12, 17, 1912. When blacks also happened to be netted in raids, whether or not they were the intended targets, the label "colored" or "negro" was always attached; for an example, see *Public Ledger,* November 4, 1912.

26. Vice Commission of Philadelphia, 11; *Evening Bulletin,* April 23, 1913.

27. Charles Ashley Hardy III, "Race and Opportunity: Black Philadelphia during the Era of the Great Migration, 1916–1930" (Ph.D. diss., Temple University, 1989), 35.

28. James Stemons to John Wanamaker, n.d., Box 4, Folder 1, and John Wanamaker to Stemons, October 6, 1910, Box 1, Folder 15, James Samuel Stemons Papers, Balch Institute of Ethnic Studies, Philadelphia, Penn.

29. *Philadelphia Tribune,* January 25, February 22, 1913.

30. *Philadelphia Tribune,* August 10, September 4, October 26, 1912.

31. *Philadelphia Tribune,* February 15, 1913.

32. Hardy, "Race and Opportunity," 36.

33. *Philadelphia Tribune,* January 3, 1914.

34. "Policeman Slain Protecting Boys, Stabbed over Heart by Colored Man, Who Was Pursuing Youngsters," *Public Ledger,* September 22–23, 1912; "Negro with Knife Kills Policeman, David Simpson, Who Was on Vacation, Stabbed Trying to Shield Boys—Companion Cut," *Evening Bulletin,* September 21, 1912.

35. Jeffrey S. Adler, "'The Negro Would be More Than an Angel to Withstand Such Treatment': African American Homicide in Chicago, 1875-1910" in *Lethal Imagination: Violence and Brutality in American History,* ed. Michael A. Bellesiles (New York: New York University Press, 1999), 299–300.

36. "Tried to Shield Boys," *Philadelphia Tribune,* September 28, 1912.

37. *Philadelphia Tribune,* December 7, 1912.

38. Ibid.

39. *Philadelphia Tribune,* November 9, 1912.

40. *Commonwealth v. John Brown,* No. 538, December Sessions, 1912, Quarter Sessions Court, Notes of Testimony, 1877–1915, Box A-2774: November 1912–September 1915, City Archives of Philadelphia, Philadelphia, Penn.

41. Ibid.

42. Ibid.

43. Richard R. Wright, Jr., *The Negro in Pennsylvania: A Study in Economic History* (1912, reprinted New York: Arno Press, 1969); Walter Licht, *Getting Work: Philadelphia, 1840–1950* (Cambridge: Harvard University Press, 1992); *Philadelphia Tribune,* September 4, 1912, February 5, 1913.

44. *Commonwealth v. John Brown.*

45. Ibid.; *Evening Bulletin,* September, 21, 1912.

46. Ibid.

47. *Philadelphia Tribune,* November 9, 1912.

48. *Philadelphia Tribune,* December 7, December 21, 1912.

49. Quoted in Allen B. Ballard, *One More Day's Journey: The Story of a Family and a People* (New York: McGraw Hill, 1984), 179.

50. For a similar view regarding Pennsylvania's second-largest city, see Abraham Epstein, *The Negro Migrant in Pittsburgh* (1918, reprinted New York: Arno Press, 1969), 52.

51. Adler came to the same conclusion for Chicago: "[W]hen African Americans murdered white Chicagoans" it was "disproportionately" due to "white aggression." He also notes that "killers were not the youngest and poorest men in the community," weakening the claims of contemporaries that black migrants were behind the violence; Adler, "The Negro Would Be More Than an Angel," 300, 304–305. For an interpretation of black migrant violence in the urban North that relies solely on the argument that black southerners transplanted their "obsessions about reputation and vengeance and deadly weapons with them," see David Courtwright, *Violent Land: Single Men and Social Disorder from the Frontier to the Inner City* (Cambridge: Harvard University Press, 1996), 60–61. The earliest primary study of black northern criminality that Courtwright cites is from 1940, and the rest of his evidence comes from what he calls "more recent and sophisticated studies of murder rates" (61).

52. For general discussions regarding black social and economic conditions in the North during the Great Migration, see Hardy, "Race and Opportunity"; Joe William Trotter, Jr., *Black Milwaukee: The Making of an Industrial Proletariat, 1915–1945,* 2nd ed. (Urbana: University of Illinois Press, 2007); Victoria W. Wolcott, *Remaking Respectability: African American Women in Interwar Detroit* (Chapel Hill: University of North Carolina Press, 2001); Kimberley L. Phillips, *Alabama North: African-American Migrants, Community, and Working-Class Activism in Cleveland, 1915–1945* (Urbana: University of Illinois Press, 1999); James Grossman, *Land of Hope: Chicago, Black Southerners, and the Great Migration* (Chicago: University of Chicago Press, 1989); Florette Henri, *Black Migration: Movement North, 1900–1920: The Road from Myth to Man* (New York: Anchor Press, 1976); Gilbert Osofsky, *Harlem: The Making of a Ghetto: Negro New York, 1890–1930,* 2nd ed. (New York: Harper Torchbooks, 1971); Allan H. Spear, *Black Chicago: The Making of a Negro Ghetto, 1890–1920* (Chicago: University of Chicago Press, 1967).

53. "The Future Is Promising," *Philadelphia Tribune,* February 22, 1913.

54. Emmett Scott, *Negro Migration during the War* (New York: Oxford University Press, 1920); Sadie T. Mossell, "The Standard of Living among One Hundred Negro Migrant Families in Philadelphia," AAAPSS 98 (November 1921):109–221; Ballard, *One More Day's Journey*; Hardy, "Race and Opportunity," especially chapter 7, "Southern Migrants and the Myth of Black Criminality," 379–417. For a similar response from Pittsburgh, see Epstein, *The Negro Migrant in Pittsburgh,* 5, 46–54.

55. James R. Grossman, "Blowing the Trumpet: The Chicago *Defender* and Black Migration during World War I," *Illinois Historical Journal* 78:2 (1985): 82–96, reprinted in Kenneth Kusmer, ed., *The Great Migration and After, 1917–1930* (New York: Garland Publishing, 1991).

56. George Edmund Haynes wrote, for example, that "during the earlier days in Detroit the old residents . . . enjoyed a large share in the general life and activity of the community. With the large increase in the number of Negroes and the coming of many of the less desirable type, there was a reaction of these older residents against a gradual tending toward the segregation of all Negroes"; *Negro Newcomers in Detroit: A Challenge to Christian Statesmanship, A Preliminary Survey* (New York: Home Missions Council, 1918), 10.

57. Frederick L. Hoffman, *Race Traits and Tendencies of the American Negro* (New York: American Economic Association, 1896); W. E. B. Du Bois, *The Philadelphia Negro* (1899, reprinted with an introduction by Herbert Aptheker, New York: Schocken Books, 1967).

58. *Philadelphia Tribune*, January 17, 1914.

59. *Philadelphia Tribune*, January 24, 1914.

60. Ibid.

61. Mossell, "The Standard of Living among One Hundred Negro Migrant Families," 178, 216–217.

62. Ibid., 175, 195.

63. Ibid., 177.

64. Based on a monthly arrest report in March 1913, the precincts reporting the highest numbers of arrests for corner lounging were scattered around the city; Police Letters Books, Series 79.27, February–April 1913, Philadelphia City Archives.

65. For a comment on gun possession as an indication of intent to commit a violent crime, see Marcus Kavanagh, *The Criminal and His Allies* (Indianapolis: Bobbs-Merrill Co., 1928), 6–7.

66. Mossell, "The Standard of Living among One Hundred Negro Migrant Families," 177.

67. Scott, *Negro Migration during the War*, 136.

68. In his study of black migrants in Pittsburgh, Abraham Epstein explained that it was "natural" to look upon the newcomer as a stranger and therefore to question his moral fitness and to "consider him the cause of the crimes and vices of the community." Based on the experience of white immigrants, he added that greater familiarity over time would dissolve this initial contempt (Epstein, *The Negro Migrant in Pittsburgh*, 46).

69. Quoted in Ballard, *One More Day's Journey*, 187.

70. Quoted in Hardy, "Race and Opportunity," 385.

71. Hardy, "Race and Opportunity," 390–392.

72. Ibid.

73. Ibid.

74. *Philadelphia Tribune*, March 16, 23, 1918.

75. *Philadelphia Tribune*, July 6, 1918; Vincent P. Franklin, "The Philadelphia Race Riot of 1918," *Pennsylvania Magazine of History and Biography* 99:3 (1975): 338.

76. *Philadelphia Tribune*, August 3, 1918.

77. Ibid.

78. *Philadelphia Tribune*, August 10, 17, 1918.

79. *Philadelphia Tribune*, August 31, 1918. The curse words have been filled in by the author; the newspapers used dashes to indicate profane language.

80. Ibid.

81. Ibid. For more on gun dispossession, see Mary Ellen Curtin, *Black Prisoners and Their World, Alabama, 1865–1900* (Charlottesville: University Press of Virginia, 2000), 35; Herbert Shapiro, *White Violence and Black Response: From Reconstruction to Montgomery* (Amhearst: University of Massachusetts, 1988), 5.

82. *Philadelphia Tribune*, August 3, 10, September 14, 1918.

83. Franklin, "The Philadelphia Race Riot of 1918," 342.

84. *Philadelphia Tribune*, August 17, 1918.

85. *Philadelphia Tribune*, August 10, 1918.

86. *Philadelphia Tribune*, August 3, 1918.

87. *Philadelphia Tribune*, August 10, 1918.

88. The crime of having a dark face quotation comes from the *Philadelphia Tribune*, August 17, 1918.

89. Franklin, "The Philadelphia Race Riot of 1918," 339–340.

90. *Philadelphia Tribune*, August 10, September 28, 1918; Franklin, "The Philadelphia Race Riot of 1918," 342.

91. *Philadelphia Tribune*, August 3, September 21, 28, 1918; Franklin, "The Philadelphia Race Riot of 1918," 341.

92. *Philadelphia Tribune*, August 17, 1918; Franklin, "The Philadelphia Race Riot of 1918," 343.

93. *Philadelphia Tribune*, August 3, 1918; Franklin, "The Philadelphia Race Riot of 1918," 343.

94. *Philadelphia Tribune*, August 10, 1918.

95. *Philadelphia Tribune*, August 24, 1918.

96. *Philadelphia Tribune*, August 31, 1918.

97. *Philadelphia Tribune*, September 14, 1918.

98. Mossell, "The Standard of Living among One Hundred Negro Migrant Families," 177.

99. Scott, *Negro Migration during the War*, 136–137.

100. *Philadelphia Tribune*, August 31, 1918.

101. William D. Fuller, "The Negro Migrant in Philadelphia," June 1, 1924, unpublished report, 21, Folder 5, URB 31, Negro Migrant Study, Urban Archives, Temple University.

102. Charles S. Johnson, *The Negro in Chicago: A Study of Race Relations and a Race Riot* (Chicago: University of Chicago Press, 1922), 590–592; Noel P. Gist, "The Negro in the Daily Press," *Social Forces* 10 (March 1932): 405–411; James R. Caroll, *The American Negro as Portrayed in the Chicago Tribune, 1901–1907* (M.A. thesis, Howard University, 1951), 77–98; George D. King, *The Negro as Portrayed in the North American Review, 1901–1910* (M.A. thesis, Howard University, 1957), 81–95. An example of the crime-baiting tactics of neighborhood improvement associations in Detroit after World War II, which was not unusual in Chicago or Philadelphia in the late 1910s and 1920s, can be found in Thomas J. Sugrue, "Crabgrass-Roots Politics: Race, Rights, and the Reaction against Liberalism in the Urban North, 1940–1964," *Journal of American History*, 82:2 (1995): 561: "A northwest-side neighborhood poster played on white residents' fears of the crime that, they believed, would accompany racial change: 'Home Owners Can You Afford to . . . Have your children exposed to gangster operated skid row saloons? Phornographic [sic] pictures and literature? Gamblers and prostitution? You Face these Issues Now!' "

103. *Philadelphia Tribune*, August 3, 1918.

104. *Philadelphia Tribune*, August 17, 1918; Franklin, "The Philadelphia Race Riot of 1918," 336. Charles Kellogg points out that the president's statement was

the result of intense pressure from high-ranking officials of the NAACP and their supporters following the East St. Louis riot in July 1917; *NAACP: A History of the National Association for the Advancement of Colored People* (Baltimore: Johns Hopkins Press, 1967), 227–228.

105. *Philadelphia Tribune,* August 3, September 14, 1918. Biographical information on Phillips comes from "A Golden Jubilee," *Church Advocate,* July 1925, found in the Charles Blockson Collection at Temple University.

106. Joseph Sternberger to Christopher J. Perry, editor of the *Philadelphia Tribune,* reprinted in *Philadelphia Tribune,* September 21, 1918.

107. *Philadelphia Tribune,* September 7, 14, 1918.

108. *Philadelphia Tribune,* August 3, 1918.

109. *Philadelphia Tribune,* September 14, 21, 1918.

110. Historian William Tuttle notes that black Chicagoans blamed the racial violence leading up to Chicago's race riot during the summer of 1919 on housing and a lack of police protection. Given the situation they faced and their "participation in the war," blacks began to "depend more and more on their own resources for protection." William Tuttle, Jr., "Contested Neighborhoods and Racial Violence: Prelude to the Chicago Riot of 1919," *The Journal of Negro History* 55:4 (1970): 267.

111. Ibid., 283.

112. Epstein, *The Negro Migrant in Pittsburgh,* 54.

113. Henri, *Black Migration,* 261.

114. *Philadelphia Tribune,* March 9, 1918.

115. *North American Review,* July 17, 1916; *Evening Bulletin,* August 25, 1916; *Philadelphia Tribune,* March 30, April 27, 1918; Hardy, "Race and Opportunity," 488.

116. Raymond B. Fosdick, *Chronicle of a Generation: An Autobiography* (New York: Harper and Brothers, 1958), 144–146; Allen F. Davis and Mark H. Haller, *The Peoples of Philadelphia* (Philadelphia: Temple University Press, 1973), 284.

117. *Philadelphia Tribune,* September 14, 1918.

6. POLICING RACISM

1. Quoted in Chicago Commission on Race Relations, *The Negro in Chicago: A Study of Race Relations and a Race Riot* (Chicago: University of Chicago Press, 1922), 343; hereafter cited as CCRR, *Negro in Chicago.*

2. Annual Report of the Committee of Fifteen (1923), quoted in Kevin J. Mumford, *Interzones: Black/White Sex Districts in Chicago and New York in the Early Twentieth Century* (New York: Columbia University Press, 1997), 23.

3. Kenneth Kusmer, *A Ghetto Takes Shape: Black Cleveland, 1870–1930* (Urbana: University of Illinois Press, 1976), 48–49.

4. CCRR, *Negro in Chicago,* 356.

5. Kusmer, *A Ghetto Takes Shape,* 50.

6. Fred D. Baldwin, "Smedley D. Butler and Prohibition Enforcement in Philadelphia, 1924–1925," *Pennsylvania Magazine of History and Biography* 84 (July 1960); Report of "The Special August Grand Jury [of Philadelphia]," 1928, Series 3, Box

7, Folder 1, Committee of Seventy Records, Urban Archives, Temple University, Philadelphia, Penn.; Humbert S. Nelli, *The Business of Crime: Italians and Syndicate Crime in the United States* (New York: Oxford University Press, 1976), 186–187.

7. "February 12, 1921, Furnished Room House–1211 Kenilworth Street," Report on Vice Conditions, Box 273, J. Hampton Moore Papers, Historical Society of Pennsylvania, Philadelphia, Penn. (hereafter cited as Moore Vice Report).

8. Kusmer, *A Ghetto Takes Shape*, 177.

9. W. E. B. Du Bois, *The Philadelphia Negro* (1899, reprinted with an introduction by Herbert Aptheker, Millwood, N.Y.: Kraus-Thomson Organization Ltd., 1967), 390–392.

10. "Appeal to Self-Respecting Colored Citizens," n.d., and Plans and Purposes Document, n.d., Box 3, Folder 3, James S. Stemons Papers, Balch Institute for Ethnic Studies, Philadelphia, Penn. (hereafter cited as Stemons Papers).

11. CCRR, *Negro in Chicago*, 602.

12. Marlon B. Ross, *Manning the Race: Reforming Black Men in the Jim Crow Era* (New York: New York University Press, 2004), 145–191; Alice P. O'Connor, *Poverty Knowledge: Social Science, Social Policy, and the Poor in Twentieth Century U.S. History* (Princeton: Princeton University Press, 2001), 75.

13. St. Clair Drake and Horace R. Cayton, *Black Metropolis: A Study of Negro Life in a Northern City* (New York: Harcourt, Brace and Co., 1945), 684.

14. "Negro Social Workers," *Opportunity*, August 1930, 230; Eugene K. Jones, "A Practical Year of Interracial Cooperation," *Opportunity*, April 1926, 98–102.

15. Anna J. Thompson, "A Survey of Crime among Negroes in Philadelphia," 1925, Box 8, Folder 131, Armstrong Association (Urban League of Philadelphia) Papers, Urban Archives, Temple University, Philadelphia, Penn. (hereafter cited as Armstrong Association papers). A slightly condensed version was published the following year in three parts under the same title: *Opportunity* 4 (July-September 1926): 217–219, 251–254, 285–286. Copies of the following reports by Ira De A. Reid were found in Box 2, Folders 5, 7, 8, 10, and 11 of the Ira De Augustine Papers, Manuscripts, Archives and Rare Books Division, Schomberg Center for Research in Black Culture, New York Public Library, New York, N.Y. (hereafter cited as Reid Papers); *The Negro Population of Denver, Colorado: A Survey of Its Economic and Social Status* (Denver Interracial Committee, National Urban League, 1929); *Social Conditions of the Negro in the Hill District of Pittsburgh* (Pittsburgh: General Committee on the Hill Survey, 1930); Ira De A. Reid, *Trojans of Color: A Social Survey of the Negro Population of Troy, New York* (New York: Department of Research, National Urban League, 1931); "Community Report No. VIII—Monmouth County, N.J.," March 1932; "Community Report No. XI—Princeton, N.J.," June 1932; "Community Report No. XV—New Brunswick and Perth Amboy, N.J.," September 1932; "Community Report No. XX—Plainfield, N.J.," August 1932; "Community Report No. XXI—Trenton, N.J.," October 1932; *Survey of Negro Life in New Jersey* (Interracial Committee of the New Jersey Conference of Social Work in Cooperation with the State Department of Institutions and Agencies, 1932). See also the following articles by Reid: "A Study of 200 Negro Prisoners in the Western Penitentiary of Pennsylvania," *Opportunity,* June 1925, 168–169; "The Negro's Relation to Work and Law Observance," *National*

Commission on Law Observance and Enforcement, Report on the Causes of Crime 1:3 (June 1931): 219–256; "The Negro Goes to Sing Sing," *Opportunity,* July 1932, 215–217; and the following articles by others: Maurine Boie, "An Analysis of Negro Crime Statistics for Minneapolis for 1923, 1924 and 1925," *Opportunity* 6 (June 1928): 171–173; Edward E. Wilson, "The Responsibility for Crime," *Opportunity* 7 (March 1929); Kenneth E. Barnhart, "Negro Crime and Education," *Opportunity* 11 (1933): 364–367.

16. Henry J. McGuinn, "Part IV: Recreation," in *Negro Problems in Cities,* ed. T. J. Woofter, Jr. (1928, reprinted New York: Negro Universities Press, 1969), 227–282; Owen Lovejoy, "Justice to the Negro Child," *Opportunity* (June 1929): 174–176; Joint Committee on Negro Child Study in New York City, "Study of Delinquent and Neglected Negro Children," in *The Negro in American Civilization: A Study of Negro Life and Race Relations in the Light of Social Research,* ed. Charles S. Johnson (1930, reprinted New York: Johnson Reprint, 1970), 335–336; Earl R. Moses, "Appendix II: Social and Economic Factors in Negro Housing; Housing Conditions among Negroes in Chicago–with Special Reference to Juvenile Delinquency," in *Negro Housing: Report of the Committee on Negro Housing,* ed. Charles S. Johnson (1932, reprinted New York: Negro Universities Press, 1969); E. Franklin Frazier, *The Negro Family in Chicago* (Chicago: University of Chicago Press, 1932); Earl R. Moses, "Delinquency in the Negro Community," *Opportunity* 11 (1933): 304–307; E. Franklin Frazier, *The Negro Family in the United States,* rev. ed. (Chicago: University of Chicago Press, 1973). See especially two separate case studies of juvenile delinquents in Chicago prepared by Benjamin O. Davis for Frazier's *Negro Family in Chicago,* 216–217: Case Study of Milton Turner and Case Study of Paul Johnson, Box 81, Folder 10, E. Franklin Frazier Papers, Moorland-Spingarn Research Center, Howard University, Washington, D.C.

17. Forrester B. Washington, "Recreational Facilities for the Negro," AAAPSS (November 1928): 272–282.

18. Anne Meis Knupfer cites a 1925 Chicago Urban League Conference on Juvenile Delinquency in *Reform and Resistance: Gender, Delinquency, and America's First Juvenile Court* (New York: Routledge, 2001); "Study regarding Recreation for Colored People in North Philadelphia Made for the Community Department of the Council of Social Agencies of the Welfare Federation of Philadelphia," March 1929, Box 2, Folder 45, Wharton Centre Records, Urban Archives, Temple University, Philadelphia, Penn.; Mary Huff Diggs, "The Problems and Needs of Negro Youth as Revealed by Delinquency and Crime Statistics," *Journal of Negro Education* 9:3 (1940): 311–312.

19. "A Survey of the Most Densely Populated Negro Section of North Philadelphia," 7, Benezet House Association Records, Friends Historical Library of Swarthmore College, Swarthmore, Penn.

20. Thompson, 19, Box 8, Folder 131, Armstrong Association papers.

21. "Committee to Study Negro Delinquency," *New York Times,* December 16, 1928; Paul Blanshard, "Negro Delinquency in New York," *Journal of Educational Psychology* 16:2 (1942): 115–123; Diggs, "The Problems and Needs of Negro Youth," 315–317. See also Sidney Axelrad, "Negro and White Male Institutionalized Delinquents," AJS 57:6 (1952): 570–571, based on 1930s evidence.

22. Cheryl Lynn Greenburg, *"Or Does It Explode": Black Harlem in the Great Depression* (New York: Oxford University Press, 1991), 34–37.

23. William I. Thomas and Florian Znaniecki, *The Polish Peasant in Europe and America* (Boston: Richard G. Badger, 1918); William I. Thomas and Dorothy Swaine Thomas, *The Child in America: Behavior Problems and Programs* (New York: A. A. Knopf, 1928), 193; Walter C. Reckless and Mapheus Smith, *Juvenile Delinquency* (New York: McGraw Hill Book Company, 1932), 319.

24. U.S. Bureau of the Census, *Children under Institutional Care, 1923* (Washington, D.C.: GPO, 1927), 301–302, quoted in Thorsten Sellin, "The Negro Criminal: A Statistical Note," AAAPSS 140 (1928): 63.

25. A Big Brother movement was launched in Philadelphia in January 1928; see *Philadelphia Tribune*, January 26, 1928; "Elks to Study Harlem Delinquency," *New York Times*, May 26, 1935.

26. In 1918 Ernest T. Atwell became the director of the Bureau of Colored Work of the Playgrounds and Recreation Association of America; Washington, "Recreational Facilities for the Negro," 282; "Negro Social Workers," 230. For more on the history of African American probation officers and juvenile justice administrators, see Geoffrey K. Ward, "Color Lines of Social Control: Juvenile Justice Administration in a Racialized Social System, 1825–2000" (PhD diss., University of Michigan, 2001).

27. Jacqueline Anne Rouse, "Out of the Shadow of Tuskegee: Margaret Murray Washington, Social Activism, and Race Vindication," *Journal of Negro History,* 81:1 (1996): 35.

28. Eugene Kinckle Jones, "Social Work among Negroes," AAAPSS, November 1928, 291.

29. Clarence Brown to "Sec of the National Ass Advancement for Colored People," received April 18, 1927, Box 264, "Crime, 1927," National Association for the Advancement of Colored People Papers, Manuscript Division, Library of Congress, Washington, D.C. (hereafter cited as NAACP papers).

30. I use the term *de facto* to note that the term "racial profiling" was not used in the early twentieth century. For an example of campaigns against police abuse, see the photo with the caption "Brooklyn Negroes Protesting against the Failure to Try a Policeman Who Assaulted a Colored Woman" in *Crisis* 32:2 (1926): 80. The Colored Civic League protest group in Philadelphia was moved to action when a white policeman shot a homeless black man; see *Philadelphia Tribune*, March 22, 28, 1928.

31. Emmett Scott, *Negro Migration during the War* (New York: Oxford University Press, 1920), 136; Sadie T. Mossell, "The Standard of Living among One Hundred Negro Migrant Families in Philadelphia," AAAPSS 98 (November 1921): 216–217.

32. Henderson H. Donald, "Dependents and Delinquents," *Journal of Negro History* 6:4 (1921): 460–462.

33. Ibid., 460–462, 465. Donald's data came from a U.S. Department of Labor study supervised by National Urban League director George Edmund Haynes.

34. Mary White Ovington, *Half a Man: The Status of the Negro in New York* (New York: Longmans, Green & Co., 1911), 72–73, 198–200.

35. Reprinted in "Negro Crime," *The Crisis* 2 (June 1911): 56–57.

36. Edwin H. Sutherland, *Criminology* (Philadelphia: J. B. Lippincott Co., 1924), 104.

37. Donald, "Dependents and Delinquents," 461.

38. In addition to making no mention of southern migrant criminality ten years later, Sutherland wrote that black crime "statistics probably reflect a bias against the Negro because of the prejudice against the race," adding that "even if the statistics are completely reliable," they are not comparable by race given the vast differences "economically, educationally, and socially" between whites and blacks. Edwin H. Sutherland, *Principles of Criminology* (Philadelphia: J. B. Lippincott Co., 1934), 111.

39. Marlon B. Ross, *Manning the Race: Reforming Black Men in the Jim Crow Era* (New York: New York University Press, 2004), 148–149.

40. Richard R. Wright, Jr., "The Economic Condition of Negroes in the North: Tendencies Downward; Second Paper: Negro Criminal Statistics," *The Southern Workman* 40 (May 1911): 292.

41. Charles Flint Kellogg, *NAACP, a History of the National Association for the Advancement of Colored People* (Baltimore: Johns Hopkins University Press, 1967), 209–235; Robert Zangrando, *The NAACP Crusade against Lynching, 1909–1950* (Philadelphia: Temple University Press, 1980).

42. Herbert Seligman to Clifford Plummer, October 20, 1919, Folder "Crime, Rape Stats, Oct. 1919," Box 265, NAACP Papers. Plummer handwrote his response on the bottom of Seligman's original letter.

43. Walter L. Hetfield, Jr., to Henry Seligman, October 22, 1919, Folder "Crime, Rape Stats, Oct. 1919," Box 265, NAACP Papers.

44. For more on Johnson's role as author, see David Levering Lewis, *When Harlem Was in Vogue* (1981, reprint New York: Oxford University Press, 1989), 48, and "The Intellectual Luminaries of the Harlem Renaissance, *Journal of Blacks in Higher Education* 7 (Spring 1995): 68–69; John H. Stanfield, *Philanthropy and Jim Crow in American Social Science* (Westport, Conn.: Greenwood Press, 1985), 20; Richard Robbins, *Sidelines Activist: Charles S. Johnson and the Struggle for Civil Rights* (Jackson: University Press of Mississippi, 1996), 34.

45. Robert E. Park and Ernest Burgess, *An Introduction to the Science of Sociology* (Chicago: University of Chicago Press, 1922); Patricia Madoo Lengermann, "Robert E. Park and the Theoretical Content of Chicago Sociology," *Sociological Inquiry* 58 (Fall 1988): 361, 363; O'Connor, *Poverty Knowledge*, 18, 47–49; James B. McKee, *Sociology and the Race Problem: The Failure of a Perspective* (Urbana: University of Illinois Press, 1993), 129–130; Mark Haller, "Introduction," in *Organized Crime in Chicago: Part III of The Illinois Crime Survey, 1929*, ed. John Landesco (1929, reprinted with new introduction, Chicago: University of Chicago Press, 1968), ix–x.

46. Frazier, *The Negro Family in Chicago*. Although Frazier analyzed black juvenile delinquency statistics, his contributions were not made as a black crime expert; his primary interests were studying the black family and advancing the use of statistics on northern black rates of illegitimacy, male desertion, "broken homes," and welfare alongside rates of homeownership and occupational differentiation to demonstrate class and "cultural differences" among blacks. These ideas

would contribute to the broader statistical discourse on black pathology in the future, where crime statistics would have to share center stage. Daniel Patrick Moynihan would, for example, draw heavily on Frazier's statistical analysis of a "tangle of pathology" tied to unwed mothers and absentee fathers in his 1965 report, *The Negro Family: The Case for National Action*. It is beyond the scope of this chapter—as a coda to a Progressive era analysis—to unpack the full import of Frazier's work, which anticipated new directions in the cultural arguments about black inferiority in the post-World War II period. One of Frazier's intellectual biographers notes that "Frazier's bold scholarship became the touchstone for the great sociology/pathology debates of the second half of the twentieth century"; Jonathon Holloway, *Confronting the Veil: Abram Harris, Jr., E. Franklin Frazier, and Ralph Bunche, 1919–1941* (Chapel Hill: University of North Carolina Press, 2002), 123–156. For more on Frazier's intellectual biography, see Anthony Platt, *E. Franklin Frazier Reconsidered* (New Brunswick, N.J.: Rutgers University Press, 1991), 89–90, 135, 166–168; Darryl Michael Scott, *Contempt and Pity* (Chapel Hill: University of North Carolina Press, 1997), 43–50; McKee, *Sociology and the Race Problem*, 200–209.

47. Nicholas Lemann, *The Promised Land: The Great Black Migration and How It Changed America* (New York: Vintage Books, 1991), 120–121; "Justice for Blacks," *New York Review of Books* 45:4 (March 5, 1998); Scott, *Contempt and Pity*, 44.

48. None of the Chicago School sociologists are mentioned in the front matter or in the biographical entries of the commission's official participants and staffers (CCRR, *Negro in Chicago*, xiii–xxi, 652–655).

49. Walter White, "American Race Riots: Review of *The Negro in Chicago*," *The Nation*, November 1, 1922, 475–476; "Race Relations: Review of *The Negro in Chicago*," *The Bookman*, December 1922, 500–502. As a historical document concerned with public attitudes about blacks as criminals, especially in relation to vice districts and policing, *The Negro in Chicago* was an unsurpassed primary source during the first four decades of the twentieth century.

50. Mia Bay, *The White Image in the Black Mind: African American Ideas about White People, 1830–1925* (New York: Oxford University Press, 2000), 201.

51. O'Connor, *Poverty Knowledge*, 51; Clifford R. Shaw, Frederick Zorbaugh, Henry D. McKay, and Leonard S. Cottrell, *Delinquency Areas* (Chicago: University of Chicago Press, 1929); Clifford R. Shaw and Henry D. McKay, *Social Factors in Juvenile Delinquency*, vol. 2 of National Commission on Law Enforcement and Observance, *Report on Causes of Crime* (Washington, D.C.: GPO, 1931); Clifford R. Shaw, *The Natural History of a Delinquent Career* (1931, reprinted New York: Greenwood Press Publishers, 1968).

52. Haller, "Introduction," in *Organized Crime*, xiv.

53. CCRR, *Negro in Chicago*, 327.

54. Ibid., 329–331.

55. Ibid., 351, 354.

56. Theodore M. Porter, *Trust in Numbers: The Pursuit of Objectivity in Science and Public Life* (Princeton: Princeton University Press, 1995).

57. CCRR, *Negro in Chicago*, 329–330.

58. Sutherland, *Criminology* (1924), 103; Ronald L. Akers, "Linking Sociology and Its Specialties: The Case of Criminology," *Social Forces* 71:1 (1992): 3. John H. Laub and Robert J. Sampson crown Sutherland the "dominant criminologist of the 20th century" but also call him the "dominant sociologist of crime," adding that his research was firmly rooted in sociology rather than in the "multiple-factor theory of crime" associated with many others, including his Harvard counterparts Sheldon and Eleanor Glueck. Sutherland's theory, unlike that of the Gluecks, write Laub and Sampson, "required him to destroy individual-level, or nonsociological, perspectives on crime"; John H. Laub and Robert J. Sampson, "The Sutherland-Glueck Debate: On the Sociology of Criminological Knowledge," AJS 96:6 (1991): 1403–1404. For more on the history of "nonsociological" fields of criminal research, such as criminal anthropology, eugenic criminology, and psychiatric criminology, see Nicole Hahn Rafter, *Creating Born Criminals* (Urbana: University of Illinois Press, 1997).

59. Sutherland, *Principles of Criminology* (1934), 111. Sutherland continued to use the same language in at least the next two editions (1939, 1947) of his textbook.

60. George B. Vold, "Edwin Hardin Sutherland: Sociological Criminologist," *American Sociological Review* 16:1 (1951): 2–9.

61. Frazier, *The Negro Family in Chicago,* xi. Burgess, Shaw, and McKay showed statistically that the highest crime and delinquency areas of major industrial cities, such as Chicago, had also been the "zone of settlement" for wave after wave of European immigrants since the late nineteenth century. As each group's economic and cultural status improved, it left high-poverty, high-crime zones, only to be replaced by a new group. Hence the physical space of condemned buildings, multifamily dwellings, and industrial and commercial overzoning caused crime and delinquency, not the other way around. The fact that each group eventually moved on to a better neighborhood, what these scholars called ethnic succession, proved the inherent assimilability of each group. Therefore the problem was not the people themselves, but rather the community from which they stumbled initially on their journey to achieve the American Dream. Blacks were included in this formulation, particularly in Frazier's work, but none of the Chicago School sociologists fully accounted for Black Belt segregation and antiblack violence. Ernest W. Burgess, "The Growth of the City," in *The City,* ed. Robert E. Park and Ernest W. Burgess (Chicago: University of Chicago Press, 1925); "The Determination of Gradients in the Growth of the City," *Publication of the American Sociological Society* 26 (1927): 178–184; Shaw et al., *Delinquency Areas;* Shaw and McKay, *Social Factors in Juvenile Delinquency;* Shaw, *The Natural History of a Delinquent Career.*

62. Quoted in Johnson, *Negro in American Civilization,* 323–324.

63. In the late spring of 1920, following the killing of Elias Clayton, Elmer Jackson, and Issac McGhie, the *New York Times* wrote that "lynching of Negroes in Duluth is far from the first that occurred in the North. Human nature is much the same in both sections of the country"; James Allen, Hilton Als, John Lewis, and Leon F. Litwack, *Without Sanctuary: Lynching Photography in America* (Santa Fe, N.M.: Twin Palms Publishers, 2000), 175.

64. Maurine Bois, "An Analysis of Negro Crime Statistics for Minneapolis for 1923, 1924 and 1925," *Opportunity* 6 (June 1928): 171–173; Sellin, "The Negro Criminal," 54–55; Sutherland, *Principles of Criminology* (1934), 11. For a sample

of Sellin's most influential work on crime statistics, a seemingly separate enterprise from his work on racial crime statistics, see Thorsten Sellin, "The Basis of a Crime Index," *Journal of Criminal Law and Criminology* 22:3 (1931): 335–336, and "The Uniform Criminal Statistics Act," *Journal of Criminal Law and Criminology* 40:6 (1950): 679–700.

65. Thorsten Sellin, "Is Murder Increasing in Europe?" AAAPSS 125 (May 1926): 31.

66. Ronald P. Falkner, "Crime and the Census," AAAPSS 9 (January 1897): 43–44; Louis N. Robinson, "History of Criminal Statistics," *Journal of Law and Criminology* 24:1 (1933): 125–139.

67. Within a year of publishing the 1928 article, Sellin's stock soared. He held the position of editor of the *Annals of the American Academy of Political and Social Science,* in which the article appeared, for the next four decades. He was director of the Social Science Research Council from 1933 to 1936 and chair of the University of Pennsylvania Sociology department from 1945 to 1959. In the 1950s he became a leading international death penalty researcher and assumed the presidency of the International Society of Criminology from 1956 to 1965. He established the Center for Studies in Criminology and Criminal Law at the University of Pennsylvania in 1960; it was named for him in 1985 (today it is the Jerry Lee Center of Criminology). See Marvin E. Wolfgang, "Thorsten Sellin," *Proceedings of the American Philosophical Society* 140:4 (1996): 581–586; Eric Pace, "Thorsten Sellin, Criminology Expert, Dies at 97," *New York Times,* September 20, 1994, D22; Marvin E. Wolfgang, ed., *Crime and Culture: Essays in Honor of Thorsten Sellin* (New York: John Wiley & Sons, 1968). For all the accomplishments that Sellin is remembered for, he is not noted by criminologists today for his pivotal research on racial criminalization in the 1920s and 1930s.

68. U.S. Department of Commerce, Bureau of Census, *Prisoners in State and Federal Prisons and Reformatories* (Washington, D.C., GPO, 1929–1930), 31, and *Prisoners in State and Federal Prisons and Reformatories* (Washington, D.C., GPO, 1931–1932), 19. My analysis of these government reports and the impact of Johnson's, Sutherland's, and Sellin's research on them is also based on a comparison with a more tentative assessment of the problem of racial crime statistics in U.S. Census Bureau, "Negro Population, 1790–1915" (Washington, D.C.: GPO, 1918), 438.

69. Nathaniel Cantor, "Crime and the Negro," *Journal of Negro History* 16 (January 1931): 61–65. In "The Causes of Crime," *Journal of Criminal Law and Criminology* 23:6 (1933): 1029–1034, Cantor further dismissed race as a cause of crime, insisting that economic inequality was the "fundamental" problem. For biographical data on Cantor, see *American Sociological Review* 23:2 (1958): 203; "Dr. Cantor Dead: A Sociologist, 59," *New York Times,* December 6, 1957, 30.

70. W. E. B. Du Bois, "Negro Crime," *Crisis* 32 (May 1927): 105.

71. Carter G. Woodson, "Review of *The Negro and Crime in Virginia* by Bernard Peyton Chamberlain," *Journal of Negro History* 23:1 (1938): 110.

72. Thomas J. Woofter, *The Basis of Racial Adjustment* (New York: Ginn & Co., 1925), 130–132.

73. While not explicit in the quote, Reuter was particularly concerned about police behavior in the North: "Such police discriminations are more general in the

Northern than in the Southern communities"; Edward Byron Reuter, *The American Race Problem: A Study of the Negro* (New York: Thomas Y. Crowell Co., 1927), 356–358.

74. See also Winthrop D. Lane, "Ambushed in the City: The Grim Side of Harlem," *Survey* 53 (March 1925): 692–694; Walter Reckless, *Vice in Chicago* (1933, reprinted Montclair, N.J.: Patterson, 1969), 31; William T. Root, Jr., *A Psychological and Educational Survey of 1916 Prisoners in the Western Penitentiary of Pennsylvania* (Pittsburgh: Board of Trustees of Western Penitentiary, 1927), 217.

75. G. Croft Williams, *The Negro Offender* (New York: Russell Sage Foundation, 1922), 4–5.

76. Marcus Kavanagh, *The Criminal and His Allies* (Indianapolis: Bobbs-Merrill Co., 1928), 133–146.

77. CCRR, *Negro in Chicago*, 621.

78. Woofter, *The Basis of Racial Adjustment*, 130.

79. Root, *A Psychological and Educational Survey of 1916 Prisoners*, 214.

80. CCRR, *Negro in Chicago*, 646. Contrast this with the fact that in 1904 Du Bois had to bolster his argument by relying upon the testimony of a white southern journalist. The use of black experts during this period is one of the most explicit signs of how much had changed in the broader debate about black criminality in the 1920s and 1930s.

81. Kelly Miller, "Review of *The Negro in Chicago*, by Charles S. Johnson and the Chicago Commission on Race Relations," AJS 29:4 (1924): 499–503.

82. Thompson, "A Survey of Crime among Negroes in Philadelphia," 219, 253–254.

83. Reid, *Negro Population of Denver*, 279, Folder 7, Box 2, Reid Papers.

84. Reid, *Trojans of Color*, 28–29, Folder 5, Box 2, Reid Papers.

85. Reid, *Social Conditions of the Negro in the Hill District of Pittsburgh*, 63, Folder 8, Box 2, Reid Papers.

86. Ira De A. Reid, "The Negro in the Major Industries and Building Trades of Pittsburgh" (M.A. thesis, University of Pittsburgh, 1925), Folder 18, Box 1, Reid Papers; Reid, "A Study of 200 Negro Prisoners in the Western Penitentiary of Pennsylvania," 168–169.

87. Reid, "Community Report No. VIII—Monmouth County," 26; "Community Report No. XV—New Brunswick and Perth Amboy," 37, Folder 10 and 11, Reid Papers. Reid changed the wording slightly in "The Negro Goes to Sing Sing," 217: "The presence of an unusually large Negro population in [New York's] Sing Sing, therefore, finds its genesis in a sufficiently large number of other factors to invalidate the opinion that high rates of crime and incarceration are due to an inherent racial criminality."

88. Wilson, "The Responsibility for Crime," 96–97.

89. Kusmer, *A Ghetto Takes Shape*, 178.

90. Frankie Y. Bailey and Alice P. Green, *"Law Never Here": A Social History of African American Responses to Issues of Crime and Justice* (Westport, Conn.: Praeger, 1999), 84. For similar findings based on southern police practices, see Randall Kennedy, "History: Unequal Protection" and "History: Unequal Enforcement," in *Race, Crime and the Law* (New York: Vintage Books, 1997), 29–135.

91. Quoted in H. C. Brearley, "The Negro and Homicide," *Social Forces* 9 (1930): 247. White criminologist Hans Von Hentig examined the same evidence of police homicides from the Illinois Crime Survey and wrote, "We should not, however, forget that an excessive number of colored victims are killed under the headings of justifiable homicide or police killings." He calculated that black male homicides were three times more likely to be solved than white male homicides; "The Criminality of the Negro," *Journal of Criminal Law and Criminology* 30:5 (1940): 632–633.

92. Ida B. Wells, "Murder in Chicago," *Crisis*, August 1930, 282.

93. Marilynn Johnson, *Street Justice: A History of Police Violence in New York City* (Boston: Beacon Press, 2003), 57–86, 181–191; Robert Zangrando, *The NAACP Crusade against Lynching, 1909–1950* (Philadelphia: Temple University Press, 1980), 8; Joseph Boskin, *Urban Violence in the Twentieth Century* (Beverly Hills, Calif.: Glencoe Press, 1969), 15, 47.

94. Mark H. Haller, "Urban Crime and Criminal Justice: The Chicago Case," *Journal of American History* 57:3 (1970): 630–635.

95. Buffalo *Courier-Express*, July 25, 1947. Quoted in A. A. Abraham, "Juvenile Delinquency in Buffalo and Its Prevention," *Journal of Negro Education* 17:2 (1948): 129.

96. "Kelly Miller's Column: How To Restrain the Negro Criminal," February 9, 1935, Folder 80, Box 71–73, Kelly Miller Papers, Moorland-Spingarn Research Center, Howard University, Washington, D.C.

97. Wilson, "The Responsibility for Crime," 97.

98. George Fald to James Weldon Johnson, January 21, 1922, Folder "Crime, 1922-Jan-May," Box 264, NAACP Papers. A black sociologist wrote in 1932, "Why is the rate of homicide among Negroes so high? Apparently one reason is because so many Negroes are shot by policemen for 'resisting arrest.' It must be kept in mind that all of the statistics regarding homicide are based on the persons who were killed—not on the persons who did the killing"; Kenneth E. Barnhart, "Negro Homicides in the United States," *Opportunity*, July 1932, 213.

99. Rupert Clarke to Walter White, July 23, 1931, Folder "Crime, 1931," Box 265, NAACP Papers.

100. New Haven *Evening Register*, May 12, 13, 1931; New York *World Telegram*, May 13, 14, 1931; New Haven *Journal Courier*, May 13, 1931. All newspaper clippings were found in Folder "Crime, 1931," Box 265, NAACP Papers (hereafter cited as Gilyard Press Clippings).

101. Frances Kellor, "The Criminal Negro: A Sociological Study," *The Arena* 25: 1–5 (1901): 314.

102. Gilyard Press Clippings: New Haven *Journal Courier*, May 13, 1931; Manchester *Herald*, May 13, 1931; New York *World Telegram*, May 14, 1931.

103. "N.A.A.C.P. Protests Unjust Arrests of Innocent Negroes," Press Release, September 11, 1925, Folder "Crime, 1925," Box 264, NAACP Papers.

104. Editorial, *Philadelphia Tribune*, October 27, 1927.

105. Monroe N. Work, ed., *Negro Year Book: An Encyclopedia of the Negro* (Tuskegee: Negro Year Book Publishing Co., 1931), 289–292, and *Negro Year Book* (1938), 147.

106. Southern Commission on Interracial Cooperation, *Burnt Cork and Crime: Stories Summarized from Press Reports* (Atlanta: Southern Commission on Interracial Cooperation, 1935), quoted in Guy B. Johnson, "The Negro and Crime," AAAPSS 217 (September 1941): 96.

107. Editorial, *Philadelphia Tribune*, October 27, 1927.

108. Walter White to George W. Crawford, Esq., May 18, 1931, Folder "Crime, 1931," Box 265, NAACP Papers.

109. Claude McKay, *A Long Way Home* (New York: Lee Furman, 1937), 8–9, quoted in Irma Watkins-Owens, *Blood Relations: Caribbean Immigrants and the Harlem Community, 1900–1930* (Bloomington: Indiana University Press, 1996), 5.

110. Sellin, "The Negro Criminal," 52.

111. Given Sellin's stature, his research strengthened the position of African American researchers as they sought evidence and support for their attacks on racial crime statistics. Du Bois wrote in 1931 that Sellin's article had been "illuminating"; W. E. B. Du Bois to Edwin R. Embree, May 12, 1931, in *The Correspondence of W. E. B. Du Bois*, ed. Herbert Aptheker (Amherst: University of Massachusetts Press, 1997). Ira De A. Reid also credited Sellin for being a major influence on the subject of race and crime: He "has again and again pointed up the fallacious use of statistics that is frequently employed to support a racial index to crime thesis"; "Race and Crime," *Friends Journal,* November 30, 1957, in Folder 4, Box 2, Reid Papers. In the 1960s and 1970s black researchers and civil rights leaders were still citing Sellin's early research; see Whitney M. Young, "Those Crime Figures," *New York Amsterdam News,* September 4, 1965; Alphonso Pinkney, "Laws Regulating Criminal Behavior Interact with Racism to Maintain Minority Oppression," *Washington Post,* October 20, 1977, 130.

112. Thorsten Sellin, "Race Prejudice in the Administration of Justice," AJS 41:2 (1935): 212–217.

113. *Philadelphia Tribune,* December 29, 1927.

114. Wilson, "The Responsibility for Crime," 97; "machinery of justice" is taken from "the machinery of justice is entirely in the hands of the white man," in Woofter, *The Basis of Racial Adjustment*, 125.

115. The Moore Vice Report actually spans thirteen months, but four white agents of unknown gender took over the investigation after four months. Of the roughly two hundred pages of the journal, approximately two-thirds were written by the black female agent.

116. My interpretation of her identity as a black clubwoman is informed by the similarities between her writing and that of the members of the National Association of Colored Women described by historian Deborah Gray White in *Too Heavy a Load: Black Women in Defense of Themselves, 1894–1994* (New York: W. W. Norton, 1999). None of the entries written by the white agents approach the colorful language and anxiety about black respectability found in the entries of the black female agent.

117. "January 29,1921, Re-visit-the Royal Palace—1732 Lombard St," 34, Moore Vice Report.

118. Ibid.; "January 7, 1921, Claver's Auditorium—Lombard St. above Twelfth," 9, Moore Vice Report.

119. Evelyn Brooks Higginbotham, *Righteous Discontent: The Women's Movement in the Black Baptist Church, 1880–1920* (Cambridge: Harvard University Press, 1993).

120. "April 1st, 1921," 135, Moore Vice Report.

121. The entire thirteen-month journal, covering two hundred single-spaced typewritten pages on legal-size paper, includes one mention of southerners: "The women are of a class that although they work out [as prostitutes] are willing to go out with a man for the extra money. Most of them are West Indian and Southern negroes, who have recently come North"; "January 13, 1921, Bengal Café," 14, Moore Vice Report.

122. "March 9, 1921, Furnished Room House 718 Lombard Street," 108; "January 8, 1921, 506 South 11th Street," 7; "January 8, 1921, Furnished Room House—410 S. 11th Street," 9; "January 8, 1921, Furnished Room House, 504 S. 11th Street," 10; "March 4, 1921, 502 South 11th Street—Furnished Room House, 96–97; "March 31, 1921, Furnished Room House, 518 So. 10th Street," 134; "February 18, 1921, 1313 Lombard Street—Furnished Room House," 75, Moore Vice Report.

123. *Philadelphia Tribune,* November 11, 1927.

124. "January 21, 1921, Street Report," 22; "January 25, 1921, Pool Hall on Broad Street . . . ," 28; "March 5, 1921, 1236 Waverly Street," 97–98; "January 25, 1921, University Pool Room—1706 South Street," 27; "January 25, 1921, Street Report," 26; "January 31, 1921, Revisit Hamilton's Café," 37; "February 17, 1921, Revisit Hamilton's Café," 72-73, Moore Vice Report.

125. "February 5, 1921, 1306 Kater Street," 46, Moore Vice Report.

126. Moore Vice Report, passim. The undercover agent did not tally numbers for South Philadelphia, but such an interpretation is reasonable based on her many references.

127. Committee of Fourteen, *Annual Report* (1928), 33, quoted in Greenburg, *"Or Does It Explode,"* 38. Looking at the same records, another historian calculates that whites owned 95 percent of the speakeasies in Harlem, while the remaining 5 percent were "owned and managed" by blacks; Thomas C. Mackey, *Pursuing Johns: Criminal Law Reform, Defending Character, and New York City's Committee of Fourteen, 1920–1930* (Columbus: Ohio State University Press, 2005), 53.

128. Greenburg, *"Or Does It Explode,"* 38.

129. CCRR, *Negro in Chicago,* 622; Woofter, *Negro Problem in Cities,* 275, 280–281; Haller, "Urban Crime and Criminal Justice," 620.

130. "Club Paree Reopens as an Exclusive White Night Club / Discrimination in Police Department," *Philadelphia Tribune,* December 27, 1927. The following year the *Tribune* continued to focus on police raids: "Police Raid Negro Homes; Miss Whites / Fearing Demotions or Suspension, Captains Make Negroes 'Goats' / White Places Winked At." The article stated that "police captains in districts heavily populated with Negroes have gone on a frenzied rampage of what are reported to be illegal raids in an effort to save their necks from the ax of demotion or suspension. . . . The sanctity of the home means little to these desperate commanders. The racial identity means much, however. . . . The Negroes are being made the 'goats' in this sudden gesture at a 'snow white' district. . . . In two of the South

Philadelphia districts not one white raid was reported, although an extraordinarily large number of raids on colored homes were reported." *Philadelphia Tribune,* September 13, 1928.

131. "Been Raided," *Philadelphia Tribune,* September 13, 1928.

132. Sutherland, *Principles of Criminology* (1934), 111; Watkins-Owens, *Blood Relations,* 139.

133. Ferdinand Morton, "Memorandum *re* Conditions in Harlem," April 25, 1932, 2, Series C, Box 305, NAACP Papers, quoted in Greenburg, *"Or Does It Explode,"* 301.

134. "Chicago Police Covering up Criminal Connections by Attacks on Negroes," New York *Amsterdam News,* December 29, 1926.

135. Reckless, *Vice in Chicago,* 15, 30.

136. Quoted in Victoria W. Wolcott, *Remaking Respectability: African American Women in Interwar Detroit* (Chapel Hill: University of North Carolina Press, 2001), 111. Regarding the discriminatory police treatment black women experienced—as prostitutes or not—historian Cheryl D. Hicks writes, "Many women found that seeking and experiencing leisure was a double-edged sword, as police frame-ups occurred often. Women (and men) found that the cheap and pleasurable practice of visiting friends in their tenement rooms was a dangerous form of leisure. The simple act of enjoying the company of friends could mean an arrest for solicitation"; Cheryl D. Hicks, "Confined to Womanhood: Women, Prisons, and Race in New York State, 1890–1935" (Ph.D. diss., Princeton University, 1999), 41. See also Kevin J. Mumford, *Interzones: Black/White Sex Districts in Chicago and New York in the Early Twentieth Century* (New York: Columbia University Press, 1997).

137. Watkins-Owens, *Blood Relations,* 146.

138. "March 2, 1921, Street Report," 95, Moore Vice Report.

139. Drake and Cayton, *Black Metropolis,* 695.

140. CCRR, *Negro in Chicago,* 355–356.

141. Kellogg, *NAACP, A History,* 23, 61, 146, 214.

142. "Faked 'Murder by Negroes' to Hide Suicide Due to Finance," Press Release, May 22, 1931, Folder "Crime, 1931," Box 265, NAACP Papers.

143. "Mob Killed Wrong Negro, Girls Fear," Press Release, October 10, 1924, Folder "Crime, 1923, 1924," Box 264; "'Black Brute' Absolved of Crime after Torture by Pennsylvania Police," Press Release, n.d., Folder "Crime, Undated," Box 265; "Police Shoot Negroes in 2 Cities, N.A.A.C.P. Asking Justice," March 8, 1929, Folder "Crime, 1929, July-August," Box 265, NAACP Papers.

144. "Jersey City Branch Defeats Curfew," Press Release, n.d.; *New York Times,* December 8, 1920; Walter White to Frank I. Cobb, December 9, 1920; *The Echo* (Red Bank, N.J.), December 11, 1920, all in Folder, "Crime, 1920, '21, '23–'28," Box 264, NAACP Papers.

145. *Daily Times* (Chattanooga, Tenn.), December 11, 1920.

146. New York *Herald,* December 9, 1920; *New York Times,* December 8, 1920, all in Folder, "Crime, 1920, '21, '23–'28," Box 264, NAACP Papers.

147. Walter White to Frank Cobb, December 9, 1920, Folder, "Crime, 1920, '21, '23–'28," Box 264, NAACP Papers.

148. "Police Shoot Negroes in 2 Cities, N.A.A.C.P. Asking Justice," March 8, 1929, Folder "Crime, 1929, July–August," Box 265, NAACP Papers.

149. For examples, see *Philadelphia Tribune,* May 22, 1930, February 12, 1931.

150. "A Sample of Police Brutality," *Philadelphia Tribune,* May 30, 1929, 2; "Police Brutality Discussed at Meeting in Indianapolis," *Philadelphia Tribune,* August 27, 1931, 14; "Citizens Protest Police Brutality," *Philadelphia Tribune,* June 11, 1936, 16; "NAACP Joins White Groups in Protesting: Police Brutality Brings Interracial Cooperation in Camden," *Philadelphia Tribune,* December 14, 1933, 9.

151. By the 1920s, as many scholars note, European immigrants increasingly secured a permanent foothold as "white" based on a number of factors, including immigration restriction, unionization, ethnic succession, anti-black homeowners' resistance, and mob violence. See Mathew Frye Jacobson, *Whiteness of a Different Color: European Immigrants and the Alchemy of Race* (Cambridge: Harvard University Press, 1998); Mathew Pratt Guterl, *The Color of Race in America* (Cambridge: Harvard University Press, 2001); Thomas A. Guglielmo, *White on Arrival: Italians, Race, Color, and Power in Chicago, 1890–1945* (New York: Oxford University Press, 2003). To the factors above, I would add that Prohibition era interethnic organized crime and attempts to fight it helped further the breakdown of white ethnic distinctions; see Humbert Nelli, *Italians in Chicago, 1880–1930: A Study in Ethnic Mobility* (New York: Oxford University Press, 1970), and *The Business of Crime: Italians and Syndicate Crime in the United States* (New York: Oxford University Press, 1976); Jenna Weissman Joselit, *Our Gang: Jewish Crime and the New York Jewish Community, 1900–1940* (Bloomington: Indiana University Press, 1983).

152. *New York Times,* January 2, 1930, 32.

153. Johnson, *Street Violence,* 135.

154. Lawrence Rosen, "The Creation of the Uniform Crime Report," *Social Science History* 19:2 (1995): 217, 221; Sellin, "The Uniform Criminal Statistics Act," 682.

155. U.S. Wickersham Commission, *Report on Criminal Statistics,* vol. 3:3 (Washington, D.C.: GPO, 1931), 10–12; *New York Times,* October 13, November 23, 1929. Jerome H. Skolnick and James J. Fyfe, *Above the Law: Police and the Excessive Use of Force* (New York: The Free Press, 1993): "More than any other single action, it [*Uniform Crime Reports*] introduced and legitimized *numbers* as measures of police effectiveness" (130).

156. As late as 1950, the *Uniform Crime Reports* were still not comprehensive. They covered urban populations only, amounting to about half of the U.S. population; Sellin, "The Uniform Criminal Statistics Act," 682. Today all major news outlets continue to publish the latest crime trends revealed by the annual *Uniform Crime Reports,* and social scientists continue to use the data for statistical analysis.

157. There were fifteen cities in total: New York, Buffalo, Boston, Newark, Philadelphia, Cincinnati, Cleveland, Detroit, Chicago, Dallas, El Paso, Denver, Los Angeles, San Francisco, and Seattle; U.S. Wickersham Commission, *Report on Lawlessness and Law Enforcement,* vol. 11 (Washington, D.C.: GPO, 1931), 15.

158. Based on 1930 records kept by the Legal Aid Society of New York's Voluntary Defenders Committee, Johnson calculated that African American men (5 percent of Manhattan's population) made up 36 percent of the clients reporting

brutality; Johnson, *Street Violence,* 136; Wickersham, *Lawlessness and Law Enforcement,* Appendix IV, 225–232. Johnson also notes that Ernest Jerome Hopkins, an investigative reporter for the *San Francisco Examiner* hired by the commission to conduct fieldwork on police abuses, published his own book in which he left out black northerners but "wrote eloquently about the discriminatory use of the third degree against immigrants and police terror in the South"; Ernest Jerome Hopkins, *Our Lawless Police* (New York: Viking Press, 1931); Johnson, *Street Violence,* 136.

159. "A Letter to the Wickersham Commission," *Philadelphia Tribune,* August 20, 1931.

160. "Crime, a Problem for the Whole Nation: National Conference Planned," *Literary Digest* 118 (October 20, 1934): 22; "National Crime Conference, Washington," *Newsweek* 4 (December 22, 1934): 5; Zangrando, *The NAACP Crusade,* 93–94. Two years earlier, at the NAACP's annual meeting in Washington, D.C., a discussion of the Scottsboro convictions and anti-black jury bias prompted this statement: "In the recent investigation conducted by the Wickersham Commission there was regrettably too little attention given to this phase of our legal machinery. . . . There is no present relief in sight"; quoted in Floyd J. Calvin, "N.A.A.C.P. Holds Significant Meeting in Shadow of White House," *Pittsburgh Courier,* May 28, 1932.

161. Ira De A. Reid, "Notes on the Negro's Relation to Work and Law Observance," in U.S. Wickersham Commission, *Report on Causes of Crime,* vol. 13:1 (Washington, D.C.: GPO, 1931), 219–255.

162. The commissioners were also impressed by the evidence presented at the National Interracial Conference that blacks were racially discriminated against in employment. The tone of their statement implied that this was surprising: "The Negro appears to have a special problem in relation to unemployment as well as to crime," they wrote; "Foreword," *Report on Causes of Crime,* vol. 13:1, 167. Sellin's paper at the National Interracial Conference was published as Thorsten Sellin, "The Negro and the Problem of Law Observance and Administration in the Light of Social Research," in Charles S. Johnson, *The Negro in American Civilization* (New York: Henry Holt, 1930).

163. Reid, "Notes on Work," 222. As sociologist Tukufu Zuberi notes, late-twentieth-century racial statisticians routinely conduct these kinds of analyses by "controlling for the correlation of variables in their regression models," but often without recognizing the limits of determining causality or the indeterminacy of using "race as a proxy for other social and biological causes"; *Thicker Than Blood: How Racial Statistics Lie* (Minneapolis: University of Minnesota Press, 2001), 93–97.

CONCLUSION

1. Nathaniel Cantor, "Crime and the Negro," *Journal of Negro History* 16 (January 1931): 66.

2. Historian Cheryl Lynn Greenburg argues, for example, that "Harlem crime rates documented police bigotry and corruption as much as they revealed Harlem's poverty and unsatisfactory conditions"; Greenburg, *"Or Does It Explode": Black Harlem in the Great Depression* (New York: Oxford University Press, 1991), 195.

3. Hans Von Hentig, "The Criminality of the Negro," *Journal of Criminal Law and Criminology* 30:5 (1940): 668. In a footnote, he cited Chicago Commission on Race Relations, *The Negro in Chicago: A Study of Race Relations and a Race Riot* (Chicago: University of Chicago Press, 1922).

4. Du Bois quoted Hoffman saying in his 1922 annual survey of homicides that "it will be noted that the cities experiencing the highest rates are those having a large colored population." Taking great exception, Du Bois responded, "Mr. Hoffman . . . may still be counted as he was when he published that vicious book 'Race Traits and Tendencies of the American Negro'—as one of the most persistent and subtle enemies of the Negro race." W. E. B Du Bois, "Crime," *Crisis* 23:5 (March 1922): 200–201.

5. I reviewed race tables in all reports from the 1930s through the 1950s, but my analysis pertains to the period 1933–1946; see U.S. Department of Justice, *Uniform Crime Reports* (Washington: GPO, 1930–1956). The standard explanatory paragraph that accompanied the race table under the heading "Data Compiled from Fingerprints" underwent repeated and often subtle changes over the years. Between 1936 and 1940, for example, the foreign-born category gradually slipped from the lead sentence in the main explanatory paragraph but remained in the second to third sentences, after which all mention ceased. From 1935 to 1956, all race tables included the categories "Indian," "Chinese," "Japanese," "Mexican," and "All Others." Little text accompanied these statistical categories. The 1939 report stated, for example, "Other racial groups were much less frequently represented, as indicated in the following figures."

6. T. J Woofter, Jr., *Negro Problems in Cities* (1928, reprinted New York: Negro Universities Press, 1969), 125.

7. "Data Compiled from Fingerprints," *Uniform Crime Reports,* 1940, 223.

8. "Paternalist generalities" comes from David Levering Lewis, *W. E. B. Du Bois: Biography of a Race* (New York: Henry Holt, 1993), 206.

9. For similar comments, see ibid., 208.

10. W. E. B. Du Bois, "The Conservation of the Races," *Occasional Papers* 2 (American Negro Academy, 1897), reprinted in David Levering Lewis, ed., *W. E. B. Du Bois: A Reader* (New York: Henry Holt, 1995), 26; W. E. B. Du Bois, *The Philadelphia Negro* (1899, reprinted with an introduction by Herbert Aptheker, Millwood, N.Y.: Kraus-Thomson Organization Ltd., 1973), 390–392.

11. W. E. B. Du Bois, "Criminals," *Crisis,* January 1931, 29; "Courts and Jails," *Crisis,* April 1932, 39.

12. Focusing on Chinese immigrant vice in early twentieth century San Francisco, David Courtwright argues that every groups' crime manifests itself to varying degrees through cultural expressions; David Courtwright, *Violent Land: Single Men and Social Disorder from the Frontier to the Inner City* (1996, reprinted Cambridge: Harvard University Press, 2001), 160–162. But Jeffrey Adler warns not to overemphasize cultural distinctiveness: "First, despite the distinctive experience born of racism, African American homicide, was remarkably similar in character to white homicide. African American Chicagoans were not the reckless and pathological criminals described by conservative observers"; Adler, "The Negro Would be More Than an Angel to Withstand Such Treatment," 309.

13. Humbert S. Nelli, *The Business of Crime: Italians and Syndicate Crime in the United States* (New York: Oxford University Press, 1976), 168.

14. Edwin H. Sutherland, *Principles of Criminology* (Philadelphia: J. B. Lippincott Co., 1934), 115.

15. Mark H. Haller, "Introduction," in *Organized Crime in Chicago: Part III of The Illinois Crime Survey, 1929*, ed. John Landesco (1929, reprinted Chicago: University of Chicago Press, 1968), xiii. Émile Durkheim, *Suicide: A Study in Sociology*, trans. John A. Spalding and George Simpson (1951, reprinted New York: Free Press, 1966); Robert K. Merton, *Social Theory and Social Structure* (New York: Free Press, 1957).

16. Daniel Bell, "Crime as an American Way of Life," *The Antioch Review*, 1953, 131–154.

17. In his 1970 study of first- and second-generation Italian immigrants in Chicago during the early twentieth century, historian Humbert S. Nelli uses the sociological concepts that were built into modern explanations of ethnic criminality: "In the new urban home—cynical, cruel, vulgar, avaricious Chicago—Sicilians and Italians, northern as well as southern, joined together for mutual benefit and profit. Because of its function as a means of economic betterment and social mobility, crime occupied a place in the acculturation of Italians in the United States, along with immigrant community institutions, education, the padrone system, and politics." Humbert S. Nelli, *Italians in Chicago, 1880–1930: A Study in Ethnic Mobility* (New York: Oxford University Press, 1970), 155; see also Nelli, *The Business of Crime;* Jenna Weissman Joselit, *Our Gang: Jewish Crime and the New York Jewish Community, 1900–1940* (Bloomington: Indiana University Press, 1983). These historical analyses deemphasize crime as a problem of group culture rather than of social inequality.

18. Frederick L. Hoffman, *Race Traits and Tendencies of the American Negro* (New York: American Economic Association, 1896); Du Bois, *The Philadelphia Negro;* Franz Boas, *The Mind of Primitive Man* (New York: Macmillan, 1911); Charles S. Johnson and the Chicago Commission on Race Relations, *The Negro in Chicago: A Study of Race Relations and a Race Riot* (Chicago: University of Chicago Press, 1922); Gunnar Myrdal, *An American Dilemma: The Negro Problem and Modern Democracy*, 20th anniversary ed. (New York: Harper & Row, 1962).

19. Myrdal, *The Negro Problem and Modern Democracy*, 529.

20. Merton, *Social Theory and Social Structure;* Bell, "Crime as an American Way of Life." Historian Roger Lane whose work stood for two decades as the only book-length historical analysis of black criminality in the urban North similarly Americanized immigrant criminality and pathologized black criminality, see Roger Lane, *Roots of Violence in Black Philadelphia, 1860–1900* (Cambridge: Harvard University Press, 1986).

21. Ibid., 929, 969.

No history book could ever be written without the support and hard work of librarians and archivists. I would like to thank the staffs of the Balch Institute of Ethnic Studies in Center City Philadelphia; the Charles L. Blockson Afro-American Collection and the Urban Archives at Temple University, especially Margaret Jerrido and Brenda Stevenson; the Criminal Justice/National Council on Crime and Delinquency Library at Rutgers University, especially Phyllis Shultze; the Friends Historical Library at Swarthmore College; the Historical Society of Pennsylvania; the Library Company of Philadelphia; the Manuscript Division at the Library of Congress, especially Adrienne Canon and Ahmed Johnson; the Moorland-Spingarn Research Center at Howard University, especially Joellen El Bashir and Esme Bhan; the Nursing History Center at the University of Pennsylvania; the Philadelphia City Archives; the Schomburg Center for Research and Black Culture in New York City; and the diligent Interlibrary Loan staff of the Indiana University Libraries.

I received crucial research funding from Rutgers University, Indiana University (IU), and the Andrew W. Mellon Foundation/Vera Institute of Justice. Though not in dollars and cents, the IU History department administrative staff provided generous assistance with both their kindness and willingness to help facilitate manuscript production. Likewise, the editors, production staff, and anonymous reviewers led by Kathleen McDermott at Harvard University Press graciously shepherded the manuscript to publication.

Among the many people who contributed to my training and helped to shape the subject matter of this book, I owe many thanks to my undergraduate and graduate professors. At the University of Pennsylvania, Herman Beavers, Neil Leonard, John Roberts, Howard Stevenson, Janet Tighe, Joseph Washington, and Robert Wilson, introduced me to the study of African American life, history, and culture. Nikki Taylor, by her own example, deserves much credit for inspiring me to pursue a Ph.D. in History. At Rutgers University, I am indebted to Mia Bay, Herman Bennett, Carolyn Brown, Paul Clemens, David Fogelsong, Al Howard, Sonia Jarvis, Jonathan Lurie, Norman Markowitz, Gregory Mixon, David Oshinsky, Clement A. Price, and Deborah Gray White. It is impossible to recount the innumerable ways in which my fellow graduate students helped to shape my thinking: Zain Abdullah, Christian Alcindor, John Aveni, Jennifer Brier, William Jelani Cobb, Christopher Fisher, Tiffany Gill, Matthew Guterl, Justin Hart, Daniel Katz, Peter Lao, James Levy, Amrita Myers, Amina Pilgrim, Kalena Reid, Stephanie Sims, and Martin Summers. Special recognition goes to my dissertation committee whose supervision, counsel, tough love, and respect guided this book from inception to rough draft. David Levering Lewis was a constant presence in my life as my advisor, always pushing me to write better and faster and to get my work done. Virginia Yans read my work with the sharpest of eyes, making sure that my arguments matched the evidence. Jim Livingston, as is his trade mark, helped me to think about the big questions of political economy and historical narrative. And Thomas Sugrue gave generously of his time to help guide my initial formulations as well as to read and comment on the entire manuscript.

I was fortunate to benefit from the advice and suggestions of several individuals who did not have to take an interest my work. Ralph Austen, Alex Bontemps, and Sterling Stuckey were instrumental in encouraging me to become an historian. Mark Haller and the late Eric Monkkonen provided the perfect balance of skepticism and encouragement to a rooky researcher with far too many unpolished questions. Members of the American Studies department at Purdue University, the American Italian Historical Association, especially Jerry Krase, David Roediger, and the late Rudolf J. Vecoli, the Social Science History Association, and faculty at the John Jay College of Criminal Justice provided thoughtful feedback on my research at various stages of development. Keith Wailoo gave candid and indispensable advice about how to write a book, and was a first-rate mentor at Rutgers while leading me and several others in a year-long research assistantship; my peers also gave generous feedback on the book: Curt Caldwell, Stephanie Pfeiffer, Laura Waxman; and especially, Richard Mizelle and Stephen Pemberton. My colleagues at the Vera Institute of Justice welcomed me into the real world of criminal justice reform and research. Michael Bobbitt, Robin Campbell, Tina Chiu, Ernest

Duncan, Zaire Flores, Karen Goldstein, Linda Green, Karen Greene, Nicole Henderson, Michael Jacobson, Anita Khashu, Ali Knight, Clinton Lacey, Francesca Levy, Jeff Lin, Van Lu, Hester Lyons, Delma McDonald, Wayne McKenzie, Keesha Middlemass, Andres Rengifo, Tim Ross, Don Stemon, Christopher Stone, Gloria Tate, Andy Toth, Nick Turner, Daniel Wilhelm, Jon Wool, Phil Valdez, Geoff Ward, and Alicia Young helped me to make history relevant to their otherwise contemporary concerns. My Vera co-conspirator and brother-in-research arms Joao Costa Vargas taught me valuable lessons about the limits of the scholarly work that we do and the unmet challenges of the world we live in.

Friendship and collegiality are essential ingredients to finishing a book. I have many wonderful people to thank for their curiosity, patience, and critical feedback. William Jelani Cobb is a constant presence in my life, even if by phone, always offering timely scholarly and publishing advice. Sharlimar Douglass continues to be my own private tutor on black womanist theory and practice. Matthew Guterl, my old seminar mate from Rutgers, and his wife Sandra Latcha and their two adorable children have become part of our Bloomington family. I owe Matt more than I should admit for helping me to see this book through to completion. Matt along with Kon Dierks, Sarah Knott, Amrita Myers, and Kirsten Sword, members of an IU writing group, deserve many thanks for their two rounds of critical feedback on the manuscript. Among my IU friends and colleagues who offered publishing advice, read portions of the manuscript, or gave encouragement when I needed it, I would like to thank Steven Andrews, A. B. Assensoh, Stephen Berrey (now at University of Michigan), Jon Bodnar, Kevin Brown, Maria Bucur, Claude Clegg, Deborah Cohen (now at University of Missouri-St. Louis), Nick Cullather, Deborah Deliyannis, Arlene Diaz, Ellen Dwyer, Ben Eklof, Wanda Ewing, Jeff Gould, Valerie Grim, Michael Grossberg, Ted Hall, Carl Ipsen, Sylvester Johnson, Matthias Lehman, Ed Linenthal, Jim Madison, Marissa Moorman, Frank Motley, John Nieto-Phillips, Eric Sandweiss, Robert Schneider, Micol Seigel, Steve Selka, Quincy Stewart, Steven Stowe, David Thelen, Jeffrey Veidlinger, Ed Watts, Jeff Wasserstrom (now at UC-Berkeley), Steven Wagschal, Dror Wahrman, Garfield Warren, Vernon Williams, and Ellen Wu. Several graduate students shared key insights about my work through criticism and/or conversation about their own research: Ryon Cobb, Delphine Criscenzo, Tanisha Ford, Siobhan Carter-David, William Gillis, Andrew Kahrl (now at Marquette University), Rashawn Ray, Judah Schept, Kim Stanley, Carl Suddler, and Jeremy

Young. Delphine was an excellent research and editorial assistant, who, along with Cyndy Brown, provided critical last minute assistance.

Lodging, hot meals, life-giving energy, and financial support came from many sources far removed from the academy. There are many close friends whose care and generosity sustained me and my family over the many years of this project. Claude and Lea Knight turned several research trips to Philadelphia into mini vacations because of their four-star hospitality. Anthony and Chris Rome made my stays at their place in Washington, D.C. feel like home away from home. Benjamin and Danielle Austen, friends of more than half my life, gave me many pep-talks, head-rubs, and laughs when I needed to know that they believed in me. Ben also generously read portions of the manuscript deftly wielding his editorial pen. In addition to his steadfast support and encouragement, everyone needs tough love to stay on track and Garfield Johnson dispensed small doses when necessary. Amon and Luz Johnson, Jon Chimene and Stephanie Mazza, as well as Charles Price, always cheered me on and either fed me, lent me money, or entertained me when in their company. Mashod Evans, my first undergraduate student, convinced me that teaching history well could inspire someone's life. The Davis's, Fielder's, Ince's, Newman's, and Redd's, as well as my Oakridge Street friends and Bethel Bloomington family gave me the sense of community I needed in order to be grounded over the many years of writing.

Words are not enough to express exactly how much my family means to me and how appreciative I am of all of their emotional and financial support. I have been truly blessed to have extraordinary parents in my life who have always believed in me. Kimberly Bettina Muhammad and Ozier Muhammad brought me into this world and made it as beautiful and nurturing as two parents could. As models of hard-working, successful people they also showed me that I could be passionate about my work and that I could do something meaningful with my life and be paid for it. Their care for others and concerns about the kind of world we live in have influenced me in countless ways, starting me on a journey that has thus far brought me to this book. My stepmother Lisa Redd's spirit, affection, and love of life are unsurpassed in this world, and I have benefitted greatly from drawing on her experience as a journalist. Over the many years that I was unemployed and married to their daughter, my in-laws Doris and Norris Jennings treated me like their own, opening their home to me for much needed quiet time to write. My father-in-law Robert Lawson with his awful memories of being bored to death in history classes inspired me to make history relevant and exciting. My sister-in-law Melanie Lawson watched our kids on many a weekend, freeing me to work. Many aunts, uncles, and cousins have been my staunchest supporters.

Little might have come of my ideas were it not for the love of my life. Stephanie Lawson-Muhammad put her heart into this book in a way that no other could and gave me everything she had at times to make sure that I met deadlines. Down in the trenches with me, she made my life so much more beautiful and complete. Our children, Gibran Mikkel, Jordan Grace, and Justice Marie, budding artists, poets, and authors themselves, are the embodiment of our brightest hopes and biggest dreams. I dedicate this book to them, to Stephanie, and to my parents.

Abraham, A. A., 251

Addams, Jane, 7, 9, 68, 88, 103, 105, 117–125, 128, 133, 136, 138–139, 144, 153–154, 158, 164, 271

Adler, Jeffrey S., 6, 54, 288n22, 288n23, 348n51, 366n12

African Methodist Episcopal churches (A.M.E.), 149, 175, 178, 196

Anderson, Matthew, 176, 183

Armstrong, General Samuel Chapman, 18, 38, 52, 171–172, 180

Armstrong Association of Philadelphia (AAP), 163, 180–183, 185, 188, 190, 211, 218

Association for Equalizing of Industrial Opportunities (AEIO), 163, 184–186, 188–190

Association for the Protection of Colored Women (Philadelphia), 163, 177, 181, 187, 207

Baker, Ray Stannard, 28–29, 160–161

Ball, M. V., 43–45, 48–49, 51, 54, 57, 86, 90, 145, 269

Baptist churches, 176–177, 179, 182–183, 185, 187, 189

Bartholomew, Francis R., 153–154, 185

Battersby, R. T., 262–263

Bell, Daniel, 275

Benezet House, 230

Bennet, William S., 103, 110

Benson, William E., 107–108

Blackmar, Frank, 29, 84

Blankenburg, Rudolph J., 189–199, 204, 224

Boas, Franz, 9, 90, 98–99, 103, 105–106, 109–114, 119, 122, 125, 137, 139–141, 243, 276

Bois, Maurine, 242

Bond, Adella, 213–215, 220–221

Boston (MA), 28, 39, 54, 101, 103, 105–106, 131, 134–138, 170, 235

Bowen, Louis De Koven, 117, 121, 127–129, 140

Brandt, Lillian, 106

Breckinridge, Sophonisba P., 117, 128

Brown, John, 201–204

Bruce, Philip Alexander, 50–51

Bulkley, William L., 108

Burgess, Ernest W., 236, 238, 241

Burke, William, 196

Burroughs, Nannie, 190

Bushee, Frederick, 101, 103, 105, 134, 138

Calkins, Gary L., 57

Cantor, Nathaniel, 243–244, 269–270

Chamberlain, Bernard Peyton, 244

Chester (PA) Race Riot, 211, 213, 228

Chicago (IL), 5–7, 12, 26, 28, 36, 46, 51, 53–54, 56, 59, 63, 65, 68, 78, 81, 106, 109, 118–121, 123–127, 129–133, 144, 146, 154, 158, 161, 192, 206, 223, 226, 229, 231, 236–243, 249, 251, 259–262, 266, 275

Chicago Commission on Race Relations (CCRR), 228, 235, 237, 239–241, 245, 249; or the Johnson Report, 246
Chicago Race Riot, 127, 236–237, 239
Chicago School of Sociology, 7, 12, 231, 236–238, 269
Chicago Vice Commission, 121, 133, 226, 233
Christiansburg Industrial Institute, 169
Clarke, Rupert, 252–253
Coates, Thomas G., 201, 204
College Settlement House (CSH), 147, 155, 161
Collender, Reginald, 213–214
Commission on Interracial Cooperation, 244, 254
Committee of Fourteen, 259
Creditt, W. A., 183
Crime prevention, and Americanization, 9, 12, 30, 103–104, 143, 157–159, 273; and financial costs, 11, 129–130, 144; and racism, 9, 76, 124, 126, 127, 146, 160–161, 193, 205, 224–225, 231
Crime statistics, and race, 1–8, 12, 19–20, 34, 86, 90, 105, 269–271, 273–274, 277; and *Uniform Crime Reports*, 13, 77, 91, 266, 270. *See also* Education, and crime statistics; Police; Racial Criminalization
Cunningham, R. M., 42–43, 45, 48

Daniels, John, 105–106, 108, 134–141, 160
Darwin, Charles, 18–19, 22
Davenport, Charles V., 110
Davis, Allen F., 103, 124
Davis, Charles, 241–242
Dickerson, G. Edward, 188, 201, 216, 260
Dixon, Thomas, Jr., 83, 85, 90
Donald, Henderson H., 232–235
Douglass, Frederick, 26, 135
Du Bois, W. E. B., 3, 10, 25, 58, 60, 74–75, 77, 87, 88, 90, 92–93, 97, 104–105, 114, 129, 139, 145, 147, 164–166, 172–173, 175, 180, 183–185, 187, 189, 207–208,

223, 227–228, 238; and criticisms of police, 116; criticisms of racial criminalization, 62–73, 76, 78, 81, 85, 91, 94, 95, 112, 141, 143, 168, 170, 178–179, 193, 243, 247, 262, 269–272, 284n12, 314n151, 318n191, 330n149, 366n4; and *The Philadelphia Negro*, 65, 67–68, 70–73, 81, 114, 134, 146, 178, 227, 272, 276
Durkheim, Emile, 275, 300n84, 303n21

Earp, Edwin L., 84
Eastern State Penitentiary, 43, 214
Education, and crime statistics, 1, 97; as anti-crime solution, 18, 38, 75, 90, 169–172, 180; as crime stimulus, 4, 51–52, 57, 94–96, 262; and criminal records of black college students, 96–97, 170–171; and debates about race relations, 83, 93, 273
Emerson, Helena Titus, 115
Emlen, John T., 180–181
Ethnic succession, 13, 271, 275, 357n61, 364n151
Evans, John R., 219

Fald, George, 251–252
Falkner, Ronald P., 76–77
Federal Bureau of Investigations (FBI), 91, 266, 270
Fortune, T. Thomas, 28, 185
Fosdick, Raymond, 224
Frazier, E. Franklin, 236, 241, 355–356n46, 357n61
Frederick Douglass Center, 109, 132
Friends Neighborhood Guild (FNG), 157–159, 161
Frissell, H. B., 172–173

Garner, J. W., 84
Giddings, Franklin H., 79, 317n187
Gilman, Charlotte Perkins, 85
Gilyard, Raymond E., 253–254, 261
Gossett, Thomas, 23, 28
Grammer, Carl E., 181

Hall, G. Stanley, 18, 75–76, 124
Haller, Mark, 251, 275
Hampton Institute, 18, 38, 52, 73, 75, 97, 169–172, 180
Harris, Frank, 251
Haynes, George Edmund, 126, 144, 181–182
Helper, Hinton Rowan, 16–18, 21–22
Henderson, Charles R., 7, 46, 89
Henderson, Robert, 199–201, 203–204
Hentig, Hans Von, 270, 360n91
Hoffman, Frederick L., 6, 19, 37; and progressives, 38, 39, 41, 47, 57, 303n24; and *Race Traits and Tendencies of the American Negro*, 35–36, 38, 41, 46, 49, 51–53, 59, 73, 169, 207, 242, 276; and racial criminalization, 45–56, 91, 270, 366n4; and racial Darwinism, 38–45, 86, 88, 95, 281n2, 303–304n25
Hull House, 103, 105, 117–119, 126, 129, 154, 195

Illinois Crime Survey, 249, 266, 275
Inasmuch Mission, 194–196
International Association of Chiefs of Police (IACP), 266, 270

Jackson, A. L., 262
Jersey City (NJ), 262–263
Johnson, Charles S., 12, 236–241, 246, 267, 276
Johnson, Guy B., 254
Johnson, James Weldon, 251–252, 261–262
Johnson, Lyndon B., 77
Johnson, Marilyyn S., 49, 266
Jones, Eugene Kinckle, 182, 231
Juvenile delinquency, 12, 99, 116, 118–121, 123–125, 127–128, 168, 182, 197, 230–231, 238, 251, 314n151

Katznelson, Ira, 13, 74
Kavanagh, Marcus, 245
Kelley, Florence, 68
Kelley, Robin D. G., 7, 289n24, 290n31
Kellor, Frances, 88–90, 94, 97–100, 103, 105–108, 117, 122, 132, 134, 138, 254,

319n1, 320n9, 325n74, 325n75, 333–334n197
Kelsey, Carl, 92–93, 104–106, 108, 110, 119, 125, 139, 144, 180, 185
Kusmer, Kenneth, 226, 249, 290n32

Landesco, John L., 236, 238, 241, 274–275
Lane, Roger, 121, 282n4, 287n20, 307n57, 314n151, 329n136, 329n138, 367n20
Lasch-Quinn, Elisabeth, 128, 134, 140
Lavery, Hugh, 217
Layten, Sadie, 177, 190, 207, 247
League of Civic and Political Reform (LCPR), 163, 184–185, 187–190, 193, 198
Lee, B. F., Jr., 181, 185
Lewis, David Levering, 24, 29–30, 52, 67, 73, 85, 129, 180
Lewis, Preston, 217–219
Liberalism, 10, 13, 146, 294n52
Lichtenberger, J. P., 119, 138–139, 144
Lombroso, Cesare, 47, 89
Lowden, Frank O., 236

MacKay-Smith, Alexander, 185
Mann Act (also White Slave Traffic Act), 133, 194, 333n188, 345n6
Mayo-Smith, Richard, 33, 301n86
McCord, Charles H., 127–128
McGill, S. Waters, 128
McKay, Claude, 255, 259
McKay, Henry D., 236, 238, 241, 266
McKinley, William, 158–159
McLaughlin, Steve, 201–204
McVay, Thomas, 217
Merriam, Charles, 261
Merton, Robert, 275
Miller, Kelly, 11, 60, 62–64, 78, 95–96, 112, 166, 247, 251
Moore, E. W., 183
Moore, J. Hampton, 256, 260
Morgan, Frances Armstrong, 38, 52, 307n67
Morton, Samuel George, 16, 22
Mossell, Sadie T., 60, 208–210, 220, 232
Mumford, Kevin J., 121, 133, 329n137
Myrdal, Gunnar, 276–277

National Association for the Advancement of Colored People (NAACP), 9, 12, 29, 97, 104, 114, 116–117, 122, 124, 130, 141, 143, 163–164, 172, 178, 207, 223, 228, 231–232, 235, 237, 244, 246, 251–252, 254, 256, 259, 261–262, 267, 324n68, 344n171

National Association of Colored Women, 58, 231

National Commission on Law Observance and Enforcement (also Wickersham Commission), 266–268, 365n160

National Interracial Conference, 267, 365n162

National League for the Protection of Colored Women, 106, 134

National Urban League (NUL), 12, 107, 114, 126–127, 145, 163, 181–182, 211, 228–231, 242, 246, 248, 262, 284n10

Negro Fellowship League, 130–131

Negro Problem, 1, 15, 17, 19, 20, 25, 30, 33–39, 42, 45, 52, 54–55, 58, 62, 65–69, 74, 85–87, 90, 91, 134, 138, 153, 169, 171, 173, 178, 205, 273

Nelli, Humbert, 274, 367n17

New York City, 5–6, 28, 36, 40, 43, 48–49, 53–56, 59, 74–75, 80–81, 97, 106, 114–117, 122, 126, 131, 141, 146, 154, 166–167, 177, 180, 192, 206, 226, 231, 251–255, 259–260, 263, 266

North House Association, 157

Nott, Josiah C., 22–23

Octavia Hill Association, 149–151, 153, 161

Ovington, Mary White, 9, 97–98, 103–105, 114–117, 120, 122–124, 134, 139–140, 154

Page, Thomas Nelson, 82–83, 85, 90, 93, 105, 108

Park, Robert E., 236, 238, 241, 290n31

Patterson, Orlando, 3, 282n4, 284n12

Philadelphia, 5–6, 10, 22, 28, 36, 40, 43, 51, 53, 59–60, 65–71, 81, 92, 106, 121, 131, 145, 146–228, 230, 232–235,

238, 242, 247, 249–250, 255–260, 263, 265–266

Philadelphia Race Riot, 211–223, 228, 242, 249

Philadelphia Vice Commission, 177, 191–193, 196–198, 207, 211, 345n2

Phillips, Henry L., 177, 198, 211, 221

Philpott, Thomas, 126, 161

Plessy v. Ferguson, 36, 163

Plummer, Mary, 132

Poe, Clarence H., 94–95, 119, 262

Police, 6, 119, 152; and brutality, 12, 49, 188, 201, 204, 217–219, 221, 232, 249–253, 287n21, 293–294n50; and calls for community assistance, 11, 116, 126, 155, 190, 193, 207, 222, 229, 249, 261; and crime statistics, 12, 196–198, 216, 229, 233–236, 239–243, 269, 346n17, 360n91, 360n98, 365n2; injured or killed by black men, 200–201, 214, 217; and misconduct (and corruption), 49, 115, 140–141, 148, 194–195, 211, 223–224, 231, 247–248; and mob violence, 9, 132, 199, 200, 215–216, 237, 250; and racial bias, 2, 4, 10, 93, 108, 215, 225, 230, 232–233, 240, 244, 246, 253–255, 262–263, 270, 272, 277, 363n130; and racial profiling, 232; and vice districts, 12, 115–116, 134, 193, 195–198, 227, 256, 258–260; and Wickersham Commission, 266–268, 365n158

Porter, George D., 195, 198–199

Porter, John L., 202

Prohibition, 6, 197, 226, 232, 256, 259, 265, 274

Prostitution, 27; and black women, 68, 92, 99, 107, 121–123, 223, 260, 314n144, 314n151, 329n136; and vice districts, 227, 256; and white and European immigrant women, 117–118, 120, 123–124, 141, 192, 198, 333n191. See also Mann Act; Police

Racial criminalization, 3, 5, 8, 12, 35, 221. See also Du Bois, W. E. B.; Hoffman,

Frederick L.; Philadelphia Race Riot; Police; Wells, Ida B.

Racial Darwinism, 9, 28, 32, 38, 42, 86, 88, 95, 99, 108, 111, 115, 137, 140, 245, 281n2, 303–304n25

Racial scapegoating, 60, 254, 311n107

Racial violence, 2, 4, 11, 26, 29, 37, 46, 50, 59, 61, 72, 78, 93, 122–124, 130, 132, 143–144, 163–164, 173, 200–205, 207, 210, 229, 232, 241, 272. *See also* Chester (PA) Race Riot; Chicago Race Riot; Philadelphia Race Riot

Reckless, Walter, 260

Reconstruction, 4, 15, 17–18, 26, 30, 33, 36, 48, 51, 85, 135–137, 153, 215

Reid, Ira De A., 248, 267, 270, 361n111

Reuter, Edward B., 244–255, 358n73

Riis, Jacob, 54–55, 105

Ripley, William Z., 101, 103, 110, 317n187

Robinson, James, 204, 224

Roosevelt, Theodore, 159–160, 170–171

Root, William T., 246, 248

Ross, Edward A., 25

Rowland, A. J., 185

Rutledge, William P., 266

Samuel Seabury Commission, 259

Scarborough, William Saunders, 58

Scott, Emmett, 210, 220, 232

Seligman, Herbert, 235

Sellin, Thorsten, 2–3, 12, 242, 255–257, 269–270, 284n10, 358n67, 361n111

Shaler, Nathaniel S., 15, 17–20, 23, 25, 29–31, 33–34, 36–37, 39, 44–45, 53, 56–57, 75, 82, 86–88, 295n9

Shaw, Clifford R., 236, 238, 241, 266, 357n61

Simpson, David, 200

Sing Sing Prison, 267

Smith, Thomas B., 211, 218, 224

Social Darwinism, 7, 24, 26–28, 41, 47, 143, 149, 303n25

South End House, 103, 134

Starr, Frederick, 56, 62

Starr Centre, 147–151, 153–154, 164–165, 169–170, 177

Stemons, James S., 10, 92, 166–168, 172–174, 177–180, 182–194, 198, 208, 224, 228, 238, 247, 268

Stevens, Andrew F., 216, 222–223

Stone, Alfred Holt, 84, 174, 315n166

Sugrue, Thomas J., 73, 143

Suicide, 40–42, 44–45, 47, 51, 254, 261, 300n84, 303n21

Sutherland, Edwin H., 234, 241–242, 266, 269–270, 274, 275, 355n38, 357n58

Taylor, Graham Romeyn, 236–237

Terrell, Mary Church, 58

Thomas, William Hannibal, 79–82, 85, 90, 183

Thomas, William I., 231, 236

Thomas Durham Elementary (Philadelphia), 207–208

Thompson, Anna J., 12, 60, 230, 247–248, 284n10

Tindley, Charles A., 174–175, 177–178, 183, 185, 187

Trotter, Joe, 290n32, 335n226

Tuskegee Institute, 75, 89, 96, 106, 163–164, 169–172, 180, 183

Undercover vice agent, 227, 256–258, 260

Uniform Crime Reports (UCRs), 13, 77, 91, 266, 270, 364n156, 366n5

University Settlement House, 152

Vardaman, James K., 97, 170

Vollmer, August, 266

Vrooman, Harry, 47

Walker, Francis Amasa, 31–32, 35–36, 39

Wallace, P. A., 185

Waring, J. H. N., 107–108

Washington, Booker T., 18, 58, 96, 105, 107–108, 159–160, 163–164, 168–170, 173, 180–183, 185, 189, 268

Washington, Forrester, 211, 230
Weatherly, U. G., 84, 138–139
Wells, Ida B., 3, 10, 73, 87, 94, 139, 164, 238; and antilynching efforts, 58–62, 310n96; and criticisms of police misconduct, 249; and criticisms of racial criminalization, 78, 86, 111–112, 130–131, 247, 254, 269; and probation work, 231; and progressive reform(ers), 106, 124, 129–132, 144
Welsh, Herbert, 171–173
Western Pennsylvania Penitentiary, 246
Wharton, Susan, 147–150, 153–154, 163–166, 168–170
White, Deborah Gray, 58, 131
White, Walter, 12, 237, 254–255, 261–263
Wickersham, George B., 194, 266

Willcox, Walter, 74–75, 77, 82, 84–85, 88, 90, 183, 315n166
Williams, Fannie B., 105, 109, 123, 139, 238
Williams, G. Grant, 195, 214–215, 219, 222
Wilson, Edward E., 248–249, 251
Wilson, William H., 216, 218, 222–223
Wilson, Woodrow, 168, 199, 221
Woodson, Carter G., 244
Woofter, Thomas J., Jr., 244, 246
Woolley, Celia Parker, 106, 132
Work, Monroe N., 60, 78, 254
Wright, Carroll D., 39, 46–48, 67
Wright, Richard R., Jr., 60, 78, 81, 106, 175, 180, 218, 234, 343n41

Zuberi, Tukufu, 33, 99, 365n163

Hoeks disappearance lit. 35
statistics - 36.
'race on the road to extinction' 35   a vanishing race 40
vs white suicide + disease 40.
Lombrosa 47.
police corruption, 1894
Insurance 50   repackaging of proslavery belief
wrote crime into race 31   for a postbellum audience 35.
Hoffman's effort to "render racism invisible" 56
prof. black targets of mob violence 59.
lynching 61

Heather Ann Thompson - Blood in the Water
J. Baldwin "The white Man's Guilt" 1965
Dubois. Souls a Black Folk
Boas - The Mind of Primitive Man.